EMU:

Assessing the Impact of the Euro

Edited by
Richard Baldwin, Giuseppe Bertola and
Paul Seabright

This volume is a special issue of the journal, *Economic Policy*. It contains revised versions of the papers presented at the Thirty-Seventh Economic Policy Panel Meeting held in Athens on 10–12 April 2003, with the support of the Bank of Greece. Financial support from the European Central Bank is also gratefully acknowledged.

The Economic Policy Panel meets twice annually to discuss papers that are specially commissioned by the editors to provide timely and authoritative analyses of the choices confronting policy-makers. The articles use the best of modern economic analysis, but are also easily accessible to a wide audience and highly readable. Each paper is discussed by a rotating Panel of distinguished economists whose comments are published to provide the reader with alternative interpretations of the evidence and a sense of the liveliness of the current debate.

Economic Policy is published in association with the European Economic Association for the Centre for Economic Policy Research, the Center for Economic Studies of the University of Munich, and Département et Laboratoire d'Economie Théorique et Appliquée (DELTA), in collaboration with the Maison des Sciences de l'Homme. The Senior Editors are Georges de Ménil, Richard Portes and Hans-Werner Sinn. The Managing Editors are Richard Baldwin, Giuseppe Bertola and Paul Seabright.

First published 2003 by Blackwell Publishing Ltd

Library of Congress Cataloging-in-Publication Data applied for

British Library Cataloguing-in-Publication Data applied for

ISBN 1-405-11973-X (paperback)

Set in Hong Kong by Graphicraft Ltd
Printed and bound in the United Kingdom by Page Bros, Norwich

For further information on
Blackwell Publishing, visit our website:
http://www.blackwellpublishing.com

EMU:

Assessing the Impact of the Euro

Blackwell

ABOUT THE EDITORS

Richard Edward Baldwin is Professor of International Economics at the Graduate Institute of International Studies, Geneva. He publishes academic articles in the areas of international trade, European integration, economic geography, political economy and growth. His most recent coauthored book, *Public Policy and Economic Geography*, appeared in 2003 (PUP). He also writes on current policy issues and here his most recent book is *Nice Try: Should the Treaty of Nice be Ratified*, published in 2001 (CEPR). He is a Research Associate at the NBER and CEPR and was a Senior Staff Economist for the President's Council of Economic Advisers in 1990–1991. He has been an advisor to many international organizations including the World Bank, OECD, the European Commission, and the ECB.

Giuseppe Bertola is Professore Ordinario di Economica Politica, Facoltà di Scienze Politiche, Università di Torino. He was on leave as Full-time Professor at the European University Institute (1997–2003) and in 1989–93 was Assistant Professor and Assistant Director of the International Finance Section, Princeton University. He is Managing Editor of *Economic Policy*, Condirettore of *Giornale degli Economisti e Annali di Economia*, and a Research Fellow of CEPR. His research and publications focus on the macro-economic effects of labour market institutions, on income distribution, consumer credit, and official interventions in exchange rate and interest rate markets. He has worked as a scientific and academic adviser for the International Monetary Fund, the European Commission, the Bank of Italy; as an editorial board member for *European Economic Review*, *Review of Economic Studies* and *Macroeconomic Dynamics*; and as a Scientific Committee member at CESifo (Munich), CerP and LaborRR (Turin), CREI (Barcelona) and IGIER (Milan).

Paul Seabright is Professor of Economics at the Université des Sciences Sociales de Toulouse, a Director of Research at the Institut d'Economie Industrielle and a Research Fellow at CEPR. He has published widely in both theoretical and applied microeconomics. He is a member of the European Commission's Academic Advisory Panel on Competition Policy Questions and of the CEPR Steering Committee of the CEPR's annual series of reports on Monitoring European Integration. He has been a consultant to the private and public sector and to international organizations. He is the author of *The Company of Strangers: A Natural History of Economic Life*, forthcoming from Princeton University Press in the spring of 2004.

CONTENTS

CONFERENCE PARTICIPANTS

GEORGE ALOGOSKOUFIS
*Athens University of Economics
and Business*

IGNAZIO ANGELONI
European Central Bank

MICHAEL J. ARTIS
European University Institute, Firenze

RICHARD BALDWIN
*Graduate Institute of International
Studies, Geneva*

LEONARDO BARTOLINI
Federal Reserve Bank of New York

DAVID BEGG
Birkbeck College, London

GIUSEPPE BERTOLA
*European University Institute, Firenze,
Università di Torino*

SOFOKLIS BRISSIMIS
Bank of Greece

JUAN D. CARRILLO
Columbia Business School

STEPHEN G. CECCHETTI
Ohio State University

STIJN CLAESSENS
*Universiteit van Amsterdam and
World Bank*

LORENZO CODOGNO
Bank of America

PAUL DE GRAUWE
European University Institute

GEORGES DE MÉNIL
DELTA, Paris

GEORGE ECONOMOU
Bank of Greece

MICHAEL EHRMANN
European Central Bank

CARLO A. FAVERO
IGIER, Università Bocconi, Milano

JORDI GALÍ
*CREI, Universitat Pompeu Fabra,
Barcelona*

NICHOLAS C. GARGANAS
Bank of Greece

KONSTANTINE GATSIOS
*Athens University of Economics and
Business*

GHIKAS HARDOUVELIS
Prime Minister's Office, Athens

JONATHAN HASKEL
Queen Mary and Westfield College

PATRICK HONOHAN
World Bank, Trinity College, Dublin

LOUKA TARSITSA KATSELI
University of Athens

MARGARITA KATSIMI
*Athens University of Economics
and Business*

WINFRIED KOENIGER
IZA, Bonn

TRYPHON KOLLINTZAS
*Athens University of Economics
and Business*

OMAR LICANDRO
European University Institut

ALEJANDRO MICCO
Inter-American Development Bank

KAREN HELENE MIDELFART
*Norwegian School of Economics and
Business Administration, Bergen*

DAVID MILES
Imperial College, London

THOMAS MOUTOS
*Athens University of Economics
and Business*

PAUL MYLONAS
National Bank of Greece

NICHOLAS PALEOCRASSAS
Bank of Greece

LUCAS D. PAPADEMOS
European Central Bank

SPYROS PAPANICOLAOU
Bank of Greece

APOSTOLIS PHILIPPOPOULOS
*Athens University of Economics
and Business*

RICHARD PORTES
CEPR and London Business School

CAROL PROPPER
University of Bristol

RAY REES
Universität München

WOLFRAM F. RICHTER
University of Dortmund

PLUTARCHOS SAKELLARIS
University of Maryland

PAUL SEABRIGHT
*Université des Sciences Sociales
de Toulouse*

HANS-WERNER SINN
*Center for Economic Studies,
Universität München and CESifo*

ERNESTO STEIN
Inter-American Development Bank

GEORGE STUBOS
Bank of Greece

GEORGIOS SYMIGIANNIS
Bank of Greece

GEORGE TAVLAS
Bank of Greece

PANAYOTIS THOMOPOULOS
Bank of Greece

MARCEL THUM
Technical University of Dresden

JAUME VENTURA
CREI, Universitat Pompeu Fabra

NIKOLAOS VETTAS
University of Athens

JEAN-MARIE VIAENE
Erasmus University Rotterdam

MARK A. WYNNE
Federal Reserve Bank of Dallas

Introduction

The euro has been in existence just long enough to generate sufficient data for a first look at its actual performance, having been introduced in January 1999. This book presents eight studies that use post-1999 data to provide a first look at how the euro is actually affecting trade, financial markets, macroeconomic policy-making, and Europe's economic performance. All the articles, which were originally presented at the April 2003 *Economic Policy* Panel hosted by the Bank of Greece in Athens, were published in the October 2003 issue of *Economic Policy* after being subjected to the journal's usual rigorous process of refereeing, reviewing and revising. Plainly, the book does not provide the definitive evaluation of the euro – that must wait for many more years of data – but these studies by leading European and North American economists do marshal the best available evidence in providing an early assessment of the euro's performance – what might be called the euro's '10 000 km check-up'.

The book also contains a post-dinner speech delivered by European Central Bank Vice-President Lucas Papademos to the *Economic Policy* Panel at the Athens meeting.

In this introduction, we strive to put each article into the broader policy context.

TRADE EFFECTS OF THE EURO

The classic currency union trade-off highlighted by Robert Mundell in 1960 weighs a trade gain against a stabilization loss. While the existence of both the trade gain and the stabilization loss has always seemed intuitively plausible to most observers, measurement of the trade effect proved elusive. Indeed until Andy Rose published his path breaking paper in the April 2000 issue of *Economic Policy*, the received wisdom was that the trade effect of exchange rate volatility was negligible. What Rose found was that the pro-trade effect of a currency union was huge, with a common currency boosting trade between nations by as much as 300%. Subsequent studies confirmed the existence of the effect, but found it to be smaller. For example, using a different statistical technique, an article published in the October 2001 issue of *Economic Policy* by Torsten Persson finds the effect to be something like 10–20%.

The applicability of these findings to the euro has always been questioned since. Rose's results stemmed from data on currency unions involving very poor and very, very small nations. Fortunately, the time for extrapolating from evidence on other currency unions is at an end. Alejandro Micco, Ernesto Stein and Guillermo Ordoñez use data on the actual trade performance of euroland nations to check whether the euro has boosted trade. They find that the euro has already had a noticeable impact on trade, even at this early stage. Their results suggest that the euro has so far boosted the trade of euroland nations by between 4 and 16%. It is reassuring that these estimates are in line with Persson's statistical technique attempts to correct for the size and poverty mismatch between nations with currency unions and nations without them. By using a sample of countries that includes only industrialized nations, Micco *et al.* have, in effect, performed a similar matching exercise.

The findings of Micco *et al.*, however, raise many questions as the discussion by Karen Helene Midelfart points out. The extensive sensitivity analysis performed by the authors makes it clear that euroland membership is not a magic formula for trade – the trade effect is quite different for the various euro nations – ranging from a negative impact for Greece to a very big positive impact for the Netherlands. Moreover, the authors find that adoption of the euro tends to boost a nation's trade with all nations, not just other euroland members. This suggests that adoption of the euro promotes trade in a way that is more akin to a unilateral trade opening than it is to formation of a customs union.

While much additional research needs to be done before the profession can confidently assert that it knows how and how much the euro boosts trade, the Micco *et al.* paper does establish that the euro has already boosted trade.

INFLATION DIVERGENCE

Inflation rates have diverged much more widely than expected among the member states of the EMU. Indeed, the range of inflation rates in the euro zone, which had fallen to two percentage points by 1999, widened to over three percentage points in each of the two succeeding years. Why did this happen? Conventional theories of inflation divergence within a currency union have emphasized asymmetric demand shocks, or differences across countries in productivity growth in the traded goods sectors that translate into differences in demand for non-traded goods (the latter being known as the Balassa–Samuelson effect). Patrick Honohan and Philip Lane argue that the divergence at the start of EMU was due to neither of these two factors, but rather to the different exposure of the member countries to international trade with non-euro nations, which gave them a different sensitivity to the weakness of the euro on international currency markets in the early months of the Union. The Balassa–Samuelson productivity growth effect has not yet played an important role – even in respect of the outlier Ireland – although it will probably be more significant over a longer run, especially as the accession countries join.

This paper generated a great deal of interest and vigorous discussion at the panel. There was widespread agreement that the authors have uncovered a broadly plausible hypothesis – in the sense that differences in trade patterns are of the right order of magnitude to explain the inflation divergence observed so far. Whether the recent appreciation of the euro sees a convergence in inflation will be a key test of whether the hypothesis is ultimately convincing.

There was also much discussion of whether inflation divergence matters. Some panellists argued that it does, that the political economy of national policy-making, as well as the tendency of wage setting to be driven by institutions at the level of nation states, ensure that divergence of national inflation rates continues to be a potential concern for the foreseeable future. Others argued strongly that national rates do not matter, and one panellist even suggested that the publication of national inflation statistics is unfortunate because it focuses public attention on variables that should not concern macroeconomic policymakers. Indeed, the ECB's announced target is to ensure price stability in euroland as a whole, a subject that the next paper explores at length.

DEFINING PRICE STABILITY

The ECB sets itself a very specific target for monetary policy. The goal is to keep a euroland-wide price index – the so-called Harmonized Index of Consumer Prices (HICP) – rising at an annual rate that is near but below 2%. The very specificity of this target naturally raises two questions: 'Is 2% the right figure?', and 'Is the HICP the right price index?' With four full years of data available on the HICP's perform-ance, Stephen Cecchetti and Mark Wynne study these issues. Their main finding is that the 2% figure is too low; a range of something like 1.25–2.5% would be more appropriate, given the well-known upward bias in inflation measures and the dangers of deflation. In particular, they argue that an inflation floor of 1.25% would reduce the risk of a deflation-by-mistake situation to a very low level. Plainly, such estimates are inevitably fuzzy, but the Cecchetti–Wynne reasoning is a significant and novel contribution to the question of ECB goals. The authors also point out that the statistical basis of the HICP is far from perfect. Although the HICP was put together in an admirably professional manner, given the time constraints and large number of nations involved, Cecchetti and Wynne argue that the European Union should spend a great deal more money ensuring that the HICP is the best it can be. After all, the economic welfare of hundreds of millions of Europeans is at stake.

MONEY MARKETS: EUROSYSTEM AND THE FED

Unification of the euroland interbank money markets is not the monetary union's most obvious accomplishment. It was, nevertheless, an impressive and important achievement. Like many other macroeconomic European aggregates, the integrated money market is comparable in size to its counterpart in the United States, but quite different in many structural details. And while its stability and reactions to monetary policy impulses are not as prominent as other monetary economic aspects, banks do need to perform large volumes of transactions in order to be able properly to intermediate their customers' liquidity supply and demand. Leonardo Bartolini and Alessandro Prati assess the record of the European System of Central Banks' monetary-policy-implementation framework in fostering a smooth and liquid environment for banks' management of high-frequency transactions. The paper offers the first comprehensive estimation on new data of a standard descriptive interest-rate empirical model, applied to American 'Fed funds' rates by many previous contributions. It documents that euro and dollar short-term rates and liquidity conditions feature very similar patterns, and both reflect the orderly money market conditions and reliable reactions to central banks' policy moves needed to foster financial and macroeconomic efficiency.

MONETARY TRANSMISSION EVIDENCE

Are economic policy-making conditions becoming more homogeneous within the euro zone? This is the subject of a paper by Ignazio Angeloni and Michael Ehrmann, with their particular focus being the monetary policy transmission process. They use post-1999 data to examine some of the channels through which monetary policy influences the economy, and pose two main questions: Has the transmission mechanism changed after – and because of – EMU? And, if so, is it becoming more homogeneous across countries? The authors concentrate on three transmission channels: the banking, interest rate and asset market channels. They argue, first, that the transmission of interest rate changes through banks has become more potent and homogeneous across countries because of EMU. Secondly, they claim that the interest rate channel appears to have changed even before EMU, and now affects national economies in a broadly similar way. Thirdly, they argue that the asset market channel (proxied by the stock market effects of monetary policy) also seems to work rather homogeneously across national markets (no comparison with pre-EMU is available here).

Discussion of the paper focused partly on the statistical robustness of the findings and partly on alternative economic interpretations. It is not always clear, for instance, what should count as the 'no change' null hypothesis against which to measure the developments observed. While a full evaluation must await further data there was widespread agreement that the authors have provided a very interesting first picture of developments based on post-EMU evidence.

Continuing the focus on financial markets, the next paper examines the impact of currency union euroland government bond markets.

EMU AND GOVERNMENT BOND SPREADS

One of the main advantages of EMU is increased transparency and efficiency of financial markets: the price and returns of financial instruments denominated in the same currency can reflect their future payoffs, rather than market participants' valuation of exchange rate changes. Since EMU, the yields on euroland government bonds have converged, but non-trivial spreads still exist. These spreads may depend on the different liquidity-relevant details of the securities themselves and the markets where they are traded, but they may also reflect the creditworthiness of the issuing authorities. Lorenzo Codogno, Carlo Favero and Alessandro Missale analyse these spreads empirically. They ask the data whether changes of government bond spreads respond to changes in country-specific fiscal variables. This is an important question, because even small government bond spreads have a large impact on government outlays when public debt is as large as it is in some EMU countries, and because their changes in response to fiscal events are a gauge of market discipline on national government's fiscal policies.

The paper offers intriguing evidence that changes in fiscal positions may affect yields and thus the cost of national debts. The evidence is not overwhelming and, of course, market reactions to the limited changes of fiscal positions observed in the past few years may or may not be extrapolated to the kind of runaway fiscal policies that the Stability and Growth Pact tries to rule out. To the extent they can, however, they are important, and the paper's innovative methodology will undoubtedly foster much further research as new data come in.

Another channel by which EMU affects fiscal policies is the Stability and Growth Pact, the topic of the next paper.

FISCAL POLICY IN EMU

The Stability and Growth Pact imposes rather rough constraints on national fiscal deficits. They have been widely criticized as hindering euroland nations from pursuing stabilizing policies. Jordi Galí and Roberto Perotti ask the data whether such concerns are empirically warranted. They find that the cyclical behaviour of government deficits appears to play a more virtuous stabilizing role after Maastricht, when EMU countries stopped the upward-trending and procyclical fiscal deficits that were boosting some of their government debt stocks. The paper finds rather similar patterns of changes in cyclicality and public investment not only before and after EMU, but also across EMU and non-EMU countries. Thus, the data offer no evidence that formal constraints have hampered fiscal policy's stabilization role to date.

The point is that EMU governments did not use fiscal policy wisely, historically. They are doing a better job of it now. If anything, the Stability and Growth Pact may perform a useful role in preventing past 'dissolute' policies. It does not appear to have so far prevented virtuous fiscal policy.

The last paper in the book returns to the issue of trade effects.

LIFE ON THE OUTSIDE

Evidence on the economic effects of monetary union is, if anything, even more interesting for some of the countries outside the euro zone than for the current members, since the decision whether or not to adopt the euro will be taken sooner or later by a number of current outsiders. However, countries outside EMU cannot simply assume that by joining they would become like countries inside, since a greater ability to benefit from membership may have been part of what distinguished the insiders in the first place. David Barr, Francis Breedon and David Miles make a systematic comparison of countries in EMU with the EU countries outside, focusing principally on trade creation between EMU member countries. Since their primary interest is in the trade gains that outsiders would experience if they joined, the authors make a much more thorough attempt than Micco, Stein and Ordoñez to statistically correct for the possibility of reverse causality, i.e. that high trade flows caused euro membership rather than the other way around. Even after allowing for the possibility that the decision to join the monetary union was not random, the authors find that the trade effects of monetary union are significant. They estimate that, had the UK been inside EMU, the sum of its imports and exports would have been substantially greater.

For comparative purposes, they also make preliminary estimates of the effect of monetary union on three other dimensions of economic performance: foreign direct investment, the development of financial markets and overall macroeconomic performance, though they recognize that their ability to control for other factors is more limited for these other indicators. The evidence suggests that inward investment in the countries outside would have been greater had they joined EMU, but that the impact of this on GDP would be no more than 0.3% of GDP for the UK and less than that for the other 'outs'. Financial market activity shows no clear sign of having been affected by EMU, and London's position as Europe's financial centre remains, as yet, largely unchallenged. On standard measures of aggregate performance – inflation, unemployment and output – no clear pattern of EMU effects has yet emerged.

There was much discussion at the panel of these findings, particularly in comparison with the paper by Micco *et al.* Some panellists expressed surprise that the authors' careful attempt to control for the different character of insiders and outsiders should have made so little difference to their estimates of the trade effects of monetary union, especially given the important differences they document between these two groups of countries. There was also considerable scepticism expressed about the possibility of judging the other three dimensions of economic performance on the basis of the limited data so far. Still, the paper gives significant support to the notion that monetary union may lead to an important increase in trade between member countries, and has made a notable contribution to resolving some of the evidential and methodological issues that have bedevilled discussion of this hypothesis so far.

Policy challenges of euro area enlargement

Speech by Lucas Papademos
Vice-President of the European Central Bank
at the 37th Economic Policy Panel Meeting
Athens, 11 April 2003

Dear colleagues,
Ladies and Gentlemen,

I

I am delighted to have the opportunity to address you in the context of the 37th Economic Policy Panel Meeting. I am particularly pleased to be among distinguished economists and friends from the academic and research communities as well as from central banks. The ECB and I personally appreciate the valuable contributions to economic analysis and policy-making of this Forum, which is organised by three leading European research centers.

Athens, and the Bank of Greece in particular, is the venue of this Economic Policy Panel Meeting. The choice is based on a rotation system but it turns out to be an appropriate one. I am not saying this because I am a native son, but because Athens is a place steeped in history, and not only ancient history. Next week, history will again be made in this city: ten countries in central, eastern and southern Europe will sign the Accession Treaty to join the EU, stamping a formal seal on the largest ever expansion of the Union.

An EU of 25 Member States will soon be a reality. Not quite so soon – but sooner than we might have imagined a few years ago – a substantial enlargement of the euro area will also become a reality. The challenges associated with this prospect will no longer be only the object of *academic* interest; they will also become the subject-matter of *real policy* decisions. For this reason, I thought it would be useful to address some policy issues and challenges relating to the future adoption of the euro by the acceding countries.

II

How can it be ensured that the integration of the new Member States into the euro area will proceed smoothly? What should be the overall economic policy strategy, including fiscal, monetary, exchange rate and structural policies of the acceding countries, in preparation for the euro? And, equally important, what should be the preparations on our side, within the EU and, specifically, within the ECB? After all, we should not forget Benjamin Franklin's warning that "failure to prepare is preparing to fail." These are the issues I would like to address tonight, and I will try to be as brief as possible.

Speaking to a group of economists, the first topic that should naturally be discussed is whether theory can tell us something about the preconditions that must be fulfilled for a monetary union to function smoothly. More specifically, whether theory can help us identify the essential conditions which can facilitate entry and ensure successful participation of new Member States in the euro area. In general, a necessary condition both for the smooth functioning of monetary union and the successful participation of new Member States is the attainment of a high degree of convergence. I use the concept of convergence in a broad sense to include not only nominal convergence but also convergence in real terms: institutional and structural convergence. How important is each aspect of convergence and what is the necessary or minimum degree of real convergence required? A starting point for tackling this topic is the theory of Optimal Currency Areas and the criteria that determine the symmetry of external shocks and the capacity of a country to absorb shocks. In line with this theory, the new Member States should actively seek to fulfil these criteria in preparing to join monetary union and thus should strive to make their economic structures more similar to those of the euro area. And they should introduce the necessary measures to increase the degree of trade and financial integration, the flexibility of prices and wages, and factor mobility.

But perhaps it is the other way round: Is it possible to put Robert Mundell's "cart before the horse" and rely on the endogeneity of his criteria? In other words: is it likely that joining monetary union will reduce transaction costs and market imperfections, and thus entail increased trade and financial integration as well as price and wage flexibility? Can entry into the euro area be expected to lead to an adjustment of economic structures and a synchronisation of business cycles? Recent research, such as that summarised by Micco, Stein and Ordoñez on the effects of EMU on trade[1], and that presented by Angeloni and Ehrmann on the monetary transmission mechanism in the euro area[2], suggests that the answers to these questions are generally positive. I think Mundell himself would tend to agree with this conclusion.

[1] Alejandro Micco, Ernesto Stein and Guillermo Ordoñez: *"The Currency Union Effect on Trade: Early Evidence from EMU"* (at http://www.cepr.org/meets/wkcn/9/963/papers/stein.pdf)

[2] Ignazio Angeloni and Michael Ehrmann: *"Monetary Policy Transmission in the Euro Area: Any changes after EMU?"*, ECB Working Paper no. 240, 2003.

Nevertheless, the answers to these questions cannot be regarded as definitive. Further work in this area will be useful as the answers have important policy implications for the manner in which each of the accession countries prepares for the eventual adoption of the euro. More specifically, they may also determine the priorities to be set in achieving nominal and real convergence: whether inflation and public sector deficits are reduced fast, in the expectation that the necessary structural adjustments in the real sector "will look after themselves" once the country is inside the euro area; or whether "catching-up" in real terms takes priority and the public sector should aim at financing infrastructure investment, improving market efficiency and flexibility, and cushioning social and economic change. In my view, the approach to the euro by the acceding countries should be a balanced one, involving, on the one hand, macroeconomic policies aiming at nominal convergence, which is absolutely necessary for EMU entry, and, on the other hand, structural and institutional reforms, which will be essential for securing faster growth within the euro area.

As we know, most of the acceding countries are in a process of "catching-up" in real terms and economic conditions differ considerably among them, in nominal, real and structural terms. This fact implies that it is unlikely that we can define a unique path to the euro that would be appropriate for all. It is impossible to formulate a single strategy and a set of policies that can be applied uniformly to all the acceding countries. There are, of course, certain similarities among some of these countries, with regard to their state of nominal convergence or their exchange rate strategies, but there are also differences, including differences in fiscal positions and financial structures. For this reason, the chosen economic and monetary policy strategies on the way to the euro vary, and their effectiveness will have to be assessed on a case-by-case basis.

Although initial conditions differ, the final aim of the new Member States is the same: the adoption of the euro as soon as appropriate conditions are established. So, "all roads lead to Rome", or, given our subject, I should perhaps say "to Frankfurt". Indeed, most acceding countries have declared that they plan to join the euro area as soon as possible, and some have announced specific target dates, in 2006 and 2007. The plurality of approaches to the euro, however, should not stand in the way of the equality of treatment when it comes to examining the degree of convergence.

The Treaty is very explicit on the need for nominal convergence, and even quantifies what is to be understood by it, in the famous Maastricht convergence criteria. I would like to address the challenges stemming from these nominal criteria, notably for monetary and exchange rate policies and public finances, before turning to issues related to real convergence.

III

As a central banker, I naturally start, and predictably so you might say, by emphasising that the achievement of sustained convergence to price stability is the fundamental prerequisite for the adoption of the euro. Consequently, the primary objective of each country's monetary policy should be to attain convergence to price stability, irrespective of the specific conditions – economic or institutional – which may warrant the adoption of different national strategies, at least for some time. What is crucial is that nominal convergence is sustainable. The successful performance of an economy within the euro area hinges precisely on that. Thus, the appropriate strategy should aim at securing the sustainability of inflation convergence. What are the challenges in this regard?

I would emphasise three of them: First, there is the Balassa–Samuelson effect, which is often mentioned in discussions, but which should not be overstated. According to a number of estimates, the magnitude of this effect is unlikely to be more than 1%. Second, we should not lose sight of the fact that in several acceding countries a range of prices is still administered. The necessary progress towards price liberalisation is likely to be gradual, but nevertheless has the potential to impede a smooth path towards inflation convergence. Third, accession itself could be expected to boost economic activity. Such an acceleration of output growth could put upward pressure on prices. All these factors will need to be taken into account, especially by those acceding countries that aim at the earliest possible adoption of the euro. It should also be kept in mind that, once these countries are inside the euro area, inflation differentials are likely to persist for some time. This theme is dealt with in more detail in the paper by our Irish colleagues[3]. The Greek experience also highlights the persistence of inflation differentials.

In this context, we should also be mindful of structural differences in the dynamics of economic growth between the new Member States and the current euro area. For instance, recent research at the ECB[4], based on the empirical evidence of the past seven years, finds that the acceding countries' growth is higher on average but is characterised by wider fluctuations when compared to the euro area and other EU countries. In addition, business cycles in the Central European acceding countries (Hungary, Poland, Slovenia, Czech Republic, Slovakia) have on average been less synchronised with the euro area than the so-called "euro pre-ins" (United Kingdom, Sweden and Denmark). However, the business cycles in these acceding countries did not show a worse alignment with euro area fluctuations when compared to the cycles in some euro area members on the "periphery" (Greece, Portugal and Ireland).

This leads me to my next point: considerations regarding the symmetry of growth dynamics and the size and degree of openness of an economy influence the choice of the exchange rate strategy of acceding countries, notably the desired degree of

[3] Patrick Honohan and Philip Lane: "*Divergent inflation rates in EMU*" (at http://www.cepr.org/meets/wkcn/9/963/papers/honohan.pdf)

[4] Ralph Süppel: "*Do Central European Accession Countries Benefit From Exchange Rate Flexibility?*", only submitted for publication as ECB Working Paper in 2003.

exchange rate flexibility or fixity. There is consensus, however, that the different orientations of the exchange rate policies currently pursued will gradually have to converge, not least because the new Member States are required to treat their exchange rate policies "as a matter of common interest" following EU accession. One aspect of this is ERM II membership. What is the role and purpose of ERM II in the process of monetary integration of the new Member States into the euro area? We, at the ECB, see ERM II as a useful framework to foster convergence and thus support the policy efforts to adopt the euro. In our view, (*i*) the voluntary nature of the mechanism, (*ii*) the combination of features of fixity and flexibility which are provided by the fixed but adjustable central parity and the relatively wide fluctuation band, and (*iii*) the multilateral character of its management make participation in ERM II a valuable testing phase before euro area entry in many ways: for testing the appropriateness of the central rate and of the eventual conversion rate of the national currency to the euro; and for testing the consistency of domestic macroeconomic policies and the sustainability of convergence.

That said, it would be naïve to believe, and I do not want to imply, that joining ERM II is a panacea. The new Member States will undoubtedly be confronted with a number of challenges. One is the likely upward pressure on the exchange rate, which might arise from the catching-up process, from further structural reforms – particularly in the financial sector – and/or from potential asymmetric shocks. In particular, large capital inflows and the need to pursue a tight monetary policy to complete the disinflation process might lead to a prolonged period of overvaluation of the national currency, which might nevertheless be to some extent transitory. On the other hand, strong productivity growth combined with low inflation could lead to a durable appreciation of the exchange rate, which needs to be reflected in an adjustment of the central parity. Obviously, these phenomena have to be taken into account when deciding the modalities of ERM participation and in the conduct of monetary policy within that framework. They should also be taken into account when assessing exchange rate stability in the context of the convergence examination. This was indeed the case for both Ireland and Greece.

After all, exchange rate stability within ERM II is no pie in the sky. It *can* be achieved, and sustainably so, if monetary policy is credibly geared towards convergence to price stability and provided that fiscal and structural policies are supportive of this orientation. It obviously also requires an appropriate choice of the central rate which is in line with the fundamentals and can be expected to remain in line with the fundamentals if the right policies are pursued.

This brings me to my final point on nominal convergence: fiscal policy. I think we all agree that economies going through a catching-up phase undoubtedly require substantial public investment in infrastructure, both physical and in terms of human capital, in order to close the development gap with the mature economies of Europe. To that end – it is argued – deficit spending is not only legitimate but, seen from a perspective of inter-generational income distribution, even rational and advisable.

Deficit spending, however, is not devoid of problems, not least because it can set in motion a dynamic that is difficult to contain. The experience of my home country in the 1980s is telling in this respect. In about a decade of deficit spending partly related to public investment, Greece's public debt had more than doubled, to over 120% of Gross Domestic Product. Even though public finances were consolidated later on in preparation for the euro, public debt today – despite a sustained effort lasting almost 10 years – still stands at over 100% of GDP. The need to service this "debt mountain" continues to severely restrict the room for manoeuvre for fiscal policy.

Moreover, the argument that increased public investment in infrastructure justifies deficit spending is further weakened by the fact that the EU's structural funds provide substantial resources for regional development projects. The new Member States – just like Greece, Ireland or Portugal – can expect net transfers from the Union of around 4% of GDP.

Last but not least, the Treaty provisions on excessive deficits and the convergence criteria clearly and appropriately stipulate sustainable public finances as a guiding principle for the economic policies of all Member States. After all, substantial public investment, successful catching-up and sound fiscal positions can go hand in hand. As pointed out in the paper by Gali and Perotti[5], the Stability and Growth Pact has not impaired the ability of EU governments to conduct discretionary countercyclical fiscal policy effectively and it cannot be considered responsible for the observed decline in public investment. More generally, there is ample evidence that fiscal consolidation is often, if not usually, associated with higher growth[6].

IV

Thus far, I have dwelled on nominal convergence. As I stressed earlier, this is essential for EMU entry. It is also relatively easy to assess and the Union has experience in measuring and evaluating it. Convergence in real terms, by contrast, is much less well-defined and hence subject to controversy. Some interpret it in rather narrow terms to simply denote convergence in real incomes. If this form of real convergence was a prerequisite for the adoption of the euro, then – according to estimates by the IMF – it would be many years, if not decades, before the new Member States (Malta and Cyprus apart) could enter the euro area. But this form of real convergence is not necessary.

I suggest, however, that real convergence in the broader sense is important. What I have in mind is the convergence of institutional and administrative structures and of the legislative framework; infrastructure modernisation; trade and financial

---

[5] Jordi Galí and Roberto Perotti: *"Fiscal Policy and Monetary Integration in Europe"* (at http://www.cepr.org/meets/wkcn/9/963/papers/perotti.pdf)

[6] See Giavazzi F. and M. Pagano (1990), *"Can severe fiscal contractions be expansionary? Tales of two small European countries"*, NBER Macroeconomics Annual, 5, pp. 75–111; Perotti R. (1999), *"Fiscal policy in good times and bad"*, Quarterly Journal of Economics, 114, pp. 1399–1436; Giavazzi F., Japelli T. and M. Pagano (2000), *"Searching for non-linear effects of fiscal policy: Evidence for industrial and developing countries"*, NBER Working Paper Series, 7460; Alesina A., Ardagna S., Perotti R. and F. Schiantarelli (2002), *"Fiscal policy, profits and investment"*, American Economic Review, 92, pp. 571–89.

integration. On many of these fronts, the new Member States have achieved significant progress: the data on trade flows and foreign direct investment speak for themselves. With the signing of the Accession Treaty, the new Member States have accepted the *acquis communautaire*, and thus should have in place a regulatory framework equivalent to that of the current EU. Needless to say, acceptance of the EU rules is not enough; what really matters is implementation. In this field, a lot of work still needs to be done in many of the acceding countries, for instance in modernising the judicial system or reforming administrative practices – not least to enable them to make effective use of the expected influx of EU funds.

The attainment of real convergence obviously involves enormous challenges in practice. Implementing the necessary structural, institutional and legislative reforms may not be easy as it requires political resolve and social consensus. "Necessary reforms, political resolve, social consensus" – all that sounds as if I am talking not about the new Member States but about some of the current euro area countries! In this context, I should also point out that when it comes to labour and product market flexibility, many of the new Member States are in fact ahead of several EU countries, and the task of "catching-up" definitely lies with some of the current Member States. In particular, those acceding countries that have been operating currency board arrangements in a sustainable fashion over a long period have developed alternative adjustment mechanisms, which involve greater price and wage flexibility and will be crucial for their successful participation in the euro area.

V

These remarks bring me closer to home and to the end of my speech. What are the challenges of enlargement for the EU, and specifically for the ECB? A I have to be brief, I should like to mention two: the impact of future euro area enlargements on the ECB's monetary policy and on its decision-making structures.

Several arguments have been advanced about the allegedly inflation bias of the new Member States: one is that inflation dynamics in these "catching-up" economies are different, influenced by the Balassa–Samuelson effect and other factors; another is that invisible inflationary pressures may be artificially suppressed in the drive to fulfil the convergence criteria; a third is that in these countries there is no established "stability culture". For all these reasons, it is sometimes maintained that many new Member States would have a preference for higher inflation and a less ambitious definition of price stability. Although these factual arguments are partly correct, the conclusion is not warranted.

Some have even speculated that the review of the ECB's monetary policy strategy, which is currently underway, may be influenced and anticipate the alleged inflation bias of the governors from the new Member States. This is simply not the case. There is no connection between the review of our monetary policy strategy – which is expected to be completed in May – and future euro area enlargements.

There should be no doubt that in an enlarged euro area the ECB will continue to fulfil its mandate, which is to formulate and implement the single monetary policy in order to maintain price stability in the euro area as a whole. This is done on the basis of aggregate euro area data, which are averages of the national data, weighted by country GDP shares in the euro area total. I mention this to remind you of the proportions of this enlargement. Even though the 10 new acceding countries will add some 70 million citizens to the 300 million of the current euro area, their combined GDP is of the magnitude of around 5% of euro area GDP. It is therefore somewhat far-fetched to predict that specific developments in the new Member States will "drown out" the signals emanating from the data of the current euro area.

Moreover, it should be recalled that inflation in many new Member States is below or close to the euro area average and their national central banks and governors are committed to the price stability objective. The members of the Governing Council of the ECB participate in the discussions and decision-making as independent per-sonalities pursuing the ECB's euro area-wide mandate. I can confirm this on the basis of my own experience both in my former position at the Bank of Greece and in the present one at the ECB.

Finally, great efforts have been made to prepare the ECB's infrastructure and its decision-making structures for enlargement. The new voting system for the Govern-ing Council, adopted in March by the Heads of State or Government, will ensure that decisions continue to be taken in a timely and efficient manner, also when the membership of the Governing Council increases to over 30. Although the new voting system is not as simple as we would have liked, it fulfils a number of generally accepted principles, such as the "one person, one vote" and that of "representative-ness", which is considered important in an enlarged euro area. Given the legal limits imposed by the so-called "enabling clause" of the Nice Treaty, I believe that the new voting system for the Governing Council is suitable to accommodate a future substantial enlargement of the euro area. Much has been written and said about this system – some of it rather critical – and I could dwell on this subject for much longer. But given that this is a dinner speech, I doubt whether doing so would be a good idea. After all, "the supply of words on the world market is plentiful, but the demand is falling" – as former Polish President Lech Walesa once aptly remarked. I hope that demand has held up reasonably well for so long tonight. Thank you for your attention.

Trade effect

The euro's trade impact is clearly important for the nations that have already joined euroland. But the size and nature of the trade effects are even more important for the EU members who have not joined the euro: the UK, Denmark, Sweden and the ten new nations scheduled to join next year. What are they missing? Will they face trade diversion if they do not join? For example, the debate on whether or not to join the euro is raging in the UK where it has been polarized to an extraordinary degree. This debate is in desperate need of economic analysis, in order to help clarify the potential impact of the euro on a number of dimensions, one of which is trade. This paper, we hope, will contribute to the debate, by providing estimates of the currency union effect on trade, for the specific case of the countries in the European Union. For this purpose, we use a panel data set that includes the most recent information on bilateral trade for 22 developed countries from 1992 to 2002. During this period 12 European nations formally entered into a currency union. This unique event allows us to study the effect of currency union on trade among a relatively homogeneous group of industrial countries. Controlling for a host of other factors, we find that the effect of EMU on bilateral trade between member countries ranges between 4 and 10%, when compared to trade between all other pairs of countries, and between 8 and 16%, when compared to trade among non-EMU countries. In addition, we find no evidence of trade diversion. If anything, our results suggest that the monetary union increases trade not just with EMU countries, but also with the rest of the world.

— *Alejandro Micco, Ernesto Stein and Guillermo Ordoñez*

The currency union effect on trade: early evidence from EMU

Alejandro Micco, Ernesto Stein and Guillermo Ordoñez

Inter-American Development Bank

1. INTRODUCTION

Adopting the euro involves costs and benefits. The most commonly identified cost is the loss of monetary policy as a national stabilization tool. The most commonly identified benefit is the increased trade and investment that a common currency might foster.

For example, the UK Chancellor of the Exchequer, Gordon Brown, extolled the microeconomic benefits of membership when he announced in June 2003 that Britain was not ready to join euroland due to a lack of macroeconomic convergence. The main micro gains he listed were lower transaction costs and greater cross-border trade. He asserted that 'British trade with the euro area could increase substantially – perhaps to the extent of 50 per cent over 30 years . . . Indeed, our assessment on trade and output is that inside the euro UK national income could rise over a 30 year period by between 5 and 9 per cent' (Brown, 2003).

We thank Daniel Leigh for excellent research assistance, and Jeff Frankel, Eduardo Levy Yeyati, Ernesto López-Cordova, Andrew Powell, Andy Rose, Alan Winters and two anonymous referees, as well as conference participants and discussants at the 2003 *Economic Policy* Panel in Athens, the 2002 LACEA meetings in Madrid, the 2002 Regional Integration Network meetings in Punta del Este, and internal seminars at the Inter-American Development Bank (IDB), for useful comments and suggestions. The opinions expressed in this paper are those of the authors and not necessarily those of the IDB. The Managing Editor in charge of this paper was Richard Baldwin.

Expectations regarding the euro's trade effect are partly based on a study, published in this journal in 2000, that examined the experience of post-war currency unions throughout the world. That path-breaking study, Rose (2000), suggested that currency unions increased trade by 300%. This naturally attracted a bevy of academic comments and critiques. Most of these suggested that Rose's first estimates were too high. Yet, despite this remarkably persistent 'counter attack', Rose's general conclusion still stands. As it turns out, currency unions do have an important effect on trade.

Perhaps the most telling critique of Rose's work – or more precisely of its relevance for Europe – is that Rose's estimates rely overwhelmingly on currency unions involving poor and/or small nations. One does not need to be a euro-sceptic to wonder whether such findings are directly applicable to Europe's single currency.

Fortunately, the time for extrapolating from evidence on other currency unions is at an end. We now have enough data on the actual trade performance of euroland nations to check whether the euro has boosted trade.

Using post-1999 data, the results presented in our paper suggest that the euro has already had a noticeable impact on trade, even at this early stage. The estimates we obtain for the euro's impact on trade, using different samples and different methodologies, range between 4 and 16%. While this effect is not as spectacular as the early Rose estimates, it is still statistically significant, and economically important. Furthermore, we find no evidence that EMU has diverted trade of member countries away from non-members. In fact, EMU countries seem to have increased their trade with non-EMU countries, as well as with fellow EMU members.

Our findings are clearly important for the nations that have already joined euroland. But to some extent, these nations are faced with a *fait accompli*. Our results are probably most important for the EU members who have not joined the euro: the UK, Denmark, Sweden, as well as for the ten new nations scheduled to join next year. What are they missing? Should they join the monetary union? The debate on whether or not to join the euro is raging in the UK where it has been polarized to an extraordinary degree. This debate is in desperate need of economic analysis, in order to help clarify the potential impact of the euro on a number of dimensions, one of which is trade. This paper, we hope, will contribute to the debate, by providing estimates of the currency union effect on trade, for the specific case of the countries in the European Union.

The euro's trade effect also matters in another way, maybe one that is equally important. Recent findings suggesting that macroeconomic convergence, one of the criteria that weighed in on UK's recent euro decision, may itself be fostered by adoption of the single currency. Specifically, the work of Frankel and Rose (1997, 1998) suggests that increased trade integration leads to increased correlation of business cycles. If monetary unions lead to increased trade, and increased trade leads to higher correlation, then a country could easily achieve convergence *ex post*, even if it does not meet the criteria *ex ante*. The whole argument, however, hinges on the impact of the currency union on trade. Without a positive impact, the argument falls apart, whether or not trade leads to cycle correlation.

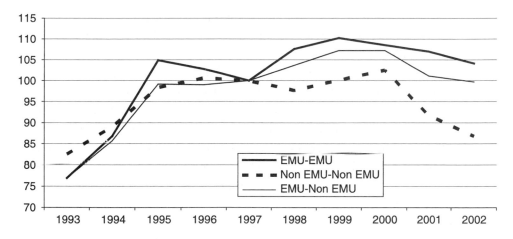

Figure 1. Evolution of trade by country pairs

Notes: The series (1997 = 100) show the trade evolution between classified country pairs. Specifically, for every country in the sample, we calculate a trade index with EMU countries and one with non-EMU countries. The EMU–EMU series is the unweighted average of the EMU country's EMU trade indices. The non-EMU–non-EMU series is the unweighted average of the non-EMU country's non-EMU trade indices. The EMU–non-EMU series is the average of all 'cross group' indices. Nations in the sample: Australia, Austria, Belgium-Luxembourg, Canada, Denmark, Finland, France, Germany, Greece, Iceland, Ireland, Italy, Japan, New Zealand, the Netherlands, Norway, Portugal, Spain, Sweden, Switzerland, the United Kingdom, and the United States.

Source: Authors' calculations with IMF Direction of Trade Statistics.

1.1. A first look at the data

A complete consideration of the euro's trade impact requires serious econometric analysis, and we shall provide this in abundance in subsequent sections. Yet, if a single currency does have anything close to the dramatic trade effects alleged, we should be able to pick it up with the naked eye.

Figure 1 shows how bilateral trade flows evolved during the four years since the euro's adoption in 1999 and, for comparison, the same flows for the six prior years. There are two main points to take away from the figure. First, the data show that in the run-up to the creation of the single currency, intra-euroland trade flows increased more than bilateral flows between non-euroland nations. Second, the numbers also suggest that trade between euro and non-euro nations also increased, albeit not as much as intra-euroland flows. Subsequently, this pattern repeats itself when most bilateral flows dropped from 1999 (due to the global growth slowdown); flows on average fell, but the flows involving euroland nations fell by less.

This sort of evidence is a very long way from proof that the euro affected trade, but it is suggestive and may help some readers believe our more sophisticated statistical analysis.

1.1.1. Nation by nation figures. The data in Figure 1 lumps all euroland nations together. A slightly more nuanced view of the trade data can be had by looking at changes in euro-members' trade shares before and after the euro's 1999 birth. This

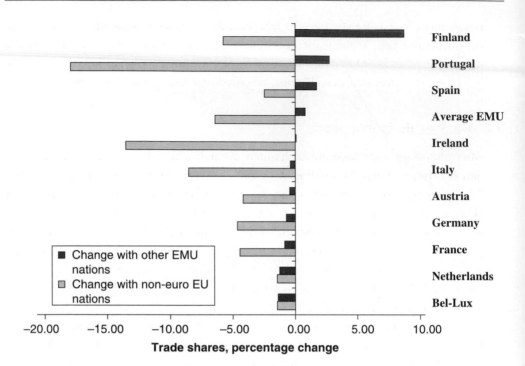

Figure 2. Changes in trade shares by country

Notes: Trade shares are expressed as a percentage of total trade within the sample (see Figure 1 for a list of nations); the numbers shown indicate the percentage change between the 1996–7 average share and the 2000–1 average share. See Table B1 in Appendix B for more detail.

Source: Authors' calculations with IMF Direction of Trade Statistics.

is done in Figure 2, which shows the percentage changes in the shares of each of the euro nation's trade with other euro members on the one hand and with non-euro EU members on the other. (The figure is based on the data reported in Table B1 in Appendix B.) While trade performance varies from country to country, there are some clear patterns that emerge from the figure. On average, the euroland countries increased their share in the trade of other euroland members, but the overall increase was small (around 0.8%) and concentrated in a few countries. However, even this modest performance – which may be modest in part due to the better growth performance of the US and other non-European nations – shines in comparison to that of the rest of the EU countries. As a group, these countries lost more than 6% of their share in the euro zone's trade, with the loss reaching double figures in the cases of Ireland and Portugal. In fact, the non-euro EU countries lost share in each and every one of the countries in the euro zone. And in all these countries, without exception, they did worse than the euro members.

Again, this sort of information is merely indicative, but it does serve to strengthen the idea that the euro may have altered trade flows. In particular, Figures 1 and 2 suggest that the EU countries that stayed out of the euro did miss something with regards to their trade with euroland. They also suggest that the dramatic currency union effect found elsewhere in the literature does not seem to be present in Europe, or at least not yet. At the same time, the discussion makes it clear that we need to control for other factors that have powerful effects on trade, such as national incomes, before we can conclude that the euro has made a difference when it comes to trade.

1.2. What we do in this paper

After discussing some theoretical channels through which the euro could affect trade and briefly reviewing the existing literature, we open the formal analysis in Section 3 by studying several variants of the so-called 'gravity model' of trade for a sample of 22 developed countries, as well as for a smaller sample of the EU 15. This model, which is now the standard-bearer in empirical studies of bilateral trade, allows us to tease out the impact of the euro, controlling for other standard influences on trade such as EU membership, distance and the size of the buying and selling nations. As mentioned above, the results in this section indicate that the single currency has had a positive impact on trade flows.

The subsequent section takes a closer look at the trade effects. In particular, we look at the impact of the euro on euroland's trade with non-euro nations. If membership in a currency union affected trade in the same way membership in a customs union did, we should expect 'supply switching' – or more colloquially 'trade diversion' – from non-euro nations to those in euroland. It is therefore of great interest that we find no evidence that EMU has diverted trade of member countries away from non-members. In fact, EMU countries seem to have increased their trade with non-EMU countries, as well as with fellow EMU members. While this evidence is merely suggestive, it does provide a first hint on *how* the euro might affect trade. Using the euro may make trade easier for its members, boosting both euro and non-euro trade flows. But, intra-euroland trade flows may be boosted even more, since the effect operates on both ends of the trade relationship.[1]

Since the history of empirical analysis is littered with examples of seemingly strong findings that collapsed when slightly different data and or statistical techniques were applied, the next section of our paper presents a sequence of robustness checks.

The paper concludes with a summary of our findings and a discussion of policy implications.

2. THEORY AND ANTECEDENTS

Empirics without theory is a risky undertaking. One simply cannot distinguish between causation and correlation without some analytical framework. We begin, therefore, with a brief discussion of the theory, before turning to a brief review of existing studies.

---

[1] We are grateful to Richard Baldwin for proposing the 'trade booster' interpretation.

2.1. Why should the euro affect trade?

The channels through which monetary union may potentially affect trade are many. The famous *One Market, One Money* study (Emerson *et al.*, 1992) provides a more formal presentation of the many microeconomic links. Here we informally present the links that we believe are most relevant in Europe today.

A common currency eliminates bilateral nominal exchange rate volatility, and thus reduces the uncertainty and risk involved in trade transactions. While there are ways to hedge against this risk, doing so may be costly. Furthermore, as Kenen (2003) points out, it is not always possible to fully hedge against large, long-lasting changes in exchange rates, since producers are uncertain not only about the price they will receive for their exports, but also about the demand for their products. Thus, the producer does not know how much foreign currency she will earn, and how much she should sell in the forward market.

Despite this argument's intuitive appeal, the evidence regarding the impact of exchange rate volatility on trade has not yielded conclusive results. (See Klaassen, 2002 for a discussion on why it is so difficult to find an effect of exchange rate risk on trade using time series analyses.) While there is some empirical evidence suggesting that exchange rate volatility has a negative effect, these effects are generally quite small (except perhaps in the case of developing countries), have decreased over time, and vary widely in significance depending on the study in question. For an early survey of this literature, see Edison and Melvin (1990).

The effects of joining a currency union, however, go beyond the reduction of exchange rate volatility. Currency unions eliminate the transaction costs arising from the need to operate with multiple currencies when trading across countries with different monies. These costs are independent of the volatility channel. In fact, De Grauwe (1994) reports that the cost of exchanging Belgian francs for guilders or deutsche marks is similar to the cost of exchanging them for French francs, pounds sterling or US dollars (approximately 0.5%), despite the low volatility of the Belgian franc vis-à-vis the guilder or the mark. Emerson *et al.* (1992) estimated these costs to be as high as 0.5% of GDP for the European Union as a whole, and as much as 1% of GDP for the case of the smaller, more open member countries, whose currencies are not used much internationally.

Sharing a common currency has an additional effect: it results in irrevocably fixed exchange rates, thus eliminating exchange rate volatility between the currency union partners for the foreseeable future. This, in turn, may increase market transparency, and foster competition among firms in different countries. Finally, in giving up their national monies and adopting a much more liquid currency, the monetary union may also provide its member countries with a vehicle to hedge exchange rate risk in their trade transactions with non-member countries. In this case, one would expect the euro to increase trade flows not only among euro members, but with other trading partners as well.

2.2. The findings of previous empirical studies

Until very recently, there were no studies measuring the direct impact of common currencies on trade. The only hint that the effect might be substantial came from the huge home market bias found in the 'border effect' literature looking at trade between Canadian provinces and US states (see McCallum, 1995 and Helliwell, 1998, who found that trade between two Canadian provinces was 10–20 times greater than trade between a province and a US state, other things equal). These findings, particularly among countries with strong cultural links, similar tastes and common membership in a free trade area, suggested that the need to transact in multiple currencies, in the case of trade between provinces and states, might be playing an important role. While recent theoretical developments associated to the gravity model have explained away part of this home bias, the border effect remains substantial (see Anderson and van Wincoop, 2001; Head and Mayer, 2002).

Empirical estimates of how bilateral trade flows are affected by a common currency – what has come to be called the 'currency union effect' – have multiplied since Rose's first paper in 2000. A comprehensive survey and an assessment of where the literature stands today by Rose (2002) finds that the currency union effect approximately doubles trade. The next section provides our analytic review of some of the main studies on the impact of currency union on trade, focusing on how the various methodologies and data samples render the studies more or less relevant to the euro's impact on trade. It should also provide a good sense of where our paper fits within this literature.

2.3. The currency union effect on trade: a review of the literature

The first paper to study the impact of common currencies on trade was Rose (2000), who added a common currency dummy to a gravity model of bilateral trade. By including dependencies, territories and colonies in his sample of 186 'countries', he was able to get 300 country pairs with common currencies, allowing for the estimation of the currency union effect. To his own surprise, and that of the rest of the profession, Rose found that a common currency increases bilateral trade by a factor of three, other things equal. In terms of the relevance of his findings for the euro, however, one important shortcoming is that most country pairs with common currencies in his sample are either currency unions formed by very small or very poor countries, such as those in the Eastern Caribbean Currency Area, or very small or poor countries adopting the currency of larger ones, such as Tonga adopting the Australian dollar. (For a discussion of the differences between the impact of a currency union and that of the unilateral adoption of the currency of others, see Levy Yeyati, 2003).

Rose's first study was based on cross-section analysis. Therefore, the question it answers is whether countries that share a common currency trade more than others that do not. As Glick and Rose (2001) argue, this is not exactly the right question from a policy perspective. What one would want to know, as a policy-maker, is the impact of a currency union on those countries that adopt it. To answer this question, Glick and Rose (2001) study the impact of currency union using panel data from 1948 to 1997. This extended period allows the authors to have enough country pairs with periods in which they shared currencies, as well as periods in which they did not. Glick and Rose's answer to the 'right' policy question is that adopting currency unions doubles trade. But the sample ends in 1997, before the creation of the EMU. Thus, while Glick and Rose answer the right policy question, their answer is relevant mostly for the case of very small and/or poor countries.

These controversial findings by Rose and his co-authors were followed by a large number of studies seeking to 'shrink' the currency union effect. The two papers among Rose's critics that we discuss are those of Persson (2001) and Tenreyro (2001), but the prize for best title goes to Volcker Nitsch, for his paper 'Honey, I just shrank the currency union effect' (2001).

Persson (2001) argues that the fact that some of the explanatory variables in Rose (2000) may have non-linear effects, combined with the fact that the selection of country pairs into currency unions is non-random (and may depend on those explanatory variables), may bias the results. Persson proposes an alternative methodology, based on matching techniques borrowed from the labour literature, and finds the effect of currency union on trade to be 65% under one variant and 13% under another.

Tenreyro (2001) also stresses the problem of endogenous selection into a currency union, but emphasizes the problem of omitted variables that may at the same time affect trade links and the propensity to join currency unions, and thus lead to a positive bias in the OLS estimates. As an example, two countries might have a history of conflict, which may reduce bilateral trade flows and at the same time make them unlikely currency union partners. After addressing this problem by modelling explicitly the decision to enter into a currency union, she obtains a currency union effect of 50%, although the effect is not statistically significant. But while Tenreyro and Persson's methodologies solve the problem of non-random selection into currency unions, they do not solve the problem that concerns us: their estimates are still relevant for the type of countries that, in their sample, tend to form currency unions: the very small and poor ones.

Two papers that provide some hints about the currency union effect on trade in large countries using historical data from the gold standard period are Estevadeordal et al. (2002) and López-Cordova and Meissner (2002). Both of these papers use smaller samples of industrial countries, plus a small group of large developing countries. Estevadeordal et al. find that common participation in the gold standard increased trade between 34 and 72%. López-Córdova and Meissner, find the gold standard effect to be 60%. In addition, they find that currency unions double trade, a result that is very similar to that found by Glick and Rose (2001).

Another paper that has addressed this problem is Rose and van Wincoop (2001). This paper, based on a model of bilateral trade by Anderson and van Wincoop (2001), estimates the *potential* euro effect on trade, using data on pre-EMU currency unions. According to the theory, bilateral trade between a pair of countries depends on their bilateral trade barrier *relative* to average trade barriers with all partners (i.e., their multilateral trade barrier or 'multilateral resistance'). Since reducing barriers vis-à-vis an important trading partner also reduces multilateral resistance considerably, the impact of the currency union on trade should be smaller in the case of countries that are large and proximate. The methodology allows the authors to estimate the trade effect of different potential currency unions. For the case of the euro, the estimated effect is of the order of 60%. But this estimate depends crucially on a number of assumptions, such as the elasticity of substitution between goods.

It is now possible to estimate the effects of the euro on trade between its members in a direct way, since data on trade are already available for 1999 through 2002. This is exactly what we do in this paper. Given the importance of the issue for the countries in the EU and the recent availability of data, it is not surprising that a number of scholars have independently started to work on this issue. See, for example, Bun and Klaasen (2002), De Nardis and Vicarelli (2003) and Barr *et al.* (this volume). These studies arrive at broadly similar results to ours, namely that the euro's trade impact is positive but modest in size compared to the estimated impact derived from evidence on other currency unions.

3. GRAVITY AND MONEY

Our empirical methodology is based on the gravity model, a model which has been extremely successful in predicting bilateral trade flows ever since its introduction by Linnemmann (1966).

3.1. The gravity model

In its simplest formulation, the gravity model states that bilateral trade flows depend positively on the product of the GDPs of both economies and negatively on the distance between them, in analogy to Newton's gravitational attraction between two bodies. See Box 1 on its theoretical foundations.

Typical variables added to the simplest gravity specification in the empirical trade literature include GDP per capita or population, as well as dummy variables indicating whether the two countries share a common border, a common language, or common membership in a free trade area (FTA). In the case of European Union nations, we also add an EU dummy to reflect the much deeper integration involved in the single market. However, the EU has deepened over time, so we add an 'EU Trend' variable, which captures the impact of the EU on trade, as it evolves through time. Finally, to control for idiosyncratic, year-specific effects – like global changes in transport and telecommunication costs, due for example to changes in oil prices, or increases in security costs after September 11th – we include yearly dummies. Details on all these variables can be found in Appendix A.

Box 1. The economics behind the gravity equation

The dependence of bilateral trade on the product of the GDPs was derived most naturally from models of trade with increasing returns to scale and product differentiation, such as that in Helpman (1987) and Helpman and Krugman (1985). There are, however, earlier theoretical foundations for the gravity model, such as Anderson (1979). Deardorff (1984) surveys the early work on this subject. For a brief discussion of the origins and theoretical foundations of the gravity model, see Frankel (1997). In these models with imperfect substitutes, the number of varieties produced in each country increases with size and, as a result, the quantity of goods imported from each country is proportional to its GDP. Within this framework, trade barriers (such as transportation and other transaction costs) increase the relative price of imported goods, and therefore reduce trade (for an early paper that introduced shipping costs into the imperfect substitutes model, see Bergstrand 1985). More recently, Deardorff (1998) showed that, under certain assumptions, the gravity equation can also be derived from the classical Hecksher–Ohlin model, which emphasizes differences in factor endowments across trading countries. The whole literature is nicely put into perspective by Evenett and Keller (2002), who discuss the different implications of these theories, and test them using bilateral data on intra-industry and inter-industry trade.

3.1.1. Adding a common currency to the gravity model. Against this benchmark, we study the impact of EMU on bilateral trade by introducing an additional dummy variable, which takes a value of one when the two countries in the pair belong to the EMU. We call this variable EMU 2, indicating that both countries in the pair are part of EMU.

The large swings experienced by the euro since its creation raises concerns about potential valuation effects. Consider, for example, the sharp depreciation of the euro following its introduction in 1999. If dollar prices of goods produced in the euro zone fall as a result of depreciation, the value of trade between two EMU countries will fall as well, relative to trade between other countries, and the EMU effect on trade could potentially be underestimated. One way to deal with this issue would be to control for bilateral unit value indices in order to capture the change in import and export prices. Unfortunately, these indices are not available. For this reason, in order to control for these valuation effects we include in most regressions an index of the real exchange rate for each of the countries in the pair (the index is the ratio between the nominal exchange rate of each country vis-à-vis the US dollar and the country's GDP deflator). Reassuringly, the inclusion of these indices does not change the results significantly.

3.1.2. Using panel data with country-pair fixed effects.

Much of the literature on the trade effect of currency unions was based on cross-section analysis. Therefore, the question it answers is whether countries that share a common currency trade more than others that do not. As Glick and Rose (2001) argue, this is not exactly the right policy question. What one would want to know, as a policy-maker, is the impact of a currency union on those countries that adopt it. To focus on the right policy question, and following Glick and Rose (2001), in most of our regressions we will include country-pair fixed effects, in order to isolate the euro effects over time, and leave out the cross-sectional variation. Thus, all time-invariant variables that are specific to a country pair – bilateral distance, common language and the like, as well as other unobservable characteristics of the country pairs – will be subsumed in these country pair dummies. In this way, if for any reason two euro countries have traditionally traded a lot, this will be captured in the country-pair dummy, and will not affect the EMU coefficients in the regression. We believe that the use of these country-pair dummies provides the cleanest possible benchmark against which to assess the euro effect on trade.

3.1.3. Data used in the regressions.

Following the practice established by Glick and Rose (2001), our dependent variable is the log of total merchandise trade (exports plus imports) between pairs of countries, in a given year deflated by the US CPI. We use two samples of nations. The first includes all 22 industrial countries included in the IMF's Direction of Trade Statistics data set. The second includes only the EU 15 (because of the Belgium-Luxembourg customs union there are only 14 observations in the EU sample). While the first sample has the advantage of the larger size, the second one has the appeal that countries are more homogeneous, geographically proximate, and all belong to the same single market. Since these countries tend to share similar experiences, it is less likely that the results will be contaminated by other factors that are not properly accounted for. Of the 91 country pairs in the EU sample, 55 share the euro. Other data are from the World Bank's World Development Indicators (population and GDP), or the CIA's World Factbook (coordinates for the calculation of distances, language, borders, etc.). See Appendix A for more details.

3.2. Estimating the trade impact of the euro

Table 1 shows the results for four variants of the basic equation using our full sample of developed countries. Column 1 shows the estimates when we exclude the country pair dummies, and include instead all the traditional difficulty-of-trading proxies such as bilateral distance, common border, etc. Column 2 shows results when pair dummies are used. Columns 3 and 4 repeat the column 1 and 2 specifications with the exchange rate variables added.

Table 1. The euro's trade impact – a range of estimates, developed country sample

EMU 2	0.198	0.039	0.230	0.054
	(0.040)***	(0.013)***	(0.042)***	(0.013)***
Real GDP	0.793	1.220	0.798	1.145
	(0.009)***	(0.056)***	(0.009)***	(0.059)***
Real GDP per capita[a]	0.218		0.240	
	(0.033)***		(0.035)***	
Free Trade Agreement	0.101	−0.012	0.088	−0.005
	(0.050)**	(0.021)	(0.051)*	(0.021)
EU	0.148	0.042	0.180	0.043
	(0.055)***	(0.021)**	(0.055)***	(0.021)**
EU Trend	−0.003	0.001	−0.001	0.001
	(0.004)	(0.001)	(0.004)	(0.001)
Landlocked	−0.495		−0.471	
	(0.032)***		(0.031)***	
Island	0.136		0.155	
	(0.045)***		(0.046)***	
Distance	−0.752		−0.738	
	(0.024)***		(0.025)***	
Area	−0.012		−0.023	
	(0.008)		(0.009)***	
Contiguity	0.248		0.286	
	(0.044)***		(0.046)***	
Common Language	0.816		0.803	
	(0.042)***		(0.043)***	
Real Exchange Rate of Country 1			−0.338	−0.158
			(0.117)***	(0.044)***
Real Exchange Rate of Country 2			−0.611	−0.270
			(0.139)***	(0.057)***
Implied proportional impact on trade:				
EMU 2 Impact[b]	0.219	0.040	0.259	0.055
(s.e.)[b]	(0.049)***	(0.014)***	(0.053)***	(0.014)***
Observations	2541	2541	2541	2541
R-squared[c]	0.93	0.45	0.93	0.46
Country Pair Dummies	No	Yes	No	Yes
Year Dummies	Yes	Yes	Yes	Yes

Note: Robust standard errors in parentheses; * significant at 10%; ** significant at 5%; *** significant at 1%.
[a] Real GDP per capita is only included in the regressions without country pair dummies because of the high colinearity between those dummies and the population.
[b] The EMU2 impact is calculated as exp(EMU2)-1; standard error (s.e.) by delta method, see Greene (2000).
[c] Within R-squared are reported in columns 2 and 4.
The equation estimated in column 4, which is our preferred regression, was:

$$\ln T_{ijt} = \alpha_{ij} + \beta_1 \ln Y_{it}Y_{jt} + \beta_2 FTA_{ijt} + \beta_3 EU_{ijt} + \beta_4 EUTrend_{ijt} + \beta_5 RER_{it} + \beta_6 RER_{jt} + \beta_7 EMU2_{ijt} + \gamma_t + \varepsilon_{ijt}$$

where T represents bilateral trade (sum of imports and exports), the Y's are real GDPs of the two nations, *FTA* is a dummy that indicates common membership in an FTA. *EU* indicates common EU members, *EUTrend* is explained in the text, the *RER* variables are the real exchange rate variables explained in the text, and *EMU2* is a dummy that takes the value 1 when both countries in the pair belong to EMU after 1999.

All regressions include year dummies. Excluding the year dummies does not affect the results in any significant way (see the web appendix).

The big story in Table 1 comes from the estimated effect of the EMU dummies, but before turning to these we want to be sure that the controlling variables are all estimated sensibly. We note that all the traditional gravity variables have the expected sign, and their coefficients are similar to those typically found in the gravity literature. In column 1, for example, the coefficient for distance is around −0.75. The coefficients for GDP and GDP per capita add up to about one, and free trade areas are estimated to increase bilateral trade by around 11% while, not surprisingly, the impact of the EU is a much larger 31%.[2] The EU trend is not statistically significant. Our results for the last two columns suggest that a real exchange rate appreciation tends to increase bilateral trade, a result that is consistent with our concerns regarding potential valuation effects.

3.2.1. The euro boosts bilateral trade.

The critical results concern the size of the euro's trade impact. Here the results suggest that the impact of EMU is important, even though smaller than previous estimates (Rose 2002, in his analysis of this literature, finds the currency unions approximately double a nation's trade). To ease interpretation, the table translates the coefficients on the EMU 2 dummy into the proportional impact on trade. Altogether, the results show that two countries in euroland trade somewhere between 4 and 26% more than other country pairs, all else equal. Interestingly, the results excluding the pair dummies suggest the intriguing, but hard to believe, finding that the impact of EMU is comparable to that of EU membership itself.

Similar estimates on a sample of EU nations only yields similar results (see Appendix B). We note that these findings, while much smaller than those obtained by Rose and co-authors, confirm the notion that currency unions foster trade. The findings are also broadly similar to those obtained in a number of other studies that independently emerged since we disseminated our first draft in early 2002. See, for example, Bun and Klaasen (2002), De Nardis and Vicarelli (2003) and Barr *et al.* (this volume).

3.2.2. Reverse causality: the 'endogeneity bias'.

Observe that the currency union effect is systematically smaller when pair dummies are included. One explanation for this relates to the possibility of reverse causality. Since the benefits associated to the reduction of transaction costs in trade flows are frequently cited as one motive for nations to join a monetary union (Gordon Brown, for example, mentioned it in his address to the UK Parliament), and these benefits are larger the greater the extent of trade between the countries in question, it is conceivable that euroland members joined because they engaged in a lot of trade with each other before joining. Under this hypothesis, our results may be telling us that high trade flows were indeed used by nations as a criterion for membership. Unusually high trade flows, in short, lead to adoption of the euro, not vice versa.

---

[2] To compute the impact of the EU, we add to the coefficient of FTA that corresponding to the EU dummy, and the coefficient of the EU Trend multiplied by mean of the trend. Thus, the impact is calculated as $\exp(0.101 + 0.148 - 0.003 * (-6.72)) - 1 = 0.31$.

The inclusion of pair dummies goes some way to removing this 'endogeneity bias'. For example, if two countries, say the Netherlands and Germany, have traditionally traded a lot, the Netherlands–Germany pair dummy will pick this up. This reduces the chances that the estimates confuse their adoption of the euro with their traditionally strong trade relationship.

The fact that the euro's impact is estimated to be much lower when the pair dummies are included – something like one-fifth the size – suggests that reverse causality, i.e. the endogeneity bias, may be a real concern. (See Box 2 for more detail on the reverse causality issue.) Given this, our preferred regressions include pair dummies, as well as the real exchange rates, in order to control for the valuation effects discussed above. The EMU effect on trade corresponding to these regressions, reported in the fourth column of both Table 1 and Table B2 in Appendix B, amounts to 5.5%, in the case of the developed country sample, and 7.6% in the case of the EU sample.

Box 2. More on the endogeneity bias

The beauty of the country-pair fixed effects is that they absorb all other unobservable characteristics of the country pairs (and of the individual countries) that are invariant over time and impact bilateral trade. Examples of such characteristics include: openness to trade, a history of conflict among a country pair, and more. Note that including country fixed effects instead of country-pair fixed effects, while accounting for country-specific time invariant factors that may help explain bilateral trade flows, do not help address the endogeneity problem discussed above.

Pair dummies do not, however, completely eliminate the scope for endogeneity. Countries could adopt the euro after a surge in trade within the sample period. Keeping the sample period relatively short (we use the period 1992–2002) mitigates this concern. In any case, it is reassuring that in the next section, when we look at the impact of the euro on trade over time, we do not observe a substantial increase in trade among EMU countries before their decision to join the monetary union. This suggests that endogeneity concerns should not be too serious once we have included country-pair dummies.

An alternative way to deal with endogeneity is to use instrumental variables. This is the approach pursued in another paper in this book by Barr et al. Those authors use the correlation of cycles as an instrument for currency union, since the Optimal Currency Area (OCA) literature suggests that there should be a close association between currency unions and cycle correlation among country pairs. However, the recent work on endogenous OCA (see Frankel and Rose, 1997, 1998) shows that cycle correlation is also strongly associated to trade intensity, suggesting that this instrument is not ideal. Be that as it may, it is reassuring that the Barr et al. estimates of the trade effect are roughly similar to ours – positive and statistically significant, but as yet much lower than the early estimates by Rose (2000).

3.3. The timing of the euro's impact

The results discussed so far suggest that the EMU has had a moderate but statistically significant effect on trade. While it is nice to be able to capture the EMU effect in a single estimate, the results of the previous section do not provide information regarding the timing of the effect.

As discussed in Section 2, the euro could affect trade via many different channels. All of these channels could take time to work, so we might not see an immediate impact of the euro. Alternatively, many of these effects could be anticipated in advance and so the euro's impact might be felt even before it was formally created in 1999.

We want to let the data speak as freely as possible on the timing issue, so we include separate euro dummies for each year from 1992 to 2002. The idea is to follow the trade performance of the countries that joined the euro over time, and check whether there is a jump around the time of the formal creation of EMU. Given this goal, it is convenient to redefine our EMU 2 dummy so that it takes a value of one for two EMU countries throughout the whole sample period, even before the formal creation of EMU. As an example, EMU 2 takes a value of one for Germany–Spain in 1993 (or any other year), even though the EMU did not exist at the time. Moreover, due to its late arrival into EMU, Greece is counted as non-EMU for the purposes of this exercise (See Table B6 in Appendix B for a set of results when Greece is counted as an EMU country.)

The estimation results are shown in Table 2. The first pair of columns correspond to our estimates using the set of all developed nations (see Figure 1 for a list of nations), while the second pair present estimates using data only for EU members. Note that, following the discussion of the previous section, we included country-pair dummies in both regressions.

The estimates in the top panel of Table 2 show how and when the euro affected intra-euroland trade. To facilitate the analysis, we plot the trade-impact equivalent of the coefficients in Figure 3 for both samples. As the figure plainly shows, the effect increases in 1999 in both samples, but the real jump seems to occur in 1998. Table B5 in Appendix B show that the jump is statistically significant. While in the developed country sample the impact of EMU continues to increase gradually after that, in the case of the EU sample there is another noticeable jump in 2001.[3]

The obvious question is why the jump in 1998, given that EMU was formally created in 1999. Recall that the road to the EMU started with the elimination of capital controls, and intensification of policy and central bank coordination in 1990 (Stage 1 of the EMU), the year 1998 was a pivotal year in the process of monetary unification. In fact, whether the euro would become a reality was still in doubt as late as 1997. Italy and Belgium had levels of debt that exceeded the convergence criteria by a wide margin. In France, a socialist government had come into power, amid

---

[3] We compared trade in 2000 and 2001 for each of the country pairs in the EU sample, to check whether the jump is due to outliers. It is not. In fact, out of only 23 country pairs whose trade increased in 2001, 18 were pairs formed by two EMU countries. Meanwhile, out of the 23 country pairs whose trade fell by more than 10%, only 4 were formed by two EMU countries.

Table 2. The euro's trade effect over time

	Developed sample		EU sample	
	Coefficient	(s.e.)	Coefficient	(s.e.)
EMU2 – 1993	−0.018	(0.031)	−0.007	(0.035)
EMU2 – 1994	0.038	(0.031)	0.025	(0.032)
EMU2 – 1995	0.051	(0.031)	0.016	(0.034)
EMU2 – 1996	0.036	(0.031)	−0.000	(0.033)
EMU2 – 1997	0.044	(0.030)	0.018	(0.030)
EMU2 – 1998	**0.098**	**(0.031)*****	**0.064**	**(0.032)****
EMU2 – 1999	**0.117**	**(0.030)*****	**0.073**	**(0.032)****
EMU2 – 2000	**0.104**	**(0.034)*****	**0.076**	**(0.035)****
EMU2 – 2001	**0.135**	**(0.035)*****	**0.166**	**(0.034)*****
EMU2 – 2002	**0.154**	**(0.041)*****	**0.164**	**(0.041)*****
Real GDP	1.138	(0.058)***	1.062	(0.075)***
Free Trade Agreement	−0.010	(0.021)	0.045	(0.030)
EU	0.009	(0.022)	−0.047	(0.053)
EU Trend	−0.001	(0.001)	−0.001	(0.004)
Real Exchange Rate of Country 1	−0.174	(0.044)***	−0.187	(0.060)***
Real Exchange Rate of Country 2	−0.264	(0.057)***	0.374	(0.098)***
Observations		2541		1001
Within R^2		0.46		0.67

Notes: Robust standard errors in parentheses; * significant at 10%; ** significant at 5%; *** significant at 1%. The estimation includes country-pair fixed effects, and yearly fixed effects. The equation estimated is:

$$\ln T_{ijt} = \beta_{ij} + \beta_1 \ln Y_{it}Y_{jt} + \beta_2 FTA_{ijt} + \beta_3 EU_{ijt} + \beta_4 EUTrend_{ijt} + \beta_5 RER_{it} + \beta_6 RER_{it} + \sum_{\tau \in [1992,2001]} \beta_{7t}I_t EMU2_{ij} + \gamma_t + \varepsilon_{ijt}$$

where I is an indicator variable that equals one in each successive year and *EMU2* is a dummy that takes the value one when both countries in the pair belong to EMU, regardless of the year. For example, I_{93} * *EMU2* has a value of one for the Spain–Germany country pair for the year 1993, even though the EMU did not exist at the time. All other variables are defined in Table 1.

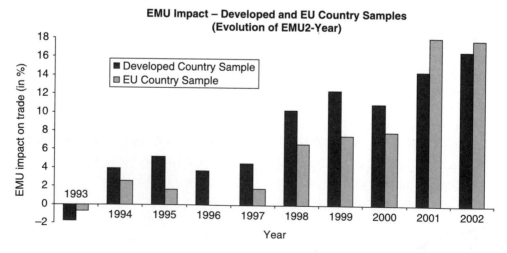

Figure 3. EMU effect over time

Notes: Results come from Table 2 converted to % impact using the following formula: exp(EMU2-year) − 1.

campaign promises to focus more on the lingering unemployment problem, and less on meeting the convergence criteria; once in office, however, the Jospin government committed itself to monetary unification. Even Germany had trouble meeting the convergence criteria, as deficits increased as a result of the unification efforts. In 1998, any lingering concerns regarding the future of EMU were put to rest. On 25 March 1998, the European Commission and the European Monetary Institute published their convergence reports, recommending that 11 countries – Austria, Belgium, Finland, France, Germany, Ireland, Italy, Luxembourg, the Netherlands, Portugal and Spain – be admitted into the EMU. At the beginning of May, the decision was formally announced during a meeting of the Heads of State in Brussels, during which the bilateral irrevocable conversion rates were set among the member currencies. This was followed on 1 June 1998 with the official creation of the European Central Bank.

In addition to providing a sense of the evolution of the EMU effect over time, the results reported in Table 2 can also be used to provide alternative estimates of the size of EMU's early years trade effect, by comparing the size of the coefficients before EMU (for example, during the period 1995–7) to the coefficients after EMU (for example, 1999–2001). A nice thing about this way of assessing the impact of EMU is that one can restrict the comparison to the years just before and just after the creation of EMU, and thus reduce the chances that the results are tainted by other changes that might have occurred over the sample period, but which may have little to do with EMU itself. These comparisons suggest that the impact of EMU on trade between its members ranges between 7 and 10%, depending on the sample and the years used for the before/after comparison, and that this impact is statistically significant (see Table B3 in Appendix B for details).

4. EURO ADOPTION: RECIPROCAL PREFERENTIAL LIBERALIZATION OR GREATER OPENNESS?

In the empirical exercises discussed so far, the evolution of trade among country pairs that adopted the euro is measured against a benchmark provided by the evolution of bilateral trade among all other country pairs. However, this leaves out the question of supply switching, or what is loosely referred to in the literature as trade diversion.[4]

4.1. Estimating the impact on intra-euroland trade and trade with third nations

To check for this, we add a new dummy to the specification presented in Table 1. This new dummy takes the value one when only one of the countries involved in the bilateral trade uses the euro. As an example, this variable, which we call EMU 1,

---

[4] When Viner (1950) coined the term 'trade diversion', he meant it to signify the welfare-reducing switch from low cost suppliers to high cost suppliers (this can result from discriminatory tariff liberalization). Since adoption of the euro does not change tariffs, any import supplier switching involves a change from high-cost to low-cost suppliers and thus tends to be welfare improving.

Table 3. Trade diversion or general openness?

	1992–2002	
	Developed sample	EU
EMU 2	**0.126**	**0.084**
	(0.019)*	**(0.030)***
EMU 1	**0.086**	**0.012**
	(0.015)*	**(0.030)**
Real GDP	1.108	1.071
	(0.059)***	(0.077)***
Free Trade Agreement	−0.008	0.048
	(0.021)	(0.030)
EU	0.030	−0.044
	(0.022)	(0.053)
EU Trend	0.000	−0.001
	(0.001)	(0.004)
Real Exchange Rate of Country 1	−0.220	−0.134
	(0.045)***	(0.061)**
Real Exchange Rate of Country 2	−0.288	0.367
	(0.057)***	(0.099)***
EMU 2 Impact	**0.134**	**0.088**
Transformed S.E. (Delta Method)	**(0.015)***	**(0.029)***
EMU 1 Impact	**0.090**	**0.012**
Transformed S.E. (Delta Method)	**(0.016)***	**(0.029)**
Observations	2541	1001
Within R^2	0.46	0.65
Country Pair Dummies	Yes	Yes
Year Dummies	Yes	Yes

Notes: Robust standard errors in parentheses; * significant at 10%; ** significant at 5%; *** significant at 1%. The impact is calculated as exp(EMU2)–1, or exp(EMU1)–1 as appropriate; standard error (s.e.) calculated by the delta method.

The equation estimated in column 4, which is our preferred regression, was:

$$\ln T_{ijt} = \alpha_{ij} + \beta_1 \ln Y_{it}Y_{jt} + \beta_2 FTA_{ijt} + \beta_3 EU_{ijt} + \beta_4 EUTrend_{ijt} + \beta_5 RER_{it} + \beta_6 RER_{jt} + \beta_7 EMU2_{ijt} + \beta_8 EMU1_{ijt} + \gamma_t + \varepsilon_{ijt}$$

where the variables are defined in Table 1 and *EMU1* is defined in the text.

would take a value of one in the case of the US and Spain, for the year 1999 (or any post-EMU year), but would take a value of zero for Spain–Germany, regardless of the year.

The idea is that the sign of the estimated coefficient on this new dummy will reveal something about the trade effects mechanism. If adoption of the euro operated in the same way as a preferential trade liberalization, that is to say, it led to supply switching away from non-euroland partners, the EMU 1 coefficient should be negative. Alternatively, a country's adoption of the euro may just make it a more open economy and therefore boost its trade with all nations.

Table 3 presents the regression results both for the developed country and the EU samples. Comparing column 1 in Table 3 to its correspondent in Table 1 column 4, we see that allowing for the euro's impact on trade with third nations actually increases our estimate of the intra-euroland effect from 5.5% to 13.4%. This result is consistent with our estimates for EMU 1, which suggest that euroland's trade with non-euro nations is also boosted by the euro's adoption. When we exclude the possibility that the euro stimulates trade with third nations – as we did implicitly in Table 1 – the comparison is between intra-euroland trade flows and *all other trade flows*, including those between euro and non-euro nations. If, as Figure 1 suggested, euroland's trade with third nations is also promoted by the single currency, this lumping together of all other trade flow raises the standard of comparison and thus reduces our estimate of the euro's direct effect on intra-euroland trade.

Observe that the impact of EMU 1 varies depending on the sample. The developed country sample results suggest that membership in EMU increases trade vis-à-vis all partners. Compared to trade among non-EMU countries, trade between an EMU country and a non-member increases by 9%. In contrast, the EU sample results suggest that the trade boost with non-members is not statistically different from zero, and all the action happens between EMU partners. Consistent with this, our estimated impact for EMU 2 in the EU sample is much closer to that we report in Table B2 in Appendix B (8.8% compared to 7.6%). While the exercise does not provide definitive answers, we believe that, once we include the EMU 1 dummy, the results using the developed country sample may be more reliable. The reason is that in the EU sample, there are very few country pairs formed by non-EMU countries left, and these are the pairs that are used as the benchmark for comparison.

4.2. The impact over time

To study the euro's direct and indirect impact on trade flows more precisely, we estimate the single currency's year-by-year impact on trade among euro adopters, and between euro-adopters and other nations. That is, we match the exercise discussed in Table 2 but we now allow for the EMU 1 effect as well.

Table 4 and Figure 4 present our results on the evolution of the EMU 2 and EMU 1 effects over time. The results in Table 4 broadly confirm the time-pattern of the euro's trade effect. In the developed country sample – which provides a broader range of observations on non-euroland nations and is thus probably more reliable – the euro significantly boosts intra-euroland trade starting in 1998, with the effect clearly increasing in magnitude in 2001 and 2002. For ease of analysis, Figure 4 plots the proportional-trade-impact equivalents of the EMU 2 and EMU 1 coefficients for the developed country sample. The figure shows that the temporal pattern of EMU 1 is similar to that of EMU 2. The time pattern for the EU sample (not shown in the figure) is broadly similar, but the onset of the trade boosting effect is delayed until 2001 and 2002. Table B4 in Appendix B provides alternative estimates for EMU 2 and EMU 1 obtained by comparing the yearly coefficients before and after the formal creation of EMU. For example, for the developed country sample, comparing 1995–7 with 1999–2001 yields estimated impacts of 15.8 and 8.6% for EMU 2 and EMU 1, respectively.

What is clear from this analysis is that euroland's adoption of a common currency has not harmed euroland's trade with other nations – a result that is consistent with what Frankel and Rose (2000) found for a much larger sample of countries.

Table 4. Trade diversion or general openness: timing of the impact

	Developed sample		EU sample	
	Coefficient	(s.e.)	Coefficient	(s.e)
EMU2 − 1993	−0.031	(0.041)	−0.025	(0.059)
EMU2 − 1994	0.060	(0.040)	0.037	(0.056)
EMU2 − 1995	0.093	(0.043)**	0.056	(0.058)
EMU2 − 1996	0.065	(0.041)	0.033	(0.060)
EMU2 − 1997	0.096	(0.042)**	0.011	(0.056)
EMU2 − 1998	**0.189**	**(0.043)****	**0.084**	**(0.065)**
EMU2 − 1999	**0.217**	**(0.040)****	**0.109**	**(0.064)***
EMU2 − 2000	**0.214**	**(0.047)****	**0.098**	**(0.068)**
EMU2 − 2001	**0.263**	**(0.046)****	**0.245**	**(0.065)****
EMU2 − 2002	**0.284**	**(0.051)****	**0.305**	**(0.074)****
EMU1 − 1993	−0.035	(0.039)	−0.020	(0.060)
EMU1 − 1994	0.014	(0.037)	0.015	(0.057)
EMU1 − 1995	0.042	(0.040)	0.047	(0.059)
EMU1 − 1996	0.015	(0.037)	0.038	(0.060)
EMU1 − 1997	0.038	(0.039)	−0.008	(0.057)
EMU1 − 1998	**0.093**	**(0.039)***	**0.022**	**(0.066)**
EMU1 − 1999	**0.103**	**(0.036)****	**0.041**	**(0.065)**
EMU1 − 2000	**0.106**	**(0.040)****	**0.023**	**(0.068)**
EMU1 − 2001	**0.133**	**(0.039)****	**0.089**	**(0.064)**
EMU1 − 2002	**0.138**	**(0.043)****	**0.161**	**(0.072)***
Real GDP	1.096	(0.058)***	1.057	(0.077)***
Free Trade Agreement	−0.019	(0.020)	0.048	(0.030)
EU	−0.023	(0.022)	−0.045	(0.053)
EU Trend	−0.004	(0.001)**	−0.001	(0.004)
Real Exchange Rate Country 1	−0.253	(0.045)***	−0.204	(0.061)***
Real Exchange Rate Country 2	−0.274	(0.057)***	0.375	(0.099)***
Observations		2541		1001
Within R^2		0.48		0.68
Year Dummies		Yes		Yes
Country Pair Dummies		Yes		Yes

Notes: Robust standard errors in parentheses; * significant at 10%; ** significant at 5%; *** significant at 1%.

5. ARE OUR FINDINGS ROBUST?

In this section we check the robustness of our results to alternative estimation methods, and to changes in the country sample. For space considerations, we will focus the robustness analysis on the developed country sample. However, results are qualitatively similar using the EU sample instead.

5.1. Alternative estimation methods

As the theory reviewed in Emerson *et al.* (1992) shows, the presence of adjustment and sunk costs (linked, for example, to the establishment of distribution and service

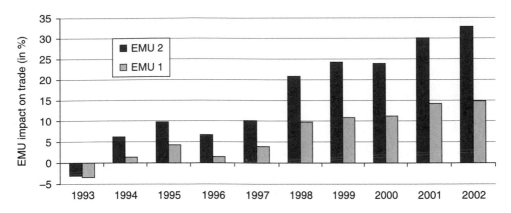

Figure 4. Evolution of intra-euroland and trade diversion effects (developed nations)

Notes: EMU 2 is the trade impact on intra-euroland trade; EMU 1 is the trade impact on euroland nations' trade with third countries.

Source: Authors' calculations with Table 4 results for developed country sample.

networks) may produce inertia in bilateral trade levels. High bilateral trade today, beyond what is explained by fundamentals – GDP, FTAs, etc. – may imply high levels of bilateral trade tomorrow, and create error autocorrelation in our panel model. To deal with this serial correlation problem, we estimate a dynamic panel that includes the lagged bilateral trade as an independent variable. We compute this dynamic model using Arellano and Bond (1991) and considering that EMU started in 1998 instead of 1999, as suggested by the discussion above.

Table 5 presents the results for the developed country sample using our regular sample period (1992–2002) as well as one that allows for a longer time horizon (1980–2002). The results for the short sample (column 4, in which both EMU 2 and EMU 1 are included) suggest that the increase in trade among EMU members is around 9% in the short run, while the effect of EMU 1 is half as large. The dynamic panel allows one to calculate the long-run effect which, for the case of EMU 2 in the short sample, is 34%. (The long-run effect is computed dividing the EMU 2 coefficient by the lagged trade coefficient.) While the 9 and 4.5% effects are smaller than those obtained in Table 3, column 1, it is important to stress that these figures correspond to the effects on impact (during the first year), while the results discussed above were looking at the effects over a longer period of time. In fact, these dynamic panel results appear to be entirely consistent with our previous results.

We note that Bun and Klassen (2002) and De Nardis and Vicarelli (2003) use a similar approach to compute the effect of EMU on trade. However, they focus exclusively on EMU 2, and thus do not allow for the possibility of a trade boosting effect (or for trade diversion). Compared to the dynamic panel, an advantage of the methodology used in Table 4, in which we follow the impact of EMU over time, is that we do not need to impose a date for the start of the EMU effect, and rather let the

Table 5. Dynamic panel estimation results

Dependent variable: Log of bilateral trade	Developed sample			
	1980–2002		1992–2002	
EMU 2	**0.072**	**0.109**	**0.055**	**0.089**
	(0.019)***	**(0.021)*****	**(0.021)*****	**(0.025)****
EMU 1		**0.061**		**0.045**
		(0.017)***		**(0.018)***
Lag of Log of Trade	**0.577**	**0.565**	**0.307**	**0.304**
	(0.022)***	**(0.023)*****	**(0.058)*****	**(0.058)****
Log of GDP	0.529	0.513	0.577	0.569
	(0.041)***	(0.041)***	(0.068)***	(0.068)**
Free Trade Agreement	0.061	0.056	0.046	0.044
	(0.015)***	(0.015)***	(0.020)**	(0.020)*
European Union	−0.039	−0.056	0.051	0.036
	(0.020)*	(0.021)***	(0.031)*	(0.031)
EU Trend	0.001	−0.001	0.009	0.007
	(0.001)	(0.002)	(0.002)***	(0.002)**
Real Exchange Rate Country 1	−0.334	−0.344	−0.354	−0.352
	(0.033)***	(0.033)***	(0.055)***	(0.055)**
Real Exchange Rate Country 2	−0.251	−0.255	−0.509	−0.499
	(0.031)***	(0.031)***	(0.058)***	(0.058)**
EMU2 Short-run effect	*0.075*	*0.115*	*0.057*	*0.093*
EMU2 Long-run effect	*0.133*	*0.213*	*0.196*	*0.340*
EMU1 Short-run effect		*0.063*		*0.046*
EMU1 Long-run effect		*0.114*		*0.160*
Arellano-Bond test – No autocorrelation order 1 (z)	−22.5***	−22.2***	−9.6***	−0.97***
Arellano-Bond test – No autocorrelation order 2 (z)	0.7	0.7	2.9**	2.9**
Year Dummy	Yes	Yes	Yes	Yes
Observations	4851	4851	2079	2079

Notes: Robust standard errors in parentheses; * significant at 10%; ** significant at 5%; *** significant at 1%.

data do the talking. In fact, the dynamic panel results are quite sensitive to the choice of a starting date. In addition, the dynamic panel assumes that the dynamics following the creation of the EMU are exactly the same as the dynamics following any other shock that affects bilateral trade, such as changes in GDP or in real exchange rates.

5.2. Alternative samples

We now check whether the impact of EMU is fairly widespread among its member countries, or whether our results are driven by the experiences of just a few of them. As a baseline for these robustness checks, we will use the regression in column 4 of Table 1 (without trade diversion), and the regression in column 1 of Table 3 (with trade diversion), both corresponding to the developed country sample.

The first check we perform is to exclude one EMU country at a time from the sample. The results are presented in Table 6. For space considerations, we only report

Table 6. Estimation with single euroland nations excluded from the sample

	Developed sample		
Country dropped	EMU2	EMU2	EMU1
None (original sample)	0.054***	0.126***	0.086***
Observations	*2541*	*2541*	
Austria	0.049***	0.122***	0.088***
Belgium-Luxembourg	0.055***	0.125***	0.086***
Finland	0.061***	0.138***	0.094***
France	0.054***	0.122***	0.083***
Germany	0.047***	0.115***	0.081***
Greece	0.071***	0.153***	0.099***
Ireland	0.060***	0.127***	0.083***
Italy	0.053***	0.124***	0.085***
Netherlands	0.046***	0.105***	0.071***
Portugal	0.062***	0.142***	0.097***
Spain	0.050***	0.125***	0.091***
Observations	*2310*	*2310*	

Notes: * significant at 10%; ** significant at 5%; *** significant at 1%. Each of the rows present the results of two regressions, one that excludes *EMU 1* and one that includes this variable. For space considerations, only the coefficients for *EMU 2* and *EMU 1* are reported in the table.

the estimated coefficients corresponding to EMU 2 and EMU 1. The results are very robust to the exclusion of one country at a time. As an example, while the coefficient for EMU 2 without introducing trade diversion was 0.054, the range of the coefficients excluding one country at a time goes from 0.046 (excluding the Netherlands) to 0.071 (excluding Greece), and is always highly significant. The only country that seems to be an outlier in this table is latecomer Greece, whose exclusion from the sample tends to inflate all the EMU coefficients.

In Table 7 we repeat the exercise, excluding groups of countries from the sample instead of individual ones. We exclude, in turn:

- the relatively less developed EMU countries (Greece, Ireland, Portugal and Spain).
- the original six EU members (Belgium, Luxembourg, France, Germany, the Netherlands and Italy).
- the Nordic countries (Denmark, Finland, Iceland, Norway and Sweden).
- the DM block countries (Austria, Belgium and Luxembourg, Denmark, Germany, France and the Netherlands).
- all EMU countries except the original DM block ones (Germany, Belgium and Luxembourg, Austria and the Netherlands).

A couple of things are worth noting. First, the exclusion of the relatively less developed EMU countries increases the magnitude of the EMU coefficients, while the exclusion of the original six and in particular, the DM block countries, reduces it. This suggests that, while the overall results are quite robust, as a general rule the impact of EMU seems to be higher in the case of the more advanced countries.

Table 7. Estimation with groups of nations excluded from the sample

	Developed sample		
Group dropped	EMU2	EMU2	EMU1
None (original sample)	0.054***	0.126***	0.086***
Observations	*2541*	*2541*	
Relatively less developed[a]	0.089***	0.184***	0.119***
Observations	*1683*	*1683*	
Original EU core[b]	0.038*	0.087***	0.061***
Observations	*1705*	*1705*	
Nordies[c]	0.048***	0.097***	0.056***
Observations	*1683*	*1683*	
DM block[d]	0.003	0.056*	0.065***
Observations	*1320*	*1320*	
All EMU except original DM block[e]	0.098***	0.217***	0.161***
Observations	*1155*	*1155*	

Notes: Robust standard errors in parentheses; * significant at 10%; ** significant at 5%; *** significant at 1%.
[a] Dropped countries: Greece, Ireland, Portugal and Spain
[b] Dropped countries: Belgium and Luxembourg, France, Germany, the Netherlands and Italy
[c] Dropped countries: Denmark, Finland, Iceland, Norway and Sweden
[d] Dropped countries: Austria, Belgium and Luxembourg, Denmark, Germany, France and the Netherlands
[e] Dropped countries: Finland, France, Greece, Ireland, Italy, Portugal and Spain.

The second observation refers to the last row, in which we exclude all EMU countries with the exception of the original DM block ones. These countries have had tight exchange rate links for decades, and it is reasonable to believe that they would have been part of any monetary union in Europe. This dispels any concerns about these countries adopting the euro as a result of a surge in bilateral trade within the sample period, which was our remaining endogeneity concern. In other words, in these countries it is clear that EMU is driving changes in bilateral trade, and not vice-versa. As shown in the table, not only is the EMU significant, but its impact in these countries seems to be larger than in any other group of countries.

Finally, Table 8 isolates the EMU effect in each of the individual EMU countries. It is best to explain the procedure with an example. In the regressions for Germany, we split the dummy EMU 2 into two different dummies. The first one is a dummy 'Germany EMU 2' that takes a value of one for pairs formed by Germany and other EMU countries, zero otherwise. The second is a dummy called 'Other EMU 2', which takes a value of one for all other pairs of EMU countries. Similarly, we create a dummy 'Germany EMU 1', which takes a value of one for pairs formed by Germany and non-EMU countries, as well as a dummy for 'Other EMU 1'. One advantage of this procedure is that we can test whether the individual country EMU 2 effect is significantly different from the effect in the rest of EMU.

The table suggests that there are indeed a few countries that are different from the rest. Spain and the Netherlands are the two countries in which the EMU seems to have had the largest effect. In both countries, their individual EMU 2 coefficients are

Table 8. Euro's impact, member by member

	Developed countries sample					
EMU2	**Benchmark**	*0.054****	*0.126****	**Benchmark**	*0.054****	*0.126**
EMU1			*0.086****			*0.086**
Other EMU2 (1)	**Austria**	0.051***	0.123***	**Ireland**	0.062***	0.132
Austria EMU2 (2)		0.067***	0.137***		0.009	0.096
Other EMU1			0.088***			0.084
Austria EMU1			0.061**			0.105*
Difference EMU2 (1)–(2)		0.016	0.013		−0.053	−0.03
Other EMU2 (1)	**Belgium-Lux.**	0.044***	0.116***	**Italy**	0.051***	0.123*
Belgium-Lux. EMU2 (2)		0.096***	0.169***		0.066***	0.135*
Other EMU1			0.083***			0.084*
Belgium-Lux. EMU1			0.120***			0.100*
Difference EMU2 (1)–(2)		0.052	0.052		0.015	0.01
Other EMU2 (1)	**Finland**	0.070***	0.142***	**Netherlands**	0.039***	0.110*
Finland EMU2 (2)		−0.013	0.055***		0.120***	0.193*
Other EMU1			0.095***			0.072*
Finland EMU1			−0.007			0.217
Difference EMU2 (1)–(2)		−0.083***	−0.087***		0.081***	0.083*
Other EMU2 (1)	**France**	0.049***	0.121***	**Portugal**	0.074***	0.150*
France EMU2 (2)		0.076***	0.149***		−0.030	0.03
Other EMU1			0.083***			0.100*
France EMU1			0.117***			−0.03
Difference EMU2 (1)–(2)		0.027	0.028		−0.104***	−0.110
Other EMU2 (1)	**Germany**	0.047***	0.119***	**Spain**	0.033**	0.104*
Germany EMU2 (2)		0.083***	0.156***		0.146***	0.217*
Other EMU1			0.082***			0.084*
Germany EMU1			0.125***			0.100*
Difference EMU2 (1)–(2)		0.036*	0.037*		0.113***	0.112*
Other EMU2 (1)	**Greece**	0.075***	0.144***			
Greece EMU2 (2)		−0.084***	−0.024			
Other EMU1			0.093***			
Greece EMU1			0.021			
Difference EMU2 (1)–(2)		−0.159***	−0.168***			

Notes: Robust standard errors in parentheses; * significant at 10%; ** significant at 5%; *** significant at 1%.

statistically different from those of other EMU countries, in each of the specifications used. At the other end of the spectrum, the impact of EMU in Greece is significant, but with the wrong sign. Portugal also has the wrong sign in some of the specifications, but the effect is not statistically significant.

Notice that countries such as Finland and Portugal, which in the stylized facts presented in Figure 2 were at the top of the ranking regarding the increase in trade share corresponding to the euro zone, are not necessarily the countries with the biggest estimated EMU impact on trade.

This apparent contradiction is not difficult to explain. The reason is that the regressions weigh all observations equally, no matter the size of the trading partner or the magnitude of the bilateral trade flows. In contrast, in the stylized facts presented in the introduction, the magnitude of the bilateral trade flows plays an important role. For example, the increase in the trade share corresponding to EMU in Finland is driven mostly by the bilateral trade experience with this country's three most important trading partners, Germany (which increased its share considerably), Sweden and the UK (both of which lost share). In contrast, trade with fellow EMU countries Portugal and Belgium-Luxembourg fell sharply, in percentage terms. These latter observations are important in the regression analysis, but their impact tends to be lost in the analysis of trade shares.

In summary, while there are important differences across countries regarding the impact of EMU on trade, the impact reported in the previous sections are generally widespread, and the overall result does not seem to be explained by the experience of one or two particular countries.

6. Conclusions

While the motivation for Europe to advance toward monetary unification was to a large extent political, economic factors also played an important role. Among the latter, the promise of greater market integration was probably the single most important economic reason for the move to establish the euro. Four years after the creation of EMU, however, we still know very little about the economic impact of the monetary union on its member countries. Is the promise being fulfilled? The question is of great importance, not only for the current EMU members, but also for the rest of the EU, as well as the countries that are in line for accession. What are they missing? Should they join the club? The debate is raging today in countries such as Sweden and the UK, which are facing the decision of whether or not to join EMU in the near future. Furthermore, the nature of the debate (as reflected, for example, by the UK Chancellor of the Exchequer Gordon Brown's five economic tests) makes it clear that the decision of whether or not to join EMU will be based, to an important extent, on economic grounds.

The main concern among euro-sceptics relates to the loss of monetary and exchange rate independence. Relinquishing the national currency takes away one important tool for macroeconomic stabilization, which becomes critical when the degree of convergence to the euro area is low, particularly in the absence of alternative adjustment mechanisms. Euro advocates, in turn, see the adoption of the euro as an important step to acquire an influential role in the process of European integration. In addition, they emphasize the microeconomic benefits of monetary union, stressing the potential impact on trade, and pointing to the large effects suggested by the existing literature. To the extent that monetary union boosts trade, they argue, convergence will follow. But is this literature, based mainly on the experience of small and poor countries establishing monetary unions, or adopting the currency of others, relevant for the countries in the European Union? Four years into the EMU, we still have more questions than answers, and little empirical analysis that could inform the debate.

In this paper, we attempt to provide some answers regarding the impact of EMU on trade, using a panel data set that includes the most recent information on bilateral trade and two different samples of industrial countries. Controlling for a host of other factors, we find that common membership in euroland has positive and significant effects on bilateral trade. Specifically, the impact of shared membership in euroland ranges from 4 to 10%, when compared to all other country pairs, and from 8 to 16%, when compared to trade between two non-euro countries. Consistent with these results, we find no evidence of trade diversion. On the contrary, some of our results suggest that the euro leads to higher trade not just with other euroland members, but also with the rest of the world.

Our estimates are much smaller than the doubling of trade found by Glick and Rose (2001), using similar techniques, but on a much larger sample dominated by the experience of very small and poor countries, a result that also coincides with Rose's (2002) assessment of this literature. They are also smaller than Rose and van Wincoop's (2001) out of sample estimates of the effects of EMU. However, the effect of EMU on trade is significant, and economically important, particularly if we consider that our sample only covers the first four years of the monetary union.

Discussion

Karen Helene Midelfart
Norwegian School of Economics and Business Administration, and CEPR

It goes without saying that the impact of the euro on trade is a question of high relevance and interest. And the impact of the euro on trade is not only about taking out the gains from even deeper integration; the whole endogenous Optimal Currency Area (OCA) argument hinges on the impact of the currency union on trade. The essence of this argument being that the extent to which the establishing of a currency union increases trade matters for the cycle correlation among its member countries, and is thus critical to the union's success. Finally, examining the effect of the euro on trade is essential in order to understand what the outsiders may be missing.

This study by Micco, Stein and Ordoñez is well structured and competently done. In their search for trade effects, the authors employ a modified version of the gravity model using panel data and country-pair fixed effects. The data the authors rely on are IMF data for total merchandise trade (export plus import) for the period 1992–2002. They work with two different data sets; one with the 22 industrialized countries (EU 15, Australia, Canada, Iceland, Japan, New Zealand, Norway, Switzerland and the United States) and one restricted to the EU 15 countries. Using different methodologies and data sets they estimate the effect of the currency union to range between 5 and 20%. While this is both a statistically and economically significant effect, it is still much smaller than what other authors have found using other models and data sets. Employing data for the EMU and a more standard gravity model, Rose and Wincoop (2001) for instance estimate the currency union effect to be around 60%.

A number of the previous studies on currency unions and trade suffer from a set of weaknesses that seem to inflate their estimates. Micco *et al.* choose a framework that deals with quite a few of the problems characterizing the earlier studies, such as the issues of non-random selection into currency unions (see Persson, 2001), and of omitted variables strengthening trade links and thus increasing the propensity to join currency unions.

Unlike the bulk of the existing studies, Micco *et al.* seek to offer direct results on the effect of the euro. Part of these other studies base their empirical analysis on data for currency unions formed by small and/or poor countries. Others are based on time series for the EMU ending before the euro was actually introduced, and are thus only able to calculate implied trade effects of a common currency.

As many new questions as new answers

But while Micco *et al.* have provided an important contribution to the analysis of the effects of the EMU, their study almost raises more questions than it answers. There are in particular a couple of issues that deserve to be mentioned.

First, based on analyses of the EU 15 and of the 22 industrialized countries, they concluded that EMU does not appear to entail trade diversion. But what about the impact of the EMU on member countries' trade with developing countries? Their data sets do not allow this question to be addressed, but it is nevertheless one of great policy relevance. In order to unveil any potential trade diversion, broadening the data set to include more countries might not be sufficient. In order to get a correct and complete picture one should probably employ a sectoral disaggregated data set. This would, for example, allow us to see whether there has been any trade diversion in labour intensive industries with southern Europe out-competing the Far East.

Second, the authors point out that the effect of EMU on trade is essential for assessing the role played by the endogenous OCA argument with respect to trade. However, whether EMU fosters trade only answers part of the question. Crucial for the OCA argument is whether the type of trade EMU has encouraged has made the member countries more or less vulnerable to asymmetric shocks. This depends on whether the EMU has encouraged intra- or inter-industry trade, as the latter may imply increased specialization and diverging industrial structures, while the former may only imply tighter economic links among the member countries. In order to assess how increased trade has tightened the economic bands among the EMU members, analysis of the effect of the currency union on pan-European production networks – possibly by employing data on trade intermediates or parts and components – is also called for. And interesting to explore, finally, is if the currency union has had a differential impact on intra- versus extra-EMU trade in terms of the type of trade it encourages.

Third, Micco *et al.* provide important results on the impact of being inside versus outside the EMU and on the change in the insider effect over time. EMU denotes the final part of the European integration. It is well known that this integration process has had dramatic effects on trade in the EU (estimated by the Commission to be around 20–30% already in 1996). What we don't know – but would like to know – is what share of the rise in trade can be ascribed to product market integration prior to the introduction of the euro, what increase in trade is about anticipating the impact of a common currency, and what increase is really the result of the implementation of a common currency.

To summarize, this is an important contribution to the debate on the effects of the EMU, but it leaves a number of questions open for future research.

Jean-Marie Viaene
Erasmus University, Tinbergen Institute and CESifo

What is the true significance of the birth of the euro for international trade developments of participating countries and of their trading partners? Good news according to the study by Micco, Stein and Ordoñez. The purpose of their paper is to measure the early effects of the third stage of economic and monetary union (EMU) on trade and, to that end, they estimate a gravity model of bilateral trade over the period 1992–2002. Two different samples of industrial countries are used. The full sample includes 22 industrialized countries, the second one is restricted to the current members of the European Union (i.e. 14 countries as Belgium and Luxembourg are merged). The latter sample therefore includes the sub-group of current EMU countries and the sub-group of EU countries that have not adopted the single currency. Their finding is that, by joining the EMU, any two participating countries increase their bilateral trade between 5 and 20%. In addition, there is no evidence of trade diversion with non-member countries. Hence, these results imply that, regarding trade, the microeconomic gains of a currency union dominate the lost macroeconomic flexibility of running an independent monetary policy.

Compared to the existing literature, the paper contains three important contributions: (1) the authors use sufficiently long samples of relatively homogenous countries to obtain indifferently time-series, cross-section or panel data estimates; (2) they find effects of currency union on trade that are smaller (and more realistic) than comparable empirical studies; (3) their intensive use of robustness checks gives a reliable range of estimates.

Given its emphasis on empirics, the study spends little time on the many ways in which the single currency could affect international trade. But, what are the reasons for the good news? First, the elimination of currency exchange costs is an obvious benefit. Also, the increased transparency in the international comparison of prices facilitates the arbitrage of goods across national boundaries. Simultaneously, search engines of the internet have provided the technology to perform arbitrage more efficiently. Second, the emergence of the euro as a reserve currency qualifies it as a prime currency of invoice for trade with non-member countries. For the euro zone, this is an additional element of stability as these trade flows are not subject to exchange rate changes and volatility. Third, with the announcement and introduction of the euro, real returns to capital have converged almost completely among participating countries. This would not have been possible without the 1992 financial deregulation and creation of a single European capital market. For countries with historically high interest rates, this meant a boost to new investments, higher growth and trade. Though this concerns mainly European countries with historically higher inflation, peripheral countries with liberalized capital markets gain as well. For example, Africa's CFA zones, which have operated as currency areas tied to the French franc, are now implicitly tied to the euro.

Why isn't there any bad news? First, a reason might be that, in this paper, the authors estimate the early effects of EMU on trade. In essence, they quantify the effects on trade described above, which are of a short-term nature and are expected to be exhausted with the passing of time. Whether these positive trade effects will be maintained in the long run is an important empirical question. Second, the last and more relevant part of the sample is characterized by strong growth worldwide and mainly by a depreciating euro with respect to the US dollar and other currencies. These are circumstances that are favourable to trade creation with the rest of the world. Finally, a conventional wisdom is that the introduction of the euro reduces exchange rate volatility. While it does by definition within the euro zone, it is not excluded that variability in the exchange rate with non-member countries increases. This is detrimental to trade if proper hedging instruments do not exist or are too costly.

Panel discussion

In reply to the discussion of Karen Helene Midelfart, Alejandro Micco and Ernesto Stein agreed that it is interesting to look deeper into the effects on inter- versus intra-industry trade, especially for assessing the effects on welfare. However, disaggregated data that would allow this issue to be addressed is not yet available. Ernesto Stein disagreed with Karen Helene Midelfart that trade diversion matters more for trade with developing countries. Instead, he expected trade diversion to play a more important role among similar countries. Furthermore, he mentioned robustness checks using different groups of countries. If the transition countries are included in the control group, the EMU effect on trade becomes smaller because trade of the transition countries has increased substantially over time.

Stijn Claessens thought that the results concerning the changes in trade volumes were more interesting than the results for levels. Moreover, he proposed that the authors should look at capital flows and FDI in order to investigate whether these serve as substitutes for trade. Ernesto Stein agreed that such analysis would be interesting but not feasible because data on FDI and capital flows are currently not available for a sufficiently long time period.

Patrick Honohan and David Begg pointed out that the results are consistent with those reported by Rose in that the trade effects are largest for small countries such as Finland and Portugal. Ignazio Angeloni thought that the results point to complementarities between trade and banking, given the results in his paper with Michael Ehrmann. He asked the authors to provide some motivation for why monetary union should induce more trade with other members of the monetary union. Stijn Claessens suggested the elimination of exchange rate volatility as one reason for the increase in trade after EMU. Alejandro Micco and Ernesto Stein replied that especially for small countries there might not have been sufficiently liquid derivative markets to hedge currency risk. After EMU this risk has been eliminated and this might have fostered trade. This explanation suggests that the effects of EMU are largest for small countries as pointed out by Patrick Honohan. However, such a mechanism is not well supported in the regression analysis.

Leonardo Bartolini wondered about the robustness of the results with respect to the distance measure. This is particularly important because distance is highly significant in the regressions. Moreover, the effect of distance might be non-linear. Alejandro Micco replied that the specification with bilateral dummies fully addresses this point.

Carol Propper urged the authors to include time dummies for all countries in the regressions to check the robustness of the results given the importance of the time variation for the identification of the model. David Begg thought that the fixed effects are endogenous and that this introduces a downward bias for the estimates. He suggested estimating the fixed effects only on the early part of the sample. Alejandro Micco agreed and remarked that studying time variation of pairs of countries would be desirable. Moreover, a more dynamic specification would be nice but sample limitations do not allow such analysis to be performed because the degrees of freedom become too small. Ernesto Stein added that in a previous draft quite similar regression results are reported for a longer sample period starting in 1980. Given that EMU was not anticipated well before the Maastricht Treaty, this suggests that endogeneity of the fixed effects does not substantially affect the results. However, he agreed that this issue needs further investigation for the current econometric specification.

David Begg remarked that the estimated effect is unlikely to be the full effect that can be expected to materialize in the future. David Miles was interested in the welfare effects resulting from the increase in trade. David Begg added that evidence on price margins and competitive advantage could provide more insights on whether the trade effect is different from the effect on welfare.

Steve Cecchetti thought that this paper might generate a literature on the economic reasons for the trade effects. He asked the authors to check the transfer pricing practices of multinational corporations in order to find out how much of the effect is resulting from pure accounting and how much from real trade.

APPENDIX A: DATA

This appendix describes the data used in our estimations.

Trade: Bilateral trade is measured in millions of dollars and is taken from the Direction of Trade Statistics (DOTS) published by the IMF. We use the simple average of the bilateral imports and exports declared by both countries (average of 4 data). For those cases in which just one of the countries reports bilateral trade, we just take the average of the two available measures. In all cases we use FOB exports and CIF imports. Trade is deflated by the US CPI taken from the IMF International Financial Statistics.

It is worth mentioning that neither of our samples contains observations with zero trade, which saves us the trouble of dealing with this aspect of the gravity model.

Real GDP: This variable is taken also from the World Development Indicators (WDI). The WDI converts figures for GDP from constant domestic currencies into US dollars using 1995 official exchange rates. For a few countries where the official exchange rate does not reflect the rate effectively applied to actual foreign exchange transactions, the World Bank use an alternative conversion factor. This information is available only until 2001 in the WDI. We compute the real GDP in 2002 using real GDP growth reported by the OECD Main Indicators. To calculate the real GDP per capita we divide by the total population in the WDI.

Gravity Variables: Data on Distance, Common Borders, Island Condition, Landlocked Condition, Common Language and Area were obtained from the CIA World Factbook (http://www.cia.gov).

FTAs (Free Trade Agreements): This dummy takes the value one when a country pair belongs to the same Free Trade Area. The data is taken from Frankel (1997) and complemented with data provided by the IDB Integration Department.

EU (European Union): This is a dummy that takes the value one when both countries in a country-pair belong to the European Union.

EU Trend (European Union Trend): This variable is based on the 'transposition deficit' data compiled by Internal Market Scoreboard and published on the website http://europa.eu.int/comm/internal_market/en/update/score. The transposition deficit measures the percentage of internal market directives, which have not been written into national law, after the deadline for doing so has passed. We multiply this measure by (−1) in order to obtain an increase in the measure as the EU becomes deeper. We used the information corresponding to November of each year.

Real Exchange Rates vis-à-vis USA: This variable is the ratio between the nominal exchange rate of each country vis-à-vis the US dollar and the country's GDP deflator. If we multiplied this index by the US GDP deflator we would obtain the bilateral Real Exchange Rate vis-à-vis the USA. Since our regressions include time dummies, multiplying our variable by the US GDP deflator would yield identical results.

APPENDIX B: ADDITIONAL EMPIRICAL RESULTS

Here we present results that serve to strengthen the findings discussed in the text.

Euroland members' trade shares in detail

In the upper panel of Table B1 we report, for each of the countries in EMU, the share of trade with EMU, with other EU countries, with other countries in Europe (Iceland, Norway and Switzerland), and with other countries in the sample (Australia, Canada, Japan, New Zealand and US), both before and after the formal creation of EMU. These shares are expressed in the table as a percentage of total trade within the sample. We use the average of 1996 and 1997 for the before EMU shares, and the average of 2000 and 2001 for the after EMU shares. These shares are the basis for the stylized facts presented in Figure 2 in the text.

The first thing that jumps out from this comparison is that the share corresponding to EMU countries is practically unchanged. Computing a simple average across the EMU countries, there is a very small increase of 0.35 percentage points. Only Finland, Portugal and Spain experience noticeable increases in the EMU share (of 3.7, 2 and 1.2 percentage points, respectively). Meanwhile, Belgium experiences a decline in the EMU share of one percentage point. In all other countries, the share of EMU remains the same, or changes less than one percentage point.

The picture is a little different if we just concentrate on intra-EU trade, in order to compare these trends to the results using the EU sample (see the lower panel of Table B1). In this case, the share corresponding to EMU partners in trade of EMU countries increases for each of the EMU countries, particularly in Ireland (3.5 percentage points), Finland (3.3), Portugal (2.5) and Italy (1.2). On average, the increase in the share of EMU is of 1.25 percentage points.

While this may seem like a negligible increase, it is important to keep in mind that, for EMU countries, the share corresponding to other EMU countries within their total EU trade was around 77.5% even before EMU. It is easy to calculate that this increase in share would be consistent with an EMU effect on trade of 7.6% (which is the effect estimated in Table B2). If trade with EMU is 77.5%, then an increase of 7.6% will imply a new share of 77.5 * 1.076 / (77.5 * 1.076 + 22.5) = 78.75, consistent with the increase in 1.25 percentage points discussed above. Thus, most of the impact of EMU on trade we estimated using the EU sample is reflected in changes in the composition of EMU countries' trade.

In contrast, a similar calculation for the case of the developed country sample suggests that the change in the shares reflects an impact of EMU of just 1.5%, much smaller than the impact estimated in the regression analysis. The discrepancy can be attributed to a couple of factors. First, by focusing on trade data alone, we are failing to keep all else equal, as we do in the regressions. In other words, the difference can be traced in part to differing patterns of EMU countries vis-à-vis the rest of the countries in the sample, in variables such as income and exchange rates. Second, in the trade shares analysis we are comparing trade flows among euro countries with trade flows between euro and non-euro countries, and this comparison group, according to our results, also experienced a trade boosting effect as a result of the euro. None of these factors play an important role within the EU sample: trade-boosting effects are weaker, and the experience of the countries in terms of income, exchange rates and the like was more similar.

Table B1. Euro countries' trade shares with their partners

	Austria	Bel-Lux	Finland	France	Germany	Ireland	Italy	Nether.	Portugal	Spain	EMU
Shares considering all developed countries											
EMU											
96–97	77.7	72.4	44.3	67.0	59.6	37.3	66.0	66.1	76.9	74.1	64.1
00–01	77.3	71.4	48.1	66.4	59.1	37.3	65.7	65.3	78.9	75.3	64.5
Perc. Change	**−0.487**	**−1.388**	**8.403**	**−0.837**	**−0.757**	**0.027**	**−0.377**	**−1.223**	**2.591**	**1.661**	**0.761**
Point Change	**−0.378**	**−1.005**	**3.726**	**−0.560**	**−0.451**	**0.010**	**−0.249**	**−0.808**	**1.992**	**1.231**	**0.351**
Other EU											
96–97	7.3	14.4	32.5	14.8	16.4	37.4	13.7	17.4	13.2	13.5	18.1
00–01	7.0	14.2	30.7	14.2	15.7	32.5	12.6	17.1	10.9	13.2	16.8
Perc. Change	−4.075	−1.414	−5.642	−4.352	−4.490	−13.109	−8.334	−1.448	−17.357	−2.413	−6.264
Point Change	−0.299	−0.204	−1.833	−0.646	−0.736	−4.901	−1.144	−0.252	−2.297	−0.325	−1.264
Other Europe											
96–97	6.3	2.5	6.4	5.1	7.6	3.2	5.8	3.9	3.0	2.6	4.6
00–01	6.7	2.4	6.3	5.2	7.1	3.7	5.3	3.7	3.0	2.4	4.6
Perc. Change	5.478	−3.271	−1.696	1.793	−6.786	13.894	−7.286	−6.371	1.272	−4.646	−0.762
Point Change	0.346	−0.082	−0.108	0.092	−0.518	0.451	−0.419	−0.252	0.038	−0.119	−0.057
Rest											
96–97	8.7	10.7	16.8	13.1	16.4	22.0	14.5	12.6	6.9	9.9	13.2
00–10	9.0	11.9	15.0	14.2	18.1	26.5	16.4	13.9	7.2	9.1	14.1
Perc. Change	3.817	12.115	−10.631	8.520	10.385	20.153	12.462	10.421	3.856	−7.989	6.311
Point Change	0.332	1.291	−1.785	1.114	1.705	4.440	1.812	1.311	0.267	−0.787	0.970
Shares considering only European Union countries											
EMU											
96–97	91.4	83.4	57.7	81.9	78.4	50.0	82.8	79.2	85.3	84.6	77.5
00–01	91.7	83.4	61.1	82.4	79.1	53.5	83.9	79.2	87.8	85.1	78.7
Perc. Change	**0.312**	**0.004**	**5.796**	**0.647**	**0.819**	**7.032**	**1.395**	**0.048**	**2.939**	**0.621**	**1.961**
Point Change	**0.285**	**0.004**	**3.345**	**0.530**	**0.642**	**3.514**	**1.154**	**0.038**	**2.508**	**0.525**	**1.254**
Other EU											
96–97	8.6	16.6	42.3	18.1	21.6	50.0	17.2	20.8	14.7	15.4	22.5
00–01	8.3	16.6	38.9	17.6	20.9	46.5	16.1	20.8	12.2	14.9	21.3
Perc. Change	−3.305	−0.022	−7.912	−2.921	−2.974	−7.023	−6.704	−0.181	−17.077	−3.412	−5.153
Point Change	−0.285	−0.004	−3.345	−0.530	−0.642	−3.514	−1.154	−0.038	−2.508	−0.525	−1.254

Notes: The numbers in the table are expressed in percentages. The Perc. changes are the percentage variation between the periods. The Point changes are the differences between the periods.

Source: Authors' calculations.

Table B2. The euro's trade impact: a range of estimates on the EU sample

Dependent variable: Ln of bilateral trade	1992–2002 European Union countries			
EMU 2	**0.250**	**0.060**	**0.261**	**0.073**
	(0.043)*	**(0.013)***	**(0.047)***	**(0.014)***
Real GDP	0.828	0.996	0.827	1.073
	(0.013)***	(0.074)***	(0.013)***	(0.077)***
Real GDP per capita[a]	0.068		0.105	
	(0.039)*		(0.043)**	
Free Trade Agreement	0.048	0.042	0.024	0.047
	(0.095)	(0.029)	(0.089)	(0.030)
EU	−0.194	−0.073	−0.302	−0.045
	(0.165)	(0.053)	(0.160)*	(0.053)
EU Trend	−0.002	−0.003	−0.010	−0.001
	(0.012)	(0.004)	(0.011)	(0.004)
Landlocked	−0.712		−0.696	
	(0.032)***		(0.032)***	
Distance	−0.733		−0.747	
	(0.037)***		(0.038)***	
Area	−0.070		0.069	
	(0.013)***		(0.013)***	
Contiguity	0.275		0.282	
	(0.049)***		(0.049)***	
Common Language	0.652		0.656	
	(0.073)***		(0.068)***	
Real Exchange Rate of Country 1			−0.177	−0.130
			(0.134)	(0.060)**
Real Exchange Rate of Country 2			−1.094	0.368
			(0.174)***	(0.099)***
EMU 2 Impact[b]	**0.284**	**0.062**	**0.298**	**0.076**
Transformed S.E. (Delta Method)	**(0.055)***	**(0.014)***	**(0.061)***	**(0.015)***
Observations	1001	1001	1001	1001
R-squared[c]	0.94	0.64	0.94	0.65
Country Pair Dummies	No	Yes	No	Yes
Year Dummies	Yes	Yes	Yes	Yes

Notes: Robust standard errors in parentheses
* significant at 10%; ** significant at 5%; *** significant at 1%
[a] Real GDP per capita is only included in the regressions without country pair dummies because of the high colinearity between those dummies and the population
[b] The EMU2 impact is calculated as exp(EMU2)-1
[c] Within R-squared are reported in columns 2 and 4.

The currency union effect using only EU nations

Table B2, corresponding to the EU sample, shows similar results to those in Table 1. The results suggest a positive and significant impact of EMU, even though smaller than previous estimates that associate currency union with an approximate doubling in trade (Rose, 2002). The results of the regression in column 4, which is our preferred one, suggest that the impact is slightly larger in this restricted sample: EMU increases trade among it members by 7.6%, compared to 5.5% for the case of the developed country sample. Notice that, unlike the case of the larger sample, here the FTA and EU variables are not significant. This is not surprising, since we are identifying the EU effect only off the entry of Sweden, Finland and Austria in 1995.

Table B3. Alternative measures of the EMU effect on trade

	Developed country sample	EU sample
1999–2000 vs. 1996–7	0.073	0.068
	(19.7)***	(13.6)***
1999–2001 vs. 1995–7	0.078	0.098
	(25.8)***	(35.2)***

Notes: *** Significant at 1%. F tests of the differences between the mean of the coefficients in the selected years are reported in parentheses.

Table B4. Alternative measures of the EMU 2 and EMU 1 impact

	Developed country sample		EU sample	
	EMU 2	EMU 1	EMU 2	EMU 1
1999–2000 vs. 1996–7	0.145	0.081	0.085	0.017
	(34.0)***	(13.7)***	(5.9)**	(0.6)
1999–2001 vs. 1995–7	0.158	0.086	0.124	0.026
	(48.0)***	(20.5)***	(17.4)***	(0.3)

Notes: ** Significant at 5%; *** Significant at 1%. In parentheses are reported the F tests of the differences between the mean of the coefficients in the selected years.

Alternative estimates and tests of the currency union effect

In Table B3 we present four other estimates of the currency union effect on trade, which are drawn from the regressions presented in Table 2, and result from the comparison of the before and after coefficients of the yearly EMU 2 variables, leaving the year 1998 out. Thus, this exercise suggests that the impact of EMU on trade between its members ranges between 7 and 10%, depending on the sample, and the years used for the before/after comparison, and that this impact is highly significant. For example, the first of the four estimates is calculated averaging the yearly EMU 2 coefficients corresponding to 1996 and 1997 in regression 1 of Table 2, and doing the same for the years 1999–2000. The estimate is simply calculated as exp (average coefficient 96–97 – average coefficient 99–00) – 1.

We undertake a similar exercise allowing for the EMU 1 dummy and thus controlling for negative trade diversion.

Table B4 presents alternative estimates of the EMU 2 and EMU 1 effects, based on the regressions shown in Table 4. The trade booster effect of EMU is confirmed for the developed country sample, where the impact of EMU 2 is approximately twice that of EMU 1. In the EU sample, the impact of EMU 1 is positive, but not significant.

Differences tests

Table B5 provides additional support regarding the significance of the currency union effect. The table tests the equality of each pair of yearly EMU 2 coefficients in Table 2, for each of the samples. The story that emerges clearly from the table is that each and every one of the years that follow the creation of the EMU is significantly different from each of the pre-EMU years, with the only exception of 1998.

Table B5. Year-wise test for differences in the euro's trade effect

	1993	1994	1995	1996	1997	1998	1999	2000	2001	2002
Differences tests – Developed country sample										
1993										
1994	0.06**									
1995	0.07***	0.01								
1996	0.05**	0.00	−0.02							
1997	0.06***	0.01	−0.01	0.01						
1998	0.12***	0.06***	0.05**	0.06***	0.05***					
1999	0.14***	0.08***	0.07***	0.08***	0.07***	0.02				
2000	0.12***	0.07**	0.05**	0.07***	0.06***	0.01	−0.01			
2001	0.15***	0.10***	0.08***	0.10***	0.09***	0.04	0.02	0.03		
2002	0.17***	0.12***	0.10***	0.12***	0.11***	0.06*	0.04	0.05	0.02	
Differences tests – EU sample										
1993										
1994	0.03									
1995	0.02	−0.01								
1996	0.01	−0.03	−0.02							
1997	0.03	−0.01	0.00	0.02						
1998	0.07**	0.04*	0.05*	0.06***	0.05**					
1999	0.08***	0.05**	0.06**	0.07***	0.06***	0.01				
2000	0.08***	0.05**	0.06**	0.08***	0.06***	0.01	0.00			
2001	0.17***	0.14***	0.15***	0.17***	0.15***	0.10***	0.09***	0.09***		
2002	0.17***	0.14***	0.15***	0.16***	0.15***	0.10***	0.09**	0.09**	0.00	

Notes: Robust standard errors in parentheses; * significant at 10%; ** significant at 5%; *** significant at 1%.

Estimates counting Greece as a euroland member throughout

In order to have meaningful comparisons across time, as we did in the regressions reported in Table 2 and Table 4, it is important to keep the euro dummies constant throughout the sample. This practice, however, gives rise to a minor problem since euro membership has expanded since 1999. Specifically, 11 European Union member states adopted the euro as their national currency on 1 January 1999, having been judged as meeting the famous Maastricht convergence criteria by the Council of Ministers. On 19 June 2000, the Council judged that Greece fulfilled the convergence criteria and thus approved its accession to the euro area as a twelfth member as from 1 January 2001.

Given that our data extends only to 2002, we excluded Greece from the EMU group of countries in the text. It is worth noting that this does not affect the results in the rest of the tables, where the EMU dummies corresponding to Greece and its partners simply switch to a value of 1 in 2001. In Table B6 we report the main results of the EMU effects over time, counting Greece as a euroland member from the start. The results are qualitatively similar to those in Tables 2 and 4.

WEB APPENDIX

Available at hattp://www.economic-policy.org

Table B6. Results over time with Greece as an EMU member

	Developed sample		EU sample		Developed sample		EU sample	
	Coeff.	S.D.	Coeff.	S.D.	Coeff.	S.D.	Coeff.	S.D.
Real GDP	1.154	(0.059)***	1.089	(0.078)***	1.114	(0.059)***	1.091	(0.078)***
Free Trade Agreement	−0.008	(0.021)	0.048	(0.030)	−0.016	(0.021)	0.052	(0.031)*
EU	0.021	(0.022)	−0.042	(0.054)	−0.004	(0.023)	−0.040	(0.054)
EU Trend	−0.000	(0.001)	−0.001	(0.004)	−0.002	(0.002)	−0.001	(0.004)
Real Exchange Rate of Country 1	−0.149	(0.045)***	−0.126	(0.063)***	−0.223	(0.046)***	−0.144	(0.064)***
Real Exchange Rate of Country 2	−0.249	(0.057)***	0.430	(0.100)***	−0.247	(0.058)***	0.453	(0.100)***
EMU2 − 1993	−0.019	(0.032)	0.016	(0.034)	−0.041	(0.041)	0.051	(0.048)
EMU2 − 1994	0.024	(0.031)	0.035	(0.032)	0.019	(0.039)	0.125	(0.053)**
EMU2 − 1995	0.050	(0.032)	0.046	(0.033)	0.046	(0.044)	0.180	(0.049)***
EMU2 − 1996	0.037	(0.032)	0.039	(0.031)	0.024	(0.043)	0.132	(0.057)**
EMU2 − 1997	0.014	(0.030)	0.009	(0.029)	0.024	(0.044)	0.093	(0.051)*
EMU2 − 1998	**0.068**	**(0.032)****	**0.056**	**(0.032)***	**0.132**	**(0.044)*****	**0.207**	**(0.045)*****
EMU2 − 1999	**0.083**	**(0.031)****	**0.066**	**(0.032)****	**0.155**	**(0.042)*****	**0.222**	**(0.046)*****
EMU2 − 2000	**0.068**	**(0.034)****	**0.066**	**(0.035)***	**0.148**	**(0.048)*****	**0.156**	**(0.045)*****
EMU2 − 2001	**0.080**	**(0.036)****	**0.138**	**(0.035)*****	**0.187**	**(0.048)*****	**0.276**	**(0.065)*****
EMU2 − 2002	**0.101**	**(0.040)****	**0.140**	**(0.041)***	**0.203**	**(0.052)*****	**0.299**	**(0.074)*****
EMU1 − 1993					−0.044	(0.039)	0.039	(0.047)
EMU1 − 1994					−0.022	(0.037)	0.099	(0.053)*
EMU1 − 1995					−0.022	(0.041)	0.147	(0.048)***
EMU1 − 1996					−0.041	(0.038)	0.102	(0.056)*
EMU1 − 1997					−0.017	(0.041)	0.091	(0.050)*
EMU1 − 1998					**0.055**	**(0.039)**	**0.163**	**(0.045)*****
EMU1 − 1999					**0.062**	**(0.036)***	**0.168**	**(0.047)*****
EMU1 − 2000					**0.065**	**(0.041)**	**0.095**	**(0.042)****
EMU1 − 2001					**0.103**	**(0.041)****	**0.149**	**(0.064)****
EMU1 − 2002					**0.095**	**(0.044)****	**0.171**	**(0.073)****
Observations	2541		1001		2541		1001	
Within R-squared	0.46		0.66		0.47		0.66	
Year Dummies	Yes		Yes		Yes		Yes	
Country Pair Dummies	Yes		Yes		Yes		Yes	

References

Anderson, J. (1979). 'A theoretical foundation for the gravity equation', *American Economic Review*, 69(1), 106–16.

Anderson, J. and E. van Wincoop (2001). 'Gravity with gravitas: a solution to the border puzzle', NBER Working Paper No. 8079.

Arellano, M. and S. Bond (1991). 'Some test of specification for panel data: Monte Carlo evidence and an application to employment equations', *Review of Economic Studies*, 58(2), 277–97.

Bergstrand, J. (1985). 'The gravity equation in international trade: some microeconomics foundations and empirical evidence', *Review of Economics and Statistics*, 67(3), 474–81.

Brown, G. (2003). '9 June 2003 Statement by the Chancellor of the Exchequer on UK Membership of the Single Currency', UK House of Commons, London. http://www.hm-treasury.gov.uk/topics/topics_euro/topics_emu_index.cfm

Bun, M. and F. Klaassen (2002). 'Has the euro increased trade?', Tinbergen Institute Discussion Paper, No. 02-108/2.

De Grauwe, P. (1994). *The Economics of Monetary Integration*, Oxford University Press, Oxford.

Deardorff, A. (1984). 'Testing trade theories and predicting trade flows', in *Handbook of International Economics*, vol. 1, Elsevier Science Publishers, Amsterdam.

— (1998). 'Determinants of bilateral trade: does gravity work in a classical world?', in *The Regionalization of the World Economy*, University of Chicago Press, Chicago.

De Nardis, S. and C. Vicarelli (2003). 'The impact of the euro on trade: the (early) effect is not so large', European Network of Economic Policy Research Institutes, Working Paper No. 017.

Edison, H. and M. Melvin (1990). 'The determinants and implications of the choice of an exchange rate system', in *Monetary Policy for a Volatile Global Economy*, AEI Press, Washington, DC.

Emerson, M., D. Gros, A. Italanier, J. Pisani-Ferry and H. Reichenbach (1992). *One Market, One Money: An Evaluation of the Potential Benefits and Costs of Forming an Economic and Monetary Union*, Oxford University Press, Oxford.

Estavadeordal, A., B. Frantz and A. Taylor (2002). 'The rise and fall of world trade, 1870–1939', *Quarterly Journal of Economics*, 118(2), 359–407.

Evenett, S. and W. Keller (2002). 'On theories of the gravity equation', *Journal of Political Economy*, 110(2), 281–316.

Frankel, J. (1997). *Regional Trading Blocs in the World Economic System*, Institute for International Economics. Washington DC, October.

Frankel, J. and A. Rose (1997). 'Is EMU more justifiable ex post than ex ante', *European Economic Review*, 41(3–5), 753–60.

— (1998). 'The endogeneity of the optimum currency area criteria', *The Economic Journal*, 108(449), 1009–25.

— (2000). 'An estimate of the effect of currency unions on trade and growth', NBER Working Papers No. 7857.

Glick, R. and A. Rose (2001). 'Does a currency union affect trade? The time series evidence', NBER Working Paper No. 8396.

Greene, W. (2000). *Econometric Analysis*, Prentice Hall, New York.

Head, K. and T. Mayer (2002). 'Illusory border effects: distance mismeasurements inflates estimates of home bias in trade', CEPII Working Paper 2002–01.

Helliwell, J. (1998). *How Much Do National Borders Matter?*, Brookings Institution Press, Washington, DC.

Helpman, E. (1987). 'Imperfect competition and international trade: evidence from fourteen industrial countries', *Journal of the Japanese and International Economies*, 1, 62–81.

Helpman, E. and P. Krugman (1985). *Market Structure and Foreign Trade*, MIT Press, Cambridge, MA.

Kenen, P. (2003). 'Making the case for the euro', *The International Economy*, Winter, 51–4.

Klaassen, F. (2002). 'Why is it so difficult to find an effect of exchange rate risk on trade?', *Journal of International Money and Finance*, forthcoming.

Levy Yeyati, E. (2003). 'On the impact of a common currency on bilateral trade', *Economic Letters*, 79 (1), 125–9.

Linnemmann, H. (1966). *An Econometric Study of International Trade Flows*, North-Holland, Amsterdam.

Lopez-Córdova, E. and C. Meissner (2002). 'Exchange-rate regimes and international trade: evidence from the classical gold era', *American Economic Review*, 93(1), 344–53.

McCallum, J. (1995). 'National borders matter: Canada-US regional trade patterns', *American Economic Review*, 85(3), 615–23.

Nitsch, V. (2001). 'Honey, I just shrank the currency union effect', *The World Economy*, 25(4), 457–74.

Persson, T. (2001). 'Currency union and trade: how large is the treatment effect?', *Economic Policy*, 33, 433–62.

Rose, A. (2000). 'One money, one market: estimating the effect of common currencies on trade', *Economic Policy*, 30, 7–46.

— (2001). 'Currency union and trade: the effect is large', *Economic Policy*, 33, 433–62.

— (2002). 'The effect of common currencies on international trade: where do we stand', URL: haas.berkeley.edu/~arose.

Rose, A. and E. van Wincoop (2001). 'National money as a barrier to international trade: the real case for currency union', *American Economic Review*, 91(2), 386–90.

Tenreyro, S. (2001). 'On the causes and consequences of currency union', *Harvard University*, Photocopy.

Viner, J. (1950). *The Customs Union Issue*, Carnegie Endowment for International Peace, New York.

World Development Indicators CD ROM (2002). World Bank.

Inflation divergence

SUMMARY

Inflation rates have diverged much more widely than expected among the member states of the EMU. We show that much of this is attributable to the differential impact on different member states of the weakness of the euro on international currency markets in the early months of the union. The Balassa–Samuelson productivity growth effect has not yet played an important role – even in respect of the outlier Ireland – although it will likely be more significant over a longer run, especially as the accession countries join.

— *Patrick Honohan and Philip Lane*

Divergent inflation rates in EMU

Patrick Honohan and Philip R. Lane

World Bank and CEPR; Institute for International Integration Studies and Economics Department, Trinity College Dublin and CEPR

1. INTRODUCTION

Although the European Central Bank (ECB) has done relatively well in achieving its target of medium-term price stability for the euro zone aggregate, regional inflation differentials since the beginning of 1999 have been quite marked. Most notably, Ireland and other peripheral nations have been persistently at the top of the inflation league table. In contrast, German inflation has been below the euro zone average. An expanded economic and monetary union (EMU) with the entry of the accession countries will surely lead to even greater inflation differentials in the future.

Why have inflation rates diverged so much in the member countries of the euro zone since the euro was introduced? Before monetary union, most of the discussion of possible inflation differentials focused on the Balassa–Samuelson effect. The expectation was that sizeable differences in productivity growth might become the main drivers of inflation differentials, since less productive but converging regions would require higher inflation rates to accommodate equilibrating trend real appreciation. After the event, many observers have interpreted the fact that inflation has been

We thank our discussants, the referees, John FitzGerald, Cedric Tille and participants in the Dublin Economics Workshop for comments. Charles Larkin and Paul Scanlon provided valuable research assistance. Lane thanks the Institute for International Integration Studies for financial support.

The Managing Editor in charge of this paper was Paul Seabright.

highest in Ireland, apparently a country with high productivity growth, as proof of the importance of this effect. In contrast, this paper argues that a different – and largely unanticipated – mechanism has been more important in the early years of EMU, namely the differential impact of euro weakness on the different member states.

While there is no suggestion that a narrowing of inflation differentials should be a goal of the ECB, persistently high inflation in any country is a matter of concern – as is persistent deflation. Understanding the sources of these inflation differentials is important to ensure public acceptance of the EMU monetary regime and in facilitating smooth adjustment, since local inflation rates carry many of the standard 'costs of inflation' by affecting those on fixed nominal incomes, real returns on savings and investments and private and public wage negotiations. To what extent was the divergence caused by asymmetric nominal shocks? To what extent was it a reflection of transitory factors versus equilibrium long-run real exchange rate adjustment? Would inflation rates have been more stable and differentials lower in the absence of EMU? Gathering initial evidence on these issues can help guide structural and fiscal policy responses not only in member states, but also in future potential joiners.

The structure of the paper is as follows. In Section 2, we ask to what extent it matters that inflation rates differ among members of a currency union. Section 3 describes the empirical inflation experience since EMU began, revealing the important role of exchange rate movements. Section 4 performs a reality check by looking in a little more detail at Ireland, which has been at the top of the inflation table since the launch of the single currency: given what is known about Ireland's rapid growth, how much can currency depreciation have contributed to its outlying inflation experience? Section 5 addresses the counterfactual of what might have happened under independent national monetary policies. Section 6 assesses the policy implications for prospective new members of the euro zone. Concluding comments are offered in Section 7.

2. DOES DIFFERENTIAL INFLATION MATTER?

The ECB can only attempt to control the area-wide aggregate inflation rate, with no tools at its disposal to address variation in inflation across member countries – nor does it attempt to do so, not even publishing sub-union inflation rates in its *Monthly Bulletin*. In what sense, then, might it matter to understand differential inflation? First, there is the question of the optimal target for euro zone inflation: some have argued that wider inflation differentials should imply a higher target for mean euro zone inflation in order to reduce the possibility of deflation in some regions or countries (see Sinn and Reutter, 2001; Kieler, 2003; cf. Kumar *et al.*, 2003). We do not wish to take a definite view on this proposition, which depends on an assumption about the shape of the costs of inflation function, except to note that its relevance might depend on the reasons for the emergence of differentials.

Second, there is a consideration of political economy. High inflation is unpopular, and politicians in high inflation countries will respond, possibly in damaging ways if they misunderstand the causes.[1] It is futile to complain that politicians should ignore national inflation or suppress national price indices to avoid this effect. Third, to the extent that the inflation differentials reflect transitory shocks, they could engender a boom-bust cycle, if there are persistence mechanisms that lead to overshooting in wage and price dynamics. This last point seems to us the most important: in the absence of a national monetary policy, other national policies may need to be brought into play to dampen real wage-unemployment cycles that might persist to a greater degree than was previously anticipated.

Underlying these observations is the fact that the member states of the EMU are still nation states with separate languages, independent fiscal policies and national wage-setting institutions which makes political decision-making respond to national inflation rates in a way that has no real analogue in (say) regional US decision-making.

Of course, some sources of inflation rate differences within the EMU are entirely innocuous or even benign. One important case, relevant to the empirical work below, is where countries begin with different price *levels*, in which case convergence towards a common price level necessarily entails a deviation in inflation rates.[2] A variant of this case is when the long-run relative price level across countries is a function of relative incomes, relative wealth levels or relative productivities: a faster-growing country may naturally have temporarily higher inflation in the transition to its new long-run equilibrium relative price level (this is a loose statement of the aforementioned Balassa–Samuelson hypothesis).

But not all inflation differentials are of this harmless variety. Even if long-run inflation rates do indeed converge throughout the union, temporary asymmetric shocks to relative prices can be expected from a variety of sources. In addition, the weaker adjustment mechanisms of a currency union may imply more frequent and prolonged relative price misalignments, or alternating phases of overheating and recession. For instance, if there are short-run supply rigidities, a localized aggregate demand disturbance will feed into domestic inflation and real exchange rate appreciation. Such inflation may be purely transitory but is potentially dangerous if it triggers persistence mechanisms that continue to operate even when the original shock has disappeared or supply responses have kicked in (see EEAG, 2002, ch. 4).

Overshooting may occur through price-wage dynamics if current inflation feeds into the path for future wage growth. It may also occur via balance sheets, if the low real interest rate that is an automatic consequence of high regional inflation inside a currency union leads to excessive debt accumulation on the parts of households or

---

[1] For example, a country experiencing sustained deflation might opt to unleash an excessive fiscal expansion, violating the rules of the Stability and Growth Pact and potentially disrupting euro zone financial markets.

[2] Another situation is where, because the basket of goods may differ from country to country, the basket average is different even if all individual prices are the same. For the small price movements that have occurred since EMU began, this is unlikely to have been a serious problem and we will not return to it.

affected businesses. In related fashion, it may also happen via the housing/property markets, by virtue of a run-up in local asset prices. Imperfections in factor and credit markets may mean that the adjustment to such overhangs can be painful. In addition, even a temporary increase in domestic relative prices (i.e. a loss in competitiveness) can lead to a permanent loss in international market share or inward foreign direct investment, if hysteresis effects are important.

As we will show, 'imported' inflation remains a threat even for a currency union, if member countries have different exposures to extra-union trade. Most directly, a member country that consumes imports from a non-member country will experience different inflationary pressures if the euro exchange rate depreciates as compared to a member country that conducts all its trade with other member countries. There are also indirect effects: the within-EMU competitiveness of a firm could be adversely affected if it relied on imported materials from a non-EMU country when its competitors were sourcing from within the EMU. Unless contractual and technical conditions allowed the firm quickly and fully to switch its source of material supplies, its profitability could be badly damaged and perhaps result in layoffs or even bankruptcy. The sharp movements in exchange rates between the euro and the US dollar make this a point of empirical relevance in the present context.

Indeed, inflation differentials in the euro zone could turn out to be larger and more persistent than in some other currency unions. Relative to the United States, inter-regional smoothing mechanisms are absent: migration is weaker and there is no strong federal fiscal system. Domestic fiscal policy is also unlikely to be an effective counterweight. As is increasingly well appreciated, the effectiveness of discretionary fiscal policy is weak and uncertain.[3] Moreover, even if fiscal policy could be usefully deployed as a stabilization device, its flexibility is constrained by the Stability and Growth Pact and concerns about long-term fiscal sustainability in several member countries.

3. DIVERGENT INFLATION EXPERIENCE IN PRACTICE

Figure 1 shows the phenomenon that needs to be explained. Both the mean and dispersion of inflation declined in the years running up to EMU, but then suddenly increased again after the first quarter of 1999. Subsequently both mean and dispersion declined somewhat again. This hump-shaped value is strikingly similar to the movement of the exchange rate with the dollar (Figures 2 and 3). In this section we will argue that the relationship is structural.

Actually, while inflation rates diverged, absolute price levels *converged* during the early months of EMU. The correlation between European real price level convergence and episodes of dollar strength is a long-standing but hitherto unnoticed empirical regularity. The dollar movement has differentially affected price movements across

---

[3] See Perotti (2003) and the references therein. However see EEAG (2003) for proposals that could improve the capability of a discretionary fiscal policy to act as a stabilizing force.

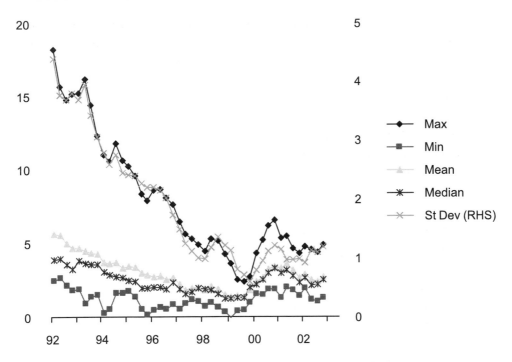

Figure 1. Distribution of euro zone inflation rates, 1992–2002

Source: Calculations based on line 64..X of the IMF's *International Financial Statistics*; quarterly data in per cent per annum.

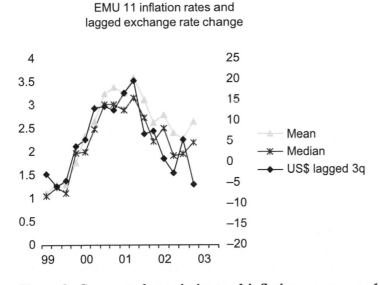

Figure 2. Currency depreciation and inflation: euro zone, 1999–2002

Note: The figure shows the mean and median inflation rates (per cent per annum) across the EMU members (excluding Greece) and, on the right-hand scale, the annual rate of exchange rate change of the euro against the US dollar lagged three quarters (DM before 1999).

Source: Calculations based on line 64..X and line 163..RF of the IMF's *International Financial Statistics*; four-quarter changes.

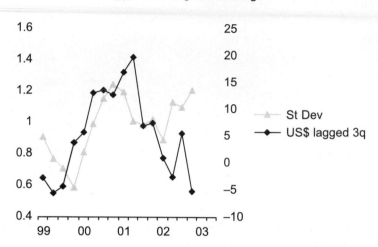

Figure 3. Currency depreciation and inflation dispersion: euro zone, 1999–2002

Note: The figure shows the standard deviation across the EMU members (excluding Greece) and the annual rate of exchange rate change of the euro against the US dollar lagged three quarters (DM before 1999), all in per cent per annum.

Source: Calculations based on line 64..X and line 163..RF of the IMF's *International Financial Statistics*; four-quarter changes.

Europe for several decades and this phenomenon has continued even under EMU.

Exchange rate movements are not the only source of differential inflation. The initial decline in nominal interest rates – a once-off asymmetric shock – does seem to have been associated with differential effects on property price levels. And, contrary to a simplistic view of the price process in a currency union, national output gaps continue to have a significant impact on national inflation rates, although government deficits have no separate effect (apart from their indirect effect on output gaps).

The section begins with a descriptive analysis of these developments and concludes with a formal model of how these factors have interacted jointly to determine national inflation rates.

3.1. Converging inflation rates to EMU . . . and then diverging!

After a long period of decline, reflecting the convergence demanded by the Maastricht Treaty, mean and median inflation in the EMU area bottomed out (somewhat ironically perhaps) in the first months of the new currency, namely during the quarter to March 1999: see Figure 1. Since then, there has been a rebound, albeit a modest one, from about 1.25% to between 2 and 2.5%.[4] By 2002, inflation rates were

---

[4] Nevertheless, the rebound in dispersion is striking relative to the sustained and almost complete convergence in bill and bond yields (cf. Adjaouté and Danthine, 2002). See also Lane (2003a) on the dynamics of the inflation distribution in Europe.

slowing again in the EMU, giving a generally hump-shape (inverted U-shape) to the plot of inflation rates since 1999 (Greece apart).[5]

Dispersion of inflation rates between member countries, whether measured by the overall spread between maximum and minimum, by standard deviation, or by the coefficient of variation, has also widened since 1999, though it remains well below the figures recorded before 1997.

The major outliers in the years before EMU began were Greece and Portugal. Since the start of EMU the clustering of countries has remained quite tight. In only one country (Ireland) has 1999–2002 inflation differed from the EMU-wide mean by more than one standard deviation. Ireland's mean annual inflation in this period was 4.1%, compared with an EMU average of 2.5. The next highest countries were Greece, the Netherlands, Portugal and Spain with between 3.1 and 3.2%.

3.1.1. Comparing inflation dispersion in EMU to the United States.

Although the dispersion of inflation rates took some observers by surprise, Table 1, reporting summary statistics on the distribution of national/regional inflation rates in the euro zone and the US over 1999–2001, shows that the dispersion, as measured for example by the coefficient of variation (CV), was not dramatically wider in the euro zone during these years. Indeed, the range for inflation is bigger for US regions in each of the years 1999–2001. This table indicates that, at least over this period, the degree of inflation dispersion in the euro zone is not out of line with that occurring in the other major advanced country currency union.[6]

Moreover, if national/regional price levels have a common long-run trend, inflation differentials should diminish over time. Although we do not have a long time series for the euro zone, Table 2 offers some relevant comparisons. For the 'Euro core' countries, the range in average annual inflation rates (measured in a common currency) was only

Table 1. Summary inflation statistics: the euro zone and US regions

	Euro zone			US regions		
	1999	2000	2001	1999	2000	2001
Mean	1.5	2.8	3.0	2.3	3.5	3.1
St Dev	0.8	1.0	1.1	0.8	0.8	0.9
CV	0.51	0.35	0.36	0.34	0.23	0.30
Max	2.5	5.2	5.2	4.2	5.8	5.4
Min	0.5	1.9	1.8	1.0	1.7	1.2
Range	2.0	3.3	3.4	3.2	4.1	4.2

Note: Per cent per annum. In this table, mean inflation rates are unweighted averages across euro zone member countries and US regions respectively. US data are based on 26 regions.

Source: European data from Eurostat's HICP database; US data from Bureau of Labor Statistics.

---

[5] Of course, Greece was not a member of EMU until 2001. Much of the empirical work below excludes Greece.

[6] Note, however, that the US data are considered noisy and this would tend to widen the dispersion.

Table 2. Long-term inflation differentials

			Range
(1)	Euro core	1972–1998	0.20
(2)	US regions	1976–1995	0.61
(3)	US regions	1926–1995	0.95

Notes: Per cent per annum. Euro core is Germany, Austria, Belgium, the Netherlands, France and Italy. In rows (1)–(2), range is in average annual inflation rates (measured in DM for the Euro core). In row (3), it is the mean range for non-overlapping decadal intervals over 1926–95.

Sources: Euro core data adapted from Walton and Deo (1999); US regions calculations adapted from Cecchetti *et al.* (2002).

0.2 percentage points over 1972–98. Indeed, this is lower than the ranges calculated for US regions over various time intervals, as is shown in rows (2) and (3). These data suggest that there is a substantial non-permanent component to inflation differentials. That said, the existing evidence is that inflation differentials are only eliminated slowly: Cecchetti *et al.* (2002) estimate the half-life of convergence for US regions to be nine years.

This comparison with the United States experience is instructive: inflation differentials in the euro zone do not appear to be extraordinary; moreover, differentials should be reversed over time. Even if the distribution of relative inflation rates continues to be similar between the euro zone and the United States, however, inflation asymmetries may be more troublesome for the euro zone than for the United States, for the reasons argued in Section 2.

3.2. Exchange rates are a major factor in explaining inflation divergence

Section 2 already flagged differential import price movements as a possible source of inflation differentials. Shifts in exchange rates are an important source of such movements. The share of each EMU member state's trade that is accounted for by other EMU members differs widely (as does the pattern of extra-EMU trade, see Table 3 below); accordingly the impact of a given movement of the euro on import prices will tend to differ widely, even if member states are price takers in international trade. Furthermore, the importance of international trade in the economy differs greatly between member states. Accordingly, the impact on domestic prices of a given movement in the euro can be quite different.[7]

We illustrate this in column (1) of Table 4. A pooled regression of quarterly changes in national nominal effective exchange rate indices on the euro-dollar exchange rate,

---

[7] Even if trade patterns were identical, variation in rates of pass-through could still lead to inflation divergence in response to an exchange rate shock. This has some relevance: a large (albeit declining) share of Irish consumer imports has traditionally been invoiced in sterling, whereas the same goods imported into Germany or France might be invoiced in euro, due to different distribution networks. The determinants of exchange rate pass through are the subject of much current theoretical and empirical work in international macroeconomics. At a broad level, we may expect the introduction of the euro to increase the proportion of imported goods that are priced in euro rather than in foreign currency, which will act to insulate euro zone prices from temporary exchange rate shocks.

Table 3. Direction of trade 2000–2001

	Non-EMU imports as a percentage of GDP	Non-EMU as a percentage of imports
EMU		
Austria	18.4	36.0
Belgium	33.9	40.9
Finland	22.5	66.9
France	12.1	44.7
Germany	19.6	58.1
Greece	17.0	53.1
Ireland	59.2	79.2
Italy	13.7	50.6
Luxembourg	33.0	26.0
Netherlands	36.3	59.9
Portugal	13.6	32.5
Spain	13.8	44.3
Average	*24.4*	*49.4*
Non-EMU EU		
Denmark	16.3	49.9
Sweden	19.4	51.4
United Kingdom	15.4	55.9
Average	*17.1*	*52.4*
Accession countries		
Bulgaria	32.9	56.3
Cyprus	27.2	60.4
Czech Republic	24.7	34.6
Estonia	51.2	61.2
Hungary	29.2	46.7
Latvia	27.5	60.1
Lithuania	29.4	65.1
Malta	57.7	55.9
Poland	13.0	47.2
Romania	16.1	47.5
Slovak Republic	39.7	54.0
Slovenia	21.5	46.4
Turkey	15.5	64.6
Average	*29.7*	*53.1*

Notes: The calculations are based on current membership of EMU.

Source: Trade data are from the IMF's Direction of Trade; GDP from the World Bank's World Development Indicators.

quarterly 1999.1–2002.2 produces an R^2 of 0.85; fixed effects are not significant. The coefficients on the dollar rate, estimated quite precisely, vary widely from 0.07 in Luxembourg and 0.11 for Austria to 0.24 for Finland and 0.35 for Ireland. Thus the impact, during the EMU period, of the change in the euro-dollar rate for the Irish effective exchange rate index was five times that for Luxembourg, taking into account the correlated changes in other exchange rates.

As a preliminary bivariate verification and quantification of the relation between exchange rates and price levels, we estimated a panel regression on quarterly data

Table 4. Pass-through and related relationships

Dependent variable	(1) $\Delta neer$		(2) Δcpi		(3) Δcpi	
	Estimate	(t-stat)	Estimate	(t-stat)	Estimate	(t-stat)
a_1	0.000	(0.4)	1.962	(3.5)	1.012	(1.8)
a_2 (at)	−0.110	(5.0)	0.023	(1.3)	−0.134	(0.9)
a_2 (be)	−0.169	(7.7)	0.071	(4.1)	−0.356	(3.5)
a_2 (de)	−0.228	(10.3)	0.037	(2.1)	−0.109	(1.5)
a_2 (fi)	−0.235	(10.7)	0.105	(6.1)	−0.300	(4.6)
a_2 (fr)	−0.192	(8.7)	0.046	(2.6)	−0.244	(2.6)
a_2 (ie)	−0.350	(15.9)	0.103	(5.9)	−0.206	(4.2)
a_2 (it)	−0.186	(8.4)	0.024	(1.4)	−0.100	(1.1)
a_2 (lu)	−0.072	(3.3)				
a_2 (ne)	−0.196	(8.9)	−0.005	(0.3)	0.060	(0.6)
a_2 (pt)	−0.163	(7.4)	−0.000	(0.0)	0.108	(1.1)
a_2 (sp)	−0.162	(7.3)	0.030	(1.7)	−0.144	(1.3)
a_2						
a_3			−0.064	(3.5)	−0.019	(1.3)
a_4 (at)			−0.024	(3.3)	−0.202	(3.4)
a_4 (be)			−0.020	(2.7)	−0.117	(2.6)
a_4 (de)			−0.018	(2.5)	−0.079	(2.5)
a_4 (fi)			−0.026	(3.5)	−0.120	(3.8)
a_4 (fr)			−0.012	(1.6)	−0.073	(1.7)
a_4 (ie)			−0.069	(7.2)	−0.125	(6.2)
a_4 (it)			−0.028	(3.7)	−0.108	(3.2)
a_4 (ne)			−0.045	(5.7)	−0.175	(4.4)
a_4 (pt)			−0.048	(5.8)	−0.196	(5.0)
a_4 (sp)			−0.041	(5.1)	−0.192	(4.6)
$ar(1)$	0.404	(5.2)	0.845	(14.5)	0.831	(11.1)
Countries/obs.	11	143	10	140	10	140
Years	1999:1–2002:2		1999:1–2002:2		1999:1–2002:2	
Method	Unweighted panel		Unweighted panel		Unweighted panel	
RSQ/DW	0.854	2.06	0.925	1.62	0.914	1.75

Note: $ar(1)$ is first order autocorrelation coefficient. Regression (1) is: $\Delta neer - a + b_i \Delta euro$; Variables: $\Delta neer$, $\Delta euro$ are log-change in the nominal effective exchange rate index and in the (reciprocal of) euro/\$ exchange rate. Regression (2) is of the form $\Delta cpi_i = a_1 + a_{2i} \Delta euro + a_3 cpi_i(-1) + a_{4i} euro(-1)$, where cpi is ifs line 64 (rebased); Regression (3) replaces $euro$ with $neer$.

linking national CPI changes to previous exchange rate movements (results of estimating a more fully specified model on annual data are presented later). We include an error correction term to capture the long-run relation between exchange rate and price level trends: we allow the long-run coefficient a_{4i} to vary across countries, to take into account variation in exposure to extra-euro zone trade. The model estimated was:

$$\Delta p_{it} = a_1 + a_{2i} \Delta e_{t-1} + a_3 p_{it-1} + a_{4i} e_{t-2} + \varepsilon_{it} \qquad (1)$$

The results of this regression are shown in Table 4 (columns 2 and 3) and display a convincingly close fit, whether it is the dollar-euro exchange rate or the nominal effective index that is used. Moreover, the largest coefficients a_{4i} are for the outlying countries for inflation as a whole (Ireland, Greece, the Netherlands and Portugal).

3.2.1. Price level convergence. Despite the existence of the common currency, it is not correct to interpret inflation differentials between members as implying a deviation from purchasing power parity (PPP) in first differences. For there is the rest of the world to take into account, and to the extent that trading partners differ, then it may be that some of the raw inflation differentials between EMU members have had the effect of reducing deviations from PPP measured on a trade-weighted basis. Moreover, if initial price levels differ, inflation differentials are required for convergence to PPP. This subsection examines the convergence of PPP-adjusted exchange rates (a measure of absolute price convergence).

Figure 4 shows the relation between productivity growth and real exchange rate appreciation for post-EMU and a representative pre-EMU period for a set of European countries.[8,9] The positive correlation implied by a crude version of the Balassa–Samuelson hypothesis is not present in this short period. Indeed, there is actually a strong negative cross-sectional correlation between productivity growth in 1997–2001 and real exchange rate appreciation in EMU (thanks largely to Ireland and Greece, and also the UK). As a matter of theory, this is not too surprising: Benigno and Thoenissen (2003) and FitzGerald (2003) have recently emphasized that fast productivity growth can lead to real depreciation. One factor is that it may generate a terms of trade deterioration; another is that productivity growth in the non-traded sector should be associated with real depreciation.

Nevertheless, a positive relationship between the price *level* (PPP times exchange rate) and the *level* of GDP per capita has existed consistently for several decades among the EMU members.[10,11] And the gradual convergence in living standards as between different countries has contributed to some long-term convergence of price *levels* across countries.[12] For example, the dispersion of the price level (measured by the coefficient of variation of PPP times the exchange rate) declined from an average of 19% in the early 1970s to 14% in 2001. But there have been wide fluctuations over the period, with this index going as high as 24% in 1978.

Interestingly, movements in the index of price dispersion have been correlated, not only with the dispersion of per capita income, but strikingly also with the DM/dollar

---

[8] We include non-EMU members here since long-run real exchange rate dynamics should be in force regardless of the exchange rate regime.

[9] See Alesina *et al.* (2001) for a simplified rendition of this explanation. See Obstfeld and Rogoff (1996) for a more comprehensive textbook treatment. Devereux (2000) makes the point that productivity growth may be more important in the non-traded sector in some countries.

[10] The positive relation between output per capita and price levels may reflect the Balassa–Samuelson mechanism but also non-homotheticity in tastes and the importance of quasi-fixed factors (e.g. land) in the non-traded sector.

[11] The slope of this line appears to have flattened, however, presumably reflecting closer good market integration (Figure 5). Detailed regression results are not reported.

[12] See also Rogers (2002) who uses a different measure for the price level (from the EIU) and finds that the greatest reduction in price dispersion took place in the early 1990s, rather than being associated with the advent of the single currency. Beck and Weber (2001), Chen (2002) and Imbs *et al.* (2002) study price dispersion across European regions but the focus is on (possibly non-linear) speeds of convergence rather than the determinants of the price gaps.

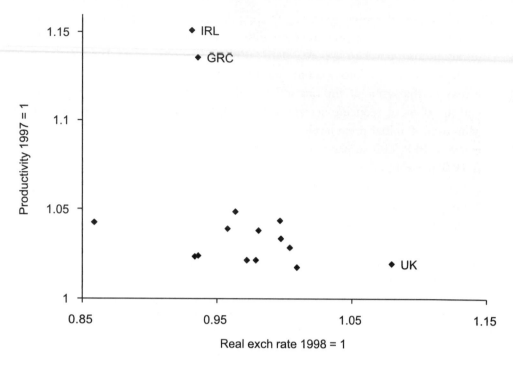

Figure 4. Productivity growth and real appreciation, 1997–2001

Notes: Real exchange rate is 'Index of relative consumer prices in a common currency'; productivity is 'productivity index'.

Source: OECD *Economic Outlook.*

market exchange rate.[13] When the US dollar is strong, prices in Europe converge. Although the empirical relationship has been quite tight, this point does not appear to have been noticed in the literature over the years.[14] It is plausible that whatever forces underlay it in the past are likely to have been the drivers once again of the price level convergence during the first three years of EMU.[15]

3.2.2. Other policy factors: fiscal policy and interest rates.   In addition to the roles played by effective exchange rate movements and price level convergence, what policy-related factors have contributed to inflation differentials within the euro

[13] The cross-sectional standard deviation of per capita GDP enters with a negative 'wrong' sign if included in this regression on its own on annual data 1970–2001, but this is due to a data discontinuity in 1991 after the unification of Germany enters the statistics. Accounting for this with a slope dummy restores the 'right' sign. The fit of the resulting equation is quite good. It implies that a 10% movement in the dollar/DM rate narrows the index by about 0.75%. The regression is:

$$\text{Coeffvar}_t = -0.14 + 0.0169 \text{ GDPpc}_t - 0.0054 \text{ Unification} * \text{GDPpc}_t + 0.075 \text{ \$/DM}_t$$
$$\quad\quad (1.4) \quad (2.9) \quad\quad\quad (7.0) \quad\quad\quad\quad\quad\quad\quad\quad (5.3) \; R^2 = 0.811 \quad DW = 1.61$$

[14] For example, Crucini *et al.* (2001) who stress that nominal exchange rate movements were of little effect in influencing real exchange rates over a five-year interval. But see Papell (2002).

[15] Among possible causes for this empirical relationship we conjecture that episodes of dollar strength might have generated a kind of Dutch disease effect, and that this effect would have been stronger in low productivity-low price countries. Exploring this and other possible explanations is not the purpose of the present paper.

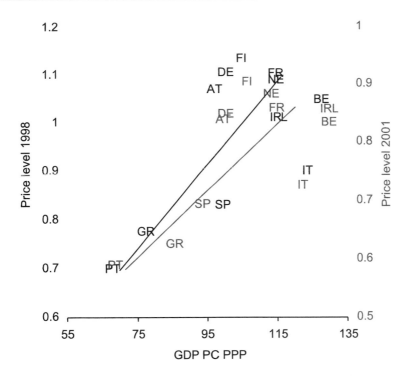

Figure 5. Price levels and GDP per capita, 1998 and 2001

Notes: Price level is purchasing power parity times exchange rate; output is gross domestic product at 1995 purchasing power parities divided by total employment, index based to Germany = 100 in each year.

Source: OECD *Economic Outlook*.

zone? In the case of interest rate and fiscal deficit policy, a common rule structure was nominally in effect (much weaker in the case of fiscal policy). But once again, as with the exchange rate, the actual impact of the evolution of interest rate and fiscal variables on inflation rates was, if anything, to contribute to divergence.

In the presence of nominal price or wage stickiness, aggregate demand factors play a role in driving inflation and real exchange rates in the short run and can push output above its long-run potential level. The pairwise correlation between output gaps and inflation rates was 0.50 over 1999–2001.[16]

One factor driving aggregate demand in some countries during this period was a sharp decline in real interest rates. The convergence of both nominal and real interest rates in the different member countries was sharp as the start date for EMU approached. But, while nominal rates remained bunched together, the spread between real interest rates widened out again subsequently as inflation diverged. Ironically, this placed some of those countries with previously high real interest rates (such as Ireland, Spain, Portugal and Greece) at the lower end of the range later:

---

[16] It is beyond the scope of this paper to discuss the empirical failings of the existing measures of output gaps. We employ the OECD measure in this study. See also European Central Bank (1999).

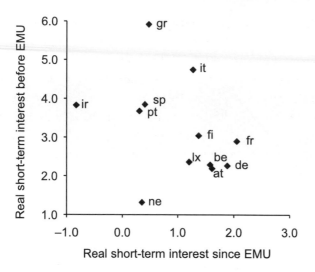

Figure 6. National real interest rates: before and since EMU

Source: Ex post real money market interest rates calculated from line 64..X and line 60B of the IMF's *International Financial Statistics*; quarterly data.

Figure 6 clearly shows a negative correlation between pre- and post-EMU real short-term rates.[17] The fall in real interest rates in those countries with higher-than-average inflation is a potentially destabilizing factor. It sustains spending levels and hence upward demand pressure on prices in exactly the countries that already have relatively high inflation, hence working against the factors that tend towards inflation convergence.

The most prominent contribution of a fall in nominal and real interest rates to demand and inflation can be through the property market. There is a fairly strong negative cross-sectional correlation between real interest rate declines in the run-up to EMU and commercial property inflation in 1995–2001 (the correlation is −0.67).[18] Beyond the wealth effect of rising property values on domestic consumption, a boom in the property market may also store up a future adjustment problem.

Turning to another policy influence on the level of domestic demand, fiscal positions are partly endogenous, especially to the business cycle and to interest rates. Furthermore, budget deficits are somewhat constrained by the Stability and Growth Pact, as well as being influenced by the scale and direction of intra-EU transfers. Nevertheless, to a large extent, within the period under review, the cyclically adjusted primary surplus has been largely under the control of national governments, although there may be a policy feedback from observed inflation. However, there appears to be no cross-sectional correlation between inflation and the cyclically adjusted primary surplus during 1999–2001: the bivariate correlation is −0.002.

---

[17] This effect thus goes beyond the original Walters' critique of destabilizing capital market effects of a currency peg.

[18] For the eight countries where data is available. There is no cross-sectional bivariate correlation with residential property inflation – Italy, with a sharp fall in interest rates, experienced only modest house price rises in 1995–2001. Starting with 1995 allows anticipatory price movements as discussed (in fact, the correlations for 1998–2001 are not significant).

With respect to another dimension of fiscal policy, changes in the indirect tax burden tend to show up in consumer prices. In principle, this is quite a complex thing to measure. If we take the change in the share of GDP taken in taxes on goods and services as a rough and ready measure, however, we will get some indication of trends in indirect taxation. Interestingly, calculating this change for the period 1998–2001, we find that the correlation with post-EMU inflation is insignificantly negative; even if the outlier Ireland (for which the ratio of consumption to GDP declined sharply during the period) is removed, the correlation, although now positive, is still insignificant.

3.3. Econometric evidence

We ran multivariate panel regressions to establish the relative contributions of some of the key factors discussed above in driving inflation differentials within the euro zone over 1999–2001. A fairly general specification for inflation differentials can be written as

$$\pi_{it} - \pi_t^E = \beta(z_{it} - z_t^E) - \delta([P_{it-1} - P_{it-1}^*] - [P_{t-1}^E - P_{t-1}^{E*}]) + \varepsilon_{it} \tag{2}$$

where π_{it}, π_t^E are the annual national and euro zone inflation rates respectively; z_{it}, z_t^E are national and euro zone variables that exert short-term influence on the inflation rate; P_{it}, P_t^E are the national and euro zone price levels and P_{it}^*, P_t^{E*} are the national and euro zone long-run equilibrium price levels.[19]

If we assert that the euro zone countries share a common long-run price level, this expression can be simplified to

$$\pi_{it} - \pi_t^E = \beta(z_{it} - z_t^E) - \delta(P_{it-1} - P_{t-1}^E) + \varepsilon_{it} \tag{3}$$

The assumption of a common long-run price level is plausible for a putative convergence club such as the euro zone, with tight trade and institutional linkages eliminating income and productivity differentials over time.[20,21] We also experimented with the alternative hypotheses that even long-run price levels may diverge due to productivity or income differences and we report results below for these cases. However, we

---

[19] We do not include country-fixed effects, since it is implausible that there exist permanent inflation differentials across euro zone member countries. This specification assumes that inflation differentials are stationary; equivalently, that national and euro zone price levels are cointegrated. Clearly, we cannot test these assumptions given the short time interval but these assumptions are firmly grounded in economic theory and so we are comfortable in treating these as maintained hypotheses. We note that much recent empirical work on real exchange rates postulates a non-linear speed of adjustment to the long-run equilibrium. Our short time span does not permit us to investigate such non-linearities. Finally, this specification implicitly assumes a common speed of adjustment at local and European levels: again, more data could allow us to relax that assumption.

[20] See also Froot and Rogoff (1995) and the empirical work by Zussman (2003). The latter finds evidence of absolute convergence in price levels among OECD countries.

[21] We earlier remarked that the degree of price dispersion in Europe appears to co-move with cycles in the euro-dollar (DM-dollar) exchange rate. To allow for this cyclical effect, one could write an expanded specification with, for example, intercept and slope dummies for periods of dollar strength and weakness. As data emerges for alternating periods of dollar strength and weakness, it will become possible to disentangle the long-term and cyclical price convergence effects.

do not find a significant role for these variables and so focus on the more restricted specification in our main discussion.[22]

In turn, the euro zone variables can be linearly combined into a time dummy, which allows us to write

$$\pi_{it} = \phi_t + \beta z_{it} - \delta P_{it-1} + \varepsilon_{it} \tag{4}$$

Following our analysis in the previous subsection, we include three variables in our z-vector. These are the rate of change in the nominal effective exchange rate (lagged by one period), the impulse in the cyclically adjusted fiscal surplus and the output gap.[23] This gives us our empirical specification

$$\pi_{it} = \phi_t + \beta_1 \Delta NEER_{it-1} + \beta_2 GAP_{it} + \beta_3 FISC_{it} - \delta P_{it-1} + \varepsilon_{it} \tag{5}$$

where π_{it} is the annual inflation rate, $\Delta NEER_{it-1}$ is the lagged growth rate of the nominal effective exchange rate, GAP_{it} is the output gap, $FISC_{it}$ is the impulse in the cyclically adjusted primary surplus and P_{it-1} is the lagged price level.[24] Note that the time dummies in the regression captures EMU-wide common movements in inflation and in the regressors, so that the regression is explaining inflation differentials in terms of idiosyncratic national movements in the determinants.[25]

Tables 5 and 6 show the results from the panel estimation for each of six inflation measures in turn: Consumer Price Index (based on HICP data); the private consumption deflator; CPI excluding energy; the import price deflator; the GDP deflator; and wage inflation.[26] Table 5 displays the pooled OLS equations; GMM estimates are shown in Table 6, where we instrument for the fiscal impulse and the output gap using lagged values of these variables.

In Table 5, the impact of the exchange rate on inflation is significant across columns (1)–(6): a country that experiences a rate of depreciation of its nominal effective exchange rate that is larger than the European average will also have relatively higher inflation.

---

[22] Rogers (2002) also employed a productivity proxy in his empirical work but found it to be insignificant for this period. As is discussed further later in the paper, these variables may become more important once the euro zone is enlarged to incorporate the accession countries. Other factors (such as the net foreign asset position) may also affect long-run relative price levels but we do not include these here due to the short time span (cf. Lane and Milesi-Ferretti, 2002).

[23] Of course, the fiscal position may primarily operate by affecting the size of the output gap. We allow for an additional independent effect, since the fiscal balance may shift the composition of expenditure towards domestically produced goods, exacerbating inflationary pressures even if the output gap is not affected. Fiscal policy may also have longer-run effects by altering unit costs and profitability but we do not pursue these channels here: see Lane and Perotti (2003).

[24] Our default inflation measure is based on the Eurostat HICP data; the price level is measured by the consumption price level in the Penn World Tables version 6.1 (this variable is highly correlated with the OECD PPP measure but is conceptually more appropriate); the nominal effective exchange rate, output gap and the fiscal surplus are from OECD sources. We lag the nominal effective exchange rate by one year in recognition of delayed pass-through from exchange rates to consumer prices. The impulse in the cyclically adjusted fiscal surplus is measured by $PRIM_{it} - \sum_{j=t-1}^{j=t-6} PRIM_{ij}/5 = 1$.

[25] In Table 5 we have reported, as well as the usual R^2, a figure for the percentage of the variation explained by factors other than the time dummies.

[26] The HICP CPI measure is the official index employed by the ECB; the private consumption deflator is the preferred measure of the Federal Reserve Board; the third measure excludes the volatile energy component; although it includes intermediate goods, the import deflator provides useful information about externally generated inflation; finally, the GDP deflator and wage inflation should be more highly influenced by domestic inflationary pressures.

Table 5. Euro zone inflation differentials: pooled OLS estimates

	(1)	(2)	(3)	(4)	(5)	(6)
Lagged change in	−0.28	−0.46	−0.30	−0.79	−0.39	−0.44
effective exchange	(−2.71)**	(−4.64)***	(−2.62)**	(−1.83)*	(−1.97)*	(2.23)**
rate						
Output gap	0.22	0.16	0.28	−0.14	0.34	0.59
	(2.65)**	(2.97)***	(3.81)***	(−0.66)	(3.62)***	(4.14)***
Fiscal stance	0.02	0.14	0.04	−0.32	0.08	0.10
	(0.32)	(1.73)*	(0.64)	(−1.39)	(0.67)	(1.13)
Lagged price level	−0.03	−0.04	−0.04	−0.03	−0.07	−0.01
	(−2.88)**	(−4.52)***	(−4.86)***	(−1.42)	(−6.20)***	(−1.12)
SE of regression (%)	0.73	0.65	0.62	1.78	0.88	0.88
Adjusted R^2	0.61	0.67	0.75	0.82	0.65	0.68
Percentage explained	0.43	0.54	0.64	0.17	0.63	0.67

Note: The dependent variables in columns (1)–(6) are the inflation differentials based on: (1) HICP; (2) Private consumption deflator; (3) HICP excluding energy; (4) Import price deflator; (5) GDP deflator; (6) Wages. Time-fixed effects included. The *t*-statistics are based on White-corrected standard errors. *, **, *** denote significance at the 10, 5 and 1% levels respectively. Percentage explained is percentage of the variation in the dependent variable explained by factors other than the time dummies, and is measured as one minus the squared residual standard error divided by the squared residual standard error of a regression on the time dummies alone.

Sources: Lagged price level is based on consumption price level from Penn World Tables version 6.1; Private consumption and import price deflator are from European Commission's AMECO database; the effective exchange rate is from the IMF *International Financial Statistics* database; all other data are from OECD *Economic Outlook* database.

Table 6. Euro zone inflation differentials: pooled GMM estimates

	(1)	(2)	(3)	(4)	(5)	(6)
Effective exchange rate	−0.28	−0.37	−0.26	−0.92	−0.36	−0.35
	(−3.43)***	(−4.07)***	(−2.88)***	(−2.51)**	(−2.21)**	(−2.40)**
Output gap	0.23	0.27	0.34	−0.34	0.37	0.71
	(3.99)***	(2.95)***	(6.13)***	(−1.49)	(2.67)**	(7.59)***
Fiscal stance	0.07	0.25	0.13	−0.58	0.11	0.21
	(1.71)	(3.22)***	(2.78)**	(−3.58)***	(1.09)	(2.13)**
Lagged price level	−0.03	−0.04	−0.05	−0.02	0.07	−0.02
	(−4.53)***	(−5.10)***	(−7.37)***	(−0.91)	(−7.31)***	(−1.40)
SE of regression (%)	0.73	0.70	0.65	1.86	0.89	0.92
Adjusted R^2	0.60	0.62	0.73	0.80	0.65	0.65
Percentage explained	0.42	0.47	0.61	0.09	0.62	0.64

Note: The dependent variables in columns (1)–(6) are the inflation differentials based on: (1) HICP; (2) Private consumption deflator; (3) HICP excluding energy; (4) Import price deflator; (5) GDP deflator; (6) Wages. Time-fixed effects included. The *t*-statistics are based on White-corrected standard errors. *, **, *** denote significance at the 10, 5 and 1% levels respectively.

Sources: Lagged price level is based on consumption price level from Penn World Tables version 6.1; Private consumption and import price deflator are from European Commission's AMECO database; the effective exchange rate is from the IMF *International Financial Statistics* database; all other data are from OECD *Economic Outlook* database.

The point estimate of −0.28 in the CPI equation means that a relative depreciation of 3.5% is associated with an additional one percentage point of inflation. This is a large effect: for instance, the Irish nominal effective exchange rate depreciated by a cumulative 11% during 1998–2000, whereas the French exchange rate weakened by only 4%.

The output gap is important except for import prices – more so for the domestically generated inflation measures (the GDP deflator and wages) than for the broader indices. The fiscal surplus is marginally significant only for the private consumption deflator. Even here, the positive sign on this variable is contrary to prior expectations: an increase in the fiscal surplus is associated with relatively higher inflation.[27] In view of its fragility, we do not dwell on this result.

Finally, the table shows that the price convergence effect is highly significant for four inflation measures, even if not for import or wage inflation. For CPI inflation, the -0.03 point estimate implies that a country with a price level one-third below the European average would experience an additional one percentage point of inflation.[28] This is significant in terms of the inflation variation observed in the euro zone but also implies that the convergence process is quite gradual.

To guard against potential reverse causation whereby the output gap and the fiscal stance are influenced by the inflation rate, we conduct instrumental variables (GMM) estimation in Table 6. It turns out that significance levels for our main variables are typically even higher under this alternative estimation procedure. We note also that the fiscal stance variable is now more significant than in Table 5; however, with the exception of the import price deflator, its sign remains perverse.

These results show that a considerable proportion of the inflation differentials in the euro zone over 1999–2001 can be systematically related to a small number of macroeconomic variables.[29] Perhaps the most novel finding is the important role played by the nominal effective exchange rate in explaining inflation differentials: euro zone member countries continue to have quite different trading patterns and hence quite varied exposure to external currency fluctuations.

We may view this source of inflation differentials as temporary along two dimensions. First, there is surely a substantial temporary component to the decline of the external value of the euro during 1999–2001: indeed, recent months have seen a sustained recovery. Second, trade patterns will continue to evolve, with a plausible shift towards a greater proportion of intra-euro zone trade. The importance of external trade will also decline if the euro zone club expands to include the 'outs' (especially the United Kingdom) and the accession countries. Moreover, to the extent that some non-joiners track the euro, this will limit the degree of volatility in nominal effective exchange rates (see Honohan and Lane, 1999). Finally, as was already noted, the introduction of the euro should over time alter pricing strategies, with more imports to the euro zone priced in euros rather than in foreign currency, shifting the impact of exchange rate shocks from consumers to producers.

---

[27] A similar positive co-movement is also found by Canova and Pappa (2003), who perform a sophisticated instrumental-variables procedure to guard against reverse causation.

[28] In 1998, the Spanish and Portuguese consumer price levels were respectively 25% and 35% below the German level.

[29] Regarding the estimation procedure, we note that serial correlation in the residuals is minor. In fact, taking the CPI inflation equation, the correlation between e_{it} and e_{it-1} is negative (-0.30). Moreover, there is no evidence of spatial correlation in the residuals: a regression of $E(e_i e_j)$ on the log of bilateral distance yields an adjusted R^2 of 0.01 (the correlation is 0.15).

With respect to the other regressors, the importance of the output gap highlights the role of short-run imbalances in generating local inflation pressures. Controlling for the output gap, however, there does not seem to be a strong role for the fiscal impulse in determining inflation. The price convergence effect can be viewed as a long-run constraining factor on inflation differentials: long-run price levels in the euro zone should move together.

Finally, it is too early to make much progress in detecting econometrically the danger, discussed informally above, of the amplitude and duration of price shocks being magnified in particular countries through destabilizing real interest rate and wage rate dynamics. As a longer data set accumulates, this will become a priority for further research.

3.4. Robustness checks

Table 7 reports results for expanded specifications in which productivity or output levels are allowed to affect long-run price level differentials. Since shifts in these variables alter the long-run equilibrium price level, we also allow innovations in these variables to influence the inflation differential in some of the regressions. These

Table 7. Expanded specifications: CPI euro zone inflation differentials, GMM estimation

	(1)	(2)	(3)	(4)
Effective exchange rate	−0.27	−0.31	−0.26	−0.25
	(−3.33)***	(−3.20)***	(−2.73)**	(−1.65)
Output gap	0.24	0.26	0.24	0.24
	(4.42)***	(3.13)***	(4.24)***	(2.66)**
Fiscal stance	0.07	0.04	0.07	0.07
	(1.73)*	(0.75)	(1.83)*	(2.07)*
Lagged price level	0.01	−0.04	−0.04	−0.04
	(−2.64)**	(−2.76)**	(−2.97)***	(−2.80)**
Lagged PROD level	0.004	0.004		
	(0.55)	(0.62)		
PROD growth rate		−0.07		
		(−0.43)		
Output per capita level			0.002	0.002
			(0.60)	(0.55)
Output per capita growth Rate				0.003
				(0.03)
SE of regression (%)	0.75	0.76	0.75	0.76
Adjusted R^2	0.59	0.57	0.58	0.56
Percentage explained	0.40	0.38	0.39	0.37

Note: The dependent variable in columns (1)–(4) are the HICP-based inflation differentials. GMM estimates. Time-fixed effects included. The *t*-statistics are based on White-corrected standard errors. *, **, *** denote significance at the 10, 5 and 1% levels respectively. PROD is the log of labour productivity in the business sector; Output per capita is based on PPP-adjusted GDP.

Sources: Lagged price level is based on consumption price level from Penn World Tables version 6.1; the effective exchange rate is from the IMF *International Financial Statistics* database; all other data are from OECD *Economic Outlook* database.

variables are not significant in any of the specifications. Moreover, despite the reduction in degrees of freedom, the results for the other regressors are largely unaffected.
However, the nominal effective exchange rate marginally loses significance when both
the level and growth rate of output per capita are included in column (4).

In Table 8, we experiment with alternative measures of the fiscal stance. These
variations do not substantially alter the results for the other variables, even if we drop
the fiscal variable entirely (column 1). The fiscal variable in levels turns out to be
significantly positive (column 2); in first differences, it is not significant (column 3).

The web appendix contains more robustness checks. We report TSLS estimates
for each of these specifications. In addition, as another sensitivity check, we report the
results for the subsamples obtained by dropping one country at a time. The main results
are quite stable: the point estimates and the t-statistics vary relatively little. The main
exception is the fiscal variable, which turns marginally positive in a couple of subsamples.

3.5. Relation to the existing literature

The empirical contribution that is closest to ours is Rogers (2002). His results are
largely complementary to ours; however, he does not include the nominal effective
exchange rate as an explanatory variable.[30] Moreover, he does not focus specifically
on the 1999–2001 period (he provides results instead for 1997–2001 that combine
pre-EMU and post-EMU data).[31] The European Central Bank (1999) also documents
a strong bilateral relation between inflation differentials and output gaps but just
using cross-sectional data for 1999.

4. THE 'OUTLIER': IRELAND'S INFLATION SURGE IN EMU

In light of the broad cross-country evidence that was marshalled in the previous section,
Ireland's experience calls for special attention. Irish inflation, below 5% for almost
15 years and averaging just under 2% per annum in the 5 years prior to EMU membership, suddenly accelerated in late 1999 and has since then been persistently at the
top of the EMU inflation league. CPI inflation touched an annual rate of 7% in the
12 months to November 2000, before retreating to the 4–5% range (Figure 7).
Conventional wisdom has it that this outlying experience is entirely homegrown,
fuelled by an overheating economy, excessive wage claims and fiscal expansion. The
rapid apparent productivity growth has suggested to many that Balassa–Samuelson
effects are at work.

---

[30] Rogers does include a measure of openness to extra-euro zone trade. However, this variable will not have a stable sign: during
periods of euro appreciation, it should have a negative sign; and a positive sign if the euro depreciates. In addition, the
composition of extra-euro zone trade also matters in determining exposure to various bilateral exchange rate movements. This
consideration is incorporated into the construction of the nominal effective exchange rate.

[31] His measures of the initial price level and the fiscal variables also differ from ours.

Table 8. Euro zone CPI inflation differentials: alternative fiscal specifications

	(1)	(2)	(3)
Effective exchange rate	−0.27	−0.23	−0.27
	(−2.88)***	(−2.81)***	(−1.87)*
Output gap	0.21	0.23	0.21
	(3.25)***	(4.34)***	(2.81)***
Fiscal stance A		0.11	
		(2.16)**	
Fiscal stance B			−0.003
			(−0.01)
Lagged price level	−0.03	−0.03	−0.03
	(−4.46)***	(−6.00)***	(−4.77)***
SE of regression (%)	0.71	0.71	0.73
Adjusted R²	0.62	0.62	0.60
Percentage explained	0.42	0.45	0.42

Note: The dependent variable in columns (1)–(3) are the HICP-based inflation differentials. GMM estimates. Time fixed effects included. The *t*-statistics are based on White-corrected standard errors. *, **, *** denote significance at the 10, 5 and 1% levels respectively. Fiscal stance A is the primary surplus in levels; Fiscal stance B is the primary surplus in first differences.

Sources: Lagged price level is based on consumption price level from Penn World Tables version 6.1; Private consumption and import price deflator are from European Commission's AMECO database; the effective exchange rate is from the IMF *International Financial Statistics* database; all other data are from OECD *Economic Outlook* database.

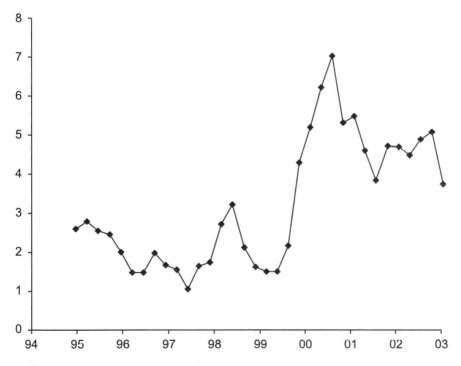

Figure 7. Irish inflation, 1995–2003

Note: Per cent per annum 12-month moving average plotted quarterly. Last observation is May 2003.
Source: Central Statistics Office of Ireland.

But, in addition to the domestic factors, EMU itself has contributed to the surge in Irish inflation in at least two ways. First, the exchange rate depreciation produced a much larger inflationary impulse because of Ireland's distinctive trade pattern (relatively little trade with EMU countries; much with the UK and the US). Membership of EMU removed the potentially effective national instrument of nominal exchange rate adjustment: dollar strength might well have been offset by an appreciation of the Irish pound, had it remained within the wide EMS band of 1993–8 instead of joining EMU.[32] Second, by lowering nominal and real interest rates, EMU added an important demand fillip, especially manifested in soaring house prices.

4.1. Exchange rate

From late 1996 to 2000, Ireland's nominal effective exchange rate depreciated by some 17% (Figure 8). This was much more than in other EMU members, essentially because Ireland has by far the smallest share of its trade with euro-area participants (31%, compared to 54% for the others). Furthermore, the extreme openness of the Irish economy means that almost a third of aggregate demand (almost 60% of GDP) is met by non-euro area imports. Although much of that trade has something of the character of an entrepôt business, nevertheless the sharp fall in the value of the currency against the US dollar and sterling from 1997 onwards has implied a much larger cost push factor than experienced by other members. Assuming a lag of several quarters in the pass-through of exchange rate to domestic CPI, Figure 8 points to a simple mechanism, namely that much of Ireland's inflation of 2000–2 can be interpreted as a pass-through effect from the depreciation.[33]

Had it not been for adherence to the common currency, historical experience suggests that a surge in the value of the US dollar and sterling would have resulted in appreciation of the Irish pound against the DM.[34] To that extent, some of this imported inflation has been due to EMU accession.

4.2. Interest rates and house prices

Given the very high interest rates previously experienced, whether measured in nominal, exchange-rate corrected, or real terms, it was always clear that EMU acces-

---

[32] In recognition of upward pressure on the real exchange rate, Ireland undertook a 3% nominal appreciation against its EMU partners in April 1998. A larger nominal appreciation at that time could have forestalled some of the inflationary pressure that was experienced after the formation of EMU.

[33] The speed of pass-through seems to have slowed in recent years; cf. FitzGerald (2001) and FitzGerald and Shortall (1998) who point to a switch from sterling-based to euro-based pricing by the large UK groups which dominate Irish retailing.

[34] For example a typical log-linear regression of the Irish pound/deutsche mark rate on the bilateral rates vis-à-vis the US dollar of the pound sterling and deutsche mark on quarterly data for the wide-band period 1993Q2–1997Q3 produces:

$$e_{DM/IEP} = 2.76 + 0.52e_{\$/\pounds} + 0.62e_{DM/\$} \quad \rho = 0.64$$
$$\phantom{e_{DM/IEP} = } (2.9) \quad (2.2) \quad\quad (6.2) \quad\quad\quad (2.6) \quad R^2 = 0.896 \quad DW = 1.71$$

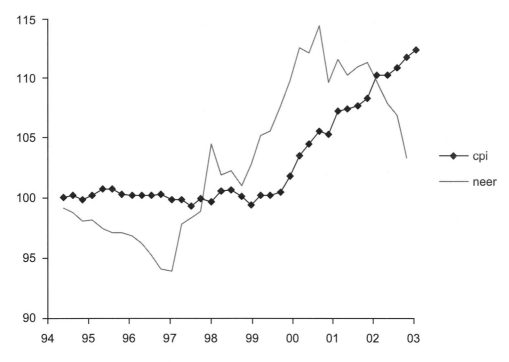

Figure 8. Irish inflation and currency depreciation, 1994–2003

Note: The figure shows CPI level, detrended by the 1994–8 trend, and the nominal effective exchange rate index.

Source: CPI is from Central Statistics Office of Ireland; NEER is from Central Bank of Ireland (trade weighted competitiveness index).

sion would lead to a sizeable step reduction in interest rates and a reduction in their volatility. [35] In the event, since EMU began, Irish real interest rates have been the lowest in the union at an average of *minus* 1% (reflecting the higher inflation rate).

This represents a sizeable change in intertemporal prices facing resident households (as well as locally exposed firms *on average*), and this may be taken to influence local asset prices, such as that of housing. The Irish property boom since the late 1990s has pushed *real* house prices to well over 250% of the levels of the early 1970s and mid-1980s. Interest rate declines are implicated in econometric studies of this boom, though the role of demographic pressures, real income growth and a possible non-fundamental (bubble) component are also debated (Bacon *et al.*, 1998; Roche, 1999).

---

[35] The decade from 1983–93, during the narrow-band EMS period, saw real interest rates averaging 7.44% per annum; excess returns on Irish money market instruments were more that 250 basis points relative to Germany during that period. In the wide-bank EMS period real interest rates fell to an average of 3.86%, but, with monetary policy holding money market rates as tight as possible it was not in the last couple of months of 1998 that nominal short interest rates (including floating mortgage rates) converged to the EMU average. Most mortgages in Ireland are still at floating rates, but in the run-up to EMU there was a big shift to mortgage interest rates fixed typically for 3–5 years. By early 1999, these accounted for 38% of total mortgages; since then, most new mortgages have reverted to the floating model.

4.3. Productivity

Little, if any, of Ireland's inflation deviation is a reflection of the Balassa–Samuelson effect. Ireland's boom has been largely one of employment growth, and not exceptional productivity gains. Much of the very high apparent productivity growth in Irish manufacturing over the past several decades is an artefact of transfer pricing, and Ireland is already close to the EMU-average of per capita GNP (Honohan and Walsh, 2002).

4.4. Wage behaviour

Partly reflecting moderate centralized wage agreements, and partly attributable to sizeable immigration, real wage rates were remarkably slow to increase during most of the 1990s, despite the rapid growth in employment and a tightening labour market. From 1997, a less restrictive wage agreement and an increasing tendency for local wage rate increases above nationally agreed levels saw the real purchasing power of wages (i.e. deflated the consumer prices) in manufacturing start to increase steadily. Even though by 2002 they had reached only 115% of their 1996 average level, and though this partly reflects a catch-up relative to a period of artificial wage-repression, the change in trend will have added some pressure to domestic consumer prices.[36]

4.5. Fiscal policy

Fiscal policy has certainly helped sustain high inflation in the last few years, especially with the rapid shift from high and rising surplus (before 2001) to deficit today. Even in the earlier years when revenue buoyancy kept the budget in growing surplus, fiscal policy was not withdrawing demand to the extent that the improved fiscal accounts reflected falling external debt service (as the external debt to GDP ratio declined), and increasing tax payments by foreign firms (exploiting the low tax regime). After 2000, the budget surplus declined rapidly with a turnaround of almost 6% of GDP in just two years, mainly due to autonomous tax reductions and spending policy increases.

4.6. Summary on Ireland

Exchange rate depreciation from 1997 has been a major driver of inflation acceleration in Ireland after 1999. Not only did it raise import prices directly but it improved wage competitiveness, thereby facilitating a sizeable increase in real wages. The fall in interest rates as Ireland joined EMU fuelled a house-price boom whose other causes were likely more important. That CPI inflation persisted after the currency

---

[36] The affordability of these wage increases even by marginal exporters to non-euro countries was, of course, enhanced by the currency depreciation that began about the same time and, as such, part of the real wage increase can be attributed to currency movements.

stopped falling reflects domestic factors (the continued rise in real wages and the sharp relaxation in the budgetary position), in addition to delayed pass-through. Ireland's persistently higher inflation (until May 2003) does not, therefore, cast doubt on the long-run convergence of inflation rates in the union. But to what extent wage and house-price inflation embody overshooting dynamics that may require painful adjustment in the future remains hard to establish with confidence.

5. COUNTERFACTUALS

In the previous sections we have documented and attempted to explain the inflation differentials among the EMU member countries over 1999–2001. In this section, we ask whether independent monetary policies would have delivered different outcomes.

As a simple illustration of the potential scale of the difference between the actual interest rates observed in the EMU members and what might have been adopted by national central banks, we calculated counter-factual country-specific interest rates using a version of the 'classical' interest rate rule proposed by Taylor (1993). The rule sets

$$R_t = 4.0 + 1.5 * (\pi_t - 2.0) + 0.125 * GAP_t \qquad (6)$$

This rule is based on an average real interest rate of 2.0%, an inflation target of 2.0%, π_t is the inflation rate and GAP_t is the OECD's calculated output gap for each country. This specification conforms to the standard principles of Taylor rules: respond aggressively to inflation signals but also take into account deviations of output from its estimated potential level.[37] Table 9 presents data on the distribution of the implied country-specific interest rates, expressed as deviations from the German rate.[38] The calculation confirms that 'freely-chosen' interest rates would have been considerably dispersed, with the range maximized in 2000 at 5.7 percentage points.[39]

Table 9. Euro zone interest rate dispersion under independent monetary policies

Year	Mean	StDev	Min	Max
1999	1.36	1.21	−0.19	3.21
2000	1.30	1.67	−0.17	5.52
2001	1.17	1.77	−0.60	4.37

Note: National interest rates as deviations from implied German interest rate. Based on Equation (3).

[37] There is a literature on the specification of Taylor rules for open economies. Variation in trade openness may mean that the optimal coefficients in the Taylor rule should vary country by country. In addition, an additional exchange rate term could be added to the rule that would imply interest rate responses to exchange rate fluctuations. However, Leitemo and Soderstrom (2001) find that adding an exchange rate term adds little to performance and the simple rule here is useful for illustrative purposes.

[38] Some other authors have implemented similar rules for the aggregate euro zone economy (Faust et al., 2001; von Hagen and Bruckner, 2002). By expressing the constructed interest rates in terms of deviations from the German level, the impact of alternative choices concerning the target nominal interest rate and inflation rate is minimized.

[39] France has the lowest implied interest rate in each year; Ireland has the maximum in 1999–2000, with the Netherlands the maximum in 2001.

A complementary approach to addressing this question is to treat the specification in Equation (2) as a regime-independent model of inflation. In this case, monetary policy would operate by affecting the values of the regressors: in particular, country-specific interest rate policies would have meant different values for the output gap and the effective exchange rate.[40]

Taking these in reverse order, it seems likely that at least some of the member countries would have acted to prevent large movements in their effective exchange rates by raising interest rates in response to the dollar appreciation in 1999–2000. For instance, as was noted in Section 4, the historical evidence for Ireland is that it would have acted to eliminate about half of the dollar-DM movement. A combination of higher interest rates and less currency depreciation would have acted to moderate inflation pressures in these countries.

With regard to the output gap, there are several reasons to believe output gaps would have been smaller under national monetary policies. Most obviously, a counter-cyclical monetary policy would have helped to close output gaps. In addition, as was discussed earlier, one source of domestic demand in the high growth economies has been the sharp fall in interest rates relative to pre-EMU levels in these countries: in the absence of EMU, any such interest rate reduction would have been smaller and would have been smoothed out under standard monetary procedures. Another contributor to output gaps has been the exchange rate depreciation in some of the countries: as noted above, the scale of depreciation in several countries would have been muted by interest rate increases under independent monetary policies.

Regarding the other variables included in Equation (2), would fiscal policy have been more restrictive in the high-inflation countries under an alternative monetary regime? With higher interest rates, it seems likely that primary deficits would likely have been lower. However, it is plausible that the price level convergence effect may have been weaker in the absence of a common currency. The common currency has increased the transparency of price differentials (especially since the introduction of notes and coin in 2002) and may have also increased trade integration.[41] In that case, the low-price countries would have experienced lower inflation and the high-price countries faster inflation.

The discussion so far in this section does suggest that a superior inflation performance might have been attainable under independent monetary policies. However, proponents of a single currency can point to some counter-arguments. First, the ongoing integration of European product and factor markets (possibly accelerated by the advent of EMU) will plausibly erode persistent inflation differentials. In line with the price level convergence effect, the scope for dispersion in traded goods prices is falling. Labour markets are also responding, with high-growth countries receiving net

---

[40] We take the initial price level as largely independent of monetary policy during this period.

[41] See Rose (2000) and the subsequent empirical literature on this point. However, Rogers (2002) argues that the price level convergence effect is no stronger among the euro zone countries than among the wider EU club.

inflows of migrants, easing pressure on wage rates.[42] Finally, there are indications of increased portfolio diversification among the euro zone countries that should partially smooth out national income shocks through risk sharing. However, we also note that the absence of a euro zone federal fiscal system means that an important risk-sharing mechanism in the US is not available to the euro zone countries.

6. IMPLICATIONS FOR ACCESSION COUNTRIES

The relevant initial conditions of the accession countries and other prospective euro members differ widely. Accordingly, while there are some general implications, these would have to be interpreted on a country-by-country basis, a task that is not attempted here.

Overall, the experience of the first several years of the system reveals that convergence of inflation rates cannot be expected to be as tight or as quick as had been anticipated by some. We view the 'price convergence' effect as generally benign and self-limiting: some temporary inflation differentials are a necessary part of the transition to long-run real exchange rate equilibrium.

With respect to the divergence in inflation rates that is induced by variation in exposure to shocks to the external value of the euro, policy should not over-react to such dispersion since the nominal exchange rate movements themselves are sure to be limited and largely self-correcting as long as monetary authorities in the leading countries continue to succeed in restraining inflation over the long term.

The accession countries and the member states which have not adopted the euro are, on average, as highly specialized in trade with the current EMU participants as the latter are themselves (Table 3). If we take the non-EMU imports as a percentage of GDP, this is not much higher on average in the accession countries and is actually lower in each of the 'out' countries, by comparison with the 'ins'. There is considerable variation. Estonia and Malta are rather highly exposed to non-EMU trade, although neither to the same extent as Ireland. These countries can be expected to experience wider fluctuations in their CPI inflation, but hardly to an extent that would make a case for delaying EMU membership.

Does CPI volatility from such a source matter for policy? In terms of monetary and exchange rate policy, if a case could be made for augmenting mean EMU-wide inflation with some function of the cross-country dispersion of inflation as the target for EMU policy, then it would follow that the external exchange rate of the euro could act as a useful intermediate objective or indicator of monetary policy. However, the assessment of whether the ECB should stabilize the external value of the euro would surely be much more heavily influenced by other factors than this consideration. On the whole, there seems little reason to over-react.

---

[42] The correlation between output gaps and net immigration during 1999–2000 was 0.70.

There is another potential dimension to exchange rate policy, namely the establishment of bilateral arrangements for stabilizing exchange rates between the euro and the currencies of 'fringe' trading partners (Honohan, 2000). With enlargement both of the EU and EMU membership, the potential gains from such arrangements will already be largely secured and, in any case, would have little impact compared to the volatility of bilateral exchange rates vis-à-vis major trading partners such as the US and Japan.

Should national fiscal deficits and surpluses be employed as a tool to damp inflation fluctuations? The standard prescription is that fiscal policy should be more counter-cyclical to compensate for the absence of an independent monetary policy (cf. EEAG, 2003, ch. 2). However, in line with Perotti (2003) and others, we found little econometric evidence of the stabilizing properties of discretionary adjustments to the budget balance beyond those captured in the output gap.[43] Moreover, the empirical investigation by Lane (2003b) suggests that governments find it hard for political reasons to push the discretionary component of fiscal policy in a counter-cyclical direction. In combination with the well-known problem of correctly timing fiscal interventions, these results suggest that national fiscal policy does not offer a 'silver bullet' in tackling excessive inflation differentials. It seems to us that further research on the appropriate role for discretionary fiscal policy in regional stabilization must be a high priority for European macroeconomists.

Perhaps the major message is for those involved in wage negotiations. Although we have argued that exchange-rate induced surges in national inflation are likely to be reversed, this view may not be shared by those negotiating on behalf of organized labour. Multi-year wage collective bargaining settlements based on an expectation of continued above-EMU average inflation could be very damaging to the competitiveness of labour in such circumstances. Given that the accession countries can be expected to support higher than average real wage increases on a sustained basis in the years ahead as their level of average productivity converges to the frontier, it will be much more difficult for negotiators in those countries to compute the appropriate and affordable rate of wage increase and the exchange-rate induced effects might easily be ignored or misinterpreted in making such calculations. As we have shown, recognizing the external sources of inflation can be of material significance in this respect.

Macroeconomic conditions at entry also need careful management. We have already seen how a sharp fall in nominal and real interest rates contributed to demand pressure in Ireland, both directly and by permitting a relaxation of fiscal discipline via the easing of budgetary constraints. New entrants should be wary of

---

[43] The point estimates we obtained – though rarely significant – implied a disinflationary effect for expansionary fiscal policy, conditional on the output gap (a result also found by Canova and Pappa, 2003). Indeed, this is the policy prescription of Duarte and Wolman (2002): income tax reductions during a boom can have a moderating impact on inflationary pressures.

allowing their economies to overheat in this way.[44] Careful attention should be paid to the rate at which currencies are pegged, especially for those countries which will experience a large fall in nominal interest rates. A more appreciated entry rate could help forestall a surge of inflationary pressures upon entry.

7. CONCLUSIONS

Despite the common currency, exchange rate movements have had a substantial impact on inflation differentials in EMU, reflecting the different degrees of exposure of member states to trade outside the euro zone. Our analysis suggests that the recent strengthening of the euro should lead to a much sharper fall in inflation in the externally orientated member countries than in the core countries that largely trade within the euro zone.

Much of the remaining pattern of inflation movements can be explained by national output gaps. The inclusion of fiscal imbalances adds no significant explanatory power. The initial fall in nominal and real interest rates – quite different across countries – likely not only contributed to inflationary pressures via raising aggregate demand in goods markets but may also have contributed to dispersion in property price movements in the run-up to and early years of EMU.

Although the observed differentials seem to have come as a surprise to some observers, they are little larger than those recorded across US regions in the same years. To some extent, inflation differentials may be more persistent within a currency union than outside it in that national inflation rates and real interest rates are inversely related inside a currency union, generating procyclical dynamics. From a policy perspective, finding institutional mechanisms that minimize the risk of real exchange rate overshooting is a high priority.

Finally, while differential productivity growth has not featured centrally in the inflation experience of existing members in the early years, it will surely be a more relevant factor when accession countries join the euro. To the extent that inflation differentials reflect price level convergence and the operation of the Balassa–Samuelson mechanism, one can view such inflation differentials benignly. However, real appreciation inside a currency union also carries risks. With a low common nominal interest rate, real interest rates in the high-inflation countries will be negative. In turn, this could fuel an expenditure boom, generating extra inflationary pressure through an emerging output gap and a rapid run-up in property prices. The potential overhang from such overheating pressures poses a serious risk for the accession countries.

---

[44] Current inflation and real interest rate conditions differ widely among candidate countries. The latest 4-quarter mean inflation is almost 10%, though less than 4% for the ten countries expected to join the EU in 2004. Real *ex post* short-term interest rates recently varied from 10–11% in Poland and Romania to negative values in Bulgaria. Real interest rates in Turkey have been extremely volatile.

Discussion

Jaume Ventura
CREI and Universitat Pompeu Fabra

Inflation rates in the euro zone converged dramatically from the signing of the Maastricht Treaty to the onset of EMU. At the time, most observers thought that inflation convergence was a key prerequisite for the success of the euro. Surprisingly, this process quickly halted and then reversed right after the adoption of the euro. Even more surprisingly, this inflation divergence does not seem to have had much of an effect on the viability of the single currency. How can we explain this turn of events? This paper by Patrick Honohan and Philip Lane provides a new, refreshing and quite convincing answer to this question. To fully appreciate their contribution, it is worth taking a step back and reviewing the state of the debate before their paper.

A popular view is that inflation divergence has been caused by asymmetric shocks. Since the data clearly shows that inflation has been high in fast-growing countries, it seems natural to conjecture that these asymmetric shocks must have been on the demand side. Unfortunately, there is little evidence for the existence of these asymmetric demand shocks. The Stability and Growth Pact and the creation of the European Central Bank have led to a convergence in fiscal and monetary policies. If anything, regulations and expectations about the future have converged across countries. In a nutshell, the search for the asymmetric shocks on the demand side has been futile so far, and I do not expect it to yield anything in the future.

Some have pointed out that we should look for the asymmetric shocks on the supply side. In fact, there is strong evidence suggesting that productivity growth has been quite different among euro zone countries. At first sight, the notion that one can explain inflation divergence with asymmetric supply shocks does not seem very promising. After all, supply shocks tend to generate low inflation in fast-growing countries and this directly contradicts the data. But there is a well-known recipe to 'convert' supply shocks into demand shocks. It is called the Balassa–Samuelson effect, and it goes as follows: assume there are two sectors, traded and non-traded. The former faces a relatively flat demand, while the latter faces a relatively vertical one. A positive supply shock in the traded sector raises income, and leads to a small or negligible decline in the price of non-traded goods. Higher income raises the demand for non-traded goods and this leads to a large increase in the price of non-traded goods. To sum up, if supply shocks (or productivity growth rates) are biased towards the traded sector they can create both growth and inflation in the same way that demand shocks do.

But is this the answer to the mystery of the divergent inflations? I do not believe so. It is true that Ireland and Greece have higher productivity growth than France and the United Kingdom. But these differentials in productivity growth are nothing new. They also existed well before the adoption of the euro during a period when inflation rates rapidly converged among euro zone countries. This observation raises some difficult questions. Why did inflation rates converge before 1999 when differentials in productivity growth were as high as in the period after 1999? What did really change in the first quarter of 1999? To be fair, the hypothesis that asymmetric shocks have caused inflation divergence has run into a cul-de-sac, and new and fresh hypotheses are badly needed.

This is exactly what the paper by Patrick Honohan and Philip Lane does. The paper argues that the introduction of the euro itself has created the force for diverging inflations. The Honohan–Lane hypothesis goes as follows: euro zone countries have different trading partners and, in particular, the importance of their trade with non-euro zone partners varies substantially. For instance, while almost four-fifths of Ireland's imports come from non-euro zone partners only a quarter of Luxembourg's imports come from non-euro zone countries. Under these conditions, a depreciation of the euro will raise prices more in Ireland than in Luxembourg. To calculate the effects of changes in the nominal exchange rate on inflation, what matters is the nominal *effective* exchange rate and not the nominal exchange rate. As a result of differences in exposure to non-euro zone trade, the former varies substantially across countries even if the latter is the same for all.

The Honohan–Lane hypothesis is simple and original, and it allows us to move away from the fruitless search for asymmetric shocks. Moreover, the authors show that it works empirically. Their estimates suggest that a 3.5% depreciation in the nominal effective exchange rate raises the inflation rate by about 1%. This is enough to explain most of the differences in inflation. For instance, the 2% inflation differential between Ireland and France can be fully explained by the fact that the nominal effective exchange rate depreciated by 11% in Ireland but only by 4% in France. I find these numbers quite convincing.

Despite this positive assessment of the Honohan–Lane hypothesis, we must keep in mind that the key test of its validity is being conducted as I write this discussion. According to the Honohan–Lane hypothesis, the recent appreciation of the euro should reverse the trend once again, and generate a new period of inflation convergence. I look forward to seeing whether events will confirm this prediction.

David Begg
The Business School, Imperial College London

Within a monetary union, divergent inflation rates are the key channel for changing real exchange rates. Sometimes this is desirable, and part of the adjustment mechanism, but sometimes divergent inflation rates are themselves sources of shocks that then initiate the need for further adjustment.

Whether inflation divergences 'matter' is therefore not a helpful way in which to pose the question. Failure of inflation rates to diverge when real exchange rate adjustment is required may be just as problematic as observed divergences in inflation rates when no other prior shocks are evident.

I therefore see the heart of the paper   its novel and important contribution – not in the discussion of when inflation divergences matter but rather in the empirical verification of the idea that, within a monetary union, different member states will typically have different patterns of external exposure and openness, and hence will be differentially affected by changes in the common external exchange rate. At its simplest, having different bilateral trade weights with third countries, they have different paths for their effective exchange rate.

Stated thus, this is an idea with which we have all long been familiar. Nevertheless, prompted by their familiarity with the Irish experience, the authors have tracked down its empirical implications and argue, convincingly, that the idea is general and consistent with the empirical evidence for the whole panel of member states in the euro zone since its launch in 1999. Ireland, being more open than Germany, experienced larger swings in its effective nominal exchange rate for any given fluctuations in the euro/dollar exchange rate. In turn, this induced differential movements in inflation that acted in the direction of equilibrating real exchange rates again.

More specifically, by encompassing several leading explanations of differential inflation – convergence to a long-run price level, the business cycle effect of output gaps through the Phillips curve, movements in the euro exchange rate, and the effect of fiscal policy – the authors show that the first three effects can clearly be detected, though any independent effect of fiscal policy disappears once the other three effects are included.

Doubtless, others will now try to extend these results. My suggestions for further research include the explicit inclusion of supply shocks (for example, successive monthly reports of the ECB have laid considerable stress on floods and animal disease as adverse shocks to which ECB monetary policy had to respond).

Next, the authors offer us a bonus, a discussion of the counterfactual of what might have happened, country by country, had member states retained an independent national monetary policy. Using a standard Taylor rule to model what national interest rates would then have been, the authors arrive at unsurprising conclusions: Irish interest rates would have been higher if they had been set in Ireland, and German interest rates would have been lower. National output gaps would therefore have been smaller.

Although I have no problem with the conclusion, I wonder if the analysis is terribly convincing. Neither output nor inflation is exogenous to the monetary policy rule. Hence, by using actual paths for output and inflation, the authors describe a hybrid of real and hypothetical rather than a true counterfactual. In such exercises, I see no coherent alternative to general equilibrium or systemic modelling.

What lessons should accession countries draw from all this? While forces for price level convergence remain strong these countries should be expected to have inflation rates above the euro zone average. Once the euro has been adopted this need present no particular problem, but any transitional monetary arrangements should be compatible with our guess about the inflation differentials that are likely on average to persist. ERM2 is therefore potentially vulnerable to currency crises if markets do not fully understand which inflation divergences are accomplishing adjustment and which are sources of further divergence. Some of us have written all this before. What we need to learn after reading Honohan and Lane is that external movements in the euro will also have predictable effects and should be interpreted accordingly by markets.

Panel discussion

Jordi Galí agreed with the discussants that the authors should focus more on how the *nominal* exchange rate affects inflation differentials. He suggested looking in greater detail at price indices that capture some of the effects the authors are interested in. The price index of imported consumer goods or the price index for domestic final goods should pick up the nominal exchange rate effect and domestic demand effects, respectively. Moreover, the nominal exchange rate hypothesis is universal so that it can be tested on US regions or a cross-section of other countries. Margarita Katsimi argued that the nominal exchange rate hypothesis should have become less relevant after EMU in 1999.

David Miles pointed out that the increase of housing prices is not specific to Ireland since housing prices have increased substantially also in other cities such as London. What could be specific to the Irish case is that much of the mortgage debt is variable rate debt. Omar Licandro asked whether the increase of house prices in Ireland could justify including housing prices into the HICP (see the paper by Cecchetti and Wynne in this volume) given that the effect on real interest rates is important. Patrick Honohan cited an IMF study identifying Ireland's recent house price inflation as close to the highest among industrial countries in the past 20 years. He stressed that the capitalization effect matters for borrowers.

Lorenzo Codogno agreed that the policy relevance of inflation dispersion is small because the market will adjust to absorb these differences. He was interested in further discussion of the structural deviations of inflation rates. Paul de Grauwe thought that inflation differentials and the understanding of their political determinants are important. Marcel Thum asked for more discussion about the politico-economic dimension of the results for accession countries. Steve Cecchetti did not find the results surprising and thought that monetary policy-makers should not care about regional differences. To some extent he found the existence of national data unfortunate because of the resulting public pressure if such differences are not taken into account by monetary policy. Paul de Grauwe was convinced that national information will continue to play an important role for the ECB's monetary policy in the future. Mike Artis added that the importance of inflation differentials stems from the fact that historically national monetary policy has reacted strongly to fluctuations of

the exchange rate in the EMU countries. Margarita Katsimi argued that the importance of inflation differentials depends on the ECB voting mechanism: national differences should matter less if the principle of one-man-one-vote is applied than if
national representation matters. Lucas Papademos pointed out that the Greek experience has been very similar to the Irish one. He thought it unlikely that inflation
differences exist forever and urged more research on understanding the adjustment
mechanism. He considered the implications for monetary policy as far from straightforward since inflation differences can no longer be accommodated by monetary
policy. Thomas Moutos argued that the effect of international specialization, frag-
mentation of production and specialization has an ambiguous effect on inflation
differences across countries so that inflation differences may even increase in the
future. Apostolis Philippopoulos wondered whether credibility differences of national
central banks have become completely unimportant after EMU as a determinant of
inflation differences. Patrick Honohan replied that inflation differences across EMU
members resulting from nominal exchange rates will become a matter of declining
importance in the future compared with inflation differences stemming from productivity growth differences. Hans-Werner Sinn added that the nominal exchange rate
channel can be important. He mentioned that for Germany a 10% devaluation
increases inflation by 5%.

Omar Licandro asked whether differences in trade patterns among US regions
compared with EMU countries can be used to explore the nominal exchange rate
hypothesis given the similarity of the inflation differentials for the US and EMU.
In particular, it would be interesting to know how much this matters for Ireland.
Ernesto Stein added that the analogy between US-regions and EMU member states
can be exploited if suitable data exist because states like Florida are more open than
Nebraska so that there is variation in trade across regions.

Mike Artis mentioned the 'Procrustes' dilemma of a one-fits-all monetary policy
rule for the euro area. For example, Ireland was used to a high interest rate policy
and had to bear a substantial policy shock after accession to EMU. Moreover, standard optimum-currency-area criteria suggest that Ireland should never have joined
EMU. In this context he missed a discussion of the Irish IT shock in the paper. He
concluded by noting the importance of developing policy instruments for the better
management of asymmetries among current and also future accession countries in
the EMU.

Stijn Claessens asked why the authors did not extend their sample to earlier years.
He suggested weighting countries by their degree of openness and controlling for the
initial level of the exchange rate. Ignazio Angeloni asked for further explanation of
how persistent inflation differentials are and how these differentials are absorbed.
Mark Wynne wondered whether measurement error in the US data, the more comprehensive sample on which HICP is based and different baskets and weights used
for the construction of the price indices could induce a spurious similarity of the
inflation differentials among US regions and EMU countries.

WEB APPENDIX

Available at http://www.economic-policy.org

REFERENCES

Adjaouté, K. and J. Danthine (2002). 'European financial integration and equity returns: a theory-based assessment', presented to the Second ECB Central Banking Conference, Frankfurt, October.

Alesina, A., O. Blanchard, J. Galí, F. Giavazzi and H. Uhlig (2001). *Defining a Macroeconomic Framework for the Euro Area (Monitoring the European Central Bank 3)*, CEPR, London.

Bacon, P., F. MacCabe and A. Murphy (1998). *An Economic Assessment of Recent House Price Developments*, Government Publications, Dublin.

Beck, G. and A. Weber (2001). 'How wide are European borders? New evidence on the integration effects of monetary unions', Goethe University, Frankfurt, mimeo.

Begg, D., F. Canova, P. de Grauwe, A. Fatas and P.R. Lane (2002a). *Surviving the Slowdown (Monitoring the European Central Bank 4)*, CEPR, London.

Begg, D., F. Canova, P. de Grauwe, A. Fatas and P.R. Lane (2002b). *Surviving the Slowdown (Monitoring the European Central Bank 4) – Update*, CEPR, London.

Benigno, G. and C. Thoenissen (2003). 'Equilibrium exchange rates and supply side performance', *The Economic Journal*, 113(486), C103-C124.

Canova, F. and E. Pappas (2003). 'Price dispersion in monetary unions: the role of fiscal policy', London School of Economics, mimeo.

Cecchetti, S., N. Mark and R. Sonora (2001). 'Price index convergence among United States cities', The Ohio State University, mimeo.

Chen, N. (2002). 'The behaviour of relative prices in the European Union: a sectoral analysis', PhD dissertation, University of Brussels.

Crucini, M.J., C.I. Telmer and M. Zachariadis (2001). 'Understanding European real exchange rates', Vanderbilt University, mimeo.

Devereux, M. (2000). 'Real exchange rates and growth: a model of East Asia', *Review of International Economics*, 7, 509–21.

Duarte, M. and A. Wolman (2002). 'Regional inflation in a currency union: fiscal policy versus fundamentals', mimeo, Federal Reserve Bank of Richmond.

European Central Bank (1999). 'Inflation differentials in a monetary union', *Monthly Bulletin*, October, 36–45.

EEAG (European Economic Advisory Group) (2002, 2003). First and Second *Reports on the European Economy*, CESifo, Munich.

Faust, J., J. Rogers and J. Wright (2001). 'An empirical comparison of Bundesbank and ECB monetary policy rules', International Finance Discussion Paper No. 705, Board of Governors of the Federal Reserve System.

FitzGerald, D. (2003). 'Terms-of-trade effects, interdependence and cross-country differences in price levels', Harvard University, mimeo.

FitzGerald, J. (2001). 'Managing an economy under EMU: the case of Ireland', *World Economy*, 24, November, 1353–71.

FitzGerald, J. and F. Shortall (1998). 'Pricing to market, exchange rate changes and the transmission of inflation', *Economic and Social Review*, 29, October, 323–40.

Froot, K. and K. Rogoff (1995). 'Perspectives on PPP and long-run real exchange rates', in G.M. Grossman and K. Rogoff (eds.), *Handbook of International Economics*, Vol. 3. North Holland, Amsterdam, 1647–88.

Honohan, P. (2000). 'Miniblocs and fringe currencies of the EMU', *Journal of Economic Integration*, 15(1), 47–75.

Honohan, P. and P.R. Lane (1999). 'Pegging to the dollar and the euro', *International Finance*, 2(3), 379–410.

Honohan, P. and B.M. Walsh (2002). 'Catching up with the leaders: the Irish hare', *Brookings Papers on Economic Activity*, 1, 1–77.

Imbs, J., H. Mumtaz, M. Ravn and H. Rey (2002). 'Aggregation and the real exchange rate', London Business School, mimeo.

Kieler, M. (2003). 'The ECB's inflation objective', IMF Working Paper WP/03/91.

Kumar, M.S., T. Baig, J. Decressin, C. Faulkner-MacDonagh and T. Feyzioglu (2003). *Deflation: Determinants, Risks, and Policy Options*, Occasional Paper 221, International Monetary Fund, Washington, DC.

Lane, P.R. (2003a). 'Monetary-fiscal interactions in an uncertain world: lessons for European policymakers', in M. Buti (ed.), *Monetary and Fiscal Policies in EMU*, Cambridge University Press, forthcoming.

Lane, P.R. (2003b). 'The cyclical behaviour of fiscal policy: evidence from the OECD', *Journal of Public Economics*, forthcoming.

Lane, P.R. and G. Milesi-Ferretti (2002). 'External wealth, the trade balance and the real exchange rate', *European Economic Review*, 46, 1049–71.

Lane, P.R. and R. Perotti (2003). 'The importance of composition of fiscal policy: evidence from different exchange rate regimes', *Journal of Public Economics*, forthcoming.

Leitemo, K. and U. Soderstrom (2001). 'Simple monetary policy rules and exchange rate uncertainty', Working Paper 122, Sveriges Riksbank.

Lucas, R.E. Jr (2000). 'Inflation and welfare', *Econometrica*, 68(2), 247–74.

Obstfeld, M. and K. Rogoff (1996). *Foundations of International Macroeconomics*, MIT Press, Cambridge, MA.

Papell, D.H. (2002). 'The panel purchasing power parity puzzle', University of Houston, mimeo, November.

Perotti, R. (2003). 'Estimating the effects of fiscal policy in OECD countries', *Journal of the European Economic Association*, forthcoming.

Roche, M. (1999). 'Irish house prices: will the roof cave in?', *Economic and Social Review*, 30, 343–62.

Rogers, J. (2002). 'Monetary union, price level convergence and inflation: how close is Europe to the United States?', Working Paper 740, International Finance Division, Board of Governors of the Federal Reserve System.

Rose, A. (2000). 'One money, one market: estimating the effect of common currencies on trade', *Economic Policy*, 30, 7–46.

Sinn, H. and M. Reutter (2001). 'The minimum inflation rate in Europe', NBER Working Paper 8085.

Taylor, J. (1993). 'Discretion versus policy rules in practice', *Carnegie-Rochester Conference Series on Public Policy*, 39, 195–214.

Von Hagen, J. and M. Bruckner (2002). 'Monetary policy in unknown territory: the European Central Bank in the early years', ZEI, Bonn, mimeo.

Walton, D. and S. Deo (1999). 'Limits to inflation: convergence in Euroland', Global Economics Paper No. 30, Goldman Sachs.

Zussman, A. (2003). 'Real exchange rate behavior in a convergence club', Stanford University, mimeo.

Defining price stability

SUMMARY

The Harmonized Index of Consumer Prices (HICP) is at the core of the monetary policy strategy of the European Central Bank (ECB). It is the basis for the quantitative definition of price stability that is the ECB's principal objective. For operational purposes, in October 1998 the Governing Council of the ECB originally announced that its definition of price stability would be an annual increase in the HICP of 'below 2 percent'. In May 2003, this was changed to 'close to 2 percent'. But is 2% the right number? Our analysis suggests that the answer is no, and that a modest upward redefinition of HICP inflation consistent with price stability is warranted. We evaluate the ECB's quest for price stability during the first years of monetary union from a measurement perspective. That is, we start by considering what the HICP is designed to measure and how accurate it is in terms of its stated objective, and then ask whether there is any sense in which HICP inflation of 2% can be said to be too low. We conclude that the conceptual underpinnings of the HICP remain sufficiently vague so that it is difficult to compare with other indexes or come to any hard conclusions about its accuracy. However, it is possible that the HICP is susceptible to the biases that are known to affect other measures of inflation at the consumer or household level, and if forced to quantify potential bias, a point estimate of 1% strikes us as reasonable. Bias of this magnitude, in conjunction with the inherent noisiness of the headline number and the well-known aversion of central bankers to deflation, lead us to conclude that a target of 2% is in fact too low.

— *Stephen G. Cecchetti and Mark A. Wynne*

Inflation measurement and the ECB's pursuit of price stability: a first assessment

Stephen G. Cecchetti and Mark A. Wynne

Brandeis University and NBER; Federal Reserve Bank of Dallas

'For all these conceptual uncertainties and measurement problems, a specific numerical inflation target would represent an unhelpful and false precision. Rather, price stability is best thought of as an environment in which inflation is so low and stable over time that it does not materially enter into the decisions of households and firms' (Alan Greenspan, 'Transparency in Monetary Policy', remarks to the Federal Reserve Bank of St Louis Economic Policy Conference, 11 October 2001).

'The ECB's Governing Council was of the view that the quality of the HICP made it feasible to set a precise definition of price stability as part of its monetary policy strategy' (Otmar Issing, 'The Relevance of Reliable Statistical Systems for Monetary Policy Making in the Euro Area', speech to CEPR/ECB Workshop on Issues in the Measurement of Price Indices, 16 November 2001).

The views expressed in this paper are those of the authors and do not necessarily reflect the views of the Federal Reserve Bank of Dallas or the Federal Reserve System. We thank Elias Brandt for research assistance and Roisín O'Sullivan for assistance with some computations. We also thank Erwin Diewert, the editor, Richard Baldwin, our discussants, Jordi Galí and Carol Propper, and seminar participants at Sam Houston State University for comments that helped us substantially improve this paper. The Managing Editor in charge of this paper was Richard Baldwin.

1. INTRODUCTION

Article 105 of the Treaty Establishing the European Community mandates that the primary objective of the European System of Central Banks shall be to maintain price stability. In October 1998 the Governing Council of the European Central Bank (ECB) adopted its 'stability-oriented monetary policy strategy'. Included was a quantitative definition of price stability as 'a year-on-year increase in the Harmonized Index of Consumer Prices (HICP) for the euro area of below 2% . . . to be maintained over the medium term.' Since the beginning of monetary union in 1999, through December 2002, inflation has been at or above this self-imposed limit of 2% in no fewer than 30 of 48 months, as Figure 1 shows.

Unlike the ECB, the Federal Reserve has consistently shied away from offering a quantitative definition of price stability. Rather, throughout his tenure, Chairman Alan Greenspan has defined price stability *qualitatively* as prevailing when inflation ceases to be a factor in the decisions of households and businesses, as the opening quote indicates. Of course, Alan Greenspan is not the first Fed chairman to prefer a qualitative rather than a quantitative definition of price stability. In 1983, Greenspan's predecessor, Paul Volcker argued that 'A workable definition of . . . "price stability" would . . . be a situation in which expectations of generally rising (or falling) prices over a considerable period are not a pervasive influence on economic and financial

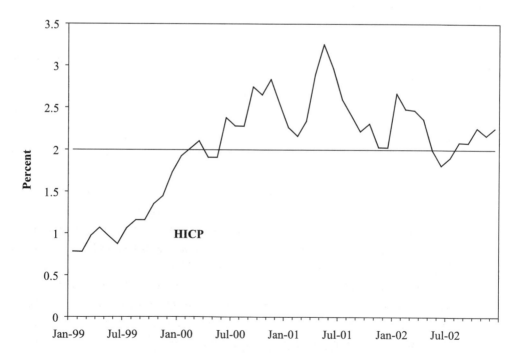

Figure 1. HICP inflation in the euro area since the launch of EMU

Source: Eurostat/Haver Analytics.

behaviour . . . "[price] stability" would imply that decisionmaking should be able to proceed on the basis that "real" and "nominal" values are substantially the same over the planning horizon – and that planning horizons should be suitably long.' Among the reasons Chairman Greenspan has given for not advancing a precise quantitative definition are the difficulties associated with inflation measurement in a dynamic economy. About a month after Chairman Greenspan's defence of the Fed's reluctance to provide a quantitative definition of price stability in the US, ECB board member Otmar Issing confidently asserted that the ECB does not share the Federal Reserve's concerns about price index accuracy.

In the recently completed assessment of its policy strategy, the Governing Council reaffirmed its view that the HICP is sufficiently accurate that it can safely be used to quantify ECB's Treaty mandate of price stability. Are they right? Is the quality of inflation statistics available to the Governing Council sufficient for them to be used as they are? And is 2% the right number?

This is the backdrop for our review of various aspects of the performance of the ECB during the first years of economic and monetary union (EMU). The creation of the HICP in time for an assessment of the convergence criteria prior to the launch of EMU was a remarkable achievement. And when it came to quantifying what is meant by price stability in the euro area there was no viable alternative to the HICP.

With that said, however, we think it is necessary and possible to do better. We will pose and attempt to answer three questions.

- What is the HICP, and what is it designed to measure? Answering this question in the context of a discussion of monetary policy leads us to ask: What does price stability mean for monetary policy-makers? We argue that the welfare basis for the price-stability objective of the ECB (and other central banks) creates a compelling case for policy-makers to focus on a cost-of-living index, as this provides the clearest measure of the impact of inflation on households. While it is relatively uncontroversial that the final objective of a central bank should be defined in terms of a headline measure of inflation such as the cost-of-living-based consumer price index, few would argue that central bankers should respond to every monthly uptick or downtick in the monthly measure.

- Is it possible to construct a measure of core inflation based on the HICP that does better than the traditional measures that are reported each month as part of the regular monthly release of the HICP? Core inflation plays a prominent role in the deliberations of most central banks. The idea is that monetary policy should be concerned with the medium-term (i.e. several-year) trend in inflation, not the month-to-month or quarter-to-quarter ups and downs. In fact, policy-makers who react to high-frequency price fluctuations are likely to add volatility rather than stabilize it. We will examine various measures of core inflation based on the HICP and confirm what has already been found in many countries, namely that traditional measures of core inflation are of limited value, and that non-traditional measures deserve greater prominence.

- How should price stability be defined? Given recent trends in central banking practice, and the ECB's Treaty mandate to maintain price stability, everyone expected the ECB to put forward a quantitative definition of price stability. And given the paucity of other comprehensive inflation measures for the euro area and the lags in the publication of the GDP-based price measures, it was not at all surprising that the definition was in terms of the HICP. However, the ECB has been criticized for setting its inflation 'target' too low, and for not making it symmetric. We will argue that 2% may be too low for a ceiling on HICP inflation, and that the ECB's definition of the rate of HICP inflation consistent with price stability should be revised upward. Measurement bias alone is not sufficient reason for an upward revision. Our point estimate of bias is in fact below 2%. However, there is considerable uncertainty associated with this point estimate. This uncertainty, combined with the aversion of most central bankers to deflation and the inherent noisiness of month-to-month inflation, is central to our argument for a higher target and range. Our rough calculations suggest 1.25–2.5% HICP inflation as a better definition of price stability. We view this as an operational minimum. Concerns about the zero nominal interest rate bound – that there will be times when further interest rate reductions are desirable but impossible – would raise this range even further.

2. THE HARMONIZED INDEX OF CONSUMER PRICES

From the launch of EMU in January 1999 through December 2002, the HICP rose by just over 9%. Over the same period, inflation in the US has been roughly the same: the Consumer Price Index for All Urban Consumers (CPI-U) went up 10.1% from the beginning of 1999 to the end of 2002. It would seem that inflation performance in the US was comparable to that in the euro area, and it may have been. But comparisons are not so simple, because the CPI-U and the HICP differ in their conceptual frameworks. The CPI-U is an approximation to a cost of living index and its construction is grounded in welfare economics. The HICP is unequivocally not a cost of living index, but it is less clear what it is. These conceptual distinctions give rise to many important differences in practical implementation, the most important of which has to do with the treatment of owner-occupied housing. In the CPI-U, owner-occupied housing services are priced on a rental equivalence basis, and have a weight (relative importance as of December 2001) of about 20%. The HICP does not (at present) include the services of owner-occupied housing in its domain of definition. There are also important differences in terms of coverage. The US CPI measures the inflation experiences of urban households only (about 85% of all households) while the HICP is supposed to measure the inflation experiences of all households resident in the economic territory of the member states.

2.1. The conceptual framework

The HICP has its origin in the Treaty requirement that for the purposes of assessing convergence prior to EMU, inflation 'shall be measured by means of the consumer price index on a comparable basis, taking into account differences in national definitions' (see Article 1 of the Protocol on the convergence criteria). Given the pressure of time in the run-up to EMU, the only viable option was to use the common components of national CPIs to produce a measure of inflation at the consumer level that was comparable across countries. The conceptual justification has been provided as something of an afterthought.

Starting from the observation that 'there is no operational definition of "inflation"', Eurostat (2001) states 'the HICP [is] a Laspeyres-type price index that is based *on the prices of goods and services available for purchase in the economic territory of the Member State for the purpose of directly satisfying consumer needs*' (p. 19, emphasis in original). The HICP covers household final monetary consumption expenditure as defined by the European System of Accounts (ESA 95). Household final monetary consumption is defined as the component of consumption expenditure incurred by households regardless of nationality or residence status, in monetary transactions, on the economic territory of the member state, on goods and services that are used for the direct satisfaction of individual needs or wants, and in one or both of the two time periods being compared (Eurostat, 2001, pp. 19–20). The HICP is intended as a 'pure' price index, meaning that 'it is only changes in prices that are reflected in the measure between the current and base or reference period. *The HICP is not a cost of living index*' (p. 19, emphasis in original).

Instead, as Astin (1999) explains, the intent is for the HICP to track the cost of actual monetary transactions. This means that no imputed prices, such as those for the services of owner-occupied housing, should be used in the HICP. The same reasoning is used to exclude the cost of borrowing money, on the grounds that it is neither a good nor a service.

The HICP was first published in March 1997, with the release of the figures for January 1997. The raw price data are collected by national statistical institutes, compiled into national HICPs and then forwarded to Eurostat, which publishes the overall HICP for the EU and the euro area (the Monetary Union Index of Consumer Prices, MUICP), as well as *about* 129 individual price series at various levels of aggregation. We say 'about' because exact numbers are hard to come by. To see the problem, we can look at the 3-digit level. The individual series titled 'Telephone and telefax equipment' and 'Telephone and telefax services' are reported, along with the combined series called 'Telephone and telefax equipment and services'. In principle all countries are supposed to report the separate series, but in practice some only report the combined series.

While the basket of goods priced for the HICP is the same across all EU countries, the individual prices are not aggregated using a common set of expenditure weights. Rather prices in each country are weighted according to expenditure patterns in that country. Thus, in 2000, for example, the expenditure division 'Food and Non-alcoholic beverages' had a weight of 24.4% in the HICP for Spain, but only 12.1% in the UK. Each country is supposed to ensure that the weights used to aggregate the individual prices are sufficiently up to date to ensure comparability. Many countries (accounting for a bit less than two-thirds of the euro area HICP) update the item weights each year or plan to start doing so soon. The HICPs for each country are aggregated into an overall index for the EU (the EICP) and the euro area (the MUICP) using country weights derived from the share of each country's household final monetary consumption in the relevant total. The EICP and MUICP are annual chain indexes, with weights updated each year. Thus the weights for 2003 are based on national accounts data on household final monetary consumption expenditure for 2001 updated to December 2002 prices.

2.2. Evaluating the HICP

A number of authors have already critiqued the HICP's conceptual basis, or lack of one. Prominent among them are Diewert (2002) and Wynne and Rodriguez (2002). As they point out, the framework is not very well developed (certainly nowhere near as well developed and understood as the theory of the cost of living index), and what conceptual basis exists suffers from a number of internal inconsistencies. One of particular note is the manner in which quality adjustment is treated. To determine when quality adjustment is called for, Eurostat notes that 'Quality change occurs whenever . . . a change in [product] specification has resulted in a *significant difference in utility to the consumer* between a new variety or model of a good or service and a good or service previously selected for pricing in the HICP for which it is substituted' (Eurostat, 2001, p. 69, emphasis added). It is difficult to make sense of this statement except in the context of the theory of the cost of living index, which Eurostat claims the HICP explicitly is not.

It is equally difficult to understand the claim that the HICP includes no imputations. If taken literally, then as Diewert (2002) points out, the index should ignore new goods and services. This would apply to both new goods and new varieties of existing goods. The appropriate treatment of new goods in the cost of living framework is to estimate a virtual price for the earlier period when the good was not available, and use this virtual price to compute the index. In the case of new varieties of existing goods, some form of quality adjustment will typically be needed, which will again entail the imputation of prices to characteristics of goods.

The lack of a solid conceptual foundation makes evaluation of the HICP itself nearly impossible. For example, how could we possibly figure out the extent of measurement error in the HICP without a clear notion of what we should be trying to measure? Error relative to what? Maybe the HICP suffers from the generic measurement problems that attend consumer price indices – substitution bias, bias due to the failure to correct for quality change properly, and so on – but who knows? Without a theoretical ideal, it is simply impossible to do the sort of evaluation that has been done for the US CPI. And indeed, Eurostat (2001, p. 36) asserts that it is inappropriate to criticize the HICP from the cost-of-living perspective. This means that most if not all of the biases that are known to affect fixed-weight Laspeyres-type measures of inflation, such as substitution bias, quality bias and new goods bias may have no meaning in the context of the HICP.

These problems notwithstanding, measurement error is of serious concern to central bankers. Achieving true price stability means knowing the accuracy of the available price indices. For the Governing Council of the ECB, this means having some sense of the size of the bias in the HICP. But as our previous logic suggests, we find it difficult to evaluate the likely extent of such a bias. An equally severe obstacle to any attempt to assess the accuracy of the HICP is limited to the amount of publicly available information on the data collection and adjustment practices of the individual national statistical offices, and how well they implement the ideal HICP.

Finally, there is suggestive evidence that the HICP may be failing even to *harmonize* price measurement across the EU. Of all the components of the HICP, the category '09.1.3 – Information processing equipment' is the one most likely to include similar if not identical products in every country, and also one most likely to be susceptible to serious quality adjustment problems. Commission Regulation 1749/1999 defines this category as including personal computers and monitors, printers, software and miscellaneous accessories accompanying them, calculators, typewriters, word processors and telefax and telephone answering facilities provided by personal computers. Figure 2 plots the recent behaviour of this component of the HICP for each country, deflated by the relevant national HICP.

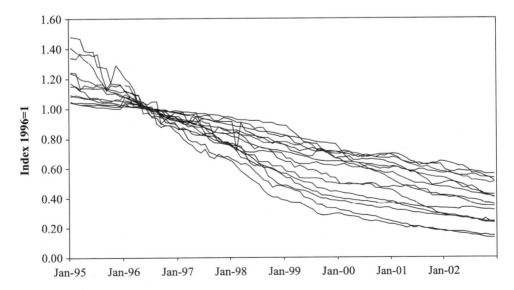

Figure 2. Relative price of information processing equipment in EU countries

Source: Eurostat/Haver Analytics.

The extraordinary range of estimates shown in this figure suggests that the HICP may be failing to achieve its most basic objective. The evidence is only suggestive: it could well be that the different inflation experiences reflect nothing more than national differences in the composition of spending on information processing equipment. In the absence of evidence to the contrary, however, we are inclined to interpret the figure as illustrating significant differences in quality adjustment procedures in the decentralized compilation of the HICP. Hoffman (1998) documents comparable problems in the German CPI, which is also decentralized.

2.3. Bias

With these observations as background what can we say about the accuracy of the HICP? Are there any grounds for believing that measurement error might be so significant that 2% inflation as measured by the HICP would constitute true price stability? Or is the HICP so accurate that true price stability would require no increase in the HICP?

There is a strong presumption on the part of many economists that price indices systematically overstate the cost of living. For example, price indices are weighted averages of individual prices and the weights are revised occasionally. But because people tend to immediately buy less of the goods whose prices have risen the most, the fixed weights misrepresent consumers' purchase patterns – they systematically give too much weight to the prices that have risen the most. Other biases are related to improvements in quality, and the introduction of new goods (see Box 1). However, some recent research has cast doubt on some of these priors, and there is no alternative to a detailed examination of the construction of the HICP to determine whether bias exists. (See in particular the papers by Silver and Heravi, 2002 and Hobijn, 2001, 2002.)

Wynne and Palenzuela (2002) provide a comprehensive review of the current state of knowledge on the accuracy of the HICP, and argue that there is very little scientific basis for a point (or even an interval) estimate of a positive bias in the HICP. But let's deny ourselves the luxury of such fence sitting and ask, if forced to produce a number for the potential bias, what would it be?

Lebow and Rudd (2003) is the most up-to-date and comprehensive review of the accuracy of the CPI-U, and they estimate that it overstates the rate of increase in the cost of living by about 0.9% a year, with a range from 0.3 to 1.4 percentage points. By comparison, the Boskin Commission (Boskin et al., 1996) estimated that the CPI-U overstated inflation by about 1.1% a year, with a range of 0.8 to 1.6. There have been no comparable studies of the accuracy of the HICP, and only a handful of studies of the accuracy of national CPIs in the EU. The best of the existing studies of the accuracy of measures of consumer price inflation in the EU (Hoffman, 1998), estimated that the German CPI overstated inflation by about 0.75% a year. So for the sake of discussion, a point estimate of an upward bias of 1.0% would be consistent with such evidence as exists.

Box 1. Sources of bias in measures of consumer price inflation

Measures of consumer price inflation that are rooted in the theory of the cost of living index may deviate systematically from an ideal measure for a variety of reasons. Loosely speaking such bias can arise because of the manner in which raw data are collected, the way they are combined into the final index, or the technique used to adjust them for changes in quality.

A typical consumer price index is intended to measure the inflation experience of a hypothetical average or representative consumer. To construct the index, the government statistical agency has to figure out what consumers buy and where they buy it. These are done with various expenditure surveys, and mistakes give rise to bias.

The first difficulty is that consumers' buying patterns change all the time, while surveys are infrequent. And in particular, as some goods become relatively more expensive and others relatively less expensive, consumers will tend to shift their expenditure patterns away from the goods that have become more expensive and towards those that have become less expensive. The willingness to make such substitutions lessens the impact of price changes on consumers' standards of living, and to the extent that statisticians fail to take such substitution possibilities into account, the overall measure of consumer price inflation they compile will be subject to substitution bias. Different price indices are more or less subject to substitution bias. Measures like the HICP and the US CPI that are based on expenditure weights that change infrequently are particularly susceptible to this problem, and are known to overstate inflation as a direct result.

Failing to account for changes in where consumers shop gives rise to something called outlet-substitution bias. If consumers have typically made the bulk of their food purchases at small neighbourhood bakeries and butcher shops, but a liberalization of the retailing industry suddenly causes a dramatic increase in the attractiveness of supermarkets that charge lower prices, a failure on the part of the statisticians to take this into account in deciding where to gather price information may again impart an upward bias to the consumer price index.

The problems posed by changes in the quality of the goods and services included in the consumer price index, and the arrival of new goods in the consumer marketplace pose the greatest challenges for statisticians in accurately measuring the cost of living. Quality bias arises when statisticians fail to take into account improvements in the quality of a good or service included in the consumer price index. For example, suppose that all cinemas introduce elaborate new sound systems that enhance the overall movie-going experience, and raise ticket prices at the same time. If consumers willingly pay the higher ticket prices because they value the greater sound quality, but statisticians simply record the higher ticket prices without account for the changed quality, then inflation will be overstated.

Finally, new goods bias arises when the statisticians fail to recognize the introduction of new goods or services on which consumers spend a significant fraction of their income. The distinction between genuinely new goods and new varieties of existing goods is not always clear cut, although few would dispute that mobile phones or DVDs are genuinely new goods, while more durable shoes or clothing, say, are simply better varieties of existing goods. Failing to recognize the introduction of new goods that are subsequently purchased by most consumers may impart an upward bias to a consumer price index because such goods typically experience rapid price declines following their introduction. Under the rules governing the construction of the HICP, new goods or services are supposed to be introduced into the index when they account for one-tenth of one percent of consumer spending.

And this point estimate is likely to be very imprecise. The comprehensive studies for the US suggest that the standard error on those estimates is roughly 0.4.[1] Our view is that this is a floor for any estimate of the uncertainty in the bias of a euro-area cost of living index. The evidence on information technology prices alone suggests the possibility of significantly higher uncertainty. Our conservative estimate is that the point estimate of 1% has a standard deviation of half of one percentage point. We will come back to these figures in our evaluation of the Governing Council's definition of price stability.

2.4. Does it make any difference?

Should policy-makers care about any of this? Would it make any difference if they were to shift attention away from the HICP and toward a cost of living index? Would such a move have had any impact at all on policy actions? We can address this issue by comparing alternative inflation measures.

2.4.1. A direct comparison using Swedish and Dutch data.   Both the Netherlands and Sweden use the theory of the cost of living index as the conceptual framework for their national CPIs, which they continue to produce alongside their national HICPs. Figure 3 shows the difference between inflation at the consumer level as measured by the HICP and the cost of living based CPI for each of these

[1] This estimate comes from Lebow and Rudd (2003) and is based on the information summarized in their Table 1. This table reports, variously, 80% and 90% confidence intervals for estimates of the bias. If 0.3% is the lower limit of an 80% confidence interval, then with a point (mean) estimate of 0.9% the standard deviation must be $(0.9 - 0.3)/1.45 = 0.41$. If instead we take the range to be a 90% confidence interval, the standard deviation is $(0.9 - 0.3)/1.65 = 0.36$. Applying the same calculus to the Boskin Commission yields comparable estimates.

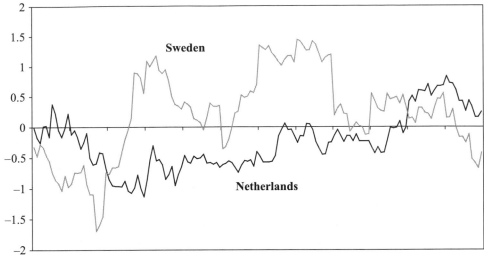

Figure 3. Difference between HICP and CPI (COL) inflation

Source: Eurostat/OECD/Haver Analytics.

countries over the past decade (that is, HICP inflation minus CPI inflation). As
Figure 3 shows, HICP inflation exceeded CPI inflation in the Netherlands for most of
2001 and 2002; a similar situation prevailed in Sweden for most of 1997 and 1998.
Other things being equal, a monetary policy that was based on developments in the
HICP would have been too tight (from a welfare point of view) in both instances.

The discrepancy between the two measures of inflation has to do with the treatment of owner-occupied housing. As we noted above, the 'no imputations' rule means
that the cost of owner-occupied housing is not included in the HICP. It is included
in the CPI, however, since consumers spend a good deal of their income on housing.
Indeed, if we compare the behaviour of prices in the expenditure class 'Housing,
water, electricity and fuels' which is computed for both the HICP and the CPI for
Sweden, we find essentially the same pattern of discrepancies as shown in the figure
above. That is, the prices of 'Housing, water etc.' as measured by the CPI were falling
from 1997 through 2000, whereas the HICP showed the same prices as rising for
most of this period. The difference between 'Housing, water etc.' prices as measured
by the HICP and the CPI amounted to 3.0 to 5.0 percentage points in the early part
of this period, and averaged 1.7 percentage points over the period as a whole (that
is, the HICP for 'Housing, water etc.' rose at an average annual rate that was 1.7%
greater than the increase in the CPI).

While the two measures of inflation at the consumer level can diverge for periods
of a year or longer, they do tend to track each other over long periods of time (formal
statistical tests confirm this, i.e. that they are cointegrated). From January 1991 to
December 2002, the mean inflation rate at the consumer level in the Netherlands as

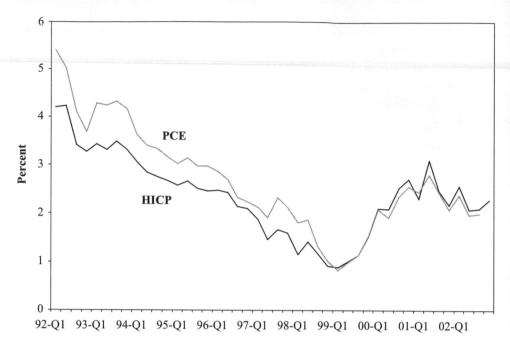

Figure 4. Comparing HICP and PCE (COL) inflation in the euro area

Source: Eurostat/Haver Analytics; European Central Bank.

measured by the HICP was 2.5%, versus 2.7% as measured by the cost of living based CPI. For Sweden the comparable figures are 2.6% HICP inflation and 2.3% CPI inflation. HICP inflation is somewhat more volatile than CPI inflation in the Netherlands (standard deviation of 1.2 as opposed to 0.8%) while the opposite is the case in Sweden (standard deviation of HICP inflation of 2.3%, versus 2.6% for the CPI).

2.4.2. An EU wide comparison: PCE versus HICP. The deflator for personal consumption expenditure (PCE) is a comparable proxy for a cost of living index for both the EU and the euro area. The PCE deflator is a measure of consumer price inflation computed as part of the national accounts, and so is available for all EU countries. Figure 4 plots both the HICP and a PCE deflator for the euro area over the past ten years.[2] The PCE is an approximation to a cost of living index that differs from the HICP in a number of ways, the treatment of housing being the primary one. As is standard for cost of living measures, the PCE attempts to measure the cost of all consumption, including especially the cost of housing to homeowners. The cost

---

[2] A variant of the PCE index is the Federal Open Market Committee's current preferred measure of inflation. Committee members, and especially Chairman Greenspan, believe it to be the most accurate cost of living index currently produced in the US. The Eurostat version of the PCE is somewhat different from its American cousin. The primary difference is in the weighting. The US variant is a chain-type index, while the PCE is an implicit deflator. The chain-type index is designed to minimize substitution bias that tends to make fixed-weight indices like the CPI overstate inflation. By contrast, deflators ignore the welfare impact of substituting from high to low price items, and so systematically underestimate inflation.

of homeownership is computed by assuming that owners rent their own houses from themselves, and then going to rental information to estimate the rent that they would have to pay to do it. In the US this is referred to as 'owner's equivalent rent', and it makes up 20% of the consumer price index. Since housing is such a large component of consumption spending, including it can have an important impact on estimates of inflation.

Looking at the details in Figure 4, we see that the HICP and the PCE deflator move nearly in lock step, especially since the inception of monetary union. The average difference is 0.28 percentage points (standard deviation 0.34) for the entire 1992–2002 period. Since 1999, the difference has been much smaller, averaging 0.08 percentage points with a standard deviation of 0.10. The two series – the HICP and the PCE proxy for the cost of living index – move together and since 1992 the HICP has been on average 0.17 percentage points lower (standard deviation 0.19).

All of this evidence together suggests that over the past decade, the HICP has tended to underestimate, but move closely with, changes in a cost of living index. This is not too surprising, given what we know about the rate of change in the price of owner-occupied housing in most EU countries since 1990. The deflators of imputed rentals for housing in almost all EU countries have tended to rise faster than the PCE deflators for most of the period since 1990. And since the PCE deflator can be thought of as (essentially) a weighted average of HICP inflation and the rate of change of the cost of owner-occupied housing, it should not be too surprising that the HICP might have had a tendency to understate the rate of increase in a cost-of-living type measure of inflation over the past decade.

2.5. Evaluating the HICP as a measure of monetary inflation

Putting aside the issue of measuring the cost of living, we can explore the extent to which the HICP is measuring what its architects say it is trying to measure.

As we already mentioned, Eurostat officials state that the HICP is a 'pure' price index reflecting changes in the nominal cost of monetary consumption. We interpret this as saying that their goal is to construct an accurate index of *monetary inflation*. Understanding what this is and how to measure it means moving away from the utility-based framework (the conceptual basis for cost of living indices). Instead of starting with households, consumers and utility maximization, our approach to the measurement of monetary inflation takes as its point of departure the idea that the observed changes in the prices of individual goods and services can be thought of as the sum of two parts: a general (monetary) inflation component, and a goods-specific or service-specific (relative-price) component.

This way of thinking about inflation can be traced back to the earliest literature on price index measurement. Writing in the nineteenth century, at a time when most countries were on the gold standard, William Stanley Jevons (1865) was interested in detecting the component of price changes that was 'due to a change on the part of gold'. Reasoning that any change in the central bank's holdings of gold must affect all prices in equal proportion, he proposed taking a simple geometric mean of all prices to identify this monetary component of price changes. That is, monetary inflation is the component of price changes that is uncorrelated with relative price changes contemporaneously.

2.5.1. The DFI measure of inflation. Both Bryan and Cecchetti (1993) and Cecchetti (1997) further elaborate this purely statistical view of inflation measurement. They argue for the computation of monetary inflation as the common element in a broad cross-section of prices using a 'dynamic factor index' (DFI). (See Box 2 for a detailed description of the DFI.) When applied to the components of the HICP, the DFI can be interpreted as a measure of monetary inflation at the household level, and a check on the accuracy of the HICP as a 'pure' price index.

2.5.1.1. An example: the cost of living index versus the DFI. To understand the difference between a cost of living index and an index such as the DFI, consider an example in which we have divided consumption into two categories, food and shelter. A cost of living index based on expenditure patterns would give food a weight of 0.3 and shelter a weight of 0.7 in the construction of the aggregate price index. A dynamic factor index aims to separate relative price changes from overall inflation, so it concentrates on finding the weights that cause the relative price changes of the two categories to cancel out. With only two goods, this is a simple exercise. Because the relative price changes are the inverse of one another with just two goods, the relative-price-cancelling weights are 50/50. The case of just two goods is extremely special; adding more goods and allowing for dynamics in the price movements immediately drives us away from equal weighting since the relative-price-cancelling weights get much more complex. In general, the relative-price-cancelling weight on each price depends on its historical variability (variance and persistence) – the less noisy and more persistent inflation is in a given price component, the higher the weight will be. Intuitively, the current change in a price that has historically been very noisy and whose changes have historically been fleeting does not tell us much about overall inflation; the DFI therefore assigns a low weight to such price changes.

Importantly, the DFI weights are based on statistical information content, not on expenditure or GDP shares. While this may seem disturbing at first, it really shouldn't be. After all, statistical analysis is about using the most informative data points to answer a well-posed question. The DFI asks what the common element is in all prices – the part conceptually analogous to pure monetary inflation – and then uses the data in the best way possible to estimate it. Since this has nothing to do with the cost of living, it is not surprising that it is unrelated to household expenditure patterns. Furthermore, because it gives higher weight to inflation in commodities (or countries) that is more persistent the DFI is consistent with the ideas that have been suggested recently in work by both Benigno and Lopez-Salido (2001) and Mankiw and Reis

Box 2. The dynamic factor index (DFI)

The problem of inflation measurement is one of the oldest in economics. Most of us learn about index numbers and are trained to think about inflation measurement from a cost of living perspective. However, an alternative statistical approach takes as its point of departure the following decomposition of the change in the price of some good or service, π_{it}, today as having a common (monetary) component, π_t, and an idiosyncratic (good-specific or relative-price) component, x_{it}. Formally,

$$\pi_{it} = \pi_t + x_{it},$$

where i indexes the set of prices and t is time. The problem of inflation measurement is to figure out the value of π_t from the individual π_{it}. To do this, Bryan and Cecchetti (1993) proposed a radically different approach to the problem of inflation measurement. Specifically, they assume that the common (monetary) component of price change is generated by a time series as follows:

$$\psi(L)\pi_t = \delta + \xi_t.$$

Furthermore, they assume that the idiosyncratic (relative-price) component is generated by the time-series model

$$\theta_i(L)x_{it} = \eta_{it}.$$

In these expressions, $\psi(L)$ and $\theta_i(L)$ are vectors of lag polynomials, and ξ_t and η_t are i.i.d. random variables. Throughout, it is assumed that both the common element, π_t, and the idiosyncratic components, x_{it} can be modelled as AR(2) processes.

The main identifying assumption of the DFI model is that the common component and the idiosyncratic components are mutually uncorrelated at all leads and lags. This is achieved by assuming that $\Theta(L) = [\theta_i(L)]$ is diagonal and that all the error terms in the model are mutually uncorrelated. This is consistent with the notion that the common component captures all of the (monetary-policy induced) co-movement in the individual price series, leaving x_{it} to reflect only idiosyncratic (relative price) movements. To set the scale of π_t, the variance of ξ_t is normalized to one. Assuming that the η_i's, and the x_{it}'s, are independent of each other is done from analytical convenience. The 'true' relative price shocks can be any linear combination of these.

The parameters of the model are then estimated via maximum likelihood using the Kalman filter. As a by-product, the Kalman filter recursively constructs minimum mean square error estimates of the unobserved components π_t and x_{it} given observations of π_{it}. The common index, the DFI, can be written as a linear component of current and past values of the observed series

$$\hat{\pi}_t = \sum_i \hat{w}_i(L)\pi_{it}.$$

The weights are reported in Table 1 and the estimated index is plotted in Figure 5.

An index of this sort can be computed using virtually any set of prices. For example, Bryan *et al.* (2002) examine the implications of including stocks, bonds and real estate, along with the price of goods and services, to derive a comprehensive measure of monetary inflation (as opposed to a measure of monetary inflation at the household level, which is the measurement objective of the HICP). And the range of prices used to compute the DFI could be further broadened to include in addition to asset prices the prices of inter- mediate goods and wages, along the lines suggested by Fisher (1920).

Table 1. Comparison of weights in the HICP and the DFI

	HICP weights	DFI weights
Austria	0.03	0.18
Belgium	0.03	0.15
Finland	0.02	0.11
France	0.20	0.10
Germany	0.31	0.09
Greece	0.02	0.02
Ireland	0.01	0.05
Italy	0.19	0.05
Luxembourg	0.00	0.10
Netherlands	0.05	0.04
Portugal	0.02	0.04
Spain	0.10	0.08

Notes: Values are for headline HICP and DFI computing using headline HICP. The DFI weights are the average over the entire sample.

Source: Eurostat/Haver Analytics and authors' calculations.

(2002) who suggest that monetary policy should target an inflation index that gives more weight to prices based on how sticky they are.

2.5.2. Comparing the HICP and DFI. Using the DFI as a basis, we can evaluate the HICP as a measure of monetary inflation at the household level – its stated measurement objective. Table 1 reports the weights that come out of the DFI com- putation. The latter are constructed from the individual HICPs of the 12 countries in the monetary union – the 'MU12' – including Greece throughout the sample.

Looking first at the table, we see that the re-weighting is fairly drastic. The com- bined weights on Germany, France and Italy fall from 0.70 to 0.24 for the headline HICP, while the weight on Luxembourg goes from roughly zero to 0.10.

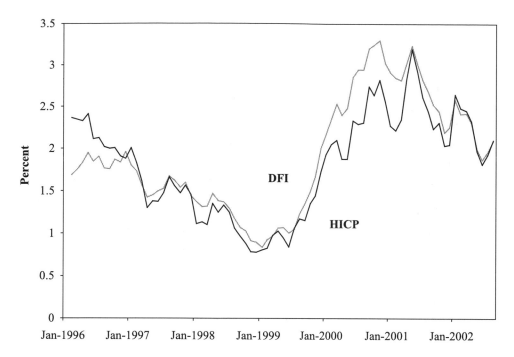

Figure 5. Dynamic factor index and HICP

Source: Authors' calculations; Eurostat/Haver Analytics.

Figure 5 plots the headline HICP together with the dynamic factor index constructed from the individual euro-area country HICPs. After seeing the numbers in
Table 1 the figure is less startling than one might have expected. The HICP and DFI
have a correlation of 0.92 – high enough that it is hardly worth doing the work to
construct the DFI. Since the inception of monetary union, the HICP has been below
the DFI by roughly 0.2 percentage points. And the standard deviation of the difference
between the two series is 0.27. We note that substituting the official national CPIs
for the Eurostat-published HICPs changes almost nothing – the HICP is below the
CPI-based DFI by 0.2 percentage points on average, with a standard deviation of 0.21,
again since January 1999. We will return to this in our assessment of the Governing
Council's use of a 0–2% range.

3. CORE INFLATION MEASURES DERIVED FROM THE HICP

Putting conceptual issues to one side, policy-makers still face important questions in
choosing a measure of inflation on which to focus in their policy deliberations.

Most people agree that headline inflation is not a good choice, as it is often distorted
by transitory relative price changes – oil price shocks and the like – that are unrelated
to the medium-run objectives of central bankers. Instead, the response is to focus on
core inflation measures. With that in mind, we examine whether the information in

the HICP can be combined in a different way that would provide the ECB with a better measure of core inflation.

Among possible candidates for core inflation measures, the traditional exclusion or 'Ex. Food & Energy' type are typically given greatest prominence. These measures attempt to reduce noise by eliminating certain classes of price changes that are (implicitly) deemed to contain no information about inflation trends. But there is a potential trade-off. While simple to compute and easy to explain, exclusion-style core measures throw out lots of information, some of which might be useful. It need not always be the case that food and energy prices never contain useful information about underlying inflation developments. And it need not be the case that all of the included components are always informative.

Examples are easy to come by. For instance, in the aftermath of the 11 September terrorist attacks on the United States, the insurance payments arising from these events caused a huge decline in the price of insurance in the PCE deflator, leading analysts to supplement the traditional core PCE with one that excluded insurance as well as food and energy. Likewise, the October 2002 Producer Price Index showed a surprisingly large 1.1% increase month over month, largely due to the elimination of various discounts introduced by automakers to sustain sales in the wake of 11 September. The reaction was to compute a measure of core PPI inflation excluding the price of new cars. To eliminate distortions caused by regular changes in cigarette taxes, some analysts produce a 'smoke-free' core US CPI. And the list goes on and on.

The point that excluded components of traditional core measures are not necessarily the least informative comes out clearly in Table 2, where we report the mean and standard deviation of 12-month inflation in the 45 major components of the HICP computed over the period from 1996:1 to 2002:8.[3] The italicized items are the ones removed from the 'All Items Excluding Energy, Food, Alcohol and Tobacco' measure of core inflation computed and reported each month by Eurostat. We have sorted the table by the standard deviation of price changes at this lower frequency. These range from 0.57 (Spirits) to 7.40 (Liquid fuels). Importantly, the italicized categories are not all at the top of the table, and that some of the other items have very high standard deviations. Oils and Fats; Coffee, Tea and Cocoa; Postal Services; and Telephone and Telefax Equipment and Services are high volatility components that are *included* in the traditional core measures. And there is little justification for excluding the beer or spirits categories.[4]

Exercises like this emphasize the *ad hoc* nature of traditional core measures of inflation. The weighted median and trimmed mean measures of core inflation proposed by Bryan and Pike (1991) and Bryan and Cecchetti (1994) (and explained in more detail

---

[3] Note that the level of detail reported in Table 2 is not the maximum level of detail reported in the HICP. We consolidated some of the four-digit class levels to ensure maximum comparability across countries.

[4] At the one-month horizon, the single most volatile price series is that for Package Holidays (COICOP/HICP code 09.6), with a standard deviation of 58.40. Our consolidation of various four-digit classes conceals some remarkable variation in individual prices series.

Table 2. Volatility of 12-month changes in components of euro area HICP

	Weight	Mean	Std. Dev.
Fuels and Lubricants	*40.1*	*3.26*	*7.40*
Oils and Fats	6.1	0.80	5.23
Coffee, Tea and Cocoa	5.5	−0.95	5.20
Vegetables incl. Potatoes and Tubers	*15.8*	*2.33*	*4.94*
Electricity, Gas and other Fuels	*49.7*	*2.49*	*4.61*
Fruit	*11.7*	*3.09*	*3.84*
Meat	42.5	1.98	2.80
Telephone/Telefax Equipment and Services	20.9	−2.49	2.35
Postal Services	2.4	1.91	2.00
Milk, Cheese and Eggs	22.5	1.52	1.86
Fish	*12.0*	*3.50*	*1.47*
Health	31.9	2.80	1.21
Tobacco	*22.8*	*3.95*	*1.20*
Water Supply and Misc. Services	26.7	3.24	1.14
Services for Maintenance/Repair of Dwellings	9.6	1.91	1.08
Footwear, including Repairs	15.7	1.79	1.03
Wine	*8.2*	*1.95*	*1.00*
Bread and Cereals	26.9	1.61	0.93
New and Used Automobiles	44.6	1.06	0.93
Clothing	64.7	1.02	0.92
Repair of Household Appliances	1.1	3.03	0.92
Rent for Housing	63.0	2.18	0.90
Non-durable Household Goods	9.9	1.28	0.90
Food Products, n.e.c.	3.9	1.34	0.89
Household Textiles	6.9	1.39	0.85
Transport: Spare Parts and Accessories	9.7	0.31	0.85
Accommodation Services	15.2	3.45	0.83
Mineral Water, Soft Drinks and Juices	9.5	1.10	0.81
Motor Cycles and Bicycles	8.6	1.18	0.81
Miscellaneous Goods and Services	69.8	1.92	0.78
Catering	70.1	2.49	0.75
Transport: Maintenance and Repairs	24.7	2.76	0.74
Transport Services	21.8	2.67	0.73
Beer	*6.9*	*0.97*	*0.67*
Sugar, Jam, Honey, Syrups, Chocolate	10.4	1.37	0.63
Products for Maintenance/Repair of Dwellings	8.7	1.92	0.62
Domestic and Home Care Services	8.3	3.05	0.61
Spirits	*3.8*	*0.90*	*0.57*
Recreation and Culture	96.9	1.06	0.55
Education	8.8	2.72	0.55
Glassware/Tableware/Household Utensils	5.8	1.68	0.50
Furniture/Furnishing/Carpet/Repair	33.2	1.46	0.47
Major Household Appliance/Small Elec. Appliances	10.8	−0.49	0.39
Tools and Equip. for House and Garden	5.1	0.68	0.37
Other Services for Personal Transportation Equip.	11.3	1.81	0.34

Notes: Sample period: 1995:1 to 2002:8. Mean and standard deviation are for the 12-month changes. Weights are for 2000 and are from Eurostat (2001).

Source: Eurostat/Haver Analytics; authors' calculations.

in the Appendix) seek to bring some discipline to the process. The idea behind these alternatives is to discard each month only those prices deemed to have the least information about underlying inflation developments. Some months this may mean discarding food prices; other months it may mean discarding energy or apparel prices, and in yet other months it may mean discarding the prices of goods that have recently been subjected to large indirect tax increases.[5] Not only that, but measures like the weighted median and trimmed mean have some very desirable statistical properties.[6]

Looking at the ability of the measures to track trend inflation provides further evidence that either the trimmed mean or median measures of core inflation out-perform the traditional measures. It is clear that central banks rely on measures of core inflation to provide them with some sense of where trend inflation is headed. Thus it makes sense to evaluate measures of core in terms of their ability to track trend inflation. Here we are immediately confronted with the problem of the short time-span for which the HICP has been around, and the even shorter time-span since the creation of EMU. Nevertheless, the results are worth reporting as they buttress what has been found in many other countries over longer time periods. Table 3 reports the root mean square errors (RMSEs) of various measures of core inflation, defined in terms of their deviations from a measure of trend inflation. And the results are not sensitive to our choice of how to compute the trend. (Figure 6 plots headline HICP inflation and our measure of the trend.) The smaller the RMSE, the closer the core measure is to the trend.

Several points are worth noting. First, for the vast majority of individual countries, as well as for the euro area composite, headline HICP is a better measure of the trend than the conventional core. For the euro area, the RMSE for the HICP excluding energy, food, alcohol and tobacco is higher than the one for the HICP itself. Altern-ative exclusion measures, such as the HICP excluding seasonal food or unprocessed food or energy, have the same property. To put it bluntly, these measures are worse than doing nothing.

The same cannot be said of the trimmed mean and weighted median, which are nearly always better than the headline HICP at tracking the trend for the euro area. The weighted median HICP is roughly 15% better at tracking the trend than the HICP itself, while the optimal trimmed mean is 40% better.

The estimates in Table 3 are important in helping us to understand how to construct an inflation range for policy-makers. If we assume that the inflation objective is the medium-term trend, then the numbers in the table give us an estimate of the variation in any specific measure of inflation about that trend and we can use them to compute

---

[5] This approach to core inflation measurement has been explored at the level of individual EU member states by Álvarez and Matea (1998, 1999) for Spain, Aucremanne (2000) for Belgium, Bakhshi and Yates (1999) for the UK, Le Bihan and Sédillot (2000, 2002) for Germany, and Meyler (1999) for Ireland. Vega and Wynne (2001) compute these measures for the euro area and show that the desirable characteristics they exhibit at the level of individual member states appears to hold at the euro area level as well.

[6] Bryan et al. (1997) show how these measures are more robust measures of the mean of a distribution that has fat tails. Since price change distributions often have excess kurtosis, this improves the quality of the estimates. Vega and Wynne (2001) document the presence of excess kurtosis in the HICP.

Table 3. Comparing measures of core inflation, euro-area level and individual countries

	Headline HICP	Ex Energy, Food, Alcohol and Tobacco	Optimal trim	Weighted median
Euro area	0.35	0.38	0.21	0.30
Austria	0.42	0.37	0.33	0.41
Belgium	0.60	0.60	0.43	0.64
Finland	0.48	0.36	0.33	0.58
France	0.41	0.57	0.24	0.24
Germany	0.52	0.48	0.34	0.57
Greece	0.61	0.99	1.20	1.40
Ireland	0.71	0.77	0.38	0.57
Italy	0.48	0.42	0.42	0.95
Luxembourg	0.80	0.60	0.59	0.74
Netherlands	0.64	0.76	0.60	1.33
Portugal	0.61	0.45	0.33	0.63
Spain	0.52	0.43	0.27	0.29

Notes: The euro-area figures are constructed using data that includes all 12 members of the monetary union as of 2002. The table reports the root mean square errors (RMSE) for various measures of core inflation defined as the deviation of the measures from a measure of trend inflation. Trend inflation is measured as a HP filter of monthly HICP inflation with smoothing parameter 14 400. Optimal trim for each country is the trim that minimizes the RMSE. Computations cover the period 1996 to 2002 using the 12-month change in the index.

Source: Eurostat/Haver Analytics; authors' calculations.

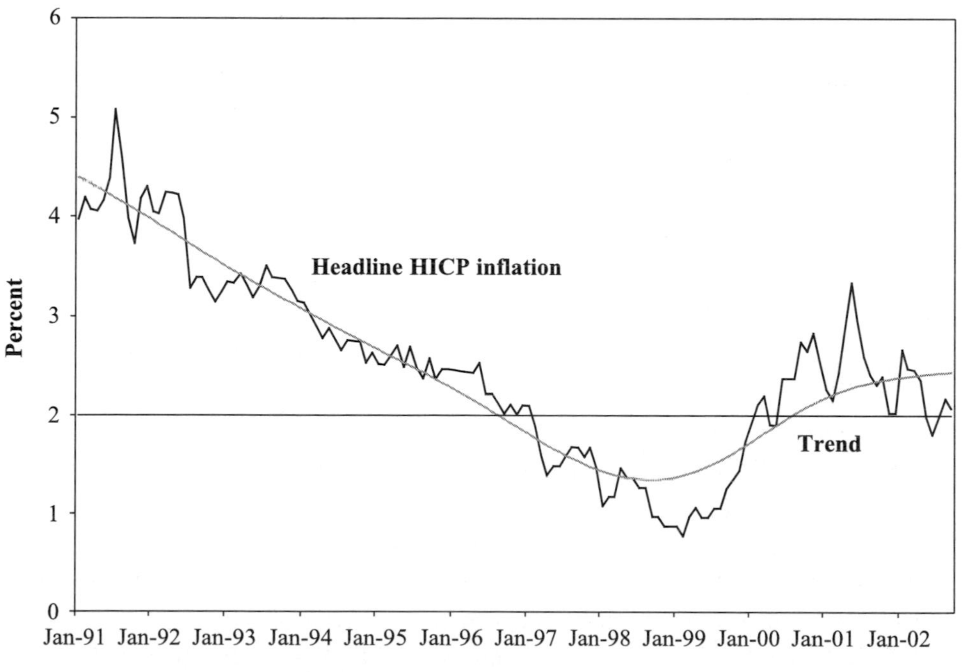

Figure 6. Headline HICP and trend inflation

Source: Eurostat/Haver Analytics; Authors' calculations.

ranges within which variation can be tolerated. Speaking in probabilistic terms, policy-makers can construct an interval within which the probability is 70, 80 or 90% that trend inflation remains on target – and the higher the probability, the bigger the range. So, for example, if the traditional core measure were in a range of 0.35 percentage points above or below the target, one would conclude that there is a 70% chance that inflation is still at the target. To be 90% sure, the range would have to be plus or minus roughly 0.6 percentage points. With the weighted median, the equivalent numbers are plus or minus 0.30 percentage points and plus or minus 0.5 percentage points. We will use this in our discussion of the current 0–2% range laid out in the ECB's monetary policy strategy, to which we now turn.

4. DEFINING PRICE STABILITY

We now have amassed a fair amount of information about the HICP. In Section 2 we concluded that, while the HICP may not have a solid theoretical grounding, it does track cost of living indices that do. But these consumption-based price measures have well-known biases that the HICP probably shares. Even when evaluated on its own terms, as a measure of monetary inflation, we find evidence of bias in the HICP. We then proceeded to examine alternative measures of inflation based on the data in the HICP and reported two basic findings in Section 3. First, the headline HICP is a noisy measure of the medium-term trend that is the focus of the ECB's policy strategy. Second, non-traditional measures of core inflation perform much better than traditional measures in tracking trend inflation.

Our final task is to bring these findings together in order to evaluate the ECB's definition of price stability. Do the data support the use of a 0–2% range for the HICP as the objective for monetary policy in the euro area? We address this question in two steps. First we compute an estimate of the central point of a range – what might be considered a 'point inflation target'. And second, we use the information we have collected to construct an interval about this target that represents a range within which measured inflation can fluctuate without concern that the target is being compromised.

4.1. An inflation target

Calculating a point inflation target is a necessarily speculative activity. We base our estimate on the following principles that, in our view, summarize the consensus of central bankers. In a perfect world, the monetary policy would work to achieve price stability. That is, the policy-makers' objective would be zero inflation, properly measured. Furthermore, this zero inflation objective should be defined in terms of a welfare-based measure of inflation, such as a cost of living index.

Since published consumer price indices contain bias relative to the cost of living ideal, the quantitative definition of the price stability objective should reflect this bias. That is, a finding of positive bias in the index used to define price stability would

Table 4. Bias and precision of various inflation measures

	Bias estimate	Precision as measured by standard deviation
Euro area cost of living indices as a measure of Inflation	1.00	0.50
HICP as a measure of cost of living	−0.25	0.33
Headline HICP as a measure of the HICP medium-term trend	0.00	0.35

argue for defining price stability at some positive measured rate of inflation rather than zero. Likewise a finding of negative bias would argue for defining price stability at some negative measured rate of inflation. In Section 2 above, we argued that while there is at present very little scientific evidence to support a claim that the HICP routinely overstates or understates the true rate of inflation, it is nevertheless reasonable to conjecture that the HICP shares the same biases as have been found in the US CPI, and likely of the same order of magnitude. First, we conjecture that measures of the cost of living in the EU are upward biased by about 1.0% per annum. This is marginally higher than the 0.9% bias found by Lebow and Rudd (2003) in the US CPI, but lower than the 1.1% bias estimate of the Boskin Commission. A point estimate of 1.0% bias in EU cost of living indexes thus strikes us as a reasonable guess.

This estimate is subject to some degree of uncertainty. Lebow and Rudd (2003) present a range from 0.3 to 1.4%, while the Boskin Commission presented a range from 0.8 to 1.6%. A more useful measure of the uncertainty associated with these point estimates is given by the standard deviation of the estimate. Above we noted that the standard deviation of the estimates for the US tend to be around 0.3 to 0.35, but that the greater uncertainty about the accuracy of cost of living indexes in the EU warrants a higher figure. We conjecture that an estimate of a 1.0% bias in European cost of living indexes should be viewed as very imprecise, and that a standard deviation of 0.5% associated with the bias estimate is reasonable. These are the figures reported on the first row of Table 4.

Since the HICP is not a cost of living index we need to make an adjustment. While at the level of individual EU countries (specifically, the Netherlands and Sweden) cost of living based CPIs and the HICP tended to track each other over long periods of time, the same did not appear to be true at the EU level. In Figure 4 we noted that the HICP tends to increase at a rate below that of a proxy for a cost of living index at the EU level by about 0.28 percentage points, and that the standard deviation of the difference was 0.34%. We rounded these figures to −0.25 and 0.33 in the second row of Table 4. Thus our point estimate of bias in the HICP is the sum of our guess of the bias in EU cost of living indexes (1.0%) and the bias in the HICP as a measure of the cost of living (−0.25%), that is, 0.75%. Coincidentally, this is exactly equal to Hoffman's 1998 estimate of the bias in the German CPI.

An estimate of the bias provides a baseline for any central bank's inflation objective. But it is only a start. The simple calculation that focuses solely on the level of the bias ignores a number of considerations that often enter into central banker's deliberations. These include uncertainty in the measurement of the bias itself as well as the desire to ensure that policy does not come up against the zero nominal interest rate floor. From a measurement perspective, we presume that policy-makers will take uncertainty into account.

Recent events have made policy-makers extremely 'deflation averse'. For more than a decade now, the Japanese economy has been mired in a deflationary recession. There is a significant body of opinion that Japan's problems are due in no small part to the failure of the Bank of Japan to prevent deflation taking hold. Persistent, broadly based price declines left borrowers without the revenue to repay debts, causing a deterioration in lender balance sheets and eventually paralysing the banking system. The Japanese experience has convinced many central bankers that deflation may pose greater risks than inflation, and seems to have made many of them more tolerant of small amounts of inflation than they are of small amounts of deflation. This has immediate implications for how to integrate uncertainty into the construction of the inflation target. In fact, for a given level of deflation aversion, the bigger the uncertainty about the bias, the higher the target should be set.

Analytically, this implies a calculation in which we first choose the policy-makers' tolerance for the possibility that the inflation target actually implies steady deflation. We take this to be a fairly small number: 2.5%, or 1 in 40. With a 2.5% tolerance, we need to shift our target measured inflation (0.75% based on our best guesses about the extent of bias in the HICP) up by an increment equal to 1.96 times the standard deviation of the estimated bias, 1.96 being the ordinate that cuts off 2.5% of the tail of a standard normal distribution. For the HICP there are two sources of uncertainty, namely that associated with the estimated bias in EU cost of living indexes (which we put at 0.5%), and that associated with the estimated bias in the HICP as a cost of living index (which we put at 0.33%). Assuming that these two sources of uncertainty are independent gives us a standard deviation of 0.60 percentage points (that is, the square root of $(0.5)^2 + (0.33)^2$). Multiplying this by 1.96 we have an adjustment of 1.18 percentage points. Adding this increment to the point bias estimate of 0.75 yields 1.93%. Our interpretation of this is that when reported HICP is rising at a rate of 1.93%, there is less than a 2.5% probability that prices properly measured are actually falling.

Figure 7 plots the relationship between measured HICP on the horizontal axis and the probability that there is deflation on the vertical axis. For any tolerance, you can read off the value for the point inflation target. Increasing the willingness to accept deflation reduces the point target, while reducing the tolerance for deflation increases it. For example, accepting a 10% probability that prices are actually falling would imply a target of 1.52%, while a probability of 1% implies a target of 2.15%. Changes in both the point estimate and precision of the bias change the figure. An increase in the point estimate shifts the entire picture to the right, while a decline in precision twists the curved line counter-clockwise raising the section to the right of the vertical line.

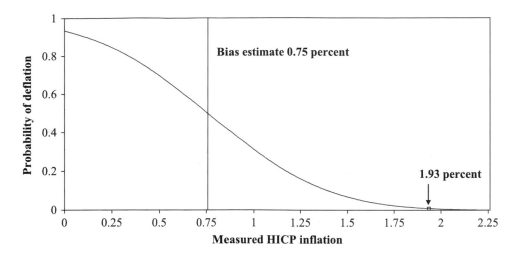

Figure 7. Probability of deflation in true price level as a function of measured HICP inflation

Source: Authors' calculations.

4.2. A target range

The second step in constructing an operating definition of price stability is to figure out the size of the target range. The ECB's monetary policy strategy states explicitly that their inflation objective is 'over the medium term'. This brings us to the information in Section 3 where we computed the precision of the various HICP-based measures of inflation. Again, we can make a statistical statement. Assume that policy-makers would like there to be only a high probability, say 90%, then a reading on the 12-month change in the headline HICP is not different from the target. Using the 90% tolerance for error, we can compute a target range by taking plus or minus 1.64 times the HICP's precision estimate of 0.35. This gives us a band of plus or minus 0.58 percentage points. If the target were 1.93% (as implied by a 2.5% tolerance for the possibility that it implies deflation) then the range is 1.35 to 2.51.

There are two ways to reduce the size of this range. The first would be to increase the tolerance for imprecise measurement, thereby reducing the multiple on the RMSE. A move to 70% reduces the target band to plus or minus 0.35. The other way to reduce the target range is to take advantage of core inflation measures. Since they have less short-term volatility, their RMSEs are smaller. If, for example, the ECB were to set its objective in terms of the weighted-median HICP, since its RMSE is 0.30, then the 90% band need only be from 1.44 to 2.42%.

While extremely speculative, these calculations suggest that the ECB's original range of 0–2% was too low. Rounding our preferred estimates, we suggest that it would be much more prudent for the ECB to adopt a target range of 1.25–2.5% for 12-month changes in the HICP. Concerns about the zero nominal interest rate constraint as well as the potential benefits that might come from small positive inflation would push the upper end of this range closer to 3%. An increased tolerance for short-term deviations of headline inflation from the medium-run trend might result in an increase in the size of the band.

The implications of shifting to a definition of price stability where HICP inflation of 2% is closer to the midpoint than the top of the range are immediately apparent. In particular, looking back over the recent history we see that from June 2000 to April 2002 the 12-month change in the headline HICP consistently exceeded 2%. This created significant challenges for the ECB, as the upper limits of its inflation target range was breached during a period when the world economy was slowing significantly. The primacy of the price-stability objective meant that there was little latitude to reduce interest rates in an effort to spur short-term growth. After all, the Governing Council had to ensure that inflation did not remain at levels that were deemed intolerably high. A shift to a range up to 2.5% would have meant that there inflation exceeded the limit only intermittently during Autumn 2000 and Spring 2001, breeching 3% in only one month, May 2001. It is our view that a shift to a higher, and more reasonable, target range would increase flexibility in a manner that is potentially very productive.

5. CONCLUSIONS

We have reviewed the primary measure of inflation used by the ECB to guide its policy deliberations, and tied the issue of inflation measurement to the important question of operationalizing the ECB's mandate for price stability. The ECB has no meaningful alternative to the HICP for tracking inflation developments in the euro area. However, the HICP is poorly understood outside the community of statisticians involved in its production. While all measures of inflation at the consumer level seem to move together over long periods of time, there appear to be significant short-term discrepancies between cost of living based CPIs and the HICP. These discrepancies have potentially important implications for monetary policy, and make it essential that the HICP be put on a firmer theoretical footing. This could be achieved either by adopting the cost of living index as the measurement objective for the HICP, or by articulating an alternative internally consistent theory of the HICP. This would then allow a more meaningful assessment of the scope for measurement error, with all that this would imply for the ECB's definition for price stability.

For now, we think it is reasonable to conjecture for the sake of argument that the HICP shares the biases that have been found in the US CPI, and ask what biases of comparable magnitude might imply for the definition of price stability. We have shown that the presence of bias, in conjunction with the inherent noise in the HICP and central bankers' aversion to deflation, suggests that the ECB's definition of price stability as prevailing at 2% may be too low. Our calculations imply that the ECB might want to recast its definition of price stability as a range from 1.25–2.5%. Figure 8 shows what inflation performance since the launch of EMU would have looked like relative to this alternative definition.

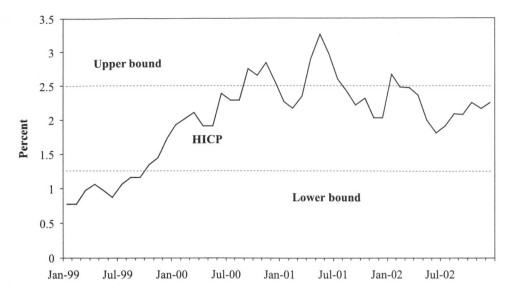

Figure 8. HICP inflation relative to the alternative definition of price stability

Source: Authors' calculations; Eurostat/Haver Analytics.

On 8 May 2003 the ECB announced the results of its evaluation of the original monetary policy strategy that had been in place since October 1998. At that time, the Governing Council confirmed the definition of price stability as 'below 2 percent . . . to be maintained over the medium term'. Simultaneously they agreed that in pursuit of this objective, they would aim to maintain HICP inflation at 'close to 2 percent over the medium term'. One interpretation of this is that the ECB has moved from a 2% ceiling to a symmetric 2% target. This is entirely consistent with the target range that we propose.

Finally, we have shown that conventional measures of core inflation derived from the HICP are worse than doing nothing. This complements what has been found for many other countries, and further reinforces our belief that there is an important role for non-traditional measures of core inflation such as the trimmed mean and weighted median in the formulation and communication of monetary policy in the euro area.

Discussion

Jordi Galí
CREI, Universitat Pompeu Fabra, and CEPR

The present paper by Cecchetti and Wynne (CW, henceforth) raises a number of important questions related to the ECB's pursuit of price stability: Does the definition of price stability adopted by the Governing Council make sense? Does it provide useful guidance when decisions on interest rates have to be made? Is it useful for the purpose of monitoring the ECB's performance? What is the best way to render it operational? Can we think of inflation measures other than the 'year-on-year increase in the HICP for the euro area' that could be more useful? In trying to answer some of these questions, CW cover a lot of territory. Given the nature of the topic it is not surprising that in many cases their answers are largely tentative or speculative; in others they just hint at some of the issues and arguments involved (the 'a first assessment' appendage in the title suggests that the authors may recognize this). But the authors may be partly to blame, however: they could have narrowed their inquiry a bit and dug deeper into one or two of the many issues they address.

The part of the basic message that I wish to comment on can be summarized as follows: HICP-based inflation measures have many shortcomings to be used as a benchmark for monetary policy; non-conventional core inflation measures (weighted median or trimmed mean) are more desirable.

Let me turn to some of the thoughts, concerns and disagreements provoked by the paper.

The HICP as a cost of living index

CW stress several times that the US CPI is a cost of living index, grounded on welfare economics, in contrast with the HICP used in the euro area. A key distinction between the two, CW argue, is that the US CPI includes some imputed prices, such as those for the services of owner-occupied housing. But if the optimal price index is one that should include the shadow value or opportunity cost of all goods and services yielding utility to the consumer, the CPI is a far cry from that ideal index. Thus, for instance, the CPI does not include an imputed price for leisure (presumably a nominal wage index) or for home-produced goods (e.g., home meals or childcare).

Interestingly, however, to the extent that an important component of the costs of inflation (and the one emphasized in classical analyses) lies in the opportunity cost of holding part of one's wealth in the form of money, it is not obvious that such imputed prices should be included in the optimal price index, since by definition they correspond to goods and services that do not generate a demand for money. In other words, in a barter economy the (classical costs) of inflation should not be the major concern.

CW's criticism of the HICP on the grounds of insufficient information about data collection and adjustment practices seems justified and is welcome. In particular, the possibly important differences across countries in those practices are nicely illustrated with the relative price of information processing equipment. Their case would be stronger if they showed that nothing like the phenomenon illustrated in Figure 2 occurs across regions in the US.

In fact, many of the goods included in that category are likely to have nearly identical absolute prices across the US (many are sold by catalogue). But in that case, significant diverging trends in relative prices of those goods is exactly what we would expect, given the persistent inflation differentials across US regions that have been emphasized in a well-known paper by Cecchetti *et al.* (2002).

On the bias associated with HICP inflation in the euro area and its policy implications

The uncertainty about that bias appears to be quite large, as the authors emphasize. It may also be useful to point to two pieces of information that reflect the ECB's own perception about that bias. First, the absence of an explicit floor in the quantitative definition of price stability has been recognized explicitly by the ECB as a cushion against a likely positive bias (see, e.g., European Central Bank, 2001c, p. 39).

Second, one can easily infer what that floor is (and hence the ECB's perceived potential bias) from the assumptions and calculations underlying the determination of the 4.5% reference value for M3 growth. A simple back-of-the-envelope calculation yields an implicit target interval for HICP inflation of 1–2% per annum (see, e.g., Box 3.3 in European Central Bank, 2001c). The implied 1% bias is roughly consistent with the numbers suggested by CW.

In the final exercise contained in their paper, CW determine a point target for HICP inflation conditional on alternative degrees of tolerance of deflation (i.e., acceptable risks of experiencing negative inflation on average for the euro area), given their estimates of the uncertainty regarding the bias. But why is the risk of deflation (on average) for the euro area as a whole the relevant variable? Given the likely persistent inflation differentials across countries, wouldn't it be more appropriate to choose a point target that guaranteed that no country in the euro area experienced negative inflation on average? This point is particularly relevant in light of the upcoming enlargement, and the likely growing spread in average national inflation rates resulting from it, as has been stressed recently by Sinn and Reutter (2001).

What measure of inflation should the ECB seek to stabilize?

The idea behind the different measures of core inflation reviewed by CW is to filter out the influence of the more volatile components of inflation (using different filtering devices, more or less sophisticated). What are the welfare-theoretic underpinnings of such an approach? CW make a quick reference, as supporting their approach, to a recent literature that has tried to determine 'from first principles' (and in the context of dynamic optimizing models with nominal rigidities) the inflation measure that the central bank should seek to stabilize in order to minimize a utility-based loss function. In my opinion, the connection between the two is more subtle and fragile than CW's remarks may suggest. Let me explain.

A key result of that literature can be summarized as follows: the inflation measure that the central bank should target is one that gives a (relatively) larger weight to components associated with sectors or countries with the stronger nominal rigidities.

That general principle has been illustrated in a variety of contexts: a multi-sector economy (Aoki, 2001; Mankiw and Reis, 2002), an economy with both price and wage stickiness (Erceg et al., 2000), and a monetary union (Benigno, 2001; Benigno and López-Salido, 2002).

Notice, though, that the mapping between inflation volatility and flexibility of prices is not an immediate and obvious one, at least in theory. To illustrate this, consider a sector in which prices are adjusted only once a year, and in a synchronized fashion (e.g., many regulated prices, schools in September, etc.). The core inflation measures proposed by CW would treat those movements as outliers, even though they correspond to sectors with highly sticky prices. More generally, the variance of sectoral/regional inflation is an endogenous variable that depends among other things on the policy pursued by the central bank. In principle, thus, the weight attached to each component should depend on 'structural' features, not on observed endogenous realizations.

In practice, however, there seems to be some favourable evidence for the mapping between flexibility and volatility. It can be found in a paper by Bils and Klenow (2002), in which direct measures of the frequency of price changes for 350 categories of goods and services are constructed (ranging from super-sticky coin-operated laundry to highly flexible unleaded gasoline). Interestingly, Bils and Klenow also estimate measures of inflation volatility for each category. The correlation between the frequency of price changes and the standard deviation of inflation innovations is shown to be positive and pretty high (0.68). While, broadly speaking, this kind of evidence gives some support to core inflation measures like the ones considered here, it is not much helpful when it comes to choosing one above the other. Hence, any related evidence that might be gathered in the future for the euro area could provide the basis for a measure that had more solid theoretical underpinnings (at least within a certain class of models).

Choosing among alternative core inflation measures

As a criterion to assess the performance of the different core inflation measures they propose, CW look at the RMSE relative to a measure of 'trend' inflation. The measure of trend inflation chosen is the HP-filtered HICP inflation (this is specified in a footnote). According to this criterion the trimmed mean seems to outperform other core inflation measures. But why is the deviation from 'trend' inflation a useful criterion? What is so special about HP-filtered inflation to turn it into a benchmark? And if indeed HP-filtered inflation represents the 'ideal' measure of inflation, against which others are judged, why not use HP-filtered inflation as a measure of core inflation directly? A possible objection that might be raised is that the HP filter is a double-sided filter and thus cannot be computed in real time. But this does not seem very relevant here: common back-casting techniques to deal with the end-of-sample problem could be easily applied in the present context.

The ECB and core inflation: not a love story

It would have been useful for CW to discuss the actual role played by core inflation measures in the formulation and communication of monetary policy in the euro area. As I have pointed out elsewhere (Galí, 2003), I believe that the ECB has given core inflation measures an unjustifiably low status in the early years of EMU. That limited role was acknowledged clearly by the ECB itself in a short article on 'measures of underlying inflation' in the *Monthly Bulletin* of July 2001, which stated that 'the concept of core inflation has proven to be fraught with ambiguities in practical applications' and that 'none of the core inflation measures can be trusted to provide consistently useful indications over time'. Given the previous verdict, it may not be surprising that measures of core inflation are not directly reported in the price section of the statistical appendix to the *Monthly Bulletin*. They are also absent from the tables and graphs of the key 'Price developments' section in the main text. In the text, a quick two-line reference is generally made to the latest figure for the 'HICP excluding unprocessed food and energy'. It is possibly just an unfortunate coincidence that such a measure was reported for the first time in the July 1999 issue: in that month core inflation went below headline HICP inflation for the first time since the creation of the ECB.

The ambiguity associated with the current definition of the ECB objective (less than 2% inflation in the medium term) could be replaced with an explicit target interval within which some agreed-upon measure of core inflation should remain at all times. After all, as CW's analysis implies, they amount to the same thing: temporary inflation developments (often sector specific) should be ignored for the purpose of assessing the performance of monetary policy, since they fall outside the control of the monetary authority. However, the definition in terms of a core inflation measure is more operational, since it would make it possible to determine whether the ECB meets its objective or not at any point in time. This would improve the accountability and render the MP process more transparent. From that perspective, the core inflation-based objective would also improve on inflation forecast targeting schemes, since inflation forecasts are conditional on many more assumptions, in addition to being less transparent and more prone to tinkering.

In any event, I think we should welcome the CW paper and hope it triggers an active research avenue on a topic that is of central importance to the practical conduct of monetary policy, and also one that can be increasingly informed by developments on the theory front. Let us also hope that CW remain active contributors to that research programme.

Carol Propper
University of Bristol

The paper is an extremely clear discussion of the HICP used by the ECB in their price stability objective. The authors set themselves three questions, provide answers to all three, and come up with practical policy recommendations: that the ECB could set their inflation target higher and would do well to increase their use of non-traditional core inflation measures. The paper provides a very competent and full technical analysis of the issue. I do, however, have a few issues I would like to raise.

First, it seems to me that in their discussion of the fact that the HICP is not a cost of living index, the authors are possibly addressing a straw man. The ECB needed, in a short time period, to have a measure of inflation that would apply to all EU countries. The approach they took was to construct a measure based on the inflation measures produced by the individual countries. This meant that certain components, such as the costs of owner-occupied housing and borrowing, could not be included in the HICP. So the present HICP is not a cost of living index, and the authors of this paper argue that this is not desirable.

It is not clear to me, however, that any of the current indices of inflation used around the world are true cost of living indices. None value home production or the quality of health care services, for example – both of which are important to an individual's quality of life and so would be included in an ideal cost of living index. One could list other similar exclusions. Given this, it seems to me more proper to state that the HICP captures some components of a true cost of living index, but compared to the US and other CPIs omits some costs, notably housing costs.

Over time, it could be possible that the HICP will come to include housing costs. Or are the authors arguing that this will not be possible? If so, is it on conceptual grounds – for example, because housing markets in the EU will always differ in some fundamental way? Or is it on practical grounds – for example, that during the next few years there will be entry into the EU of different countries? If the latter, and if the measure of inflation is that important, why couldn't one condition of entry be the construction of a domestic inflation measure that included these missing components?

Second, the authors show that domestic inflation in two EMU countries (Sweden and the Netherlands) diverges from that measured by the HICP for up to a year or so, and that these divergences are not in the same direction at one time period. The inference drawn might be that one single monetary policy will have a different impact. But aren't such divergences always going to arise in the short run in the EMU area as adjustments to shocks take some time to work through factor markets? I would fully expect such short-run divergences to exist in the USA. (In addition, some of the divergence in the author's illustrative example may be due to the omission of housing costs HICP and its inclusion in the CPIs of Sweden and the Netherlands.) But are these divergences of sufficient length to matter, given that the time scale for monetary policy is the medium term?

This brings me to my final point, which concerns the use of such measures for monetary policy. Differences in measures of inflation are important not so much in themselves but because of their impact on monetary policy. At a couple of points in the paper the authors say that under such and such a definition of inflation, monetary policy would have been too tight etc. It would be of interest to have a clearer idea of what differences in monetary policy – for example, differences in timing and in the extent of interest rate changes – the different definitions would produce. In this context it is worth noting that in the UK the RPI without housing costs (RPIX) is used as the government's inflation target, because by excluding mortgage interest payments the index does not reflect the direct impact of interest rate changes made to control inflation.

The Bank of England MPC minutes make it clear that, in the setting of interest rates, the Committee take into account quite a wide range of economic data of which the actual inflation rate is one important part. So even if there are differences in the various measures of inflation these may not translate into significant changes in the timing or the severity of monetary policy changes. The ECB is more secretive but I would guess the same is true for them. It would be nice to know whether the authors think that the under-estimation of inflation they argue to be present in the HICP actually made a difference to the policy chosen. More formally, the authors could run the different measures of inflation through some sort of Taylor Rule (an equation linking the (quarterly) interest rate to (usually) the current and thrice lagged inflation rate and a measure of the output gap). This would give us a clearer idea of how monetary policy linked to the different inflation measures would have differed. Perhaps not by much. This approach could also be used to test the usefulness of the non-traditional core measures of inflation advocated by the authors.

Panel discussion

Lucas Papademos congratulated the authors for the relevance of their paper given that the ECB will soon review the quantitative assessment of price stability. Clearly, the relevance of the conclusions depends on the accuracy and robustness of the estimates. He noted that other papers report smaller biases. Moreover, he remarked that the bias is not very large and not very significant in the medium term so that the importance of the bias should not be exaggerated. For example, the figure showing the evolution of the HICP over the last few years should not lead one to believe that monetary policy of the ECB is not effective. Instead he stressed the importance of the medium-term objectives of monetary policy of the ECB which is not meant to react to short-term fluctuations. Since the introduction of the euro, average inflation has been 2.1% and thus quite close to the target. Furthermore, he pointed out that the ECB is well aware of the existence of the bias and the resulting risk of deflation. Indeed, the ECB's policies reveal that the more relevant part of the target interval (0, 2) is the upper half. Hans-Werner Sinn added that average inflation needs to be quite high to prevent deflation in every EMU member country: the inflation rate increases in the number of countries if the probability distribution of the price indexes is independently distributed across countries. He asked the authors for a breakdown of the results by country. Paul Seabright pointed out that there are many sectors in which deflation is present. Traditionally, deflation has been attributed to productivity changes but he thought that differences in competitiveness between sectors could play a role. More competition exerts downward wage pressure. Hence, deflation across sectors changes endogenously over time together with changes in competition. Steve Cecchetti replied that the ECB should not care about the regional or sectoral possibility of deflation but that the ECB should focus on the average. However, he agreed with Paul Seabright that it would be interesting to think about a theoretical structure for the issue of sectoral deflation. He mentioned that those sectors with price declines get over-proportional media coverage but monetary policy should not react to this public pressure.

Lucas Papademos also argued that measures of core inflation are measured with high uncertainty and a bias so that core inflation cannot be used directly by the ECB for monetary policy decision-making. However, core inflation is used as input to assess the future prospect of the evolution of the price level so that it is targeted. Steve Cecchetti replied that the paper does not want to change policy-makers' objectives to use core inflation for their monetary policy decisions. He considered core inflation as useful information but too complicated for the public and thus not suitable for external use. Mike Artis argued that the HICP is a good starting point to assess the effects of price evolution on consumers. He added that the treaty formulates the target of price stability and is not concerned with how low inflation is. Moreover, he asked whether there existed any survey data on what consumers thought about the deflation problem.

Carlo Favero urged the authors to discuss whether the measurement problems affect monetary policy at all. One should rather analyse the targets than the instruments. He stressed the point raised in the discussion of Carol Propper that the authors should put more emphasis on the relevance of their findings for monetary policy. An example for an analysis covering this aspect is the article by Mankiw and Reis to which the authors refer in the paper. Related to the discussion of Jordi Galí, Lorenzo Codogno wondered whether the HICP is the best measure of the inflation trend as opposed to some measure of core inflation.

David Miles wondered how housing costs are treated in the US-CPI. He argued that the aggregate effect should be zero as capital gains and rental costs net out. In this respect the US-CPI overestimates the effect of housing on the cost of living so that it is an advantage that housing costs are not included in the HICP. Jean-Marie Viaene was not convinced that quality changes induce an overstatement of inflation. The overall effect of quality improvements and reductions is unclear (see Hobijn, 2002). Steve Cecchetti replied that it is difficult to deal with the problem that some agents are hedged against some price increases whereas others are not. He repeated that the real problem of the HICP was the lack of transparency about its construction and not that certain goods are not included compared with the US-CPI. Mark Wynne added that these issues cannot be addressed unless more information on the construction of the HICP is available.

Paul Seabright asked the authors to distinguish better between the importance of measurement of inflation for monetary policy on the one hand and ECB account-ability on the other hand. Patrick Honohan asked the authors to use different weights in the DFI analysis. Instead of applying equal weights to all countries using least squares, he asked to assign larger weights to larger countries because it is more important to get monetary policy right for these countries.

Richard Portes asked whether there is significant discussion between the ECB and Eurostat on measurement issues. Ignazio Angeloni answered that these two institutions indeed interact regularly on the whole database on monetary policy.

APPENDIX

Using the trimmed mean and weighted median to estimate core inflation

The trimmed mean measure of core inflation pioneered by Bryan and Cecchetti (1993) and Bryan et al. (1997) differs substantially from the standard exclusion-style measures. Instead of eliminating the same components of the price index every month, their procedure removes the components of the index that have the highest and lowest inflation each month.

We begin with a bit of notation. Each month we have observations on the components that are used to construct the price index. For the HICP at the 4-digit level, these are listed in Table 2 in the text. Denote the inflation in component i in month t π_{it}. The headline HICP is constructed as the weighted average of these π_{it}'s, where the weights are based on expenditure patterns. Letting w_i denote the weight on component i, we can write the headline index as $HICP_t = \sum w_i \pi_{it}$. (For simplicity we ignore the fact that the HICP is actually constructed as a fixed-weight index in levels, and so taking the weighted average of the component inflation requires using time-varying weights. We do this in the application.)

Exclusion measures, such as the HICP excluding food, energy, alcohol and tobacco, simply set the weights on the excluded goods to zero and rescale the weights on what is left.

To compute the trimmed mean, and the weighted median, of the price changes each month, the first step is to take the components along with their weights and order them from highest to lowest. For the purposes of our example, let us assume that there are 12 components of the HICP, as there are at the 2-digit level. Also, let us use parentheses around the subscripts to denote the *sorted* inflation rates. That is, let $\pi_{(12)t}$ denote the highest individual inflation rate in month t, and $w_{(12)}$ the associated weight, and so on down to $\pi_{(1)t}$ and $w_{(1)}$ for the lowest inflation rates. Table A1 shows the sorted data. For the α-percent trimmed mean, cut off all components with cumulative weight less than $\alpha/100$ and greater than $(1 - \alpha/100)$, and average what is left (again using the weights).

An example helps demonstrate the point. In Table A2, the weighted average inflation rate corresponding to the HICP is:

Headline inflation

$$= (0.05 \times 5.0) + (0.20 \times 4.5) + (0.10 \times 4.0) + (0.01 \times 3.5) + (0.24 \times 3.0) + (0.02 \times 2.5)$$
$$+ (0.10 \times 2.0) + (0.02 \times 1.5) + (0.15 \times 1.0) + (0.02 \times 0.5) + (0.03 \times 0.0) + (0.01 \times (-0.5))$$

$$= 2.72$$

Table A1.

Inflation ordered from highest to lowest	Weight in HICP of the component with that inflation	Cumulative weight for all components with higher inflation
$\pi_{(12)t}$ maximum inflation	$w_{(12)}$	$w_{(12)}$
$\pi_{(11)t}$ – second highest inflation	$w_{(11)}$	$w_{(12)} + w_{(11)}$
$\pi_{(10)t}$ – third highest inflation	$w_{(10)}$	$w_{(12)} + w_{(11)} + w_{(10)}$
⋮	⋮	⋮
$\pi_{(1)t}$ – lowest inflation	$w_{(1)}$	$w_{(12)} + w_{(11)} + w_{(10)} + \ldots + w_{(1)}$

Table A2.

Inflation ordered from highest to lowest	Weight in HICP of the component with that inflation	Cumulative weight for all components with higher inflation
5.0	0.05	0.05
4.5	0.20	0.25
4.0	0.10	0.35
3.5	0.01	0.36
3.0	0.24	0.60
2.5	0.03	0.63
2.0	0.10	0.73
1.5	0.02	0.75
1.0	0.15	0.90
0.5	0.02	0.92
0.0	0.03	0.95
−0.5	0.05	1.00

To compute the weighted median, simply scan down the third column and note that it jumps from 0.36 to 0.60. This means that the median observation is 3.0%.

The trimmed mean can be a bit tricky. Say that we want the 5% trimmed mean. This means removing 5% of the weight from the top and bottom of the distribution of inflation and averaging what is left. Looking at the table, we see that this implies dropping 5 and −0.5, and averaging the rest. But when we compute this average, we need to be careful to rescale the weights, dividing by $(1.0 - 2.0 \times 0.05) = 0.9$. So we compute:

5% Trimmed mean inflation

$$= [(0.20 \times 4.5) + (0.10 \times 4.0) + (0.01 \times 3.5) + (0.24 \times 3.0) + (0.02 \times 2.5) + (0.10 \times 2.0)$$
$$+ (0.02 \times 1.5) + (0.15 \times 1.0) + (0.02 \times 0.5) + (0.03 \times 0)]/0.9$$

$$= 2.77$$

REFERENCES

Aoki, K. (2001). 'Optimal monetary policy responses to relative price changes', *Journal of Monetary Economics*, 48, 55–80.

Astin, J. (1999). 'The European Union Harmonised Indices of Consumer Prices (HICP)', *Statistical Journal of the United Nations ECE*, 16, 123–35.

Aucremanne, L. (2000). 'The use of robust estimators as indicators of core inflation', National Bank of Belgium Working Paper.

Álvarez, L.J. and M. de los Llanos Matea (1998). 'Measures of the inflation process', in J.L. Malo de Molina, J. Viñals and F. Gutiérrez (eds.) *Monetary Policy and Inflation in Spain*, St Martin's Press, New York.

— (1999). 'Underlying inflation measures in Spain', Banco de Espanña – Servicio de Estudios Documento de Trabajo No. 9911.

Bakhshi, H. and T. Yates (1999). 'To trim or not to trim? An application of a trimmed mean inflation indicator to the United Kingdom', Bank of England Working Paper Series No. 97.

Benigno, P. (2002). 'Optimal Monetary Policy in a Currency Area', *Journal of International Economics*, forthcoming.

Benigno, P. and J.D. López-Salido (2001). 'Inflation persistence and optimal monetary policy in the euro area', unpublished manuscript, Department of Economics, New York University, October.

— (2002). 'Inflation persistence and optimal monetary policy in the euro area', ECB Working Paper series, No. 178.

Bils, M. and P.J. Klenow (2002). 'Some evidence on the importance of sticky prices', NBER Working Paper No. 9069.

Boskin, M.J., E.R. Dulberger, R.J. Gordon, Z. Griliches and D.W. Jorgenson (1996). 'Toward a more accurate measure of the cost of living: Final report to the Senate Finance Committee from the Advisory Commission to Study the Consumer Price Index', US Government Printing Office, Washington DC.

Bryan, M.F. and C.J. Pike (1991). 'Median price changes: An alternative approach to measuring current monetary inflation', Federal Reserve Bank of Cleveland Economic Commentary, December.

Bryan, M.F. and S.G. Cecchetti (1993). 'The Consumer Price Index as a measure of inflation', *Federal Reserve Bank of Cleveland Economic Review*, 29(4), 15–24.

— (1994). 'Measuring core inflation', in N.G. Mankiw (ed.), *Monetary Policy*, University of Chicago Press, Chicago.

Bryan, M.F., S.G. Cecchetti and R.L. Wiggins II (1997). 'Efficient inflation estimation', NBER Working Paper No. 6183, September.

Bryan, M.F., S.G. Cecchetti and R. O'Sullivan (2002). 'Asset prices and inflation', NBER Working Paper No. 8700, January.

Cecchetti, S.G. (1997). 'Measuring short-run inflation for central bankers', *Federal Reserve Bank of St Louis Review*, 79, 143–55.

Cecchetti, S.G., N.C. Mark and R.J. Sonora (2002). 'Price index convergence among United States cities', *International Economic Review*, 43(4), 1081–99.

Diewert, W.E. (2002). 'Harmonized indexes of consumer prices: Their conceptual foundations', *Schweiz. Zeitschrift für Volkswirtschaft und Statistik*, 138(4), 547–637.

Erceg, C., D. Henderson and A. Levin (2000). 'Optimal monetary policy with staggered wage and price contracts', *Journal of Monetary Economics*, 46, 281–313.

European Central Bank (2000). *Seasonal Adjustment of Monetary Aggregates and Consumer Prices Indices (HICP) for the Euro Area*, European Central Bank, Frankfurt am Main.

— (2001a). 'Measures of underlying inflation in the euro area', European Central Bank Monthly Bulletin, July, 49–59.

— (2001b). 'Analysis of HICP developments based on seasonally adjusted data', European Central Bank Monthly Bulletin, January, 19–21.

— (2001c). *The Monetary Policy of the ECB*, European Central Bank, Frankfurt am Main.

Eurostat (2001). *Compendium of HICP Reference Documents*, Office for Official Publications of the European Communities, Luxembourg.

Fisher, I. (1920). *The Purchasing Power of Money: Its Determination and Relation to Credit, Interest and Crises*, Macmillan, New York.

Galí, J. (2003). 'Monetary policy in the early years of EMU', in M. Buti and A. Sapir (eds.), *EMU and Economic Policy in Europe: Challenges of the Early Years*, Edward Elgar.

Greenspan, A. (1994). Statement before the Subcommittee on Economic Growth and Credit Formulation of the Committee on Banking, Finance and Urban Affairs, US House of Representatives, 22 February.

Hobijn, B. (2001). 'Is equipment price deflation a statistical artifact?', Federal Reserve Bank of New York Staff Report No. 139.

— (2002). 'On both sides of the quality bias in price indexes', Federal Reserve Bank of New York Staff Report No. 157.

Hoffman, J. (1998). 'Problems of inflation measurement in Germany', Discussion Paper 1/98 Economic Research Group of the Deutsche Bundesbank.

Hogg, R.V. (1967). 'Some observations on robust estimation', *Journal of the American Statistical Association*, 1179–86.

Howitt, P. (1997). 'Commentary', *Federal Reserve Bank of St. Louis Review*, 79, 139–41.

Jevons, W.S. (1865). 'On the variation of prices and the value of the currency since 1782', *Journal of the Royal Statistical Society*, 28, 294–325.

Le Bihan, H. and F. Sédillot (2000). 'Do core inflation measures help forecast inflation? Out-of-sample evidence from French data', *Economics Letters*, 69, 261–66.

— (2002). 'Implementing and interpreting indicators of core inflation: The case of France', *Empirical Economics*, 27, 473–97.

Lebow, D.E. and J.B. Rudd (2003). 'Measurement error in the Consumer Price Index: Where do we stand?', *Journal of Economic Literature*, 41(1), 159–201.

Lequiller, F. (1997). 'Does the French Consumer Price Index overstate inflation?', INSEE Direction des Études et Synthèses Économiques Document de travail G9714.

Mankiw, N.G. and R. Reis (2002). 'What measure of inflation should a central bank target?', unpublished manuscript, Department of Economics, Harvard University, September.

— (2003). 'What measure of inflation should a central bank target?', *Journal of the European Economic Association*, forthcoming.

Meyler, A. (1999). 'A statistical measure of core inflation', Central Bank of Ireland Technical Paper 2/RT/99.

National Research Council (2002). *At What Price? Conceptualizing and Measuring Cost-of-Living and Price Indexes*. Panel on Conceptual, Measurement, and Other Statistical Issues in Developing Cost-of-Living Indexes, edited by C.L. Schultze and C. Mackie. Committee on National Statistics, Division of Behavioural and Social Sciences and Education, National Academy Press, Washington DC.

Silver, M. and S. Heravi (2002). 'A failure in the measurement of inflation: Results from a hedonic and matched experiment using scanner data', European Central Bank Working Paper No. 144.

Sinn, H.W. and M. Reutter (2001). 'The minimum inflation rate for Euroland', NBER Working Paper No. 8085.

Vega, J.L. and M.A. Wynne (2001). 'An evaluation of some measures of core inflation for the euro area', European Central Bank Working Paper No. 53.

Volcker, P.A. (1983). 'We can survive prosperity', Speech at the Joint Meeting of the American Economic Association-American Finance Association, San Francisco, 28 December.

Wynne, M.A. and D.R. Palenzuela (2002). 'Measurement error in the HICP: What do we know? What do we need to know?', European Central Bank Working Paper No. 131.

Money markets

€ and $

SUMMARY

At the inception of economic and monetary union (EMU), an open question was whether execution of monetary policy by the Eurosystem could effectively stabilize liquidity and short-term interest rates. Potential problems could arise from the central bank's limited knowledge of the new euro area market's response to shocks, and from market participants' limited understanding of the monetary authorities' policy execution framework, which minimizes the central bank's presence in the market and assigns a key liquidity-stabilization role to standing facilities and to depository institutions' own reserve management. We find that the euro area money market has displayed a remarkable degree of stability since the inception of EMU: overnight euro rates have behaved very similarly to US federal funds rates, which are managed much more actively by the US Federal Reserve. Recent operational changes by both the Eurosystem and the Federal Reserve are leading to convergence in style of policy execution on the two sides of the Atlantic, and may foster even closer similarity in the next few years.

— *Leonardo Bartolini and Alessandro Prati*

The execution of monetary policy: a tale of two central banks

Leonardo Bartolini and Alessandro Prati

Federal Reserve Bank of New York; International Monetary Fund

1. INTRODUCTION

Before the launch of Stage Three of economic and monetary union (EMU), the European System of Central Banks had to design a monetary policy execution framework for a new money market whose response to shocks and policy changes were not well understood by either the new central bank or market participants. The central banks of the EMU member countries had previously adopted a 'hands-off' approach to policy execution, with infrequent interventions and a key role for reserve requirements in stabilizing interest rates. That approach was suitable for the banking sectors of the member countries, dominated by a handful of domestic institutions, but might prove inadequate in the larger euro area market. Many of the relevant tools, such as the Bundesbank's fixed-price auctions, required precise knowledge of banks' liquidity needs. Would the same tools be able to stabilize liquidity and interest rates effectively

The opinions expressed in this paper are the authors' own and need not reflect those of the Federal Reserve System or the International Monetary Fund. We thank Raymond Guiteras and Mychal Campos for excellent research assistance, and Ulrich Bindseil, Stephen Cecchetti, Krista Schwartz, Tuomas Välimäki, our two discussants, and an anonymous referee for many useful comments and suggestions.
The Managing Editor in charge of this paper was Giuseppe Bertola.

in the new market? Would sitting by the market's sideline be as effective in the euro area market as it was in individual countries' pre-EMU money markets?

These are important concerns, because the interbank market is a keystone of most advanced countries' financial architecture. In this market, depository institutions lend reserves to each other, mostly at overnight maturity, to offset both anticipated and unanticipated needs for liquidity. It is in this market that monetary policy is executed, and it is this market that anchors the entire term structure of interest rates. By controlling the market's liquidity, a central bank can steer short-term interest rates towards their desired level and provide smooth liquidity conditions for both banks and their customers. An ill-designed framework for policy execution can cause unnecessary market volatility; increase banks' costs, impairing their role as intermediaries of funds for the non-bank sector; and complicate the central bank's policy-making effort by blurring its reading of overall liquidity conditions.

In light of the crucial role of interbank money markets, most central banks outside of EMU have opted for a very 'hands-on' approach to liquidity management, where frequent intervention aims at providing the right amount of liquidity to stabilize short-term interest rates around target levels. For instance, the Federal Reserve has moved over the years towards more frequent intervention and less pervasive reliance on decentralized tools for liquidity management, such as reserve requirements and marginal lending/borrowing at banks' own initiative. The Federal Reserve now performs open-market interventions almost daily (and sometimes twice a day). Most other industrial countries' central banks adopt similar hands-on attitudes and are sometimes even more significantly present in the market, as in the case of the Bank of England.

At the inception of EMU, Eurosystem architects opted to follow the tradition of EMU legacy central banks, rather than the path exemplified by other major central banks active in markets of size and structure comparable to the new euro area market. This was a risky move, given the limited familiarity of the new central bank and of market participants with each other. In retrospect, the gamble appears to have paid off. Our analysis shows that the euro area market has displayed a remarkable degree of stability since the inception of EMU. Euro-area short-term interest rates behave very similarly to US rates, which we use as a benchmark and are formed in a market receiving significantly more support by the central bank. Overnight interest rates in both markets have displayed strong and qualitatively similar cyclical behaviour of volatility over reserve-related periods; virtually full and immediate response to *announced* policy changes; significant anticipation of *future* policy changes; and, most interestingly, similar asymmetry in interest rates' response to expected policy tightening and policy loosening.

This similarity is surprising because the policy frameworks of the two central banks are very different, and recent studies, mostly spurred by Hamilton's (1996) work on the US federal funds market, have documented clear theoretical and empirical links between money market behaviour and central banks' operating procedures. In fact, one need only look as far as the UK to see that operating procedures matter.

In that market, complete lack of reliance on reserve requirements is associated with much higher money market volatility than in the other main industrial countries, despite multiple daily operations by the Bank of England to control market liquidity.

The observed similarity of euro area and US money market behaviour indicates that certain ingredients of the Eurosystem and Fed's style of policy execution may have offset the many formal differences in the two institutions' policy frameworks. For instance, both institutions enjoy strong credibility of commitment to interest stabilization, and both exert asymmetric efforts to smooth interest rate behaviour in advance of policy changes. These common features appear to outweigh differences in the details of the two policy frameworks, such as differences in the frequency of open-market intervention and in the role of reserve requirements. We review such arrangements in the context of a comprehensive empirical analysis of short-term interest rate behaviour in the two areas that incorporates a detailed description of the two central banks' operating procedures. We integrate in the analysis a discussion of the impact of recent changes in Eurosystem and Fed frameworks. These are leading to convergence in the two central banks' styles of policy execution, and may in the future foster even greater similarity in day-to-day behaviour of euro area and US money markets.

2. DATA AND EMPIRICAL MODELLING STRATEGY

The data consist of overnight market interest rates and of key policy rates. Market rates are the 'Euro Over Night Index Average' (EONIA) rate in the euro area and the 'effective federal funds rate' in the United States; policy rates are identified with the minimum (or fixed) bid rate on the Eurosystem's main refinancing operations, and with the federal funds target rate for the Fed. For our purpose, comparing EONIA and effective federal funds rates is justified by the fact that these rates price essentially identical contracts (namely, unsecured, overnight, interbank loans) drawn from similar sources (transaction-weighted trades executed by major brokers). Their relationship to the policy rates is also very similar across the two markets. The Eurosystem does not formally view the minimum bid rate on refinancing operations (or the fixed bid rate used until end-June 2000) as a formal target for the EONIA rate. In practice, however, both Eurosystem rhetoric and market participants agree in interpreting this rate as the desired level for market rates, assigning to it a role equivalent to the Fed's federal funds target.

As shown in Figure 1, which plots our raw data, the euro area sample begins on 22 January 1999 and ends on 23 October 2002. (We dropped all data from 1 January to 21 January 1999, during which time the Eurosystem experimented with a narrow 50 basis point corridor for market rates.) The US sample begins on 4 February 1994, when the Fed began to announce its federal funds target rate, and also ends on 23 October 2002.

On these data we estimate an empirical model which lets the difference between the market and policy rate on day t be equal to a time-varying mean plus a time-varying volatility multiplied by an error term,

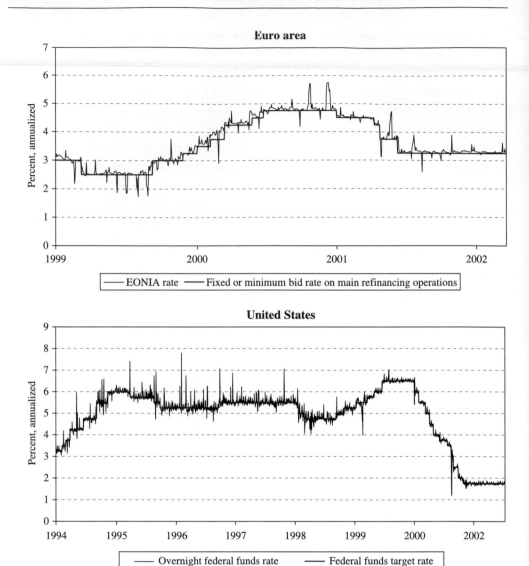

Figure 1. Overnight interbank rates and key policy rates

$$\text{rate }(t) = \text{mean rate }(t) + \text{volatility }(t) * \text{error }(t),$$

and allows the mean and volatility of the interest rate to evolve over time as a function of factors describing features of the monetary policy frameworks in the two areas, which are summarized in Table 1.

Both the Euro-system and the Fed impose reserve requirements on local depository institutions on an average periodic basis. Banks' *actual* reserves, defined as daily averages over 'reserve maintenance periods' (lasting one month in Europe and two weeks in the United States), must exceed *required* reserves, which are also defined as average fractions of 'reservable' liabilities over prior 'reserve computation periods'.

Table 1. Data and summary of institutional details (as of June 2003)

	United States	Euro area
Operating target	Overnight rate	Overnight rate
Key policy rate	Overnight target rate	Minimum bid rate in main refinancing auctions
Intervention frequency	Almost daily	Weekly for main refinancing operations, monthly or only occasionally for other operations
Reserve regime	Lagged average required reserves	Lagged average required reserves
Maintenance period	Two weeks, from Thursday to Wednesday	One month, from the 24th of each month to the 23rd of the following month
Reserve remuneration	–	Required reserves remunerated at the average rate on main refinancing operations over the period
Computation period	Two weeks, from Tuesday to the second following Monday	One month, from the 24th of each month to the 23rd of the following month
Interest corridor: Upper limit	Rates on primary / secondary credit, or target rate + 1 / 1.5%	Marginal lending rate, or minimum bid rate + 1%
Interest corridor: Lower limit	–	Marginal deposit rate, or minimum bid rate – 1%

Defining reserve requirements on an average basis is meant to induce banks to act to stabilize interbank interest rates with no need for central bank action. Since reserves held on different days of the same reserve period are equivalent for the purpose of meeting requirements, if banks expected interest rates to change within a reserve period they should try to purchase reserves in days with 'low' rates and sell reserves in days with 'high' rates. Such behaviour should bid low rates up, and high rates down, until rates are expected to remain constant within the reserve period (aside from negligible discounting).[1] This 'martingale property' of overnight interest rates holds true when banks face no impediment to holding reserves on any day of the reserve period, and allows the central bank to worry only about providing the right amount of liquidity *on a cumulative basis over the reserve period*. To the extent that interest rates tend to be constant regardless of reserve flow volatility within each reserve maintenance period, the central bank can sit out the whole reserve period, let banks bid rates in line with the rate expected to prevail on 'settlement day' (the last day of the period), and intervene only once on settlement day. If that single operation provided just enough liquidity for the expected settlement-day rate to equal its desired level, it would stabilize rates perfectly at that level in all days before settlement.

---

[1] This prediction holds also when required reserves are remunerated, as done by the Eurosystem, but not by the Fed. By remunerating required reserves at near-market rates, the Eurosystem can bring the *average* cost of holding reserves near zero, but leave their *marginal* cost positive (equal to the interbank rate), thus preserving incentives for banks to act to stabilize rates.

The conditions for the martingale property to hold exactly are rarely met in prac
tice, however. While in most countries banks tend to hold actual reserves in amounts
close to required reserves, which is evidence of a significant binding role of reserve
requirements, reserves are also held for reasons other than reserve requirements.
Indeed, several studies have provided evidence that the martingale property is statistically rejected, if not always by economically significant deviation, in the main industrial countries' money markets.[2]

Our comparison of euro area and US interbank markets is based on an empirical
model of short-term interest rates that incorporates key features of monetary policy
execution in the two markets.[3] This model (see Box 1 for details) is conceptually
similar to those used in recent research on money markets, including Hamilton
(1996), Balduzzi et al. (1998), and Prati et al. (2003). Our work improves on most
related studies not only because we use more recent data, but also because we compare interest rate behaviour in the euro area and the United States using a common
econometric methodology. To this end, we begin by estimating a model as similar as
possible for the two markets, and follow a standard general-to-specific search for a
parsimonious specification that only preserves significant coefficients.[4]

To allow for conditions under which the martingale property may either fail or be
met, we consider a rather general specification that includes among the determinants
of both mean and volatility of interest rates a set of dummy variables, one for each
day of the reserve maintenance period (counted backward from settlement day).

Other determinants of 'mean rate (t)' include dummy variables for each day of the
week; dummies for month-end, quarter-end, and year-end days and for days preceding and following these days; dummies for days preceding and following holidays; and
past, contemporaneous, and future changes in policy rates, this latter group of variables being designed – as we discuss later – to assess the impact of policy changes on
market rates. As determinants of 'volatility (t)' we also include dummies for each day
of the week, month-end, quarter-end, and year-end days; dummies for days preceding and following holidays; a dummy for the first day of each period in the euro area
(which is independent of the previous dummy, because of varying length of the euro
area's reserve period); and a dummy for days in which a policy rate changes.

[2] See Hamilton (1996) and Balduzzi et al. (1998) for the US market, Perez-Quiros and Rodriguez-Mendizabal (2000) and
Bindseil and Seitz (2001) for the euro area market, and Prati et al. (2003) for multi-country evidence.

[3] We do not review here details of the microstructure of the euro area and US interbank markets, for which Hartmann et al.
(2001) and Furfine (1999) provide excellent references. While many details are of course different across the two markets, the
interplay between market and policy rates is broadly similar, and market size also points to a similar role played by the interbank
market in our similarly sized economies. Specifically, Furfine (1999) and Angeloni and Bisagni (2002) estimate the size of the
overnight unsecured interbank markets in the euro area at about €100 billion in 1999, and in the United States at $140 billion
in 1998.

[4] Because models in this literature are usually highly parameterized, it is common to proceed with model reduction by discarding
insignificant coefficients and to present only parsimonious specifications. Estimates including insignificant coefficients typically
differ from those presented here only in the third or fourth significant digit, and are available upon request. Even general
specifications including all insignificant coefficients are not fully comparable across the two markets we consider, which feature
reserve periods of different lengths and differently linked to calendar days.

Box 1. The econometric model

Our econometric model is of an EGARCH type in the style of Nelson (1991). We begin by measuring interest rates as differences between daily transaction weighted overnight rates and contemporaneous key policy rates, denoting this difference by $\tilde{r}_t$. We then assume:

$$\tilde{r}_t = \mu_t + \sigma_t v_t, \tag{1}$$

$$\mu_t = \tilde{r}_{t-1} + d_{m_t} + d_{w_t} + d_{c_t} + \alpha_0 \Delta r_t^* + \ldots + \alpha_n \Delta r_{t-n}^* + \phi_1 \Delta r_{t+1}^* + \ldots + \phi_m \Delta r_{t+m}^*, \tag{2}$$

$$\ln(\sigma_t^2) = \lambda \ln(\sigma_{t-1}^2) + (1 - \lambda L)(d'_{m_t} + d'_{w_t} + d'_{c_t} + d'_{p_t}) + \varepsilon_t. \tag{3}$$

In (2) and (3), $m_t = T, \ldots 1, 0$, counts days until the end of the maintenance period at t; $w_t = Monday, \ldots, Friday$, is a week-day pointer at t; c_t is a pointer to other calendar days (end months, end quarters, days before and after one, two, and three-day holidays) at t; d_{m_t}, d_{w_t}, and d_{c_t} in the mean equation, and d'_{m_t}, d'_{w_t}, and d'_{c_t} in the variance equation, are the corresponding dummies for reserve period, weekday, and other calendar effect coefficients; d'_{p_t} is a dummy for days in which a policy rate changed; L is the lag operator; v_t is a mean-zero, unit variance, i.i.d. error term; and $\alpha_0, \ldots, \alpha_n$ and $\phi_1, \ldots, \phi_m$ are coefficients associated with policy rate changes occurring, respectively, $0, \ldots, n$ days earlier and $1, \ldots, m$ days later, respectively. US maintenance periods always end on Wednesdays, so weekday coefficients are not separately identified. Euro area periods are linked to calendar months, so that a linear restriction suffices to identify both weekday and maintenance period effects (we use $\sum w_t = 0$).

Because banks' ability to carry reserve imbalances to future periods is limited (some carryover is permitted in the USA but not in the euro area), we allow for first-day coefficients in the mean equation to differ from other days' coefficients. We do so by interacting the coefficients in (2) with a first-day dummy.

We model the shock in the variance equation as $\varepsilon_t = \kappa |v_{t-1}| + \theta v_{t-1}$, allowing the effect on the variance of positive and negative shocks to differ when θ is not zero. In estimation, we approximated the absolute-value function $|v_{t-1}|$, as in Andersen and Lund (1997), by setting $|v_t| = |v_t|$ for $|v_t| > \pi/2k$ and $|v_t| = (0.5\pi - \cos(kv_t))/k$ for $|v_t| < \pi/2k$, setting $k = 20$. We then estimated the model by maximum likelihood, assuming the error terms to be distributed as Student t variables. Analysis of the residuals led us to an EGARCH(1, 1) model for both samples.

Differences in sample periods, calendar and other institutional features, and the complexity of estimating jointly two very non-linear models, make simultaneous estimation for the two samples impossible. Although this restriction prevented us from conducting formal statistical tests of similarity of the two samples' coefficients, we can nonetheless provide many useful qualitative comparisons, as well as numerical comparisons that may lead the way for formal testing in future studies.

3. EMPIRICAL RESULTS

Figures 2–4 below report the main results of our estimation, whose final specification retains only variables statistically significant at the 10% level.[5] The most interesting empirical results are those regarding the behaviour of market rates around policy rates and over a typical reserve period. In the following subsections we will discuss the behaviour of interest rates around dates of policy changes (distinguishing between 'anticipation' and 'announcement' effects of policy changes on market rates), and their behaviour of interest rates over a typical reserve maintenance period ('reserve period' effects).

Other estimation results are not as relevant to the issues we address, and are reported in Table 2. These include, among others, evidence of high rates around end-months, end-quarters, and end-years in both areas (likely reflecting surges in payments and window-dressing effects) and evidence of time-varying and persistent volatility (which, in the United States, we also found to respond asymmetrically to positive and negative shocks).

3.1. Anticipation effects

The behaviour of market rates in days preceding policy changes provides a good starting point to assess a central bank's commitment to its operational task of stabilizing the interbank rate around its desired level. Changes in policy rates are implemented by the two central banks via a change in current liquidity conditions, or via a commitment (a 'signal') to change future conditions to levels supporting a new desired level for market rates. Of course, to minimize reserve holding costs, banks would prefer to hold more reserves before a rate hike than afterwards (and *vice versa* for an anticipated rate cut). When a change in the policy rate is anticipated before the end of a reserve period, this behaviour tends to bid market rates away from the current level towards the new, anticipated level of the policy rate.

A central bank could opt not to respond to this behaviour, disregard intra-period departures of market rates from their desired level, and continue to provide a smooth flow of reserves over the reserve period. Alternatively, it could respond to the behaviour of market rates by skewing reserve provision within the period: to the extent that the martingale hypothesis does not hold exactly, injecting funds before a rate hike and withdrawing them afterwards can prevent rates from anticipating the policy move.

---

[5] Day-of-the-week and day-of-the-maintenance-period dummies were retained if jointly significant at the 10% level in Wald tests. We always retained all the EGARCH parameters.

Table 2. Estimated parameters not included in Figures 2–4

	Euro area		United States	
	Mean	Variance	Mean	Variance
Monday		2.593 (4.192)		
Tuesday (difference from Monday)		0.286 (0.208)		
Wednesday (difference from Monday)		0.720** (0.219)		
Thursday (difference from Monday)		0.084 (0.221)		
Friday (difference form Monday)		0.422** (0.205)		
First day of the reserve period		5.746** (0.517)		
Day in which target rate changes				0.990** (0.325)
End of months 1,2,4,5,7,8,10,11, or the previous and following days		2.196** (0.382)		
End of quarter, or the previous and following days		3.709** (0.521)		1.838** (0.201)
End of year, or the previous and following days		3.207** (0.590)		1.574** (0.413)
Day before end of month			0.013* (0.007)	
End of month	0.052** (0.006)		0.078** (0.007)	
Day after end of month	−0.033** (0.006)		−0.038** (0.008)	
End of quarter	0.088** (0.014)		0.167** (0.026)	
Day after end of quarter	0.105** (0.014)		−0.095** (0.032)	
End of year	0.280** (0.134)		−0.788** (0.054)	
Day after end of year	−0.322** (0.074)		1.162** (0.069)	
Day before 1-day holiday				1.273** (0.367)
Day after 1-day holiday				1.286** (0.394)
Day before 3-day holiday			−0.024** (0.008)	
Day after 3-day holiday			0.202** 0.011	0.541** (0.273)
Degrees of freedom of Student's t	2.182** (0.201)		2.374** (0.167)	
EGARCH parameters:				
α	1.596** (0.767)		1.244** (0.226)	
δ	0.810** (0.029)		0.554** (0.039)	
χ	0.098 (0.112)		0.434** (0.097)	

Notes: Standard errors are in parentheses; ** and * indicate significance at 5% and 10% level.

Hence, the extent to which market rates 'anticipate' future policy changes will reflect a central bank's propensity to lean against the wind by altering the time profile of reserve provision, as well as the accuracy with which the private sector forecasts future policy changes.

Note that reserve requirements play a key role in supporting such 'anticipation effects' by linking *current* rates to expected *future* rates via banks' attempts to take advantage of interest rate gaps over the reserve period. From this viewpoint, differences between Eurosystem and Fed frameworks suggest that anticipation effects should be stronger in the euro area than in the United States. First, given its option to intervene every day, the Fed enjoys ample scope to keep market rates near target, until a target change is actually implemented, by injecting liquidity into the market prior to a target hike and mopping up liquidity afterwards. Second, the shorter (two-week) US reserve period eases the Fed's task of leaning against expected target changes: only changes expected over (up to) the next two weeks cause significant pressure on market rates. The Eurosystem faces a tougher task, given its commitment to infrequent intervention and to longer (one-month) reserve periods, which let expectations of rate changes up to one month ahead push overnight rates away from their currently desired level.[6]

To assess the importance of anticipation effects, we included actual policy rate changes as regressors in our mean equations in the days preceding each change. Their estimated coefficients capture important aspects of the interaction between central banks and market participants. Of course, policy changes are known in advance only up to a forecast error, which tends to bias their coefficients towards zero. Hence, the coefficients of future policy changes tend to be small when market participants are unable to forecast them precisely, and/or the central bank manages liquidity to keep market rates close to the current target in advance of policy changes. Conversely, the same coefficients' estimates will be close to unity if the central bank allows its planned policy changes to be forecasted easily, and refrains from altering the profile of liquidity provision within the period to keep rates near the old target prior to a policy change.[7]

Figure 2 shows the estimated cumulative response of the overnight rate to an upcoming policy change. To allow for asymmetric response of market rates to policy rate changes in different directions, we allow the 'anticipation' coefficients to differ prior to rate hikes and rate cuts.

----

[6] Eurosystem operations include 'main' refinancing operations, normally injecting liquidity into the market, and executed every Tuesday via two-week repos with next-day settlement; and 'longer-term' operations, executed monthly with a maturity of three months. The Eurosystem may also execute 'fine-tuning operations', although it has done so only sporadically.

[7] An alternative strategy to study anticipation effects would be to obtain independent estimates of expected policy changes and to study market rates' response to changes in such expectations. This methodology would isolate the effect of expected policy changes on market rates from the effects of uncertainty about policy changes, two effects that are jointly estimated in our model. To this end, however, futures, spot-next, and tom-next rates are not helpful: they provide estimates of future expected *market* rates, not of expected *target* rates, thus providing only an alternative test of the martingale hypothesis (see, for example, Angelini, 2003). In principle, survey data on expected policy rates could also be used to separate the effect of expected policy changes from the effect of uncertainty about such changes; however, these data are not available at the required daily frequency.

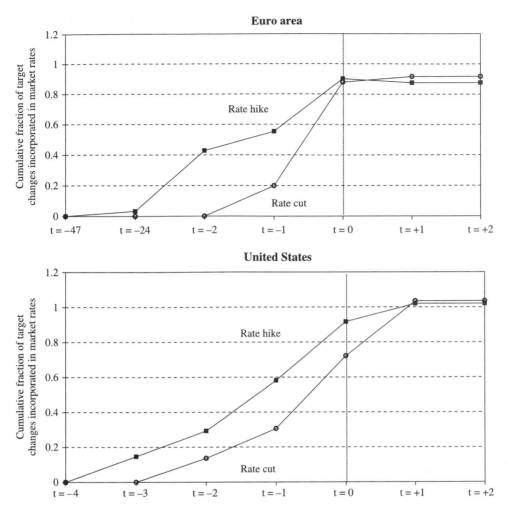

Figure 2. Estimates of anticipation and announcements effects of policy rate changes

There is evidence of significant anticipation effects in both the US and euro area money markets. Interestingly, in both markets anticipation effects are stronger during phases of policy tightening, with a particularly long lead during the tightening phase of 1999–2000 in the euro area. On the day prior to a target change, the similarity between the two markets is striking: the previous-day anticipation of target rate *hikes* is about 60% in both markets. Anticipation of rate *cuts* is smaller but also rather similar in the two markets (30% in the United States and 20% in the euro area).[8]

[8] We conducted Wald tests of a number of hypotheses of 'equality of one sample's estimated coefficient to the estimated value of the same parameter in the other sample'. For instance, the hypothesis that the estimated previous-day anticipation effect of a target rate *hike* in the United States is equal to the estimated value of the corresponding anticipation effect in the euro area was accepted with a p-value of 0.934. The analogous hypothesis of equality between the previous-day estimated anticipation effect of a target rate *hike* in the euro area and the estimated value of the same coefficient in the United States gave a p-value of 0.975. Similar tests of equality of anticipation effects on the day prior to a target rate *cut* yielded p-values of 0.073 and 0.110, respectively.

The lead with which market rates anticipate target hikes is, however, different in the two markets. In the United States, gradual movements of market rates towards the new target begin three days before a target hike, and two days before a target cut. In the euro area, the estimates plotted in Figure 2 indicate that policy rate hikes have been anticipated with much longer leads than policy rate cuts.[9] While the anticipation of a rate cut has only a two-day lead, the anticipation of a rate hike goes back to the beginning of the reserve period in which the hike took place, with some weak evidence of anticipation effects in the previous reserve period.[10]

Significant anticipation effects in both markets reveal that neither the Fed nor the Eurosystem manage liquidity so tightly as to prevent deviations of overnight rates from their desired level in the presence of expected policy changes. This may reflect their wish to smooth liquidity provision (rather than interest rates) over time. Indeed, both Ejerskov *et al.* (2003) and Välimäki (2003a, b) find that the European Central Bank (ECB) assigns importance to providing liquidity smoothly over time. Similarly, the fact that the Fed does not intervene literally *every* day, reveals that liquidity smoothing plays a role in its monetary strategy.[11]

3.1.1. Asymmetries and the format of liquidity auctions.   The asymmetric response of market rates to anticipated policy rate hikes and cuts suggests exploring political-economy motives for central banks to provide liquidity asymmetrically during policy-tightening and policy-loosening phases. After all, policy tightening has never been as popular as policy loosening. Our estimates for both markets suggest that rate cuts tend to surprise markets more than rate hikes: perhaps policy rate hikes already justified by 'fundamentals' are typically delayed more, or implemented by smaller steps, than corresponding policy cuts.

There is, however, a feature of the Eurosystem's monetary framework that can also explain the observed asymmetric response to anticipated policy rate cuts and hikes. This feature reflects the interaction between the Eurosystem's preference for smooth provision of liquidity over time with a specific format for Eurosystem auctions, in an environment of structural deficit reserve position for euro area banks.[12] To understand this interaction, consider first the equilibrium response of rates in Eurosystem auctions to an anticipated policy rate *hike*, when the central bank does not accommodate fully the higher demand for reserves resulting from this anticipation, because

---

[9] In addition, as banks anticipated rate hikes that did *not* occur in the 1999–2000 period, they had to rebalance reserves at settlement, causing the large down-swings in the EONIA rate at settlement observed in 1999–2000.

[10] The short euro area sample made individual coefficients for the tightening phase unstable and difficult to estimate. To overcome this difficulty, we estimated a separate coefficient for the day preceding a target change (13%) and an *average* coefficient for all the previous days in the same reserve period (1.9% per day, implying an anticipation effect of 41%). By estimating an average coefficient also for the reserve period preceding a target change, we found a further anticipation effect of 3%; however, this estimate was not statistically significant.

[11] For instance, Feinman (1993) argues that the Fed displayed inertia in the 1980s in response to small shocks.

[12] Detailed studies of the impact of Eurosystem auctions on the euro area interbank market include Bindseil (2002), Välimäki (2003a, b), and Würtz (2003).

that would require excessive skewing of liquidity within the reserve period. In this case, the equilibrium auction rate rises above the current policy rate (either the fixed tender rate used in Eurosystem auctions until June 2000, or the minimum bid rate used afterwards). Scarce liquidity allocated at the auction, in turn, lifts the equilibrium interbank rate up towards the new, anticipated policy rate.

Before expected policy rate *cuts*, conversely, auction participants would like to bid below the current minimum (or fixed) rate, since that rate is expected to fall and there is no reason to borrow funds now at a rate higher than that expected to prevail later. However, bids below the floor (until June 2000, the fixed bid rate; afterwards, the minimum bid rate) are rejected. Bidders will then respond by under-subscribing the auction, which keeps the equilibrium auction rate at its minimum. The resulting reduction in liquidity allocated to the interbank market keeps interbank rates from falling in advance of the rate cut, as the minimum (or fixed) tender rate restrains downward fluctuations of market rates. Thus, while anticipated increases in policy rates result mostly in a rise of market rates, anticipated rate cuts result mostly in a decline in reserves and little change in interest rates, in accord with our estimated behaviour of interbank rates prior to Eurosystem policy rate changes.

Of course, the fixed rate on Eurosystem auctions could in principle provide a ceiling for market rates in anticipation of rate hikes, in the same way that the minimum bid rate has acted as a (soft) floor in anticipation of rate cuts. However, reserve requirements normally place euro area banks in a structural (reserve) deficit position, so that Eurosystem intervention usually involves an *injection* of reserves; and the Eurosystem rationed reserves injected at the fixed-rate repo auctions. Thus, euro area banks are normally able to absorb *less* reserves than the Eurosystem wishes to inject (by underbidding in auctions), but cannot hold *more* reserves than desired by the central bank. (The opposite would be true for a banking system in a structural surplus position.) As a result, while market forces have kept euro area market rates near the (minimum or fixed) tender rate in advance of policy rate cuts, only a much larger injection of reserves by the central bank would have kept market rates near the tender rate in anticipation of policy rate hikes.

3.2. Announcement effects

The extent to which market rates depart from their desired level in the aftermath of a policy change is also instructive of a central bank's liquidity-management style. A change in a policy (or 'target') rate signals a commitment by the central bank to alter current and future liquidity to levels supporting the new target. For overnight market rates actually to adjust to the new target, market participants must trust the central bank to validate this new level by providing adequate funds through the end of the reserve period. If the credibility of this commitment is limited, the market rate may adjust only partially, or not at all, to the newly announced policy rate.

To study the response of market rates to changes in policy rates, we included actual changes in policy rates as determinants of mean market rates in days of policy changes and in n subsequent days (including up to all days in the same reserve maintenance period). The estimated coefficients for these regressors assess how much of a policy rate change is reflected in market rates up to n days *after* a change.[13]

Since in both markets policy changes are normally announced in the middle of the trading day, effective rates for these days are drawn from both pre-change and post-change transactions. Hence, the same-day coefficient of the policy change is smaller than unity even in the absence of anticipation effects and with instantaneous adjustment of rates to the new target, and is not particularly informative as regards the forecastability and reliability of central banks' policy moves.

It is more interesting to examine how long it takes for market rates to adjust fully to their new desired level. Our estimates indicate that this lag is minimal in both the United States and the euro area: the coefficients of past policy changes were never statistically significant for $n > 1$, to imply that market rate adjustment is complete within a day after a policy change in both areas (Figure 2). In the United States, same-day and next-day announcement effects sum to 44% during the policy-tightening period and to 73% during the policy-loosening period, reflecting the greater role that anticipation effects played in the former period. Similarly, in the euro area, same-day and next-day announcement effects sum to 32% during the policy-tightening period and to 72% during the policy-loosening period.

Our estimated rapid announcement effects are intuitive for the United States, where the Fed usually begins to intervene the morning after a target change and can reinforce its commitment to the new target by intervening every day through the end of the reserve period. They are more surprising for the euro area, where policy changes are normally announced on Thursdays and remain nothing more than a commitment until the following Tuesday's operation. Also, the Eurosystem executes (on average) only a pair of operations between the day of a policy change and settlement day, leaving relatively little scope for experimenting with liquidity injections and withdrawals at the new rate. Thus, the rapid adjustment of euro area market rates to policy changes is a clear indicator of the Eurosystem's credibility among market participants despite its recent inception in 1999, and of the clear signalling role played by its main policy rate in anchoring and stabilizing market rates.

3.3. Reserve period effects

Finally, our estimation allows us to examine the cyclical behaviour of euro area and US interest rates over a typical reserve period. Our goal is to identify patterns in

---

[13] See Demiralp and Jorda (2002), for a related methodology to estimate announcement effects.

interest rates that reveal our two central banks' propensity to lean against shocks from the non-bank sector and against patterns in rates induced, inadvertently, by reserve requirements.

One particular pattern that has attracted attention in previous research is the tendency of overnight rates to rise at the end of reserve periods. This pattern has been documented in data for both the United States (Hamilton, 1996; Bartolini *et al.*, 2001; Clouse and Dow, 2002) and the euro area (Perez-Quiros and Rodriguez-Mendizabal, 2000; Bindseil and Seitz, 2001). As with other predictable patterns in mean rates, a systematic rise in rates at settlement is potentially relevant for policy, because it indicates that banks fail to treat reserves held on different days as perfect substitutes, *and* that the central bank has failed to offset higher demand for funds on specific days of the reserve period. (Higher rates at settlement, in particular, have been interpreted as reflecting frictions such as transaction costs and penalties on overnight overdrafts, leading banks to accumulate the bulk of their reserves at the end of the period.)

In contrast with previous research, our estimates show weak evidence of reserve-related patterns in mean rates in both areas. Euro area rates tend to fall slightly until the day before settlement, and rise approximately seven basis points at settlement. US rates are somewhat high on Mondays (seven and two days before settlement) and on settlement days. This evidence is summarized in the top panels of Figure 3, which display estimates of the reserve period mean coefficients d_{m_i}. (As discussed below, the main reason for the difference between our results and those of previous research may be traced to differences in samples and, in recent years, to more aggressive efforts by the two central banks to offset previously observed patterns in rates.)

In contrast with the broadly non-cyclical behaviour of mean rates, we find that interest volatility displays sharp cyclical patterns in both areas, as documented in the top panels of Figure 4. In the figure, the reserve-period effects on the standard deviation of interest rate shocks (the coefficients d_{m_i} in Box 1) are plotted as ratios of the standard deviation on settlement day. These estimates show a striking similarity between the qualitative behaviour of interest rate volatility over the reserve period in the euro area and in the United States. In both, volatility is sharply higher on settlement days than on previous days. In both, interest volatility begins to rise in advance of settlement: 2 days in advance of settlement in the United States and 4 days in advance of settlement (for a reserve period that is twice as long) in the euro area.

To interpret these findings, recall that high settlement-day volatility is a direct effect of periodic reserve requirements: at settlement, individual banks scramble to unload excess reserves or fill reserve shortages. When the banking sector as a whole shows a reserve imbalance at settlement, interbank rates must adjust to induce banks to absorb such imbalance.

Rising volatility *prior* to settlement, instead, is indicative of a central bank's unwillingness (or inability) to provide unlimited quantities of funds at a fixed price in

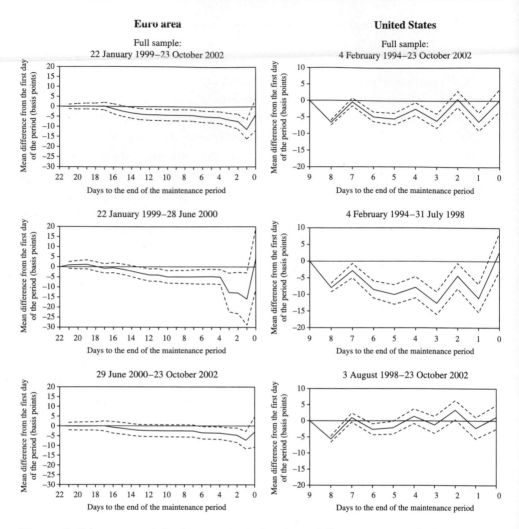

Figure 3. Mean overnight interest rate by day of the reserve period

response to liquidity shocks to the banking sector. Banks need not lay pressure on interest rates prior to settlement, if they expect the central bank to intervene before period-end to eliminate current reserve imbalances. In this case, interest volatility should remain relatively low and constant through the last-but-one day of the maintenance period (at most reflecting non-periodic factors such as daily overdraft penalties), and spike only on settlement day. If, however, the central bank does not fully offset aggregate shocks experienced by banks during the reserve period, then shocks recorded *before* settlement will be partially reflected as end-period imbalances, the more so the closer to settlement they occur. Interest volatility will then rise gradually as settlement approaches, in accord with our estimates for both our sample markets.

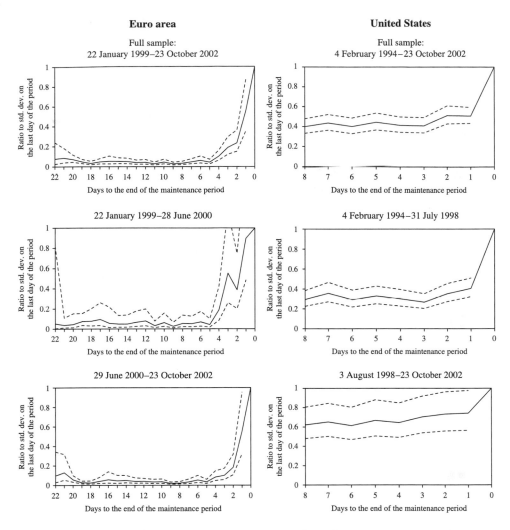

Figure 1. Overnight interest rate volatility by day of the reserve period

There are many reasons why a central bank may be reluctant to offset aggregate liquidity shocks completely.[14] The most relevant issue for us, however, is that the Eurosystem has adopted a schedule of once-per-week intervention, which usually requires executing the last operation of each reserve period several days before settlement. In this case, interest rate volatility is clearly expected to spread from settlement days to previous days.

---

[14] For instance, central banks are often reluctant to execute very large repos, fearing that the underlying collateral market might be unduly stressed. This is a concern that the Fed had in mind when it rescheduled its operations around the time of deepest liquidity of the repo market. Central banks are also often reluctant to respond fully to large shocks, fearing the need to take opposite action at a later time, a practice that has been felt could provide mixed signals of the central bank's policy stance. Finally, and perhaps more important for the Fed in recent years, a central bank may be reluctant to execute large operations if these pressure banks against their daily overdrafts limits: a large reserve drain in a single day may induce many banks to scramble to avoid daily overdrafts; a large injection may soften the market as banks try to avoid excess reserves that may be difficult to unwind before settlement.

From this viewpoint, the surprising aspect of our estimation is the absence of even greater differences in volatility behaviour between the two areas. Unlike the Eurosystem, the Fed has retained the option of offsetting shocks to banks' liquidity at high frequency. Our analysis reveals that – historically at least – the Fed seems to have been reluctant to use this flexibility fully, although, as discussed below, the cyclical behaviour of volatility has weakened significantly in recent data. Also, the Fed's frequent intervention schedule helped smooth US interest rate volatility over the reserve period, but – with all obvious caveats in place when conducting cross-country quantitative comparisons – has not led to less volatile interest rates than in the euro area. Indeed, while settlement-day volatility is quantitatively similar in the two areas (the mean absolute median difference of settlement-day interest rate changes is about 25 basis points in both areas), non-settlement-day volatility is less than one-tenth of its settlement-day level in the euro area, but only about half of its settlement-day level in the United States. As a result, away from settlement, euro area rates are less volatile than US rates.

4. ONGOING CHANGES IN POLICY IMPLEMENTATION FRAMEWORKS

Both the Eurosystem and the Fed have been rather successful in steering interbank rates near desired levels in recent years. However, both have implemented changes in their framework and 'style' of intervention. These changes are meant to improve daily management of liquidity and interest rates, and several of them make each central bank's procedures more similar to those used by the other one.

4.1. The changing role of US reserve requirements

Seeking to limit interest volatility induced by changes in required reserves, in July 1998 the Fed abandoned the regime of almost-contemporaneous reserve accounting adopted in 1984 and returned to a regime similar to that in use in the euro area (albeit with shorter reserve periods). Maintenance periods now lag computation periods by 30 days. This may or may not lead to more stable interest rates: although lagged computation reduces uncertainty by predetermining *required* reserves, it does not affect the more important sources of variability stemming from Treasury flows affecting *actual* reserves. Indeed, US interest volatility did fall over the last few years, but only started to decline a year or two after the reform, pointing to alternative reasons for recent lower volatility.

Second, some 15 years after the effective breakdown of its main emergency-lending facility,[15] in January 2003 the Fed started a new lending programme allowing banks

---

[15] The Fed's main marginal lending facility – the discount window – effectively ceased to operate in the mid-1980s when a series of episodes of financial distress, beginning with the crisis of Continental Illinois in 1984, made US banks reluctant to borrow for fear of signalling financial weakness. The Fed offers no reserve-deposit facility other than limited rolling over of excess reserves to subsequent reserve periods. By contrast, the Eurosystem uses an unrestricted below-market deposit facility and a collateralized above-market borrowing facility, operated at the initiative of banks, to provide a symmetrical corridor of fluctuation for market rates around the Eurosystem's main refinancing rate.

to borrow funds along traditional European-style practice: funds are loaned against collateral at penalty rates, with no limit on the use of such funds and no requirement that banks should seek loans elsewhere first.[16] Like the Eurosystem's marginal borrowing facility, the Fed's new facility aims at limiting market rates' fluctuations above target in times of market tightness.

The Fed has also acted to smooth policy execution and to limit its impact on securities markets. It changed the time of its daily intervention (from 11:30 to 10:30 am in 1997, and then to 9:30 am in 1999) attempting to schedule intervention at the time of deepest market liquidity. And in 1999 it expanded the set of collateral accepted under repo, chiefly by including securities issued by government-sponsored agencies. This brings the Fed marginally closer to the practice of the Eurosystem, which accepts an even broader class of securities as collateral, including private sector securities.

The most far-reaching change in Fed procedures in recent years, however, is the Fed's decreased reliance on reserve requirements as an instrument for monetary control. Until 1990, in terms of reserve ratios and eligible liabilities, the Fed's reliance on reserve requirements was comparable to that of most other industrial countries' central banks (other than the UK). At the end of 1990, however, the Fed lowered requirements on non-transaction deposits to zero, thereby promoting a major decline in required reserves. Additionally, in January 1994 the Fed clarified its regulation of deposit accounts, effectively sparking a dramatic growth in banks' practice to 'sweep' overnight balances from liabilities subject to the reserve requirement, such as checking accounts, to liabilities free of requirement, such as money market accounts. As a result of these developments, required reserves in the United States have declined from $60 billion in 1989 to $37 billion in 2002, although this decline has stopped recently.[17] A growing fraction of banks – especially smaller, local banks – has been able to satisfy reserve requirements in full by holding cash, thus becoming effectively unbound by requirements (Bennett and Peristiani, 2002).

While looser reserve requirements might be expected to increase interest rate volatility, no such evidence can be detected in recent US funds data (Bennett and Hilton, 1997; Prati et al., 2003). In fact, a trend-decline in volatility has been observed since the mid-1990s, most likely because the Fed has offset the declining role of reserve requirements by intensifying the frequency of its daily intervention. As documented in Table 4, nowadays Fed fine-tuning through repos is an almost daily event, occasionally supplemented by outright transactions (usually, purchases) aimed at offsetting persistent liquidity imbalances.

---

[16] The new programme replaces the Fed's main discount window programme and follows the format of the temporary 'Century Date Change Special Liquidity Facility' introduced experimentally between October 1999 and April 2000. The new programme offers collateralized credit to banks on a 'no question asked' basis, at a rate of 1% above target for institutions deemed to be financially sound, and at a rate of 1.5% above target for other institutions.

[17] These amounts exclude 'clearing balances', a reserve-like requirement to which US banks must pre-commit, and for which they are compensated by credits useable to purchase services provided by the Fed.

Table 3. Main reserve aggregates

	Euro area	United States
1. Required reserves	128.7	37.5
2. Applied vault cash	–	29.5
3. Required reserve balances (1) – (2)	128.7	8.0
4. Required clearing balances	–	10.2
5. Total required balances (3) + (4)	128.7	18.2
6. Reserve balances	129.2	9.7
7. Total reserves (2) + (6)	129.2	39.1
9. Excess reserves (7) – (1) or (6) – (3)	0.5	1.6

Note: Data for the reserve period ending in November 2002 for the euro area, and for November 2002 for the United States; in billions of local currency.

Source: European Central Bank, *Monthly Bulletin*, and Board of Governors of the Federal Reserve.

Table 4. US required reserves and frequency of intervention

	Average daily required reserve balances	Average days with repo operations (per 10-day period)
1/1/89 – 12/31/90	$60 bn	5.7
1/1/91 – 12/31/95	$55 bn	6.1
1/1/96 – 10/31/02	$43 bn	7.8

Source: Board of Governors of the Federal Reserve and authors' calculations.

4.2. Changes in the Eurosystem's refinancing operations

Across the Atlantic, the most noticeable change in the Eurosystem's framework since its inception in 1999 has been the switch from a fixed-rate to a variable-rate-with-minimum-bid format for refinancing auctions on 28 June 2000. This switch, as intended, eliminated the severe problems of overbidding that had marred previous Eurosystem auctions.[18] As we discuss below, it may also have helped to stabilize the Eurosystem's liquidity provision to the interbank market, although our discussion in Section 3.1.1 above suggests that problems of interest rate instability in the euro area in advance of policy rate hikes in 1999–2000 were not likely to depend on the specific fixed-rate format: both fixed-rate and minimum-rate auctions are bound to induce similar upward drifting of market rates when policy tightening is expected within the current reserve period, and underbidding when policy loosening is expected.

Two upcoming changes in the Eurosystem's operational framework are more likely to help mitigate the destabilizing role of expected policy changes discussed in the

[18] See Ayuso and Repullo (2001), Oechssler and Nautz (2001), and Välimäki (2003a) for a detailed analysis of the overbidding phenomenon in Eurosystem fixed-rate auctions.

previous section. Effective in 2004, the first main refinancing operation following the policy-setting meeting of the ECB Council (usually held on the first Thursday of each month) will settle at the beginning of the following reserve period. Our estimation suggests that this reform is likely to help to stabilize rates, since most policy changes are 'anticipated' within the same maintenance period in which they occur. Also, the maturity of the main financing operations will be shortened from two weeks to one week, so as to keep the liquidity impact of each operation within the current reserve period. This change (a theoretical underpinning for which is in Välimäki, 2003b) moves the Eurosystem closer to the practice of shorter-term repos followed by the Fed.

4.3. Sub-sample evidence

Aside from formal changes in policy frameworks, a relevant issue is whether the two central banks have implemented in recent years more subtle changes in 'style' of intervention, mostly involving changes in liquidity-provision strategies at high frequency that may have also affected the day-to-day behaviour of the two areas' money markets. To explore this possibility, and provide preliminary evidence on how both formal and stylistic changes in policy execution have affected interest rate behaviour in the two areas, we followed a simple event-study methodology by splitting our data into 'early' and 'late' samples, and comparing the behaviour of interest rates and liquidity in the two samples.

Specifically, we set the break-points for the two samples at the times of the main operating changes in the two areas: the shift from fixed-rate to minimum-bid-rate auctions in June 2000 for the euro area, and the switch from (almost) contemporaneous to lagged reserve requirements in August 1998 for the United States. Of course, this sample split may also capture other policy-driven and autonomous changes in market behaviour between the two periods.

We re-estimated the model separately over each sub-sample, using the same econometric methodology of the previous section, and the most relevant results are reported in Figures 3 and 4 above along with the full-sample estimates. In Figure 3, split-sample results reconcile our findings of essentially acyclical behaviour of mean rates, discussed in the previous section, with previous evidence of high rates around settlement. Our estimates reveal evidence of a sharp up-turn in rates near settlement for the euro area in the 'early' sample (middle panels of Figure 3), consistent with the findings of Perez-Quiros and Rodriguez-Mendizabal (2000) and Bindseil and Seitz (2001), as well as for the US sample, consistent with the findings of Hamilton (1996) and others. Over our 'late' samples, however, this evidence has all but disappeared in both areas (bottom panels in Figure 3).

Liquidity data, plotted in Figure 5, suggests that this change in interest rate behaviour could be related to changes in liquidity management by the Fed and the ECB. Both central banks have moved aggressively in the later sample to skew liquidity supply so as to offset market tightness around settlement. In the earlier sample, the

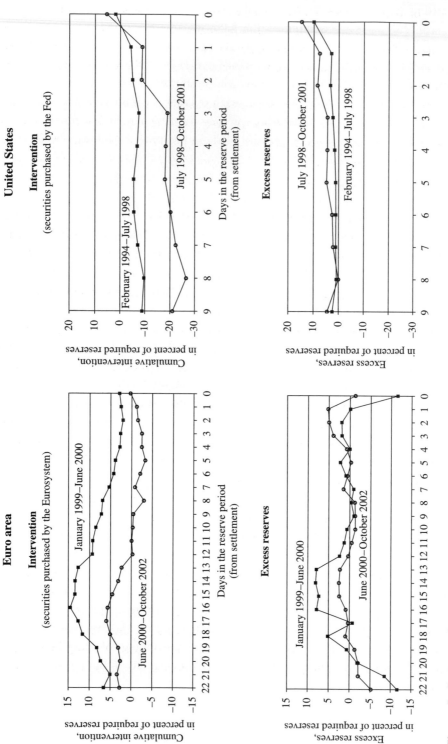

Figure 5. Intervention and excess reserves over the reserve period

Fed typically increased its supply of liquidity over the last 3 days of the period by about 6% of required reserves; in the later sample, the increase in liquidity over the last 3 days of the period was about 25% of required reserves. Similarly, the Eurosystem moved from tightening liquidity by 2% of required reserves in the last 5 days of the period in the earlier sample, to increasing liquidity by 4% of required reserves in the later sample.

Our split-sample analysis also documents changes in interest volatility after June 2000, when the Eurosystem shifted to variable rate auctions. Volatility behaviour over the reserve period did not change much after June 2000: the relevant panels in Figure 4 only show a marginally less gradual increase in volatility. Overall volatility fell from the earlier to the later sample, however. The mean absolute median difference of daily euro interest rate changes fell from 0.077 (about 8 basis points) in the earlier sample to 0.056 in the later sample, suggesting that the change in auction format may have enhanced the Eurosystem's ability to control the liquidity of the interbank market.[19] By contrast, the most visible change in US volatility pattern is that of a substantially weaker cyclical behaviour of volatility in the 'late' sample, a change likely reflecting both more aggressive and frequent intervention by the Fed, and weakening reserve requirements in the United States, discussed above.

Another feature highlighted by Figure 5 is the persistent (though weaker in late data) bulge in euro area liquidity over 8–10 days in the middle of a typical reserve period. Two factors contribute to this bulge. First, periodicity in payments and window dressing effects lead banks to demand more liquidity at end-months than on other days, and end-months typically fall in the second week of the euro area's reserve period. Second, since the Eurosystem only performs weekly intervention, to provide the needed extra liquidity at end-months it must typically also provide (undesired) extra liquidity in the few days before and after each end-month: only if the central bank intervened daily could end-month effects be offset precisely.

In summary, our split-sample analysis points to qualitative changes in the behaviour of interest rates means and volatility that are consistent with more effective management of liquidity by both institutions in the 'later' than in the 'earlier' sample. In both markets, interest rate volatility has recently declined and its cyclical behaviour has softened, while systematic patterns in mean rates have weakened. Our analysis shows that there are still differences in the behaviour of the euro area and the US money markets, and many such differences are clearly related to differences in the frequency of intervention between the Eurosystem and the Fed. Yet, it is remarkable that, both in aggregate and split-sample analysis, implementation frameworks that are formally so different can be associated with such similar market behaviour.

---

[19] The decline in volatility is significant at the 0.03 level or less, according to standard non-parametric tests. Needless to say, comparison of volatility levels across samples provides only preliminary evidence on the effect of a policy shift, since it does not separate the effect of policy shifts from that of possible changes in autonomous flows.

5. CONCLUSIONS

The Eurosystem and the Fed, the central banks of the world's two main currency areas, have adopted rather different frameworks for the day-to-day execution of monetary policy. The Eurosystem has adopted a more 'hands-off' approach to policy execution, centred on delegating to depository institutions the task of stabilizing their own liquidity at high frequency. The Federal Reserve has adopted a more 'hands-on' approach, involving daily intervention to fine-tune the liquidity of the banking system. In practice, however, certain ingredients of the two institutions' style of liquidity management have significantly mitigated differences in market behaviour between the two areas. For instance, although the Fed has retained the option of offsetting shocks to banks' liquidity at high frequency, it has not so far used this flexibility fully to stabilize pre-settlement interest volatility, nor to keep rates tightly close to their pre-change target before a target change. And while the Eurosystem's framework leaves little scope for daily fine-tuning, the quickly earned credibility of the central bank's commitment to interest rate stabilization and the intertemporal smoothing induced by reserve requirements have allowed the Eurosystem to stabilize interest rates effectively and reap essentially all the 'announcement effect' benefits of policy changes. Further, asymmetries in both central banks' provision of liquidity in advance of policy rate hikes and cuts have induced qualitative similarities in the behaviour of market rates in advance of policy changes.

This similarity is, in many ways, surprising. Few observers, even among those with large stakes in the success of EMU, would have expected the Eurosystem to be so effective so quickly in stabilizing interest rates and liquidity, and to replicate so rapidly the operational success of a much longer-established central bank such as the Fed.

Looking forward, changes in both Eurosystem and Fed frameworks, that are either under consideration or have been suggested by observers, would promote even greater similarity in behaviour between the euro area and the US money markets. The Fed is intent on pursuing a marginal lending facility that would allow it to contain upward fluctuations in market rates in the same way as the Eurosystem's marginal lending facility. The experience of the first few months of operation of the new programme is not encouraging, as there is still negligible borrowing by depository institutions. Clearly, the new programme's chances of success hinge on its ability to assuage banks' reluctance to borrow for fear that such a decision may reveal a weak financial condition. As long as a bank perceives borrowing from the Fed as revealing negative information regarding its financial condition, it may be even more reluctant to borrow after the reform at a penalty rate than it was to borrow before the reform at a subsidized rate. At the lower end of the interest rate corridor, the Fed has often advocated the possibility of paying interest on reserves (see, for instance, Meyer, 1998), but enacting such reform would require unlikely action by the US Congress.

In Europe, reforms could eliminate the instability in market behaviour associated with required minimum bids in refinancing auctions, which have been documented here and elsewhere. To address this problem, the Eurosystem has opted, for the moment, to change the settlement of auctions and the schedule of reserve periods, so as to shift liquidity injections and effects of policy changes to future reserve periods. This seems a rather indirect way to correct for an asymmetric auction mechanism that may be theoretically useful only in the presence of collusion among auction participants, which is hardly realistic in the Eurosystem auctions' environment. If planned changes in Eurosystem procedures do not achieve their goal of stabilizing interest rates, the debate on eliminating minimum bids in Eurosystem auctions, possibly leading to a symmetric auction format more in the Fed's style, would likely be rekindled.

A more dramatic development would be a move by the Eurosystem towards more frequent intervention. To mop up the liquidity stockpiled in the market in preparation for the millennium date change, on 5 January 2000 the Eurosystem utilized for the first time a US-style same-day-settlement fine-tuning measure – an off-schedule, one-week fixed-term collection of deposits. Since then, the Eurosystem has used fine-tuning measures on a handful of occasions – a slight change in intervention style that has not required amending the policy framework, which was designed from the outset to allow for a great deal of choice among different intervention tools. A move towards more frequent use of such fine-tuning operations – including, for instance, at the end of reserve periods – could help mitigate the cyclical behaviour of interest volatility, stabilize liquidity around month-ends and other special calendar days, and help to control interest rates better in advance of anticipated policy changes. However, it would probably take a reduction of required reserves such as that experienced by US banks in the 1990s or other truly major structural changes in the euro area money market to prompt the Eurosystem to increase the frequency of its intervention and modify a key ingredient of policy execution it inherited from legacy central banks.

Discussion

Ignazio Angeloni
European Central Bank

This paper covers new ground, providing a first-ever analytical comparison of the monetary policy operational frameworks of the Federal Reserve and of the Eurosystem.[20] As such, the paper makes a valuable contribution to the literature and is likely to become a benchmark for future research.

As the authors point out, the central difference in the operational approaches of the two central banks is that the Fed is 'hands on', whereas the Eurosystem is 'hands off'. The Fed intervenes almost daily, using a range of different types of open market

---

[20] The reference to the Eurosystem (combination of ECB and National Central Banks), rather than to the ECB alone, is appropriate when discussing operational matters because all monetary policy operations in the euro area are executed nationally.

Table 5. Volatility of the overnight interest rates – standard deviation of daily changes; percentage points

		Euro area (EONIA)	US (effective Fed funds rate)	UK (SONIA)	Japan (Mutan)
Average volatility of	1999	0.161	0.186	0.312	0.014
the overnight rate	2000	0.142	0.151	0.429	0.022
	2001	0.146	0.182	0.436	0.048
	2002	0.114	0.068	0.527	0.004
Average overnight	1999	2.738	4.989	5.221	0.054
rate level	2000	4.123	6.257	5.855	0.106
	2001	4.393	3.881	5.038	0.045
	2002	3.288	1.672	3.923	0.001
Average volatility	1999	0.059	0.037	0.060	0.259
divided by the	2000	0.034	0.024	0.073	0.208
average overnight level	2001	0.033	0.047	0.087	1.067
	2002	0.035	0.041	0.134	4.000

Source: ECB and Bloomberg.

operations and pegging the federal funds rate tightly around the policy target. The Eurosystem, on the contrary, intervenes normally once a week, with standardized repo auctions, without having any operational target for the interbank rate. In the euro area the daily interbank rate (EONIA) freely adjusts to market forces, helped by semi-automatic mechanisms such as the reserve requirements and the 'standing facilities' that serve the purpose of smoothing out daily rate changes. One important implication is that the Eurosystem operational framework, unlike that of the Fed, requires little day-by-day discretionary decisions by the central bank. I shall return to this feature below.

Like the authors, I am quite impressed by the similarity of daily interbank rate volatilities in spite of different 'control styles' of the two central banks. Table 5 shows volatility data for the 1999–2002 period, including the UK and Japan. The similarity between the data for the United States and the euro area is striking. The volatility of the corresponding daily rate in the UK is higher, despite the 'hands-on' approach followed also by the Bank of England. The very low volatility observed in Japan is probably attributable to the 'zero-bound' constraint on interest rates. All in all, this evidence demonstrates that a well-designed monetary control system can work well and display very little interest rate volatility even without a constant presence of the central bank in the market.

I have two specific comments on the paper and a more general one. My first specific comment relates to the analysis of the 'anticipation' effects. The authors argue that looking at how the daily rates adjust *before* policy changes says something about the extent to which the central bank accommodates the market impact of policy expectations, and hence about differences or similarities in the operational style. However, interest rate movements prior to monetary policy changes are driven mainly by the way the central bank 'prepares' the financial markets to such changes, something that has to do more with central bank communication than with operational style. The evidence in the paper speaks to a joint test of differences in communication policies and operational frameworks, with the first being probably more important. If what drives pre-meeting patterns of daily rates is communication policy, then the authors' finding that both markets adjust earlier to rate hikes than to rate cuts would indicate that both central banks prepare markets better to monetary restrictions than to monetary expansions; a very interesting finding. Trying to discriminate between these two hypotheses thus seems quite important, and could probably be done using separate measures of market expectations, such as interest rate futures.

My second remark is on the 'announcement' effects. The authors find that the overnight rate adjusts quickly *after* policy changes and interpret the results as a measure of central bank 'credibility'. However, conducting operations in a consistent way after the policy decision seems to me a rather obvious, minimal requirement, which says nothing about whether the central banks are credible in a broader sense, for example in achieving their goals. The use of the term 'credibility' in such a narrow sense is misleading in my view.

I come to my more general remark. I like the paper and agree with most of its conclusions, but the authors limited themselves to registering differences in operational framework, without suggesting reasons for these differences or expressing a value judgment on them. Yet, going deeper into what is behind the observed differences could help in understanding the ongoing changes and perhaps predicting some future ones. Let me offer a couple of thoughts. Like all market practices, operational frameworks of central banks are very inertial; changes occur with considerable lags relative to the circumstances that originate them. The Eurosystem operational framework was designed anew recently, collecting the best practices of the participating central bank. From this viewpoint, the Eurosystem's streamlined and transparent central bank operations represents more modern practice, to which the Fed may end up converging over time. The recent reform of the Fed's discount window, towards a European-like marginal lending facility, would seem to confirm this.

Other factors, however, may prevent further convergence. As I noted earlier, the 'hands off' approach fits particularly well the Eurosystem's decentralized structure, because it greatly reduces the need for daily discretionary decisions. The Federal Reserve System concentrates most operations in one location (New York) and delegates the related responsibilities to one authority (the New York Fed). This reduces some of the benefits stemming from the 'hands-off' approach, though not all, in my view.

Stijn Claessens
University of Amsterdam

Bartolini and Prati's paper shows that the ECB and Fed differ in terms of their operational frameworks (or formalities) for the execution of monetary policy, but they do not differ in style and most importantly effects of how they execute monetary policy. It also suggests that two institutions are getting similar to each other. I learned quite a bit from this paper. It is to the point, does not pretend to cover other areas, and has a nice mixture of institutional detail, empirics and qualitative discussions.

As a non-specialist, my general observation is that, although there are institutional differences among central banks, why would we expect the effects of monetary policy in terms of short-term interest rates behaviour to be different? Are there not '100 ways to skin a cat' (as argued by Borio, 2001, when comparing monetary policy operating procedures in the United States, Japan and the euro area)? Naively perhaps, I would expect similarities rather than differences, because supplying liquidity in line with the objective set for the short-term interest rates is the main operational task of all central banks. There are laws of economics and finance that even central banks have to observe, so there are very limited degrees of freedom in this area for central banks that prefer not to have an antagonistic relationship with the banking system. The paper shows that there are few differences, thus confirming what I perhaps naively expected.

The evidence of limited differences is partly a consequence of the fact that it is not clear what an ideal world would look like and how far off, if at all, the two institutions are from that ideal. This is not a shortcoming of this paper alone, as most papers leave the null-hypothesis poorly defined. At the same time, the paper may understate the differences between the two institutions that still exist. It seems to me that the data and analysis suggest there are still considerable differences in response and anticipation under the two systems. Whether there is convergence in behaviour of short-term interest rates is also hard to say, as we do not have long time spans. The data show some changes over time, but whether these are due to different aggregate monetary policy conditions, changes in institutional arrangements or other factors is unclear. Besides, the convergence is presumably driven by market factors, but these are not explicitly analysed. It would also have been very interesting to assess whether any of these differences affect the longer-term policy credibility of the central bank. This would allow one to draw from the analysis some normative arguments as to why and how a central bank ought to be involved in short-term liquidity markets.

I have a few other general comments. There is too little attention to the newness of the ECB. The paper argues that the ECB has quickly gained credibility, but it is not obvious that this is true in all dimensions. For many observers, as regards credibility in monetary policy, the ECB's role is not necessarily as clearly defined as the Fed's. In terms of the short-run intervention, it can be assumed that the ECB has gained as much respect as the Fed has, apart from some initial learning perhaps, as this is an operational issue with quick learning on both sides – markets and ECB. Credibility on target rates in other words seems more a mechanistic issue, not a policy issue. Still, the lower and more erratic anticipation for the ECB could come from either lack of credibility in monetary policy or from technical adjustments, which happened during this period.

I have some comments on empirics. As the authors explain, the two models cannot be estimated simultaneously because of institutional differences, thus precluding formal comparative tests. It would similarly have been desirable to account for market expectations when assessing anticipation effects: indexes or market prices indicating where markets are expecting rates to go could perhaps explain the differences in announcements effects across markets, and across rate hikes and cuts. But, as the authors explain, good data are not available on a daily frequency.

The analysis may shed some lights on other institutional aspects. The key question that came to my mind was whether there are reasons why central banks adopt certain liquidity policies. Is the way a central bank intervenes in the short-term interbank market affected by financial structure (the relative importance of banks and markets), banking system concentration, presence of state-owned banks, relative importance of non-bank financial institutions? Could it be that the United States with its more diversified financial system, broader economic structure with perhaps less liquidity shocks and more alternative short-run funding tools to absorb liquidity shocks offers more scope for the Fed to be just a player in the markets without need to create distance? And, in contrast, could it be that a more hands-off approach is more necessary for the ECB given the more concentrated banking systems in Europe with also more state ownership? Might this more hands-off approach especially have been necessary in the early phase of the ECB to establish independence while at the same time the authorities still have more informal means of managing the situation if need be?

To answer these questions, we would need more details on interbank markets, including the number of banks, the aggregate liquidity, the distribution in size of the players etc., that could account for the differences. In that respect, I did miss some institutional detail on the interbank markets. Do they work the same in both systems? Probably not, but little attention is given to this aspect in the paper (besides the references and some data in footnote 3). This is not the fault of the authors, as the paper does not have the space to provide this background, but it would be interesting to know whether there are market and political economy pressures that may force the Fed and ECB into certain institutional roles that suits their systems best.

Panel discussion

Leonardo Bartolini replied to the discussants that the focus of the paper is descriptive and that normative aspects are beyond its scope. He agreed that the differences in the operational framework are most likely explained by historical reasons, and argued that they can matter (as evidenced by the British money market's very different operational framework and very different behaviour).

Steve Cecchetti doubted that the Fed's new discount policy may overcome the negative signalling problems inherited from the previous regime. As regards intra-day volatility, he argued that standing facilities should substantially smooth it in the euro money market, while in the United States the Fed's absence from the market between the early morning and late afternoon allows large interest rate spikes. He wondered about the optimality of either system, and Carol Propper pointed out that the different operational frameworks may well have different operational costs.

Jonathan Haskel asked how much the ECB and Fed co-operate. Leonardo Bartolini replied that there is indeed co-operation between the Fed and ECB on understanding better the liquidity management and execution of monetary policy.

REFERENCES

Andersen, T.G., and J. Lund (1997). 'Estimating continuous-time stochastic volatility models of the short-term interest rate', *Journal of Econometrics*, 77, 343–77.

Angelini, P. (2003). 'Liquidity and announcement effects in the euro area', manuscript, Banca d'Italia.

Angeloni, I., and E. Bisagni (2002). 'Liquidity effects in the euro area', manuscript, European Central Bank and University of California, San Diego.

Ayuso, J., and R. Repullo (2001). 'Why did the banks overbid? An empirical model of the fixed rate tenders of the European Central Bank', Banco de España, Working Paper No. 0105.

Balduzzi, P., G. Bertola, S. Foresi, and L. Klapper (1998). 'Interest rate targeting and the dynamics of short-term rates', *Journal of Money, Credit, and Banking*, 30, 26–50.

Bartolini, L., G. Bertola, and A. Prati (2001). 'Banks' reserve management, transaction costs, and the timing of Federal Reserve intervention', *Journal of Banking and Finance*, 25, 1287–1318.

Bennett, P., and S. Hilton (1997). 'Falling reserve balances and the federal funds rate', Federal Reserve Bank of New York, *Current Issues in Economics and Finance*, 3, 5.

Bennett, P., and S. Peristiani (2002). 'Are US Reserve requirements still binding?' Federal Reserve Bank of New York, *Economic Policy Review*, 8(1), 53–68.

Bindseil, U. (2002). 'Equilibrium bidding in the Eurosystem's open market operations', European Central Bank Working Paper No. 137.

Bindseil, U., and F. Seitz (2001). 'The supply and demand for Eurosystem deposits: The first 18 months', European Central Bank, Working Paper No. 44.

Borio, C.E.V. (2001). 'A hundred ways to skin a cat: Comparing monetary policy operating procedures in the United States, Japan and the euro area', in *Comparing Monetary Policy Operating Procedures across the United States, Japan, and the Euro Area*, BIS Paper New Series No. 9, December, pp. 23–47.

Brunner, A.D., and C.S. Lown (1993). 'The effect of lower reserve requirements on money market volatility', *American Economic Review, Papers and Proceedings*, 83, 199–205.

Clouse, J.A., and J.P. Dow Jr. (2002). 'A computational model of banks' optimal reserve management policy', *Journal of Economic Dynamics and Control*, 26, 1787–1814.

Demiralp, S., and O. Jorda (2002). 'The announcement effect: Evidence from open market desk data', Federal Reserve Bank of New York, *Economic Policy Review*, 8(1), 29–48.

Ejerskov, S., C. Martin Moss, and L. Stracca (2003). 'Demand and supply in the ECB's main refinancing operations', European Central Bank, manuscript.

Feinman, J.N. (1993). 'Estimating the open market desk's daily reaction function', *Journal of Money, Credit, and Banking*, 25, 231–427.

Furfine, C.H. (1999). 'The microstructure of the federal funds market', *Financial Markets, Institutions and Instruments*, 8, 24–44.

Hamilton, J.H. (1996). 'The daily market for federal funds', *Journal of Political Economy*, 104, 26–56.

Hartmann, P., M. Manna, and A. Manzanares (2001). 'The microstructure of the euro money market', *Journal of International Money and Finance*, 20, 895–948.

Meyer, L.H. (1998). 'Payment of interest on demand deposits and on required reserve balances', Testimony Before the Committee on Banking, Housing and Urban Affairs, US Senate, 3 March 1998, in *Federal Reserve Bulletin*, May, 326–30.

Nelson, D.B. (1991). 'Conditional heteroskedasticity in asset returns: A new approach', *Econometrica*, 59, 347–70.

Oechssler, J., and D. Nautz (2001). 'The repo auction of the European Central Bank and the vanishing quota puzzle', University of Bonn, Discussion Paper No. 9/2001.

Perez-Quiros, G., and H. Rodriguez-Mendizabal (2000). 'The daily market for funds in Europe: Has something changed with EMU?', ECB Working Paper No. 67.

Prati, A., L. Bartolini, and G. Bertola (2003). 'The overnight interbank market: Evidence from the G-7 and the Euro Zone', *Journal of Banking and Finance*, forthcoming.

Välimäki, T. (2003a). 'Bidding in fixed rate tenders: Theory and evidence from ECB tenders' in *Central Bank Tenders: Three Essays on Money Market Liquidity Auctions*, Bank of Finland Studies E:26, Helsinki.

— (2003b). 'Variable rate liquidity tenders', in *Central Bank Tenders: Three Essays on Money Market Liquidity Auctions*, Bank of Finland Studies E:26, Helsinki.

Würtz, F.R. (2003). 'A comprehensive model on the euro overnight rate', ECB Working Paper No. 207.

Monetary transmission evidence

SUMMARY

We examine the euro area monetary policy transmission process using post-1999 data, with two main questions in mind: has it changed after – and because of – economic and monetary union (EMU) and, if so, is it becoming homogeneous across countries? Given the data limitations, we concentrate on three components of the transmission mechanism: the banking, the interest rate and the asset market channels. We find evidence that the transmission through banks has become more potent and homogeneous across countries. On the financial market channels, our evidence is somewhat weaker but suggestive. The interest rate channel appears to have changed even before EMU, and now affects national economies in a broadly similar way. The asset market channel (proxied by the stock market effects of monetary policy) also seems to work rather homogeneously across national markets (no comparison with pre-EMU is available here). A positive answer to both questions raised above represents, in our view, the best working hypothesis under current knowledge.

— *Ignazio Angeloni and Michael Ehrmann*

Monetary transmission in the euro area: early evidence

Ignazio Angeloni and Michael Ehrmann

European Central Bank

1. MOTIVATION AND EMPIRICAL STRATEGY

In this paper we attempt a first empirical assessment of the effect of economic and monetary union (EMU) on monetary transmission in the euro area. We compare post-EMU with pre-EMU data, using developments in other (non-EMU) countries as controls.[1] In doing so, it is important to bear in mind that EMU is a *process*, not a one-time event. The transition to a new currency and monetary policy was something economic agents had time to prepare for, and adjust to, over a number of years. This complicates significantly the task of identifying causal links. In any event, we address several related questions, only some of which are of causal nature: Has the euro area transmission mechanism changed lately? Has it changed *in coincidence* with EMU? Has it changed *because of* EMU? What is the direction of change?

The views expressed in this paper are not necessarily shared by the ECB or the Eurosystem. All the usual disclaimers apply. We thank seminar participants at the University of Bonn, the Bundesbank, the ECB, the participants in the 37th *Economic Policy* Panel, our discussants Paul de Grauwe and David Miles and the editors for helpful comments. We also thank Anil Kashyap for many inspiring discussions about the transmission mechanism over the last few years. The Directorate General Statistics of the ECB provided generous statistical support. Sandrine Corvoisier skilfully assisted in processing the data.
The Managing Editor in charge of this paper was Paul Seabright.

[1] From this viewpoint, we move a step forward relative to recent studies such as that conducted by the so-called 'Eurosystem Monetary Transmission Network', that used pre-EMU data to infer about the post-EMU transmission mechanism (Angeloni et al., 2003a). A review of the recent literature is contained in an earlier version of this paper: see Angeloni and Ehrmann (2003).

These questions link up with another issue of great policy relevance, the *differentiation* of monetary policy effects across countries. Several authors have argued that the pre-EMU monetary transmission process was uneven across countries, in a way that would complicate the conduct of the single monetary policy.[2] Others have noted that such differences are difficult to detect empirically.[3] Arguably, some of the cross-country differences in monetary transmission, those linked more directly to the existence of currency segmentation and to the different monetary regimes, should fade away quickly once a common currency is adopted. Therefore, looking at the two issues in conjunction seems particularly promising.

Unfortunately, studying the monetary policy transmission process in the euro area is difficult at this stage, due to the extreme scarcity of data. Ideally, one would like to compare a model of the euro area against models of the individual member countries' transmission processes, where changes of key parameters could be measured and tested. This is clearly not feasible with four years of data. Euro area-wide models estimated using 'synthetic' variables for the pre-EMU period do exist,[4] but they assume homogeneity across time and countries, blurring crucial distinctions that we want to address. Even national data are, in many cases, not complete and homogeneous enough in key areas such as inventories, housing or durable consumption.

Our research strategy is to focus on a selected number of links in the transmission process that are important, for which data are available, and where EMU-related changes are likely to occur rapidly. These criteria led us to concentrate on two building blocks: the banking sector and the financial markets. The next few paragraphs explain this choice in more detail.

In the survey of the transmission mechanism published in the *Journal of Economic Perspectives* (1995), four channels are distinguished through which monetary policy affects aggregate demand: the bank lending channel, the interest rate channel, the asset market channel and the exchange rate channel. The bank lending channel is a natural focus of our attention as it matches all three criteria above. Banks have a central role in financial intermediation in the euro area.[5] Monthly data (the lowest usable data frequency with four years of data) exist. Finally, post-EMU changes, if any, are likely to occur quickly, as banks are directly exposed to the action of the central bank and operate in the euro area interbank market, that has been fully integrated since 1999 (Hartmann *et al.*, 2001). The interest rate and asset market channels also fulfil the criteria: they are important for the transmission mechanism, high frequency data exist and the financial markets are likely to be immediately affected by the new risk-return configuration determined by EMU.

---

[2] E.g. Cecchetti (2001), Mihov (2001).

[3] Kieler and Saarenheimo (1998), Guiso *et al.* (1999) and Angeloni *et al.* (2003a).

[4] The most frequently quoted structural models are Fagan *et al.* (2001) and Smets and Wouters (2002); for a VAR study, see Peersman and Smets (2003).

[5] Micro evidence on banks tends to support that the bank lending channel, as proposed by Kashyap and Stein (1997), is a relevant element in the transmission process in a number of euro area countries (Ehrmann *et al.*, 2003, and references therein).

Different considerations apply to the exchange-rate channel. This channel compounds two separate links, one from monetary policy to the exchange rate and the other from the latter to the domestic economy. The first link is notoriously very volatile and unsystematic.[6] The second one is likely to decline in importance after EMU, since the euro area economy is much less open to international trade than the constituent countries. For these reasons the exchange rate channel is not analysed in this paper, though we regard it as an interesting avenue of future research.

The final link in the transmission mechanism is that between aggregate demand and output and prices. This breakdown depends on factors – such as wage-price setting mechanisms and other elements affecting the supply side response – that normally change slowly, depending on deep-rooted features of goods and labour markets. Structural reforms in these markets are a necessary complement of EMU, as recognized by the Lisbon process, but implementation takes time and their dividend in terms of macroeconomic performance materializes only gradually. Moreover, from our perspective, these phenomena would need to be analysed with quarterly or even annual data. For all these reasons, we do not think that such analysis is feasible at the present stage.

Summing up the rest of the paper, our evidence on the banking sector and the financial markets is presented in Sections 2 and 3, respectively. Our next and final step is to bring the separate pieces of evidence together, seeing what overall message may be drawn. We will do so in Section 4, using what has been called, in another context, the 'Sherlock Holmes' approach. Like Sherlock, we will try to solve our case by 'weaving together all the bits of evidence into a plausible story' (Leamer, 1978). We hope our story will be informative and suggest also where else to look in order to complete the picture.

2. EVIDENCE ON THE BANKING CHANNEL

2.1. Market-structure and signal-quality effects

Our focus in this section is on detecting any changes in the reaction of banks to monetary policy that may be related to the introduction of the euro, and on whether they indicate that the monetary transmission mechanism is becoming more homogeneous across countries.

One can think of two classes of reasons why behavioural changes may have occurred in banking. The first relates to the fact that, with the transition to the euro, the *nature of the monetary policy signals* has changed. A new central bank is in charge,

---

[6] Recent research on how the exchange rate channel affects output and prices in the euro area (see van Els *et al.*, 2003) assumes uncovered interest parity (UIP) holds. However, the empirical support for UIP is weak. Calvo and Reinhart (2000) suggest that the link between policy interest rates and the exchange rate has the theoretically expected sign about 50% of the time, i.e. like tossing a fair coin.

with a new strategy and a new euro-area orientation. The policy actions of the ECB convey different information relative to those of pre-existing national central banks, particularly in countries where the policy regime has changed most significantly. In particular, if the volatility of monetary policy has declined as a result (and it has, as we shall see), the response of banks to a policy signal of any given size is likely to have increased.[7]

The second potential reason for behavioural changes relates to possible modifications in the *structure of banking markets*. There can be several ways for this to take place, all stemming from the fact that the single currency removes one source of segmentation across national banking markets – the exchange rate risk. Suppose national banking markets are segmented and banking systems differ with respect to some intrinsic characteristic (say, efficiency, although the same line of reasoning could apply to other factors as well). Bank efficiency would affect lending conditions to national customers, including the response of such conditions to shocks. Once segmentation is removed, prices of banking products tend to converge due to competition; inefficient banking systems, no longer able to pass extra costs on to customers, would eventually restructure or see their market shares reduced. Price convergence does not require cross-border activity, but only contestability of markets. The converse, however, is not true: significant cross-border business would be *prima facie* evidence that markets are contested.

Bank competition across frontiers can alter the cross-border pattern of monetary transmission in several ways. Under segmented markets, each national banking system transforms domestic deposits into domestic loans, using a domestic technology, with the national central bank influencing the process via the interbank market and the cost of raising deposits. Banking efficiency is reflected in the spreads between the lending and interbank rates and between the interbank and deposit rates. Once markets integrate, competition in the loan and deposit markets tends to equalize these spreads.[8] Interbank market integration, which allows relatively inefficient banks to access the better deposit raising technology of the foreign banks, also tends to equalize deposit spreads. Alternatively, foreign deposit and loan markets can be accessed through foreign branches, with similar effects. Finally, another (more indirect) way in which lending conditions can be altered is through cross-border mergers and acquisitions (M&A). For example, M&A can induce banks to sever their customer relationship with small borrowers, a factor normally leading to loans being priced more sluggishly and inefficiently.[9]

The *market-structure* channel is probably slower to operate than the *signal-quality* channel. Whether the euro has already had an influence on the competition among national banking sectors is an open question. Some evidence on the effect of the introduction

---

[7] This follows from a simple errors-in-variables argument. If a signal is observed with noise with variance σ^2, the response by the banks to it is reduced (assuming linearity) by a factor of $\sigma^2/(\sigma^2 + s^2)$, where s^2 is the variance of the signal.

[8] We abstract here from the characteristics of the local borrowers. Alternatively, one could reason in terms of borrower-risk-adjusted terms.

[9] Sapienza (2002) analyses the link between M&A in banking and loan supply conditions and provides arguments and evidence along these lines.

of the euro on bank market penetration is contained in a more extended version of this paper (Angeloni and Ehrmann, 2003), which shows that:

- Cross-border lending and deposit taking among euro area countries has tended to increase after 1999, but no dramatic changes have taken place.
- On the contrary, cross-border interbank activity has been rising sharply, in absolute terms and relative to control cases (non-euro area countries). This confirms that the euro area interbank market is well integrated.
- Cross-border branching shows no sign of increase in the euro area after 1999; it is very extensive in small countries and very limited in large ones, and, on the whole, not too different in scale from what one observed across US states.
- There is some sign of increase in cross-border bank mergers, relative to past trends and to control cases. The level of this phenomenon, however, remains low relative to most of the comparators (notably, the USA).

With our limited data samples, identifying separately the *market-structure* and the *signal-quality* effects econometrically is not possible. The econometric evidence below, on the mechanics of bank interest rate determination and its response to policy shocks, aims at estimating the total effect without trying to disentangle the two possible causes.

2.2. Transmission of monetary policy to bank interest rates

We use monthly data on lending and deposit interest rates, across a variety of instruments and maturities, on a comparable basis for five euro area countries and for the euro area as a whole.[10] We look at how bank rates react to changes in the money market rates. These results provide answers to the questions posed in the introduction in two ways. First, changes in the pass-through parameters can tell us something about whether the transmission through bank rates has changed. Breakpoints in 1999 are an obvious focus of attention. We are also interested in the direction of change – such as whether there is more powerful or more rapid transmission. Second, our detailed sector-level and country data allows us to examine cross-country homogeneity, particularly since 1999.

We calculate three parameters:

- the impact effect (within a month);
- the maximum effect (whenever it occurs);
- the time needed to reach this maximum effect – across all rates and countries, and for the euro area average.

---

[10] Data are available on the ECB website (www.ecb.int). Furthermore, all the data used in this paper are available and documented on the *Economic Policy* website (www.economic-policy.org).

Table 1. Effect of money market rates on lending and deposit rates (country averages)

Country (no. of rates)	Impact coefficient		Maximum response		Time to max	
	1990–1998	1999–2002	1990–1998	1999–2002	1990–1998	1999–2002
Germany (8)	0.441	0.387	0.852	0.765	6.875	4.750
France (2)	0.017	0.621	0.325	1.158	6.000	5.000
Italy (7)	0.153	0.396	0.541	0.931	4.714	6.286
Spain (9)	0.404	0.470	0.717	1.184	5.111	5.444
Netherlands (4)	0.389	0.468	0.800	0.850	4.750	3.000
Euro area (10)	0.241	0.380	0.475	0.744	14.600	5.000
UK (10)	0.422	0.423	1.481	0.810	6.700	6.100
Sweden (2)	0.395	0.581	0.609	0.455	1.500	1.000
Japan (10)	0.524	0.239	0.882	0.323	5.100	2.000
US (5)	0.838	0.744	1.367	1.304	4.400	3.800
Std dev. among euro area countries	*0.186*	*0.093*	*0.215*	*0.186*	*0.932*	*1.210*
Coeff. of Var. among euro area countries	*0.663*	*0.200*	*0.332*	*0.191*	*0.170*	*0.247*

Notes: The coefficients are averages from models for various retail rates. OLS regression equation for the impact coefficient: $\Delta r_t^{bank} = \alpha + \beta \Delta r_t^{mmkt} + \varepsilon_t$. Maximum response and time to max are computed from VAR responses of retail rates to a unitary shock to money market rates (obtained from a Choleski decomposition). Regression equation: $x_t = \alpha + \beta_1 x_{t-1} + \beta_2 x_{t-2} + \varepsilon_t$, where $x_t = [r_t^{bank} \; r_t^{mmkt}]'$. Sample size: 1990:1 (or later)–2002:7.

Source: Authors' calculations.

To do this we use two models. The impact effect is estimated using a simple regression of changes in the bank rate on changes in the money market rate and a constant, whereas we use a simple bivariate VAR in levels to calculate the peak effect and the timing.[11] The results, grouped by country, are summarized in Table 1.

The table shows results for the five largest euro area countries, for the area as a whole, and for a 'control group' including UK, Sweden, Japan and USA. Impact and peak effects and the time to maximum effect (in months) are given for two sub-periods: 1990–8 and 1999–2002. Data are averaged across types of rates for each country (the number of rates available for each country is indicated).

There is a clear upward movement of both the impact and the peak response, except in Germany, where both decline slightly. Moreover, the dispersion of these two parameters across the euro area countries declines between the first and the second period.[12] There are no analogous changes in the control group. In contrast to these changes in the *size* of the coefficients, we find no evidence that the *speed* of the pass-through has become faster, either in the euro area or in the control group. In Table 2 we show the same coefficients grouped not by country, however, but by loan or deposit type. Mortgage and business loans show the largest increase in the impact coefficient between pre-1999 and the successive period. The increase in the peak coefficient is more evenly distributed. Some tests of cross-country restrictions on the impact coefficient are shown in Table 3. At the standard significance levels, only mortgage loans, business loans (long-term) and time deposits (long-term) pass the cross-country homogeneity test. Interestingly, maturity seems to matter: equality is accepted in all the long-term loan and deposit categories, and rejected in the short-term ones. It is clear that, despite the sizeable changes that have taken place between our two time sub-periods, considerable ground still needs to be covered before a full or near homogeneity of the transmission through bank rates is achieved in the euro area.

To check whether the break between the first and the second sub-period is indeed located at or around the start of 1999, we estimated the regressions of the first columns of Tables 1 and 2 using rolling-window samples of 36 months. The results are reported in Figure 1 for a selection of euro area rates, with a vertical line marking the first window that includes observations post-EMU. The coefficients generally start rising

---

[11] These simple regressions could potentially be affected by omitted variable or endogeneity bias if third factors (like the business cycle) affected both rates separately or if money market rates responded to bank rates. We have controlled for this bias in two ways: by adding the change in industrial production in the equation; and by performing Hausman endogeneity tests on all equations. We found evidence of such bias at the 5% level in only 5 out of the 80 equations we estimate for the euro area and the euro area countries, and in only 7 out of the 54 equations for the control countries, which we take as evidence that our results are generally unbiased. Both tests gave identical results. The VAR shocks were all standardized by dividing by their standard error.

[12] The somewhat surprising results for France – a nearly zero coefficient in the first period, rising to a fairly high level in the second – may depend on data quality: the two French retail rate series are in fact collected at quarterly frequency and interpolated monthly, which can induce spurious lags in the univariate equation. If the French equation is estimated with one lag, the estimated coefficients are: 0.168 pre-EMU; 0.308 post-EMU. The decline in the standard deviation and in the coefficient of variation across countries are both confirmed using these alternative estimates for France.

Table 2. Effect of money market rates on lending and deposit rates (averages by instrument)

Type of business (No. of rates)	Impact coefficient		Maximum response		Time to max	
	1990–1998	1999–2002	1990–1998	1999–2002	1990–1998	1999–2002
Euro area						
Mortgage loans (5)	0.249	0.394	0.517	0.840	3.200	4.000
Loans to consumers (5)	0.299	0.298	0.684	0.832	7.400	6.200
Loans to corporations (11)	0.350	0.534	0.811	1.110	14.636	5.000
Deposits (19)	0.297	0.404	0.565	0.836	5.105	5.105
UK, Sweden, Japan, US						
Mortgage loans (5)	0.289	0.458	0.711	0.609	3.200	2.400
Loans to consumers (6)	0.336	0.203	0.872	0.424	9.000	6.167
Loans to corporations (5)	0.554	0.478	1.132	0.810	5.000	3.800
Deposits (11)	0.746	0.510	1.567	0.830	4.364	3.091

Source. Authors' calculations; see Table 4.

Table 3. Tests for homogeneity of the impact effect of changes in money market rates to bank rates across euro area countries, grouped by instrument

Type of business (No. of rates)	1990–1998		1999–2002	
	χ^2	Significance	χ^2	Significance
Mortgage loans (4)	5.702	0.223	1.069	0.899
Loans to consumers (4)	16.395	0.003	21.596	0.000
Long-term loans to corporations (4)	4.681	0.322	3.714	0.446
Short-term loans to corporations (5)	106.504	0.000	20.167	0.001
Savings deposits (6)	48.035	0.000	39.936	0.000
Long-term time deposits (4)	20.091	0.000	6.053	0.195
Short-term time dep., current account (4)	135.865	0.000	47.887	0.000

Notes: SUR models comprising national rates only (i.e., excluding euro area rates), where each equation is estimated as $\Delta r_t^{bank} = \alpha + \beta \Delta r_t^{mmkt} + \varepsilon_t$; for further explanations see Table 1.

Source: Authors' calculations.

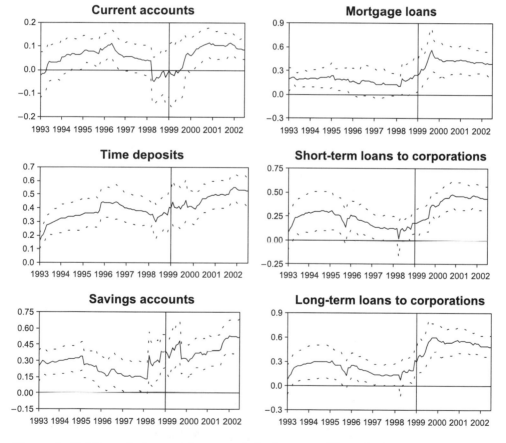

Figure 1. Rolling window estimates of the impact effect of changes in money market rates to bank rates: euro area

Notes: Solid line: rolling window coefficient estimates; dashed lines: 95% confidence bands; vertical line: first window with observation under EMU; x-axis represents the end point of the respective regression windows; further explanations: see Table 1.

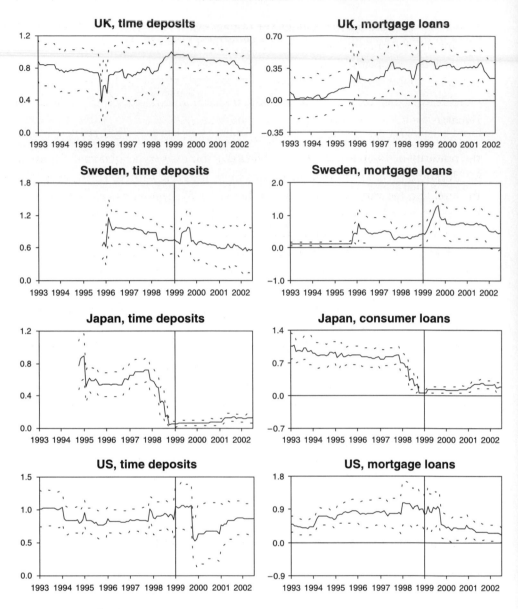

Figure 2. Rolling window estimates of the impact effect of changes in money market rates to bank rates: other countries

Notes: Solid line: rolling window coefficient estimates; dashed lines: 95% confidence bands; vertical line: first window with observation under EMU; x-axis represents the end point of the respective regression windows; further explanations: see Table 1.

once observations after 1999 enter the regression window and keep rising while new observations from the new regime are added. Figure 2 shows that no such pattern can be found for the countries outside the euro area.

As we have suggested earlier, identifying the factors behind these changes, specifically in terms of the *market-structure* versus *signal-quality* interpretation, is difficult with the data available today. The second interpretation seems to square well with our evidence: the impact of money market rates on bank rates rises in most cases after 1999, except in Germany; it is probably not a coincidence that the volatility of money market rates falls after 1999 in all countries, except in Germany.[13] However, the first interpretation could have a role, too, in explaining why the estimated responses of banks to policy signals are increasingly homogeneous across countries.

A related piece of evidence pointing to structural changes in credit markets concerns the maturity of bank loans. One established empirical regularity is that the maturity (or duration) of financial contracts tends to be inversely related, across countries, to the level and the variability of inflation (Borio, 1995). High inflation countries tend to be characterized by shorter financial contracts. The loan market of the euro area is no exception to this rule; countries with a recent history of high inflation, such as Italy and Spain, were until recently characterized by shorter average loan maturity than, say, Germany. This has a potential implication for the transmission process, since a shorter (or equivalently, floating rate) loan or mortgage contract tends to generate cash-flow responses to changes in policy-driven interest rates that are different from those of long contracts (at fixed rate). The interesting message coming from Table 4 is that such differences are in the process of being reduced (gradually, but steadily) in the euro area. For all categories of loans taken into consideration (covering loans to both non-financial corporations and households) the cross-country variance of maturity (measured crudely by the share of loans with original maturity over 5 years) is on a declining trend. The maturity in Spain and Italy is on the rise, conceivably as a result of the fact that expectations of price stability have been strengthened; in France it is roughly constant. Interestingly, Germany again stands out from the crowd: historically it had the highest share of loans beyond 5 years, but maturity is now slowly declining.

3. EVIDENCE ON THE FINANCIAL MARKET CHANNELS

In focusing on the non-bank financial sector, we are again looking for evidence that can help us characterize the post-EMU transmission process and to show whether any change has taken place, particularly with regard to the degree of cross-country homogeneity. Relative to the bank lending channel, which at least conceptually is relatively straightforward to define (though quite difficult to identify empirically), the range of financial market channels is broader, more articulate and complex to pin down. Transmission through the financial markets can take place in a number of

---

[13] Between the pre-EMU (1990–8) and the post-EMU (1999–2002) periods, the variance of three-month interest rate changes dropped from 0.24, 0.41, 0.14 respectively in France, Italy and Spain to 0.04. In Germany, it increased from 0.03 to 0.04. The *signal-quality* interpretation also seems consistent with recent estimates of De Bondt *et al.* (2003), showing that the relevance of bond yields in affecting bank lending rates declined recently relative to money market rates in a number of euro area countries. The signal conveyed by long-term rates may not be so relevant anymore, since money market rates have become more informative.

Table 4. Share of loans with original maturity over 5 years, euro area

	1997	1998	1999	2000	2001	2002Q2
Non-financial corporations						
Euro area	49.76	50.63	49.25	47.96	48.05	48.52
of which: France	53.67	56.01	57.01	54.89	56.22	55.33
Germany	64.29	65.12	61.45	60.80	60.78	61.60
Italy	24.37	25.23	26.85	26.95	27.77	29.39
Spain	36.80	38.08	39.26	38.71	41.42	42.99
Netherlands	60.21	60.05	61.40	58.24	58.50	56.95
Std. Dev. of euro area countries	*16.81*	*16.70*	*15.48*	*14.54*	*14.05*	*13.06*
Coeff. of Var. of euro area countries	*0.35*	*0.34*	*0.31*	*0.30*	*0.29*	*0.27*
Households – consumer credit						
Euro area	48.61	48.37	44.47	44.76	45.37	45.59
of which: France	22.21	22.23	23.96	25.00	27.25	27.61
Germany	66.84	66.87	58.78	58.17	59.38	59.99
Italy	17.90	17.88	18.02	20.99	24.28	25.08
Spain	36.23	40.47	42.12	43.46	45.10	44.69
Netherlands	21.12	22.28	19.29	18.90	20.20	18.92
Std. Dev. of euro area countries	*20.25*	*20.36*	*17.61*	*16.95*	*16.51*	*16.81*
Coeff. of Var. of euro area countries	*0.62*	*0.60*	*0.54*	*0.51*	*0.47*	*0.48*
Households – other lending						
Euro area	66.14	65.81	58.27	57.76	58.23	58.03
of which: France	76.75	76.65	76.20	74.85	72.50	72.97
Germany	81.61	82.54	70.70	70.45	70.59	70.15
Italy	25.70	25.56	28.83	30.45	34.40	35.31
Spain	56.98	55.76	56.51	59.63	57.65	55.12
Netherlands	44.98	44.95	45.58	41.10	43.27	41.88
Std. Dev. of euro area countries	*23.02*	*23.31*	*19.17*	*19.04*	*16.70*	*16.68*
Coeff. of Var. of euro area countries	*0.40*	*0.41*	*0.35*	*0.34*	*0.30*	*0.30*

Notes: Standard deviation and coefficient of variation are calculated for Germany, France, Italy, Spain and the Netherlands.

Source: ECB; authors' calculations.

different ways, involving difficult issues of conceptual as well as empirical identification. A short discussion on the logical framework can be of help.

Referring again to the survey in the *Journal of Economic Perspectives*, we focus here on what Mishkin (1995) there calls the 'interest rate' and the 'asset price' channels. In Mishkin's definition the interest rate channel (IRC) is the traditional Keynesian effect whereby monetary policy is transmitted, through liquidity and expectations effects, to the structure of nominal and real interest rates, and then indirectly to investment and consumption plans by non-financial firms and households. More specifically – see Angeloni *et al.* (2003a) – the IRC is the mechanism that operates in the absence of capital market imperfections, i.e. only through the intertemporal reallocation of expenditures that follows a change in expected real interest rates (which are the *prices* of such reallocation). In principle this definition excludes asset market or 'broad credit channel' effects stemming from changes in 'external finance premia', emphasized by Bernanke and Gertler (1995) and Bernanke *et al.* (1999). In practice it is very difficult to distinguish between a 'pure' IRC and these other influences, as recently pointed out by Bernanke.[14]

Attacking empirically all these subtle distinctions would be impossible with our limited data. Our pragmatic way forward is to concentrate, first, on something that approximates the IRC in its purest form, looking at how nominal and real interest rates (short and long term) on riskless assets behave across sample periods. We do this in the next subsection. After this, in the following subsection we approach one key building block of the 'asset price' channel, by comparing the impact of monetary policy on national stock markets.

3.1. Interest rate channel

To test for the effect of monetary policy through the IRC one could directly estimate dynamic models, like the ones of Tables 1 and 2, on real and nominal market interest rates, and see how the coefficients change across sub-periods. The problem in doing so is that models must be very simple, since data are scarce. For the bank rates analysed in Section 2.2 this yielded sensible results, because the laws of motion of bank rates are relatively simple: bank rates are set administratively, in less than fully competitive markets, using relatively simple adjustment schemes. The empirical literature suggests that simple specifications are normally adequate to explain bank rates, usually as a function of signals provided by the central bank.[15] On the contrary, financial market rates are determined in highly efficient markets, and their dynamics and reaction to news is much more complex.[16] This may explain why our attempts to fit simple schemes linking market rates to monetary policy were unsuccessful, for all our short sub-samples. We have therefore resorted to a less data-demanding procedure, as follows.[17]

Our basic idea is that, if the IRC has become homogeneous in the euro area after 1999, then it must be true that riskless rates in real terms follow the same law of motion in all member countries. This is certainly true for nominal rates, which after EMU are forced to coincide by arbitrage given the absence of exchange-rate risk, but not necessarily for real rates if the transmission is not homogeneous. A comparison between pre- and post-EMU evidence can be based on simple measures of unconditional co-movements of real interest rates, at different maturity, across countries. As clarified

[14] See his discussion in Angeloni *et al.* (2003a).

[15] See, among many others, Neumark and Sharpe (1992) or Hannan and Berger (1991), which suggest that the main determinant of bank pricing is a simple markup on those market interest rates that are closely controlled by monetary policy.

[16] A monetary policy tightening tends to increase nominal interest rates due to the liquidity effect, and decrease nominal rates due to its effects on inflation expectations. Furthermore, their reaction is affected by expectations on future monetary policy actions. Due to this complexity, the empirical literature has generally found only a weak relationship. Kuttner (2001) discusses the methodological requirements that are needed to estimate the effects of monetary policy on market determined interest rates in a systematic way, suggesting that a careful distinction of anticipated and unanticipated policy actions is needed.

[17] Conversely, we have applied this simplified procedure back on the data underlying Tables 1 and 2, obtaining good results (available on request).

more formally below, under plausible conditions unconditional co-movement implies that the effects of monetary policy on interest rates are similar.

We use nominal short (3-month interbank) and long (10-year government bond) rates, and proxy inflationary expectations with the 12-month forward changes of national Harmonized Indices of Consumer Prices.[18] Lacking robust evidence on the stationarity of the data,[19] we look at both levels and changes of the data. As a measure of co-movement across countries we use the *variance of the interest differential*, rather than the more common *correlation coefficient*.[20] We examine three time periods. The first, 1990–4, spans from the removal of short-term capital controls to the ERM crisis of 1992–3 and its aftermath. The second, 1995–8, covers a time when interest differentials were strongly affected by the so-called 'convergence trades' in the financial markets, driven by expectations of EMU. This has conceivably produced a convergence in interest rate levels, but not necessarily in higher-frequency movements. The third, 1999–2002, coincides with the first 4 years of EMU, and is the period in which we are most directly interested.

Table 5 contains measures of interest rate co-movement, within the euro area countries and for three control groups: the euro area versus the rest of the EU; the euro area versus the USA and Japan; and four main US Census regions among themselves.[21] To obtain the results for groups of countries, bilateral variances are aggregated using GDP weights. The *within* euro area variance, expressed as a single number, can then be compared with that *between* the euro area and the control groups, and with that *within* the USA.

The variance of *real* interest differentials in the euro area (*in levels*), dramatically declines for both short and long rates. In the control countries there is also some decline, but less strong. There is no decline among the US regions. When one looks at variances of monthly *changes* of real interest differentials, a different pattern emerges. The main reduction in the variance is between the first period (1990–4) and the second (1995–8), not after 1999; there is a similar decline between the euro area and other EU, but not with the other control groups. Within the USA the variance of the differential does not decrease. The overall message is mixed: there is a sharp convergence, but it does not take place unambiguously after EMU (it depends a lot on whether levels or changes are considered), nor does it exclusively take place among euro area members. The other EU countries (UK, Sweden, Denmark) converge too. The developments are instead quite different if one looks at other areas (euro area versus USA and Japan, or within USA).

---

[18] Using backward inflation rates gives similar results.

[19] With our short data samples, standard tests of stationarity would probably lack power. Looking at levels and changes together should provide some robustness. Some evidence on stationarity will emerge from our results.

[20] The variance of the differential seems more accurate for our purpose. A correlation coefficient of one is necessary but not sufficient for the variance of the differential to be zero: if the variances are different, the differential varies even if the two rates are perfectly correlated. Hence the variance criterion is more restrictive. On the other hand, the variance of the differential can fall if the variances change, even if the correlation remains constant or even declines.

[21] US regional price data from the Bureau of Labor Statistics (www.bls.gov/cpi/) refer to four regions: West, Midwest, South, Northeast. We also tried with city data, available from the same source (results available), finding that the variance of between-city inflation differentials is much wider than that of between-region differentials. Hence, US regional data seem to provide a closer analogue to our euro area country data. We thank Steve Cecchetti, without involving him, for useful information about these data.

Table 5. Variance of real interest rate differentials: measures of cohesion

	Interest rate levels			Interest rate changes		
	1990–1994	1995–1998	1999–2002	1990–1994	1995–1998	1999–2002
Euro area						
Short rate	2.66	2.09	0.39	0.66	0.20	0.10
Long rate	1.92	1.67	0.39	0.23	0.13	0.10
Euro area and other EU						
Short rate	4.46	2.31	1.31	0.99	0.18	0.12
Long rate	1.87	0.98	0.43	0.34	0.12	0.10
Euro area, Japan and USA						
Short rate	3.88	1.99	1.19	0.40	0.24	0.12
Long rate	1.04	2.07	0.42	0.22	0.24	0.15
US regions						
Short/long	0.23	0.15	0.32	0.07	0.05	0.19

Notes: The cohesion index is calculated as $\sum w_i w_j Z_{i,j} / \sum w_i w_j$, where $Z_{i,j}$ are bilateral variances and w_i weights proportional to GDP; euro area countries without Luxembourg and Greece. Short rate: 3-month interbank rates. Long rate: 10-year government bond rates. Real rates are constructed by subtracting one-year ahead inflation rates. Sample size: 1990:1–2002:2.

Source: Authors' calculations.

Some comparisons with our control groups are interesting. Post-EMU the euro area variances are 0.39 and 0.10, for levels and changes respectively. The comparable values for the control groups are similar or (for short-term rates) higher. In the USA, the variance of the real interest rate differential in level is 0.32, and in first difference is 0.19. These figures are qualitatively the same as in the euro area.

In order to gain further insight into the co-movement of interest rates, it is useful to expand the analysis of variances to the frequency domain. This will allow us to understand whether interest rates co-move in the low frequencies (the long-term trends), in the medium frequencies (over the business cycle), or in the high frequencies. We do so by calculating the spectrum of bilateral interest rate differentials for all country pairs, and by aggregating these densities to a euro area measure with GDP weights as above.[22] The results are provided in Figure 3. As before, we report results for the interest rate differentials calculated from interest rates in levels (left panels) as well as monthly changes of these differentials (right panels).

As usual, the density is shown for a frequency range of zero to π, where zero corresponds to the lowest frequency (the long-run behaviour), and π to the highest. In the intermediate range, a value of 0.5 on the x-axis corresponds to cycles of a frequency of about 12 months, 1.0 about 6 months, and 2.0 about 3 months.

The values on the y-axis indicate how the variance is distributed over the various frequencies, where the area below the spectrum (over the whole frequency range from

[22] For a process y_t, the spectrum at frequency ω is defined as $s_y(\omega) = \frac{1}{2\pi} \sum_{j=-\infty}^{\infty} \gamma_j e^{-i\omega j}$, where $\gamma_j = E(y_t - E(y_t))(y_{t-j} - E(y_t))$, and $i = \sqrt{-1}$. This implies that the integral over the spectrum is equal to the variance of y_t: $\int_{-\pi}^{\pi} s_y(\omega)d\omega = \sigma_y^2$. Since the spectrum is symmetric, it holds that $2\int_0^{\pi} s_y(\omega)d\omega = \sigma_y^2$ (Hamilton, 1994, ch. 6).

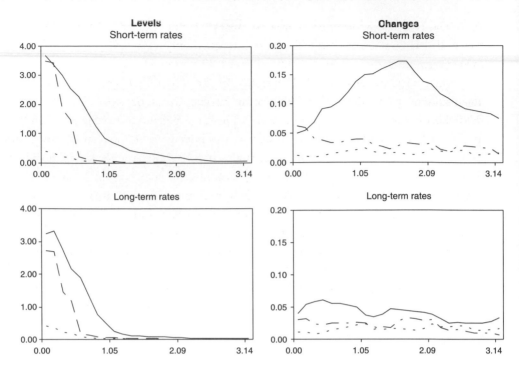

Figure 3. Spectral density of real interest rate differentials within the euro area

Notes: Solid line: 1990–4; long dashed: 1995–8; short dashed: 1999–2002.

$-\pi$ to π) equals the variance. This area shrinks considerably over the three sample periods analysed, which reflects the findings of decreasing variances presented in Table 5. More interestingly, however, we can now analyse the frequencies at which the variance reduction (and thus the interest rate co-movement) occurs.

The charts on the levels show that the variance is concentrated in the lowest frequency ranges (above 6–12 months), in all three periods. This signals that there is a trend in the real rate differentials, arguably due to the convergence process. There is a sharp reduction in the variance at these frequencies as one moves towards subsequent periods, particularly after 1999, signalling that the low frequency components of the variance are being removed as convergence is completed. The calculations with data in terms of changes (right panels) remove the trend component and permit a better inspection of the frequencies relevant for the monetary transmission process.

Focusing first on short-term rates, a hump shape shows up in 1990–4 in the spectrum between 3 and 6 months. This evidence is suggestive. Recalling the timing of foreign exchange crises in the ERM years, particularly the ones of 1992–3, it is plausible that such concentration of variance is due to divergent conduct of monetary policy to counteract exchange-rate tensions. The disappearance of the hump in 1995–8 and 1999–2002 is consistent with this suggestion. In the later periods the spectral density of short real rate differentials flattens, suggesting that the stochastic processes driving short real rates in different euro area countries has approached random noise. The typical flat spectral shape of a white noise is reached only after 1999, however. Moving to long-term rates, the picture is slightly different. The hump characterizing the spectrum in the first period is around 12–24 months. In the subsequent periods the spectrum again flattens, particularly after 1999 (comparison with the previous chart should be made keeping in mind the different scale). The large decline in variance particularly at the low frequencies is interesting insofar as this is likely to be the relevant frequency for firm investment decisions. All this confirms that the convergence in the stochastic processes driving real rates (short and long) took place well before 1999, but that after 1999 there was further progress. After 1999, real rate differentials in the euro area (levels and changes) look a lot like white noise, except that some minor residual trend component is visible in the levels of both short and long-term rates.

To rationalize this evidence[23] we use a simple framework of how the IRC operates in a two-country area without and with monetary union. We start from two simple equations making financial market interest rates and expected inflation conditional on a series of past monetary policy signals $(m_{A,t\text{-}j})$, in a generic country A:

$$r_{A,t} = k_{A,1} + \Sigma\, w_{A,j} m_{A,t-j} + \varepsilon_{A,t} \tag{1}$$

$$\pi^c_{A,t} = k_{A,2} + \Sigma\, h_{A,j} m_{A,t-j} + \eta_{A,t} \tag{2}$$

where $r_{A,t}$ is a nominal rate, $\pi^c_{A,t}$ is expected inflation and $\varepsilon_{A,t}$ and $\eta_{A,t}$ are random shocks, including other factors affecting nominal rates and expected inflation. $k_{A,1}$ and $k_{A,2}$ are constant terms, the first of which incorporates the risk premia existing in interest rates. The parameters $w_{A,j}$ and $h_{A,j}$ represent the transmission process: specifically, $w_{A,j}$ expresses lagged liquidity and expectations effects acting upon the nominal rate, while $h_{A,j}$ denotes the lagged effects of monetary policy on expected inflation. The real rate is the difference between the two:

$$\rho_A = r_A - \pi^c_A - k_A + \Sigma(w_{A,j} - h_{A,j})m_{A,t-j} + (\varepsilon_A - \eta_A) \tag{3}$$

where $k_A = k_{A,1} - k_{A,2}$. Consider two countries, A and B. The real interest differential between them is:

$$\rho_A - \rho_B = k + \Sigma(w_{A,j} - h_{A,j})m_{A,t-j} - \Sigma(w_{B,j} - h_{B,j})m_{B,t-j} + \varepsilon \tag{4}$$

where $k = k_A - k_B$ and $\varepsilon = (\varepsilon_A - \eta_A) - (\varepsilon_B - \eta_B)$.

After A and B form a monetary union, nominal rates are equalized, as are the parameters of the transmission process that affect them. So $r_A = r_B$ and $w_{A,j} = w_{B,j}$ by arbitrage. There is only one monetary shock, m_t. The real interest differential becomes:

[23] Readers puzzled by this post-data rationalization should reflect on the following quote from Sherlock: 'It is a capital mistake to theorise before one has data. Insensibly one begins to twist the facts to suit theories, instead of theories to suit facts.' Doyle (1951, *A Scandal in Bohemia*).

$$\rho_A - \rho_B = \pi_B^e - \pi_A^e = k + \Sigma(h_{B,j} - h_{A,j})m_{t-j} + \varepsilon \tag{5}$$

To verify the similarity of the transmission parameters between A and B, before and after they join the monetary union, ideally one would like to estimate fully specified versions of (1), (2) before and after EMU, and test for equality of the coefficients. As we have argued, there are problems in doing this, mainly linked to the fact that post-EMU data are too short to calculate reliable transmission parameters to financial market rates using time series data.

Our simplified framework follows directly from (4) and (5). The empirical analysis has shown three facts. First, the variances of the interest rate differentials decline over time. Second, if data in levels are considered, most of the decline takes place after 1999, while if data in terms of changes are used, a good deal of the variance reduction takes place in the earlier period 1995–8. Third, the spectra signal convergence to a white noise shape from 1990–4 to 1999–2002, with the period 1995–8 being somewhere in between: after 1999, some residual trend component is still visible in the data in levels. In Equation (4), prior to monetary union, $\rho_A - \rho_B$ is a low-variance white noise only if three conditions are met: (a) $m_{A,t-j} \cong m_{B,t-j}$ (the countries have similar monetary policies); (b) $w_{A,j} = w_{B,j}$ and $h_{A,j} = h_{B,j}$ (the transmission parameters are the same); (c) ε is a low-variance white noise. This is indeed a very stringent set of conditions, which can explain why we find large variances in the first period (pre-1994), and no white noise structure in either data in levels or changes. In Equation (5), $\rho_A - \rho_B$ is a low-variance white noise if (d) $h_{A,j} \cong h_{B,j}$ and (e) $\varepsilon \cong \eta_B - \eta_A$ is a low-variance white noise, assuming that k is indeed a constant. The residual low-frequency component observed in the level data suggests the possibility that the term k in Equation (5) may in fact embody some residual near-linear trend, which reduces to a constant when data are calculated in terms of changes. This seems indeed to be true in our data. Hence our evidence is consistent with condition (d) – the transmission parameters being the same, with some level-convergence still taking place after 1999. We do not exclude that other interpretations may be possible, however.

3.2. Stock market channel

The stock market is a key link of the transmission mechanism according to both monetarist and Keynesian views (see again Mishkin, 1995). Tobin's q theory assigns to stock prices a central role in transmitting policy shocks to firms' investment. At the same time, stock prices also affect the consumer, through wealth effects (see Meltzer, 1995). Structural macroeconometric models of the United States (such as that used by the Federal Reserve Board; see Reifschneider et al., 1999) ascribe to the stock market a major role in the transmission of monetary policy. In Europe, where stock ownership is limited but growing fast, exploring this channel is important. Furthermore, the response of stock prices reveals the markets' view of the effects of monetary policy.

A second reason for looking at the role of the stock market in our case is empirical. We have at our disposal rich high-frequency data on national and euro area-wide stock market prices, including a breakdown by country and economic sectors. We also have a new high-frequency proxy that identifies unexpected monetary policy shocks. This variable – constructed by Ehrmann and Fratzscher (2002) – compares ECB monetary policy decisions with market expectations drawn from a Reuters poll of market participants before each ECB Governing Council meeting.[24] Combining the two, we can identify exogenous monetary policy shocks and obtain precise estimates of the causal effect of monetary policy on the national stock markets. Unfortunately, these high quality data are not available before EMU, so no comparison across time can be made.

We start by analysing the national stock market indices. The focus of our interest is whether the effects on national markets are sufficiently homogeneous. Our maintained prior is that the immediate stock market impact of the news contains information on the longer run effect, relevant from a monetary transmission perspective. To isolate the effect of monetary policy surprises from those of other news, our data set includes snapshots of stock market indices between 12:30 p.m. and 15:30 CET each day. The ECB monetary policy decisions are announced on meeting days of the ECB Governing Council at 13:45. At 14:30, the ECB President's press conference starts. This meeting is a televised session in which the motivations of the policy decision are discussed. By the end of the time window, at 15:30, it can thus be presumed that further information on the meeting's outcome has been incorporated in the market. The figure in the Appendix illustrates these windows and the stock market movements on a particularly interesting day, namely Thursday, 7 November 2002.[25]

The choice of a three-hour window represents an intermediate horizon compared to the existing literature. Andersen et al. (2003) analyse exchange-rate reactions to news using five-minute intervals. However, since asset prices have a tendency to overshoot in the short run, the effects measured at such high frequencies might be overstated. An analysis of daily returns, on the other hand, might underestimate monetary policy effects especially in small samples, since a lot of additional information affects asset markets during the course of a full trading day. Only in very long samples will the additional news cancel out. We would therefore hope that an intermediate horizon

---

[24] We use the mean of the survey as our expectations measure, and define monetary policy surprises as the difference between the announced interest rate decision and this expectations measure. As shown in Ehrmann and Fratzscher (2002), these expectations are unbiased and efficient.

[25] On that day, many market participants expected an interest rate cut by both the Bank of England and the ECB. Note that the Monetary Policy Committee of the Bank of England meets on Wednesday and Thursday at the beginning of each month, and the announcement of its deliberations, at 12:00 GMT, roughly coincides with the closing of the ECB Governing Council meeting (after allowing for time difference). The US Fed had reduced the federal funds target rate the day before by 50 basis points, and markets felt this might have been part of a concerted action with the Bank of England and the ECB. The decision by the Bank of England not to move rates (announced at 13:00 CET) contradicted this speculation, hence market participants apparently reconsidered their expectations of an interest rate cut by the ECB at the time of the Bank of England announcement. In the end both central banks left their policy rates unchanged. The chart shows that the 'negative surprise' in the UK impacts at 13:00 CET both the FTSE and the continental European markets. A similar downward effect follows the ECB announcement. Further adjustments take place subsequently, before and during the ECB press conference.

Table 6. Stock market responses to ECB monetary policy surprises

	β	t-stat
Austria (ATX)	−0.517	−1.248
Belgium (BEL20)	−1.318*	−2.252
Finland (HEX)	−2.585	−1.842
France (CAC40)	−1.775*	−2.263
Germany (DAX)	−2.660**	−3.112
Ireland (ISEQ)	0.551	1.056
Italy (MIB)	−1.812**	−2.648
Netherlands (AEX)	−1.845*	−2.488
Portugal (PSI20)	−2.320**	−4.231
Spain (SMSI)	−0.665	−1.288
Eurostoxx	*−1.938**	*−2.786*

Equality of beta coefficients of national indices with prior from sectoral weights

	χ^2	Significance
All countries	21.206	0.012
Excluding Ireland and Portugal	8.667	0.277
Five large countries	7.886	0.096

Notes: *, ** indicates significance at the 5 and 1% level, respectively. SUR equations, following Pearce and Roley (1983): $\ln(x_t^{15:30}) - \ln(x_t^{12:30}) = \alpha + \beta surp_t + \varepsilon_t$; Sample size: 1 January 1999–14 November 2002.

Source: Authors' calculations.

can approximately capture the relevant effects, by giving markets time to process the new information and settle, without leaving too much time for arrival of further news.

Table 6 shows estimates of the effect of our ECB monetary surprise measure on 10 national stock market indices. We used a Seemingly Unrelated Regression (SUR) model to allow for residual covariance across the indices. The models, though simple, produce estimates that are statistically precise and close to the theoretical priors.[26] The estimated impact of a monetary tightening on stock indices is negative in all 10 countries except Ireland, where it is positive and insignificant. The majority of the slope coefficients are significant. The effect on the area-wide Euro Stoxx, a Dow Jones capitalization-weighted index including a large variety of euro area stocks, shown for comparison, is within the range of the national effects, as one would expect. Focusing on bilateral differences across national coefficients (a measure of how geographically homogeneous the response is) one sees that there are three countries whose estimated coefficients are somewhat far from the average: Germany (higher negative coefficient), Portugal (higher) and Ireland (wrong sign).

One possible explanation for these differences is the sector composition of national stock markets. If economic sectors react to monetary policy differently, and if the sector composition of national markets differ, the responses of national markets could diverge even without asymmetries in the transmission process. We have included in

---

[26] All in all, the empirical literature has not been very successful in measuring the stock market impact of monetary policy. The comprehensive survey by Sellin (2001) which reports contributions up to 1998, concludes that increases in policy rates generally lead to lower stock prices. However, several recent papers, such as Bomfim and Reinhart (2000) and Roley and Sellon (1998), on the USA, conclude otherwise. Bomfim (2000) again finds evidence for the USA that accords with the theoretical priors.

Table 6 tests of cross-country restrictions that take the sector composition into account. Specifically, we reported tests of the hypothesis that differences in the national coefficients are proportional to the 'theoretical' ones, calculated using the sector-level impact effects[27] and data on the sector composition of national indices.[28] The test across all 10 countries for which data exist is accepted at the 1% level, but not at the 5% level. It is comfortably accepted if Portugal and Ireland are excluded. The test of equality across the five largest countries is also accepted.

4. FROM OBSERVATION TO DEDUCTION, AND FURTHER INVESTIGATION

Our observations stop here. There is little more, if anything, our data can tell us. Time for our modern-day Sherlock to return to his flat, fill his pipe, and measure the living room with endless strolls, immersed in impenetrable silence. What inference can be made? Is the case settled?

He would probably start from the most obvious. Banks, a major suspect, have changed something in their behaviour. There seems to be a connection with 'the crime', *post-hoc* and conceivably also a *propter-hoc*. Their key bank decision variables, the prices on the products they offer, have started (quite suddenly indeed, Watson) to behave in a different way at the time one would expect in case of guilt.

Different interpretations are possible. Banks may have reacted to increased pressure from the euro-induced new competitive environment. Has banking become more competitive across countries? There is some evidence of an increase in bank penetration: cross-country interbank lending has increased significantly after 1999, and the interbank market has integrated quickly. But other segments, more important from the viewpoint of the transmission mechanism (like direct lending to cross-border customers) lag behind. Increased bank penetration across borders can, at best, be part of the explanation.

On the other hand, other factors could also explain this change in bank behaviour. Money and financial market interest rates – the main drivers of bank rates – have also begun to move differently; and, as Sherlock would say, one true inference invariably suggests others.[29] Market interest rates have become more stable (except in Germany) and cohesive across borders. This could explain why the pass-through of money market rates to bank rates has increased (except in Germany). True, the *post-hoc* element here is weaker: market interest rates, in real and nominal terms, had already started to move differently in the pre-EMU period 1995–8. But the change strengthened, and became permanent, only after 1999. Cross-country real interest rate comovements within the euro area today mimic closely those observed among US regions. This suggests that also the interest rate channel, another important building block of the transmission process, has changed towards more homogeneity within the area, as one would expect.

[27] Angeloni and Ehrmann (2003) calculate the impact effects of monetary policy shocks on sector stock market indices.

[28] These data are shown on the *Economic Policy* website (www.economic-policy.org).

[29] Doyle (1951, *Silver Blaze*).

If all this holds true, then one would expect to also see changes in the transmission of monetary policy to asset prices after 1999. Present and expected future rates are the discount factors that translate future income flows into current asset prices. We have seen some evidence of cross-country responses of stock markets to monetary shocks. Other things being equal, stronger interest rate co-movements across countries should tend to generate more homogeneous stock price responses across countries, for given expected streams of future dividends. Unfortunately, our data did not allow a comparison across time to be made. But we observed that, after 1999, the impact of monetary policy on stock prices is not too dissimilar across countries. Whether this is due to the reaction of *both* expected future dividends *and* expected future interest rates, or only to the latter, remains an open question.

Is our case closed? We doubt Sherlock would conclude this quite yet. But we do think that he would consider a positive answer to the questions raised at the outset (has the transmission mechanism changed after EMU; is it becoming more homogeneous) as *the most plausible working hypothesis given the current state of knowledge.* He would then probably depart for further investigation. We instead stop here for now, leaving the rest for future research. The transmission of monetary policy in the euro area after EMU is a new research subject. Many promising developments come to mind, especially when more data become available. We just mention some here.

Financial integration in the euro area, in the banking as well as the non-bank financial sectors, particularly in its relation to EMU, needs analysing and monitoring closely. This should provide continuously new evidence also on the monetary transmission mechanism and its changes. Another frontier ahead seems to be the analysis of the impact of EMU on the euro area labour and product markets. Studying the origin and the nature of inflation persistence in the euro area is a crucial first step. Since extended post-EMU data series will be unavailable for some time, in the interim cross-sectional data should be exploited as much as possible. The role of the exchange rate in the euro area transmission process should also be analysed; this is something we have completely set aside in this paper. One should look afresh at this, using recent theories on pass-through and pricing to market as a starting point (see Bacchetta and Van Wincoop, 2002). Furthermore, the behaviour of euro area consumers and specifically their reaction to monetary policy and to financial factors merit further research. Relevant differences in the effect of monetary policy on consumer behaviour between the euro area and the United States have been noted, and call for explanation (see Angeloni et al., 2003b).

Further ahead, the major challenge seems to be the construction of comprehensive models of the euro area, with proper microfoundation and a realistic characterization of the transmission process. There have been good steps in this direction – see Smets and Wouters (2002); Christiano et al. (2003) – but the goal is still very far off. Like Scotland Yard in our detective's tales, model builders are condemned by the nature of their approach always to be last in accounting for new events. Surely their story, when it comes, will be more complete and systematic than the one we have told here.

Discussion

Paul de Grauwe
University of Leuven, Belgium

This paper contains a lot of interesting information about the changes in the transmission process of monetary policies in EMU. As the authors recognize, the short period since the start of EMU puts severe limits on a satisfactory analysis of this issue. The authors have therefore decided to take a piecemeal approach, collecting bits and pieces of evidence and trying to develop a coherent story on the basis of these bits of evidence. There is of course a danger in this approach, in that the detective can be led onto a wrong track and develop a wrong story.

What do the authors establish as facts?

(1) The transmission of monetary policy to bank interest rates (deposit and lending rates) has become stronger: the impact of changes in central bank interest rates on the interest rates applied by commercial banks seems to have increased significantly since 1999. In addition, the authors claim that this transmission from the central bank interest rate to the commercial banks' interest rates has become more homogeneous. I will come back to this latter point because I will want to dispute this.

(2) The effects of monetary policy surprises on share prices are significant and appear at first sight to be relatively homogeneous. However, as the authors stress, the absence of pre-1999 data does not allow us to draw conclusions about the changes in the transmission process since 1999.

My comments are the following.

The transmission of monetary policy to bank interest rates

The authors provide interesting evidence about the transmission of monetary policy shocks (shocks in money market rates) to bank interest rates. However, their claim that this transmission has become more homogeneous is far from established. In Table 1 they show the standard deviations of the response coefficients across countries. These have declined after 1999.[30] It is unclear whether this decline is significant.

---

[30] The authors also show coefficients of variation. These, however, are not appropriate here. The coefficient of variation should only be used when one wants to compare the variation around the mean of two series that have a different dimension. For example when one compares the variation of (the levels) of the dollar/sterling rate with that of the dollar/yen rate, the coefficient of variation should be used and not the standard deviations. However, when one measures the dispersion of the transmission coefficients of monetary policy across countries (which should be between 0 and 1) there is no need to use the coefficient of variation because these transmission coefficients have the same dimension. In addition, and more importantly, the use of the coefficient of variation can lead to very misleading conclusions. The reason is that since the coefficient of variation is defined as the standard deviation divided by the mean it is very sensitive to small changes of the mean when the mean is close to zero. This is generally the case with interest rates, inflation rates, but also with transmission coefficients that come close to 0 as is the case in this paper. Relatively small changes of the mean then affect the coefficient of variation in a highly non-linear way.

For example, it appears that the decline in the dispersion of the impact coefficient is due to the extremely low value of the French impact coefficient prior to 1999. In Table 3, the authors provide significance tests of the degree of equality of the coefficients prior and after 1999. It appears from that table that there is little evidence that the transmission mechanism has become significantly more homogeneous.

Thus, I am tempted to be more cautious than the authors in my conclusion. Although I believe, as the authors do, that EMU contains a dynamic towards more homogeneity, until now there is insufficient evidence for sceptics like me to be convinced that the transmission of monetary policy shocks to bank lending rates has become more homogenous since 1999.

This conclusion may at first sight be inconsistent with other pieces of evidence provided by the authors, which is that there is a convergence of inter-bank rates and government bond rates since the start of EMU.

My explanation is the following. EMU had a strong integrating effect on inter-bank markets. In fact the start of EMU in 1999 fully integrated these markets into just one market where one interest rate prevailed. Similarly, the start of EMU had a strong integrating effect on the government bond market, leading to a strong (but not full) convergence of the government bond rates.

At the same time, however, EMU has had (up to now) little integrating effect on the retail segments of the banking markets. As a result, little convergence is observed in the lending rates that banks charge their customers in different euro zone countries. For the same reason these banks do not react in the same way to changes in monetary policies.

The effects of monetary policy surprises on share prices

The evidence provided here is quite interesting but difficult to interpret as the authors recognize. The main reason is that the absence of pre-1999 data precludes analysing the question of whether a convergence in the response of share prices to monetary policies has occurred.

I would like to make two observations:

(1) My reading of Table 6 suggests that the effect of monetary policy surprises on stock prices is relatively small. I arrive at this conclusion in the following way. From Table 6 we can compute that the mean stock market response to monetary policy surprises is −1.5. I assume that the mean monetary policy surprise is 0.25 (most of the changes in the interest rate decided by the ECB are of that order of magnitude). This means that on average monetary policy surprises led to a change in stock prices of about 0.4%. This is a surprisingly low response.

Incidentally, it would be interesting to report the R^2. This would give us some insight into the question of how much of the variability of the stock prices during the windows analysed by the authors were due to monetary policy surprises.

(2) There might be a lot of asymmetry in the transmission of monetary policy to stock prices across countries. I have also computed the standard deviation of the transmission coefficients across countries is equal to 1.02. This is considerably larger than those of the transmission coefficients from monetary policy to bank lending rates reported in Table 1. Of course, we still do not know whether these stock market responses to monetary policy surprises have converged after 1999. But it is interesting to observe that compared to the bank rate responses to monetary policy shocks, the share price responses appear to be more divergent across the euro zone.

In conclusion, I share the presumption of the authors that EMU will lead to more convergence in the transmission of monetary policies into the financial markets of the euro zone. In fact, this convergence has already happened in the money market and in the government bond markets. However, there is as yet insufficient evidence to claim that a conversion of the transmission of monetary policy has happened in the banking sectors of the euro zone countries. This lack of convergence has much to do with the fact that at the retail level the national banking systems remain fairly segmented in the euro zone.

Given the preponderance of banking finance in the euro zone this lack of convergence in the bank lending transmission limits the potential for a reduction of the asymmetries in the transmission of monetary policy to consumption, investment and output.

David Miles
Imperial College London, and CEPR

This paper uses recent evidence to assess whether there have been any changes in the monetary transmission mechanism within the Euro area. There is an enormous literature on the money transmission mechanism within developed economies. Much of that literature, and nearly all of it from the last 10 years, has involved estimating vector autoregression (VAR) models and looking at responses to what are called monetary policy shocks. This strikes me as a very unsatisfactory literature. The results always seem hard to interpret: the ranking of countries by sensitivity to interest rates is almost random and does not fit in with priors. Identification assumptions necessary to get any results seem to make a huge difference to models. And these VAR models are essentially a black box – they tell us little about the precise mechanisms at work within the overall transmission mechanism.

The paper by Angeloni and Ehrmann is admirable because it tries to look inside that black box. It focuses on some very specific parts of the transmission mechanism. In particular:

(1) The link between rates under the control of the relevant central banks (essentially short-term money market rates) and rates that affect businesses and households, namely bank borrowing and lending rates.
(2) The impact of unanticipated changes in interest rates on asset prices – specifically the impact upon stock prices.

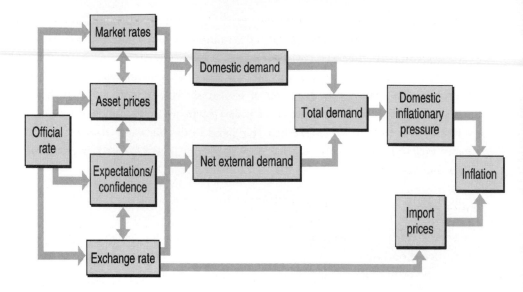

Figure 4. Stylized diagram of the transmission mechanism

The task the authors set themselves is to investigate whether these effects have changed since monetary union and how homogeneous such effects now are across the euro area.

It is important to emphasize at the outset what the paper does not do. By focusing on some very specific parts of the transmission mechanism it misses out most of the crucial links in the overall process connecting changes in monetary policy to the ultimate impacts upon the macroeconomic aggregates that matter – output, employment, unemployment and inflation. There is no evidence in this paper on how interest rate changes affect spending in different countries. There is no evidence on how changes in central bank rates affect the value of the currency – something which may generate significant cross-country differences in transmission mechanisms; nor is there any evidence on links through housing markets, which is another area where cross-country differences are likely to be significant. There are good reasons why the authors do not address these issues. But what we are left with is an analysis that really focuses on only a small number of the links shown in Figure 4 below, which describes the overall transmission mechanism. In effect, the authors are only looking at the links between the official rate and market rates and between the official rate and one particular set of asset prices – they are focusing on two of the arrows that are in the left-most part of the stylized diagram below of the monetary policy transmission mechanism.

What the authors find is that there seems to be a larger and somewhat more homogeneous impact response on commercial interest rates of changes in central bank rates since 1999. This isn't really a very surprising result. Now commercial bank rates across the euro area are responding to the same signal from the *single* central bank. It would be surprising if expectations of the degree of permanence of a European central bank rate change should be systematically different in different parts of the monetary union. Before 1999 central banks across what is now the euro area were setting rates by reference to local conditions, so it is not surprising that the impact of those central bank decisions on commercial bank rates was rather different across countries. And, because rates were more volatile than they have been since 1999, it is not surprising that on average responses of commercial bank rates were somewhat lower. The key question here is, does this tell us much about the degree to which transmission mechanisms are now similar? It is not very clear to me that it does.

Nominal rate divergence at the short end of the maturity spectrum in the euro area has, of course, all but disappeared. This is a fairly obvious implication of the formation of a monetary union. It is more interesting that the authors find that there has been a significant increase in the degree of convergence of real rates of interest. And it is less obvious that this should have happened. It implies that actual, and probably also expected, inflation rates have also converged. But once again it is not obvious that this tells us that the transmission mechanism is now fairly homogeneous. It is, however, at least suggestive. (If transmission mechanisms were wildly different we would expect actual inflation rates not to be very close with a single interest rate). But, of course, we have only had a few years of experience since the monetary union was formed and so if overall transmission mechanisms remained rather different it is too early to expect this inevitably to have shown up in substantial divergence in inflation rates.

There are other interesting snippets of evidence in the paper. There is some evidence, for example, of a convergence in the original maturity of loan contracts. This is illuminating but once again does not really tell us anything firm about convergence in transmission mechanisms. The original maturity of the length of loans is far less relevant than the duration of those loans. I believe the evidence in the paper to be about the original maturity of loans, rather than about duration. In Spain and the UK the majority of mortgage lending remains at floating rates. The maturity of those loans is long, the duration is not. In Germany mortgage loans tend to be of shorter maturity than in the UK, but since they are primarily fixed rate loans the duration is much longer. Differences in duration matter much more for the transmission mechanism than do differences in the term over which the loan should be repaid.

Toward the end of their paper the authors look at the response of stock prices to unexpected changes in interest rates. The impact effects across countries do not really look that similar; although if we exclude some of the main outliers (which include Germany and Ireland) the differences across the remaining countries are not statistically very significant. But what we are trying to gauge here is whether there has been some convergence in transmission mechanisms since monetary union. It is a great shame here that there is no evidence on the sensitivity of asset prices to unexpected rate changes pre-1999.

The authors also note, early in the paper, that there has been some increase in mergers and acquisitions and slightly more cross-border flows in banking within the euro area. But once again the link from this evidence to the issue of whether there has been overall convergence in transmission mechanisms is rather weak. To give a rather trivial example, the fact that Hong Kong Shanghai Bank Corporation bought Midland Bank in the UK some years ago really has very little to do with whether the UK monetary transmission mechanism has become more or less similar to that of Hong Kong. And the fact that US banks lend for mortgages in the UK most certainly does not make the products they sell similar to those offered in the US mortgage market. They are quite different.

The interesting questions about the monetary transmission mechanism in the euro area are all about the extent to which a change in European Central Bank rates affects demand and prices differently across member countries. Whether those differences are diminishing as a result of the monetary union and financial markets integration is really the central question. In this paper we have some suggestive facts about this but we do not have killer facts.

Panel discussion

Carlo Favero pointed out that the convergence of term premiums might simply be a consequence of the elimination of exchange rate risk. One remedy could be to look at the pass-through for long-term rates. However, his own research had shown that term premiums collapse for the long-term rates as well. He urged the authors to control for the intra-day fluctuation in the US stock market when investigating the impact of monetary policy shocks on stock prices. He also pointed out that the paper of Bartolini and Prati suggested the need to distinguish between rate hikes and cuts. David Begg suggested estimating VARs before and after 1999 instead of using survey data, because he had doubts about the quality of the survey data as an estimate of the size of the monetary policy surprise. Michael Ehrmann replied that though the Reuters data had weaknesses, the literature had found them to outperform market-based measures for the euro area and the USA. Moreover, the focus of the paper was not on the size of the surprise but its homogeneity.

Ghikas Hardouvelis urged the authors to extend the empirical study to bank-level data in order to use as much cross-sectional variation as possible, given that small magnitude of the time variation. This would allow them to control for such factors as bank size, asset and liability allocation. Concerning the analysis of monetary surprises on stock markets, he argued that Ireland might be an outlier because in the Irish case restrictive monetary policy can be good news since it contains inflation and reduces the risk premium. Thus, it would be interesting to rank countries with respect to their inflation rate and check whether there is something to this story.

Mike Artis pointed out that it is not so clear why convergence in transmission mechanisms is desirable if the propagation of shocks differs across countries. Moreover, one important component that might have induced convergence of transmission across countries had ceased to exist since 1999: the dominant idiosyncratic monetary policy of the Bundesbank which tried to give a signal to wage setters by a particular conservative inflation target.

Winfried Koeniger followed Mike Artis's remarks by adding that it would be interesting to investigate whether the heterogeneity in the transmission mechanism addresses the structural heterogeneity of countries or if it exacerbates national or regional asymmetries.

APPENDIX

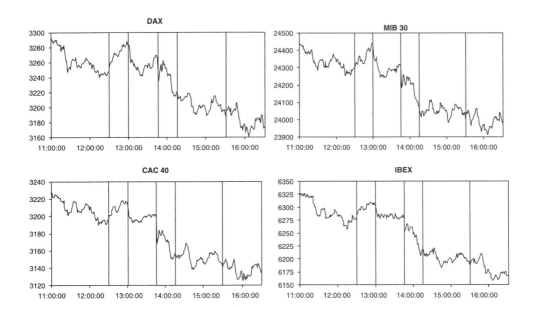

Figure A1. Stock market indices on 7 November 2002, 11:00–16:30

Notes: First vertical line: start of time window at 12:30; second vertical line: Bank of England announcement at 13:00; third vertical line: ECB announcement at 13:45; fourth vertical line: start of ECB press conference at 14:15; fifth vertical line: end of time window.

REFERENCES

Andersen, T.G., T. Bollerslev, F.X. Diebold and C. Vega (2003). 'Micro effects of macro announcements: real-time price discovery in foreign exchange', *American Economic Review*, 93(1), 38–62.

Angeloni, I., and M. Ehrmann (2003). 'Monetary policy transmission in the euro area: any changes after EMU?', ECB Working Paper Series, No. 240.

Angeloni, I., A. Kashyap and B. Mojon (eds.) (2003a). *Monetary Policy Transmission in the Euro Area*, Cambridge University Press, Cambridge, forthcoming.

Angeloni, I., A. Kashyap, B. Mojon and D. Terlizzese (2003b). 'The output composition puzzle: a difference in the monetary transmission mechanism in the Euro area and the US', *Journal of Money Credit and Banking*, forthcoming.

Bacchetta, P. and E. Van Wincoop (2002). 'A theory of the currency denomination of international trade', ECB Working Paper No. 177.

Bernanke, B. and M. Gertler (1995). 'Inside the black box: the credit channel of monetary policy transmission', *Journal of Economic Perspectives*, 9, 27–48.

Bernanke, B., M. Gertler and S. Gilchrist (1999). 'The financial accelerator in a quantitative business cycle framework', *Handbook of Macroeconomics*, Vol. 1c.

Bomfim, A.N. (2000). 'Pre-announcement effects, news, and volatility: monetary policy and the stock market', Board of Governors Finance and Economics Discussion Paper No. 2000–50.

Bomfim, A.N. and V. Reinhart (2000). 'Making news: financial market effects of Federal Reserve disclosure practices', Board of Governors Finance and Economics Discussion Paper No. 2000–14.

Borio, C.E.V. (1995). 'The structure of credit to the non-government sector and the transmission mechanism of monetary policy: a cross-country comparison'. BIS Working Paper No. 24.

Cecchetti, S. (2001). 'Legal structure, financial structure and the monetary policy transmission mechanism', in Deutsche Bundesbank (ed.), *The Monetary Transmission Process*. Palgrave, Basingstoke.

Calvo, G. and C. Reinhart (2000). 'Fear of floating', NBER Working Paper No. 7993.

Christiano, L., R. Motto and M. Rostagno, (2002). 'Banking and financial frictions in a dynamic, general equilibrium model', mimeo.

De Bondt, G., B. Mojon and N. Valla (2003). 'Term structure and the sluggishness of retail bank rates in euro area countries', mimeo, ECB.

Doyle, A.C. (1951). *Sherlock Holmes, Selected Stories*, Oxford University Press, Oxford.

Ehrmann, M. and M. Fratzscher (2002). 'Interdependence between the euro area and the US: what role for EMU?', ECB Working Paper No. 200.

Ehrmann, M., L. Gambacorta, J. Martinez-Pages, P. Sevestre and A. Worms (2003). 'Financial systems and the role of banks in monetary policy transmission in the euro area', forthcoming in I. Angeloni, A. Kashyap and B. Mojon (eds.), *Monetary Policy Transmission in the Euro Area*, Cambridge University Press, Cambridge.

Fagan, G., J. Henry and R. Mestre (2001). 'An area-wide model for the euro area', ECB Working Paper No. 42.

Guiso, L., A. Kashyap, F. Panetta and D. Terlizzese (1999). 'Will a common European monetary policy have asymmetric effects?', *Federal Reserve Bank of Chicago Economic Perspectives* 23(4), 56–75.

Hamilton, J.D. (1994). *Time Series Analysis*, Princeton University Press, Princeton.

Hannan, T.H. and A.N. Berger (1991). 'The rigidity of prices: evidence from the banking industry', *American Economic Review* 81, 938–45.

Hartmann, P., M. Manna and A. Manzanares (2001). 'The microstructure of the euro money market', *Journal of International Money and Finance* 20(6), 895–948.

Kashyap, A.K. and J.C. Stein (1997). 'The role of banks in monetary policy: a survey with implications for the European Monetary Union', *Federal Reserve Bank of Chicago Economic Perspectives*, September–October, 2–18.

Kieler, M. and T. Saarenheimo (1998). 'Differences in monetary policy transmission? A case not closed', *European Commission Economic Papers* No. 132.

Kuttner, K.N. (2001). 'Monetary policy surprises and interest rates: evidence from the Fed funds futures market', *Journal of Monetary Economics* 47, 523–44.

Leamer, E. (1978). *Specification Searches: Ad Hoc Inference with Nonexperimental Data*, J. Wiley & Sons.

Meltzer, A.H. (1995). 'Monetary, credit and (other) transmission processes: a monetarist perspective', *Journal of Economic Perspectives* 9, 49–72.

Mihov, I. (2001). 'Monetary policy implementation and the transmission in the European Monetary Union', *Economic Policy*, 33, 369–402.

Mishkin, F. (ed.) (1995). 'Symposium on the monetary transmission mechanism', *Journal of Economic Perspectives* 9(4), Fall, 3–10.

Neumark, D. and S.A. Sharpe (1992). 'Market structure and the nature of price rigidity: evidence from the market for consumer deposits', *Quarterly Journal of Economics* 107, 657–80.

Pearce, D.K. and V.V. Roley (1983). 'The reaction of stock prices to unanticipated changes in money: a note', *Journal of Finance* 38(4), 1323–33.

Peersman, G. and F. Smets (2003). 'The monetary transmission mechanism in the euro area: more evidence from VAR analysis', forthcoming in I. Angeloni, A. Kashyap and B. Mojon (eds.), *Monetary Policy Transmission in the Euro Area*, Cambridge University Press, Cambridge.

Reifschneider, D., R. Tetlow and J. Williams (1999). 'Aggregate disturbances, monetary policy, and the macroeconomy: The FRB/US perspective', *Federal Reserve Bulletin* (January), 1–19.

Roley, V.V. and G.H. Sellon (1998). 'Market reaction to monetary policy non-announcements', Federal Reserve Bank of Kansas City Working Paper No. 98–06.

Sapienza, P. (2002). 'The effects of banking mergers on loan contracts', *Journal of Finance*, 57, 329–67.

Sellin, P. (2001). 'Monetary policy and the stock market: theory and empirical evidence', *Journal of Economic Surveys* 15(4), 491–541.

Smets, F. and R. Wouters (2002). 'An estimated stochastic dynamic general equilibrium model of the euro area', ECB Working Paper No. 171.

Smets, F. and R. Wouters (2003). 'Shocks and frictions in US and Euro area business cycles: a Bayesian DSGE approach', EABCN Workshop in Madrid (ECB, mimeo), March 2003.

Van Els, P., A. Locarno, J. Morgan and J.P. Villetelle (2003). 'Monetary policy transmission in the euro area: what do aggregate and national structural models tell us?', forthcoming in I. Angeloni, A. Kashyap and B. Mojon (eds.), *Monetary Policy Transmission in the Euro Area*, Cambridge University Press, Cambridge.

Government bond spreads

SUMMARY

We provide evidence that the movements in yield differentials between euro zone government bonds explained by changes in international risk factors – as measured by banking and corporate risk premiums in the United States – are more pronounced for bonds issued by Italy and Spain. Liquidity factors play a smaller role, so policies meant to increase financial market efficiency do not appear sufficient to deliver a 'seamless' bond market in the euro area. The risk of default is a small but important component of yield differentials movements, which signal market perceptions of fiscal vulnerability, impose market discipline on national fiscal policies, and may be reduced only by further convergence in debt ratios.

— Lorenzo Codogno, Carlo Favero and Alessandro Missale

Yield spreads on EMU government bonds

Lorenzo Codogno, Carlo Favero and Alessandro Missale

Bank of America, London; IGIER, Università Bocconi and CEPR; Università di Milano

1. INTRODUCTION

By eliminating exchange rate risk between the currencies of participating member states, the inception of economic and monetary union (EMU) in January 1999 created the conditions for a substantially more integrated public debt market in the euro area. However, interest rates on euro-denominated bonds issued by different governments have not fully converged. Spreads between them may reflect differences in liquidity, as bonds that can be traded immediately with low transaction costs and minimum price changes can offer lower yields in equilibrium,[1] and/or differences in the creditworthiness of sovereign issuers.

This paper expands the results of the research project for the EC Directorate-General for Economic and Financial Affairs: 'The Decomposition of Observed Spreads in the Euro Area Government Bond Market' for which financial support from the European Commission is gratefully acknowledged. We thank the officials at the following institutions: Austrian Federal Financing Agency, Belgian Ministry of Finance, Bundesschuldenverwaltung, Dutch Agency of the Ministry of Finance, Finnish State Treasury, French Ministry of the Economy, Finances and Industry, Instituto de Gestão do Crédito Público of Portugal, Irish National Treasury Management Agency, Italian Ministry of the Treasury, Public Debt Management Office of Greece, Spanish Ministry of Economy and Finance, Bank of America, and MTS. None of the institutions mentioned above are responsible for the contents of this paper, which reflects our opinions only. We are indebted to Francesco Giavazzi, Richard Portes, Marcel Thum, all the participants at the *Economic Policy* Meetings in Athens and anonymous referees for valuable comments and suggestions. Andrea Carriero provided outstanding research assistance.
Giuseppe Bertola was the Managing Editor in charge of this paper.

[1] Gómez-Puig (2003) finds an important role for liquidity as measured by bid-ask spreads in a static panel where credit ratings identify default risk and relative levels of debt are taken as a proxy for market depth.

The aim of this paper is to study the determinants of observed yield differentials in the euro zone government bond markets. New evidence is provided on the relative importance of credit risk and liquidity by examining the role of macroeconomic fiscal fundamentals and liquidity indicators in explaining movements in yield differentials. Following Blanco (2001), we build on findings of the empirical literature on sovereign bond spreads of emerging markets, according to which spreads are sensitive to US risk factors and interest rates (see e.g. Arora and Cerisola, 2001; Barnes and Cline, 1997; Eichengreen and Mody, 2000; Kamin and Von Kleist, 1999). Then, we assess the importance of credit risk by testing whether the impact of exogenous international factors depends on local fiscal fundamentals, which are represented by the debt-to-GDP ratios.

Distinguishing between the credit risk and liquidity components of interest rate spreads has important implications for policy-making and for financial markets.

To the extent that yield spreads reflect differences in credit standings, the Stability and Growth Pact (SGP) and the European fiscal framework appear insufficient to ensure that all member states have the same creditworthiness from the market point of view. Yield differentials are important indicators of market perceptions of fiscal vulnerability and, since higher bond yields imply higher debt service costs, impose market discipline on national governments' fiscal policies. The impact of even small differentials can of course be substantial in countries like Belgium and Italy, where the debt exceeds GDP, and even a tenth of a percent spread (10 basis points) increases government outlays by more than 0.1% of GDP. The kind of runaway fiscal policies that the SGP tries to rule out and its consequent market reaction has not been recorded over the past few years. However, if even limited changes in fiscal positions as those recently observed affect yield differentials, it is sensible to expect that the impact of lax fiscal policies would be much stronger. This has important policy implications: it suggests that expansionary fiscal policies could lead to substantially higher debt service costs and thus that the scope would be limited even in the post-EMU environment.

To the extent that yield spreads instead depend on differences in liquidity of government bonds, they merely reflect the relative effectiveness of debt management policies in improving liquidity and differences in market microstructures. Policy implications would then depend on the sources of liquidity premiums. If yield differentials can be explained by the size of the overall debt issued by a specific member state, again only structural convergence could lead them to disappear. If instead yield differentials reflect specific features of primary markets where bonds are issued, such as the auction mechanism or the issuance calendar, as well as the degree of primary and secondary market efficiency, there is scope for policy action to narrow differentials further, and appropriate cost-minimizing debt management can lead to a full convergence of yields.

Understanding the determinants of yield spreads is also crucial in assessing the prospects for the European bonds market. If bonds issued by different member states continue to be perceived as imperfect substitutes, the goal of creating one market for the 'same bond' as large and liquid as the US bond market would be frustrated. However, whether this is a desirable aim depends on the reason for the segmentation.

If yield differentials were explained by differences in liquidity, their elimination would certainly be a sign of higher efficiency. If, instead, yield differentials reflected different default risks across states, they would be useful indicators for an efficient allocation of funds and a deterrent for irresponsible fiscal policies. And this may be considered as a more important goal than creating a market for the 'same bond'.

Market participants and member state debt managers appear to believe that EMU yield differentials are mostly due to liquidity factors. In order to reduce borrowing costs, debt managers have introduced substantial, sometimes costly, innovations that should have enhanced the liquidity of their bonds (see Favero *et al.*, 1999). In particular, with the launch of the euro in 1999, a number of governments have extended the time available for second-round non-competitive bidding, when specialists (the reference institutions in the primary market) are allowed to buy bonds at the average price of first-round competitive auctions. Governments have also launched repurchase programmes in order to buy back old illiquid issues in exchange for benchmark bonds. More recently, repo facilities (of the last resort type) at the Treasury have been provided to market makers. Distinguishing between credit risk and liquidity components could also help in assessing the merits of such policies.

Our analysis of yield differentials in the Euro area, however, suggests that market perceptions of default risk are a relatively important component of spreads.

2. YIELD DIFFERENTIALS IN THE EURO AREA

Interest rates on government bonds issued by EMU member states converged steadily in the 1990s as the introduction of the Euro approached. Figure 1 shows that

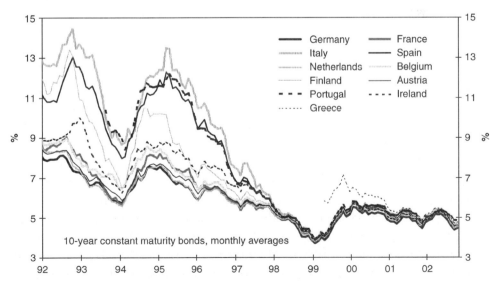

Figure 1. Government bond yields in the euro area

Note: Yields are in percentage annual terms.

Source: Datastream/Thomson Financial.

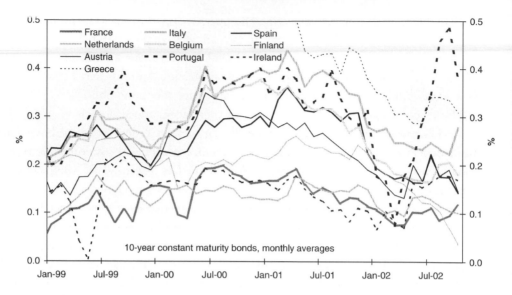

Figure 2. Post-EMU spreads of euro area versus German 10-year bond yields

Notes: Yield differentials are presented in percentage annual terms and refer to the 10-year maturity of the term structure of interest rates, hence are not affected by the small differences in the residual life to maturity of benchmark 10-year maturity bonds, the most actively traded maturity in the euro zone government securities market. German bond yields are taken as the reference rates since German bonds have maintained their benchmark status and have continued to display lower yields.

Source: Datastream/Thomson Financial.

Table 1. Average 10-year government bond yield spread versus Germany

Basis points, period Jan. 1999/Dec. 2002	AUS	BEL	FIN	FRA	GRE	IRE	ITA	NET	POR	SPA
Yield differential	24.3	28.1	19.0	13.8	54.9	14.6	32.5	13.6	32.2	25.4

Source: Datastream/Thomson Financial.

by January 1999 differences across benchmark government bond yields had largely, but not completely, vanished.[2]

Yield differentials for the EMU period are shown in Figure 2, and Table 1 reports average yield spreads for that period. Four years after EMU inception, differentials are still positive, and point to non-trivial differences in credit and/or liquidity premiums. Over the period 1999–2002, the differences between 10-year government bond yields of Germany and the other EMU member states were about 14 basis points on average in the case of France and the Netherlands, and ranged up to 32 basis points on average in the case of Italy and Portugal. Although these differences appear small, they have non-trivial consequences for public finances. For instance, if applied to the whole stock of Italian debt, the recorded yield spreads would account for additional government outlays in excess of 0.3% of GDP.

[2] For a detailed discussion on benchmark status see Dunne *et al.* (2002).

Before EMU, yield differentials within Europe were determined by four main factors:

(1) expected exchange rate movements and exchange rate risk,
(2) different tax treatments and controls on capital movements,
(3) liquidity, and
(4) default (or credit) risk.

Exchange rate factors were eliminated in January 1999 for EMU countries, and tax treatments were harmonized before monetary union, while controls on capital movements had been removed long before that. The other two factors, however, remain relevant.

As regards liquidity, bonds that can be traded immediately at low transaction costs and with minimum price changes, even in adverse market conditions, can offer lower yields to investors in equilibrium. Liquidity may vary across sovereign issues depending on trading volumes, the amounts of bonds outstanding, the trading activity of market makers, and the efficiency of the secondary market. Bonds, especially in the 10-year maturity segment, are highly standardized products, but outstanding amounts vary considerably across sovereign borrowers depending on country and debt dimensions. Therefore, issuing policies may play an important role. Secondary market character-istics such as admission and trading rules or clearing and settlement procedures may equally be critical for liquidity, and especially the willingness of market makers to quote two-way prices and stand ready to satisfy buying and selling orders. The incentives to trade and invest in specific bonds may also depend on the availability of hedging and financing instruments, such as liquid and efficient future contracts and efficient repurchase agreement markets.

As regards credit (or default) risk, namely the risk that the country may not honour, in part or in full, its obligations, it depends crucially on current and future stated and hidden debt, and debt sustainability. Debt sustainability depends on expected budget surpluses/deficits, as well as future economic activity and interest rates, which in turn are affected by domestic and international factors and policies. EMU member states have lost the option of printing money to pay for their debts, so credit risk may have become even more important even as the exchange risk disappeared. Moreover, fiscal rules such as the Stability and Growth Pact may change the market perception of default risk, and thus have an impact on interest rates (see, for example, Poterba and Reuben, 2001).

3. EMPIRICAL MODELS OF YIELD SPREADS BEFORE AND AFTER EMU

Some aspects of both credit risk and liquidity do not change over the period considered, and this makes it difficult to identify the determinants of average yield differentials. Hence, the goal of our analysis is to identify the relative importance of liquidity and default premiums in explaining fluctuations, rather than levels of yield differentials. This is accomplished by estimating the impact of macroeconomic fiscal fundamentals

Table 2. Asset swap spreads and swap differentials

	AUS	BEL	FIN	FRA	GRE	IRE	ITA	NET	POR	SPA
Sample June 1991–December 1995										
Total yield differential	n.a.	0.787	n.a.	0.536	n.a.	n.a.	4.821	0.107	n.a.	3.744
Relative asset swap spread	n.a.	0.199	n.a.	−0.053	n.a.	n.a.	0.966	0.005	n.a.	0.133
Swap differential	n.a.	0.588	n.a.	0.589	n.a.	n.a.	3.855	0.102	n.a.	3.610
Sample January 1996–December 1998										
Total yield differential	0.090	0.189	0.436	0.029	n.a.	n.a.	1.577	−0.027	1.107	1.180
Relative asset swap spread	0.094	0.147	0.022	0.061	n.a.	n.a.	0.246	0.008	0.192	0.200
Swap differential	−0.004	0.042	0.413	−0.031	n.a.	n.a.	1.331	−0.035	0.914	0.980
Sample January 1999–December 2002										
Total yield differential	0.243	0.281	0.190	0.138	0.549	0.146	0.325	0.136	0.322	0.254
Relative asset swap spread	0.243	0.281	0.190	0.138	0.469	0.146	0.325	0.136	0.322	0.254
Swap differential	0.000	0.000	0.000	0.000	0.080	0.000	0.000	0.000	0.000	0.000

Source: Datastream/Thomson Financial.

and international risk factors on yield differentials, and by testing whether the impact of international factors depends on local fiscal fundamentals. In fact, liquidity factors should be, by their nature, local and not directly related to changes in either international factors or macroeconomic fundamentals.

The analysis is complicated by the fact that liquidity-related variables affect yields at high frequencies, while risk-related variables reflect slow-moving economic fundamentals. The latter are only observed at low frequencies, and their effect may only be detected in long time series. Moreover, bond yield differentials are affected by different factors in the pre-EMU and post-EMU sample, and data on liquidity-related variables are only available for 2002.

We deal with these difficulties by focusing first on the effect of fundamentals using monthly series, and then considering the effect of liquidity factors in daily data. Importantly, we make an attempt towards keeping consistency between our two specifications.

3.1. Monthly data

Since the sample of monthly data includes pre-EMU and post-EMU observations, we need to remove from the former the component reflecting expected exchange rate fluctuations and exchange rate risk. To this end, we use the difference in 10-year fixed interest rates from the term structure estimated on swap contracts denominated in different currencies. Interest rates on swaps are virtually free from the risk of default of sovereign issuers. Swap contracts are private agreements between financial institutions (typically investment banks) to exchange a flow of interest payments at a fixed rate for one at a floating rate, usually the six-month LIBOR. The risk of swap contracts differs from that associated with a position in government bonds. An interest rate swap does not involve any principal to be potentially lost by any of the two counterparts in case of default of the other. The cost borne by a bank if the counterpart does not honour the contract, is the loss represented by the current market value of the net flow of future interest payments which could be very different from the initial one. The counterpart risk for swap rates denominated in different currencies should be the same, since the investment banks who deal in swaps operate in all markets relevant to us. Thus, the counterpart risk component of swap rates should net out in swap rate differentials. Indeed, Figure 3 shows that differentials between fixed interest rates on swaps converged towards zero as the probability of EMU increased from 1996 to 1999. Table 2 shows summary statistics on yield spreads, which separates the exchange risk components from the total yield differentials.

Hence, as in Favero et al. (1997), we measure the component of yield differentials not related to exchange rate factors as:

$$RAS_t^i = \left(R_t^i - R_t^{GER}\right) - \left(RSW_t^i - RSW_t^{GER}\right) \tag{1}$$

where RAS_t^i denotes the relative asset swap spread of country i, R_t^i and R_t^{GER} are the yields to maturity of 10-year bonds issued by country i and by Germany respectively,

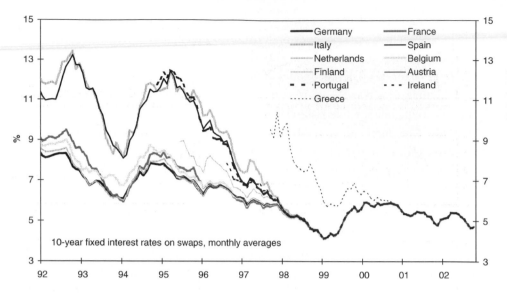

Figure 3. Fixed interest rate on interest rate swaps in the euro area

Note: Swap rates are in percentage annual terms.

Source: Datastream/Thomson Financial.

and RSW_t^i and RSW_t^{GER} are the 10-year fixed interest rates on swaps denominated in currency i and in deutschemarks respectively. It is worth noting that the relative asset swap, RAS_{t}^i, coincides with the yield differential in the EMU period.[3] We use RAS_t^i as the dependent variable in an empirical model aimed at identifying the relevance of liquidity and credit-risk related factors.

Total yield differentials and relative asset swap spreads are plotted in Figure 4, and show that the exchange rate factor did heavily affect yield differentials in the pre-EMU era, as observed by Favero *et al.* (1997) and Blanco (2001). Relative asset swap spreads show a much more homogenous time series behaviour. This is consistent with the hypothesis that netting out the exchange rate factor from yield differentials allows data coming from the pre-1999 and the post-1999 regimes to be pooled sensibly. We then implement the following empirical model on monthly data:

$$RAS_t^i = \lambda RAS_{t-1}^i + (1 - \lambda)[d_t^i(\beta_1 + \beta_2 Z_t) + \beta_3 Z_t] + (1 - \lambda)\beta_0 + u_t^i \qquad (2)$$

---

[3] As discussed by Favero *et al.* (1997) a direct measure of the default factor can be obtained by comparing the yields of bonds issued in the *same currency* by a country i and by a different sovereign issuer. In this vein, Giovannini and Piga (1994) used the yield differential between two dollar-denominated bonds: one issued by the Republic of Italy and one, of roughly the same maturity, issued by the World Bank (or by the US Treasury). This measure is, however, unsatisfactory for both empirical and technical reasons. Just as supranational issues, the bonds issued by the Republic of Italy on the global or on the Euro-syndicated market are not very liquid, as they are held by long-term investors, including central banks, are not the object of short-term arbitrage trading, are intermittent in time and do not cover all relevant maturities. The latter factor is crucial for international comparisons because, when issues are sparse, term structure effects could contaminate the data. Furthermore, unlike domestic bonds, foreign issues, and especially issues in the 'global' market, have legal guarantees for creditors (in the case of global issues in the United States, for instance, a US court is competent in the case of litigation).

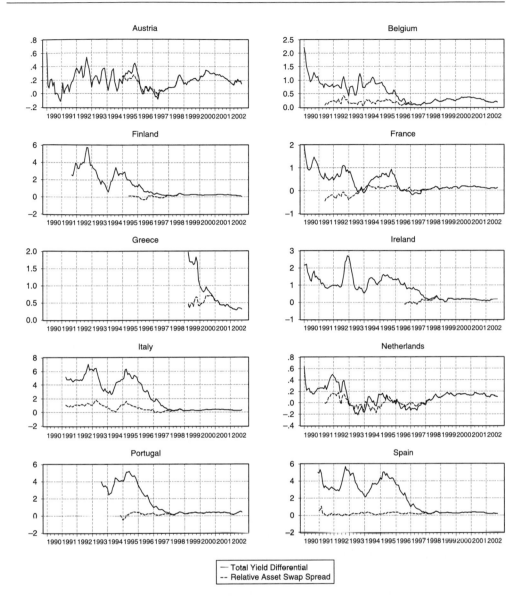

Figure 4. Yield differentials and relative asset swap spreads in the euro area

Sources: Datastream/Thomson Financial and our calculations.

where RAS_t^i is the relative asset swap spread for country i, d_t^i is the (log) deviation of country i debt-to-GDP ratio from Germany's debt-to-GDP ratio, and $\mathcal{Z}_t$ is a vector containing exogenous variables measuring or approximating risk premiums.[4] Our baseline specification for $\mathcal{Z}_t$ includes $(R_t^{SP,US} - R_t^{US})$, the spread between 10-year fixed interest rates on US swaps and the yield on 10-year US government bonds and

---

[4] We have considered other local fiscal fundamentals besides debt ratios, and in particular relative budget deficits and relative amounts of total government securities outstanding, but they were not significant once we accounted for debt ratios. We have not included future expected liabilities arising from pension systems since we have been unable to find time series of such obligations.

$(R_t^{C,US} - R_t^{US})$, the spread between the yield on Moody's Seasoned AAA US corporate bonds and the yield on 10-year US government bonds.

The model allows for slow dynamic adjustment to a long-term equilibrium value of RAS_t^i, and explains relative asset swaps in terms of exogenous factors which capture risk premiums (specifically, banking and corporate sector risk premiums in the United States). This specification is not motivated by a theoretical model, but by empirical evidence that risk tends to affect bond yields proportionally rather than additively. As international risk increases, all yield differentials generally widen. In particular, the empirical literature on sovereign bond spreads in emerging markets shows that the yield on US government bonds and/or the slope of the US yield curve are main determinants of sovereign spreads (e.g. Eichengreen and Mody, 2000; Barnes and Cline, 1997; Kamin and Von Kleist, 1999). Blanco (2001) also uses yields on US corporate bonds as a proxy for global credit risk in modelling yields on euro zone government securities. Our choice of proxies is also consistent with the evidence produced by Arora and Cerisola (2001), who document that tightening of US monetary policy and increasing uncertainty on the future stance significantly widens bond spreads of emerging markets. The dependence of yield differentials on proxies for international risk would be consistent with the results by Dungey et al. (2000), who show strong evidence in favour of the presence of a common international factor in many yield differentials.

The Z_t variables appear in the regression both linearly, and interacted with the deviation of country i debt-to-GDP ratio from Germany's debt-to-GDP ratio. This captures the idea that international risk affects yield differentials because euro zone government bonds are imperfect substitutes, either because of liquidity or because of different default risk.

The linear terms are necessary, as international factors might affect the relative asset swap spread either because of 'structural' differences in liquidity or differences in non-varying unobservable fundamentals, such as the reputation of the issuing govern-ments. Hence, the coefficients capture changes in yield spreads that can be attributed to non-varying differences in either liquidity or credit risk. In addition, such terms might capture unobservable variations in fiscal vulnerability. This would be the case if, for example, banking and corporate sector risk premiums were a leading indicator of deteriorated economic conditions and thus lower expected budget surpluses.

Interactions between international risk variables, Z_t and relative debt ratios are relevant only to the extent that the impact of global risk on yield differentials depend on differences between country i fiscal fundamentals and Germany's fundamentals. Therefore, the interaction term identifies changes in yield spreads that can be entirely attributed to default risk.

Finally, we control for an independent effect of fiscal fundamentals by entering debt ratios linearly in the regressions for the relative asset swap spread.[5] As we control

---

[5] We controlled for a linear effect of fiscal variables other than debt ratios in model (2), but they were not significant.

for time-varying fiscal variables, the constant can be interpreted as measuring the 'structural' component of relative asset swap spreads due to differences in liquidity that do not interact with international risk factors. The null hypothesis that this constant is zero thus provides a weak test of independent liquidity effects on yield differentials.

This specification makes it possible to test for parameter stability in the pre- and post-EMU periods, and allows us to identify movements in yield differentials which depend on local fiscal fundamentals and are robust to the modelling strategy of liquidity and credit-risk components. The solution of the identification problem through the interaction between international risk variables and debt indicators is based on the testable hypothesis that international risk-related factors affect yield differentials because of differences in macroeconomic fundamentals. And, very importantly for our purposes, the specification can be adapted into a model for daily data in Section 5 below, where direct measures of liquidity factors are available and slow-moving fundamentals may be taken to be constant.

4. THE EVIDENCE FROM MONTHLY DATA

The use of monthly data allows us to evaluate the effect of fiscal fundamentals on credit risk at the cost of the unavailability of measures of liquidity over the sample period. Following the discussion in the previous section, we report in Table 3 the results from the estimation of the dynamic model (2) linking the relative asset swap spread for each country to its own lag, to international exogenous measures of risk such as the spread between 10-year fixed interest rates on US swaps and the yield on 10-year US government bonds and the spread between the yield on Moody's Seasoned AAA US corporate bonds and the yield on 10-year US government bonds, and to the interaction of these measures of risk with fiscal fundamentals, measured by the (log) deviation of country i's debt-to-GDP ratio from Germany's debt-to-GDP ratio.[6] The time series behaviour of all regressors is reported in Figures 5 and 6. Table 3 contains the most parsimonious specification for each country. Such specification is obtained by omitting from a general model all coefficients not significant at the 5% level, with the exceptions of constants, which are always kept in the specification.

Table 3 shows that, for most countries, differences in debt-to-GDP ratios have no significant effects on relative asset swap spreads when considered separately. However, debt-to-GDP differentials are significant for Austria, Italy and Spain in the specification that considers their interaction with international risk variables. They are not statistically different from zero for all other countries. This evidence points to the

---

[6] We started from a more general specification for z, including also the slope of the US yield curve as measured by the difference between the yield of 10-year US government bonds and a 3-month interest rate, and some measures of stock market volatility. We excluded these variables because they were never significant in addition to our proxies for corporate and banking sector risk.

Table 3. Model estimates on monthly data

	AUS	BEL	FIN	FRA	IRE	ITA	NET	POR	SPA
Sample	1995:12 2002:10	1995:12 2002:10	1995:12 2002:10	1995:12 2002:10	1996:09 2002:10	1995:12 2002:10	1995:12 2002:10	1995:12 2002:10	1995:12 2002:10
λ	0.60 (0.067)	0.74 (0.045)	0.87 (0.045)	0.64 (0.050)	0.68 (0.068)	0.78 (0.036)	0.88 (0.045)	0.64 (0.060)	0.61 (0.057)
β_1	−0.90 (0.407)	–	–	–	–	–	–	–	−0.33 (0.12)
β_2	–	–	–	–	–	0.41 (0.195)	–	–	–
β_3	0.83 (0.425)	–	–	–	–	–	–	–	0.81 (0.12)
β_4	0.25 (0.036)	0.28 (0.034)	0.32 (0.169)	0.13 (0.030)	0.18 (0.064)	–	0.16 (0.077)	0.15 (0.063)	–
β_5	–	–	–	–	–	–	–	0.08 (0.036)	–
β_0	−0.01 (0.028)	0.02 (0.025)	−0.10 (0.125)	0.008 (0.023)	−0.004 (0.049)	0.08 (0.090)	−0.02 (0.058)	0.047 (0.052)	0.067 (0.032)
Chow Test P-value	0.38	0.16	0.29	0.70	0.00	0.84	0.10	0.70	0.94
SE of Regression	0.03	0.02	0.06	0.03	0.05	0.07	0.02	0.06	0.03
Mean Dep. Variable	0.17	0.22	0.12	0.10	0.12	0.28	0.08	0.26	0.23

Notes: Estimation method: SURE. Standard errors in parentheses. The estimated model is:

$$RAS_t^i = \lambda RAS_{t-1}^i + (1-\lambda)d_t^i[\beta_1 + \beta_2(R_t^{SP,US} - R_t^{US}) + \beta_3(R_t^{C,US} - R_t^{US})] + (1-\lambda)[\beta_4(R_t^{SP,US} - R_t^{US}) + \beta_5(R_t^{C,US} - R_t^{US})] + (1-\lambda)\beta_0 + u_t^i$$

where RAS_t^i is the relative asset swap spread for country i, d_t^i is the (log) deviation of country i's debt-to-GDP ratio from Germany's debt-to-GDP ratio, $(R_t^{SP,US} - R_t^{US})$ is the spread between 10-year fixed interest rates on US swaps and the yield on 10-year US government bonds and $(RAS_t^{C,US} - R_t^{US})$ is the spread between the yield on Moody's Seasoned AAA US corporate bonds and the yield on 10-year US government bonds.

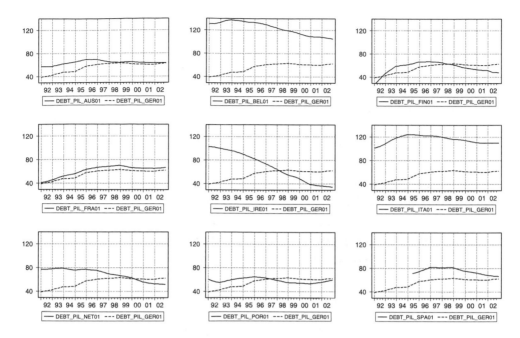

Figure 5. Debt to GDP ratios in EMU countries and Germany

Sources: EU Commission, Datastream/Thomson Financial.

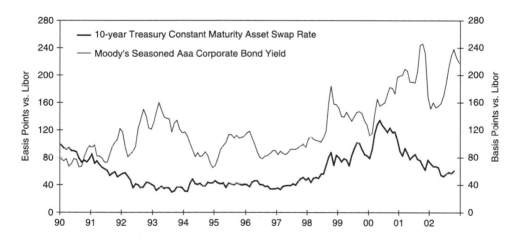

Figure 6. Exogenous measures of risk premium

Sources: US Federal Reserve St Louis and Datastream/Thomson Financial.

importance of credit risk in explaining movements in yield differentials. To assess the statistical and economic importance of the credit risk component, Figure 7 plots yield differentials and our estimate of the component explained by the interaction of fiscal fundamentals (default risk) with international risk factors linked along with its 95% confidence interval. Only in the case of Spain and Italy can a substantial part of the

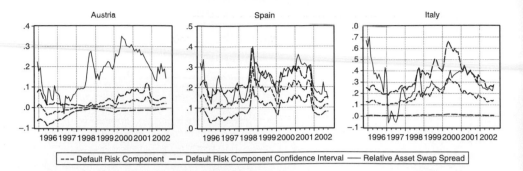

Figure 7. Estimates of yield differentials attributable to default risk

Sources: Our calculations.

total yield differential be attributed to the default risk factor, and reaches almost 20 basis points in 2002. In the case of Austria the significant response of yield differentials to risk variables does not map into a sizeable default risk component.

The international risk factors enter significantly in the linear specification for all countries except Italy and Spain. In particular, all European yield differentials (but Italy and Spain) react significantly to fluctuations in the US asset swap spread. This suggests that bonds issued by different governments are viewed as imperfect substitutes for other reasons than differences in debt ratios. International risk may have an impact because of differences in liquidity but also because of unobservable fundamentals, such as the reputation of the issuing government, or because of greater uncertainty of future budget surpluses. Finally, the constant, which captures residual liquidity factors, is significant only for Spain.

To sum up, the results from estimation on monthly data show that EU countries can be grouped according to their response to fluctuations in exogenous risk factors. At one extreme are Italy and Spain, where we have evidence that fluctuations in yield differentials can be almost entirely attributed to fluctuations in default premiums related to domestic fiscal fundamentals. At the other extreme we have Belgium, France, Finland, Ireland, the Netherlands and Portugal, where fluctuations in yield differentials respond to international risk-related factors, although independently from debt ratios. Austria is an intermediate case in that its yield differentials do respond both linearly and in an interacted fashion to international risk factors, but the response associated to local fiscal fundamentals is neither as strong nor as statistically significant as that for Italy and Spain.

4.1. Evidence from credit default swaps

A credit default swap (CDS) is a derivative contract that allows the investor to hedge against the default of a borrower. The protection buyer agrees to make periodic payments (the swap spread or premium) to the protection seller over the life of the

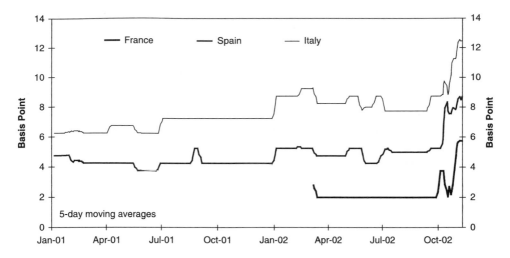

Figure 8. Credit default swap differentials versus Germany

Sources: CreditTrade and our calculations.

contract. This is in exchange for a payment in the event of default by a third party – in our case an EMU member state. The premium is usually a percentage of the face value of the government bond. Should a default event occur, the protection seller becomes liable for the difference between the face value and the recovery value of the bond. Data for such contracts are not available before 2001.

Figure 8 displays the cost of hedging against default in basis points, derived from CDS differentials for Spanish, Italian and French government bonds relative to German bonds. This provides a market-based measure of the credit-risk premium. Pricing of credit risk in CDS spreads differ from relative asset swap spreads for at least two reasons: (1) there is an optionality feature in CDSs versus asset swap spreads, as CDS spreads cannot decrease below zero while asset swap spreads may go deeply negative; and (2) CDSs have an embedded delivery option, because in case of default the protection buyer has the option to deliver a basket of bonds.

Liquidity of credit default swaps has increased, but remains extremely low compared to volumes traded in the government bond market. Therefore, this information must be taken with caution. Still, CDS spreads indicate that the credit risk that investors perceive is significant. Developments in CDS spreads seem to broadly support our findings about the importance of credit risk in the case of Spain and Italy and their relative ranking.

4.2. Does EMU generate a structural break?

Investigating if EMU generated a structural break is very important to our objective of identifying the source of fluctuations of yield differentials. In particular, January 1999 marked the introduction of important reforms of primary markets in many EMU member states. Common euro denomination would have penalized small countries, which have been forced to compete with major markets in terms of liquidity, having to offer only bond issues of a smaller size. Therefore, evidence of a structural break, possibly related to market reforms, could shed light on the importance of liquidity factors in determining yield differentials.

We address the issue of a shift in regime by a direct test for parameters stability reported as 'Chow test' in Table 3. The results of the test indicate that the null hypothesis of no structural break in January 1999 cannot be rejected at the 5% level for all countries in our sample, with the only exception of Ireland.

We also simulate our model on the basis of the parameters estimated with pre-EMU data and of the international risk factors realization in the 1999–2002 period.

The results from the dynamic simulation of our model over the period 1999–2002 are reported in Figure 9. We report the dynamics implied by the estimated coefficients applied to each series' initial condition, and do not introduce confidence intervals as the actual series always lies in the 95% confidence intervals of the simulation. Figure 9

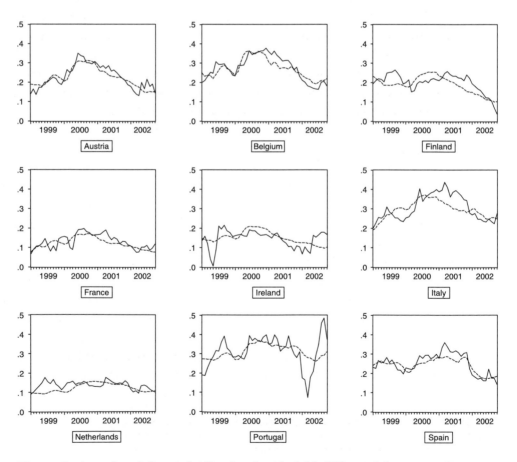

Figure 9. Actual and dynamically simulated yield differentials versus Germany

Sources: Datastream/Thomson Financial and our calculations.

shows that yield differentials in the EMU area are very well predicted given the parameters estimated with pre-EMU data and the knowledge of the international risk
factors.

The only notable exception is the Portuguese yield differential in spring 2002. The
sharp swing in that differential was probably related to rumours that the EU Commission might issue an 'early warning' for excessive deficit to Portugal. Rumours of
an early warning on Germany and Portugal spread in January 2002. But the EU
Council refused to issue the warning against Portugal (and Germany) on 12 February.
This ended the discussion. Then, after the Portuguese election, it turned out that the
actual Portuguese deficit in 2001 might have been wrongly reported by the previous
government and might have actually been higher than 3% of GDP. This would have
directly triggered an excessive deficit procedure. On 26 June the Portuguese Prime
Minister made a reference to an ECB document in Parliament saying that the deficit
was 3.9% of GDP. The official deficit figure, which had to be released by a commission founded for that purpose under the leadership of the Bank of Portugal, was
released only at a later date. On 26 July the Portuguese government officially
submitted the final deficit figure of 4.1% of GDP to the European Commission.
Then, on 16 October, the European Commission adopted a report and a recommendation arguing that the Council should declare Portugal to be in excessive deficit. That
is what the ECOFIN Council did on 5 November.[7] Interestingly, the Portuguese spread
appears to have been the only one in Europe affected by rumours of warnings,
although Germany and more recently France have experienced similar budget problems.

5. EVIDENCE FROM DAILY DATA

The econometric evidence of our baseline model points towards the importance of
differences in debt ratios for the impact of international risk factors on yield spreads
in highly indebted countries. Can liquidity-related factors increase the explanatory
power of international factors?

To gauge liquidity conditions the following measures are usually considered:[8] (1) bid/
ask spread; (2) trading volume; (3) turnover ratios (total trading volume divided by
the stock of securities outstanding, i.e. the number of times the market 'turns over' in
the period); and (4) trading intensity (number of transactions that take place over a
set period).

We have available one year of daily observations of yields on benchmark bonds
from EuroMTS data. This database records for each benchmark bond[9] the bid-ask

---

[7] The dating for all fiscal announcements in 2002 was kindly provided by Rolf Strauch and Antonio Afonso, who have recently
produced a thorough event-study of all fiscal announcements in 2002 (Afonso and Strauch, 2003).

[8] See Gravelle (1999a, b) for a formal definition of liquidity.

[9] Our data come from a snapshot of the market taken daily at 11 am. There are some recent interesting developments in the
literature on how a benchmark should be defined (see, e.g., Dunne et al., 2002). We somewhat arbitrarily define benchmarks by
considering the introduction of a new 10-year bond in the EuroMTS market.

Table 4. Model estimates on daily data

	AUS	BEL	FIN	FRA	GRE	IRE	ITA	NET	POR	SPA	Wald(b)	Wald(c)
λ	0.733	0.946	0.932	0.909	0.939	0.976	0.875	0.777	0.915	0.930	–	31.28
	(0.031)	(0.012)	(0.018)	(0.021)	(0.013)	(0.023)	(0.021)	(0.028)	(0.014)	(0.015)		(0.000)
β_0	0.064	0.036	0.215	0.039	0.200	-0.159	0.079	-0.024	0.059	0.037	82.86	–
	(0.022)	(0.043)	(0.092)	(0.023)	(0.037)	(0.344)	(0.028)	(0.028)	(0.047)	(0.048)	(0.000)	–
μ	1.168	0.305	0.097	0.258	0.231	-0.283	0.266	0.459	0.822	0.701	40.77	263.19
	(0.419)	(0.128)	(0.079)	(0.056)	(0.094)	(0.490)	(0.043)	(0.033)	(0.129)	(0.226)	(0.000)	(0.000)
β_1	0.195	0.247	-0.133	0.075	0.283	0.647	0.186	0.253	0.330	0.206	20.70	56.98
	(0.041)	(0.070)	(0.148)	(0.041)	(0.067)	(0.440)	(0.047)	(0.051)	(0.083)	(0.087)	(0.014)	(0.000)
β_2	-0.010	-0.018	-0.025	-0.012	-0.043	0.072	-0.001	-0.018	0.004	-0.034	12.78	16.44
	(0.007)	(0.018)	(0.031)	(0.005)	(0.019)	(0.095)	(0.003)	(0.009)	(0.017)	(0.018)	(0.172)	(0.087)
β_3	-0.003	0.005	-0.199	0.224	0.079	1.036	0.162	0.000	-0.048	0.119	4.98	7.03
	(0.123)	(0.196)	(0.312)	(0.104)	(0.232)	(1.161)	(0.138)	(0.098)	(0.204)	(0.224)	(0.836)	(0.722)
β_4	0.168	-0.079	1.208	0.084	-1.053	3.187	0.236	0.526	0.240	1.306	7.43	9.13
	(0.274)	(0.872)	(1.098)	(0.451)	(0.617)	(2.911)	(0.593)	(0.449)	(0.646)	(0.805)	(0.592)	(0.519)
Dum 30 Jan	0.001	0.001	-0.002	0.002	0.004	–	0.005	0.006	0.001	0.001		
	(0.010)	(0.004)	(0.006)	(0.003)	(0.004)	–	(0.006)	(0.007)	(0.006)	(0.005)		
Dum 12 Feb	-0.001	-0.005	-0.006	0.002	-0.011	–	-0.006	-0.003	-0.008	-0.007		
	(0.010)	(0.004)	(0.006)	(0.003)	(0.004)	–	(0.006)	(0.007)	(0.006)	(0.005)		
Dum 26 Jul	0.007	0.007	0.002	0.001	0.010	-0.002	0.014	0.005	0.034	0.007		
	(0.010)	(0.004)	(0.006)	(0.003)	(0.004)	(0.003)	(0.006)	(0.007)	(0.006)	(0.006)		
Dum 16 Oct	-0.008	-0.006	-0.002	-0.003	-0.008	-0.002	-0.007	0.001	-0.007	-0.002		
	(0.010)	(0.004)	(0.006)	(0.003)	(0.004)	(0.003)	(0.007)	(0.007)	(0.006)	(0.006)		
Dum 5 Nov	-0.004	-0.0003	0.002	0.002	-0.006	0.005	-0.001	-0.005	-0.002	-0.001		
	(0.010)	(0.004)	(0.006)	(0.003)	(0.004)	(0.003)	(0.006)	(0.007)	(0.006)	(0.006)		
SE of Regression	0.011	0.005	0.006	0.007	0.004	0.005	0.003	0.007	0.008	0.007		
Mean Dep. Variable	0.172	0.202	0.168	0.190	0.077	0.334	0.221	0.188	0.096	0.228		

Notes: Estimation Method: SURE. Sample 1 October 2002–12 March 2002. Standard errors in parentheses. The estimated model is:

$$R_t^i - R_t^{GER} = \lambda(R_{t-1}^i - R_{t-1}^{GER}) + (1-\lambda)[\beta_0 + \mu(RMAT_t^i - RMAT_t^{GER})SL_t + \beta_1(R_t^{SP,US} - R_t^{US}) + \beta_2(VOL_t^i - VOL_t^{GER}) + \beta_3(DEPTH_t^i - DEPTH_t^{GER}) + \beta_4(BASP_t^i - BASP_t^{GER})] + u_t^i$$

where $R_t^i - R_t^{GER}$ is the yield differential for country i; $R_t^{SP,US} - R_t^{US}$ is the spread between 10-year fixed interest rates on US swaps and the yield on 10-year US government bonds, $RMAT$ is the residual maturity of each bond, SL is the slope of the German yield curve between the 10-year and the 7-year maturities, VOL is the trading volume on the EuroMTS France, $DEPTH$ is the average quantity available at the bid and ask prices for each bond, and $BASP$ is the bid-ask spread relative to each benchmark bond. The column labelled Wald(b) reports the results of a Wald test for the null that all the coefficients in the corresponding row are zero, while in the column labelled Wald(c) we report the results of a Wald test for the null that all the coefficients in the corresponding row are equal.

spread, the trading volume, and a direct measure of market depth, i.e. the quantities available at the bid and at the ask price. To study liquidity effects, we specify a dynamic model similar to that of monthly data. Over the sample of daily observations for the year 2002 we estimate

$$(R_t^i - R_t^{GER}) = \lambda(R_{t-1}^i - R_{t-1}^{GER}) + (1 - \lambda)(\beta_0 + \beta_1 Z_t + \beta_2 X_t^i) + u_t^i \qquad (3)$$

which is the equivalent on daily data of model (2). We do not need to use relative asset swap spreads, which coincide with total yield differentials as the fixed interest rates on swaps have fully converged. We consider macroeconomic and fiscal fundamentals as constant, include an international factor measured by the spread between 10-year fixed interest rates on US swaps and the yield on 10-year US bonds, as well as the vector X_t^i of the three liquidity-related proxies mentioned above (see, for example, Fleming, 2001). We control for the difference in the residual maturities of the benchmark bonds, by interacting the differential between the residual maturity for benchmark bonds in country i and Germany with the slope of the German yield curve between the 10-year and the 7-year maturity. This correction, which is allowed to have different signs for positive and negative slopes of the long-end of the German yield curve, allows to smooth jumps in yield differentials occurring in the occasion of benchmark changes.

The results are reported in Table 4. They show that with the notable exception of France, international risk factors dominate liquidity factors in explaining yield differentials. Volumes are the best performing liquidity indicators, with a significance level close to 10% for the hypothesis of a zero impact on all countries. But the null hypothesis that all coefficients on measures of depth and bid-ask spread are zero cannot be rejected.

The null hypothesis of a zero effect of the international risk factor is strongly rejected. There are major differences across countries, but that factor is significant for all countries except France and the two countries, Finland and Ireland, where the debt ratio is substantially lower than in Germany (see Figure 5). However, in the latter countries there is also no evidence of any impact of liquidity on yield differentials. France appears to be the only country where liquidity matters more than international risk in explaining movements in yield differentials. The strongest effect of the international factor is observed for Belgium, Greece, the Netherlands, Portugal and Spain.

Overall, the results from our estimation at daily frequency suggest that international factors are more important than liquidity for the determination of yield differentials in the Euro area (except France). Several countries show a strong dependence on international factors, while evidence in favour of liquidity is weaker and limited to trading volumes. This evidence allows us to qualify the indications given by our model on monthly data. Although international risk (when not interacted with relative debt ratios) can affect yield differentials either because of differences in liquidity or in unobservable fiscal fundamentals, the fact that such effect remains when we explicitly control for liquidity indicators is – admittedly weak – evidence that differences in default risk are the main propagation mechanism.

To further assess the importance of fiscal announcements on yield differentials as indicated by the simulation of our monthly model, we have included in our daily model point dummies for five specific dates: 30 January, 12 February, 26 July, 16 October and 5 November. On 30 January the press reported a possible early warning for Germany and Portugal, the EU Council refused to issue the warning against Portugal (and Germany) on 12 February. The official deficit figures were submitted to the European Commission on 26 July, on which occasion the Portuguese government submitted the figure of 4.1% of GDP. Then, on 16 October, the European Commission adopted a report and a recommendation arguing that the Council should declare Portugal to be in excessive deficit. That is what the ECOFIN Council did on 5 November.

The coefficients on the point dummies confirm the evidence that only the Portuguese spread appears to have been affected by fiscal announcements. In particular, the dummy for 26 July is significant only for the yield spread between Portugal and Germany, showing that the submission of official figures caused an impact of 3.5 basis points in the Portuguese–German differential, with a long-run effect of about 15 basis points.

5.1. Does the presence of a liquid futures market really matter?

A potentially important variable is missing from our analysis of liquidity factors in the previous section. Anecdotal evidence from market participants attributes a great importance to the presence of an efficient and liquid future contract.[10]

A proper functioning of associated derivatives markets facilitates the active trading and management of interest rate risk. Where a well-developed futures market exists, market makers can manage their positions using futures, thereby enhancing their ability to carry out inventory-risk management in the cash market, which, in turn, promotes better liquidity. In the euro area the Bund futures contract has become predominant. It is often argued that German government bonds, which have become the *de facto* benchmark in the 10-year sector, command a sizeable premium versus other sovereign issues because of this 'derivative factor'.

In principle, our evidence in favour of the importance of international risk factors might not be robust to the inclusion of the impact of future markets in our analysis. To analyse the impact of the futures market we collected data on volumes and open interest on all futures contracts on euro zone government bonds and aggregate data

---

[10] We were unable to test for the presence of liquid and efficient repurchase agreement markets/facilities.

Table 5. Liquidity of future contracts on 10-year Eurozone government bonds

Volumes (€ 000)[a]	1998	1999	2000	2001	2002[b]
Eurex, Euro-Bund	176.0	509.5	581.1	681.9	762.9
Liffe, Bund	55.7	0	0	0	0
Matif, Euro-Notional	15.0	23.4	165.5	66.1	0
Liffe BTP	31.4	6.6	0	0	0
Mif, BTP	0.4	0.7	0	0	0
Meff, Bono	58.8	13.7	4.2	1.1	0.2
Germany	231.8	509.5	581.1	681.9	762.9
France	90.6	23.4	165.5	66.1	0
Italy	31.9	7.4	0	0	0
Spain	58.8	13.7	4.2	1.1	0.2

Open interest (number of contracts)	1998	1999	2000	2001	2002
Eurex, Euro-Bund	339.4	570.4	669.3	676.8	729.1
Liffe, Bund	106.6	0	0	0	0
Matif, Euro-Notional	118.9	133.0	310.8	108.6	1.0
Liffe BTP	104.3	27.6	0.7	0	0
Mif, BTP	1.6	2.6	0.1	0	0
Meff, Bono	92.9	21.8	13.5	8.0	2.5
Germany	446.0	570.4	669.3	676.8	729.1
France	118.9	133.0	310.8	108.6	1.0
Italy	105.9	30.3	0.8	0	0
Spain	92.9	21.8	13.5	8.0	2.5

Notes: Other smaller contracts are not considered as volumes and open interests were negligible.
[a] Non-euro denominated contracts are translated into euro at the fixed conversion rate.
[b] Data up to October.

Sources: Datastream/Thomson Financial and our calculations.

according to the underlying government bond.[11] Summary statistics are presented in Table 5. Arguably, the lack of a liquid futures contract in all EMU countries but Germany should command a liquidity premium on non-German bonds, depending on the risk to which investors are exposed by having an imperfect hedge. Figure 10 shows the German–French bond yield differential, the differential of volumes, and the open interest on futures contracts. Quite unexpectedly, the visual impression is for a positive correlation. In fact, yield differentials increased between early 1999 and mid-2000 as the German futures market became more and more dominant, and then decreased in

---

[11] Up to 1997, Liffe was the largest European futures exchange and the contracts on German and Italian 10-year government bonds were the most popular. Since mid-1998, however, trading activity has moved decidedly in favour of Eurex and Bund contracts. At the beginning of 1998, the combined volumes on Eurex and Liffe contracts on 10-year Bunds were much higher than the sum of all future contracts on other euro zone government bonds. By the launch of the single European currency the Eurex contract on 10-year Bunds was already by far the dominant contract in Europe and its volume and open interest were constantly rising. While volumes and open interest of all other contracts were waning and in some cases eventually disappearing, the contract on Matif managed to post a surprising temporary comeback, gaining more than 35% of total market share by April 2000. This was the result of an initiative by the French banking federation to boost liquidity in the market. The leap in open interest in mid-2000 was also due to a change in the method of recording (from net to gross since 23 May 2000). Still, the revival of the French contract was remarkable and offers us a wonderful opportunity to estimate the impact on asset swap spreads.

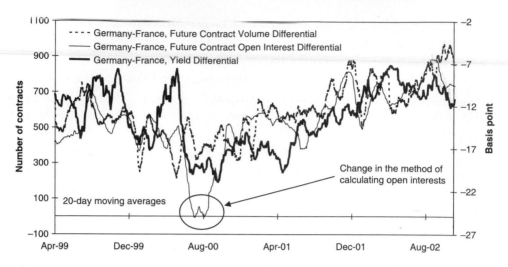

Figure 10. Germany-France yield differentials and futures contracts

Sources: Datastream/Thomson Financial and our calculations.

the course of 2001 and 2002 when the German futures market became completely dominant.

More importantly, a variable measuring relative traded volumes in futures markets is not significant when included in the equation of the French yield differential in the model estimated with daily data.

6. CONCLUDING REMARKS

Movements in yield differentials on euro zone government bonds are mostly explained by changes in international risk factors, as measured by US swap and corporate bond spreads relative to US Treasury yields. This paper provides evidence that these international factors affect spreads because they change the perceived default risk of government bonds in the euro zone. Liquidity factors play only a smaller role.

We find evidence that the impact of international risk on yield differentials in Austria, Italy and Spain, is explained by their debt-to-GDP ratios relative to Germany. Default risk explains a substantial part of changes in yield spreads in Italy and Spain. Yield differentials for all the other countries are also significantly affected by international risk factors, although independently from debt-to-GDP ratios. This suggests that bonds issued by these countries are viewed as imperfect substitutes of German bonds for reasons not related to their debt ratios. International risk may have an impact because of differences in liquidity but also because of unobservable fundamentals, such as the reputation of the issuing government, or because of greater uncertainty of future budget surpluses.

Evidence on the effects of international risk factors remains robust to the broadening of our analysis to include daily data on liquidity measures for 2002.

Greater trading volumes significantly reduce yield differentials in France, Greece, the Netherlands and Spain, while other traditional indicators, such as bid-ask spreads, have no effect. Even in such countries, however, international risk-related factors appear the main source of variation in yield differentials. France is the only country where liquidity matters more than international risk. Finland and Ireland, the two countries with the lowest debt-to-GDP ratio, also show no reaction to international risk factors.

This evidence allows us to qualify the indications given by our model on monthly data. Since international risk (when not interacted with relative debt ratios) can affect yield differentials because of differences in either liquidity or in unobservable fiscal fundamentals, we cannot conclude that liquidity has become irrelevant in the pricing of bonds in the euro area. 'Structural' liquidity factors could indeed explain the different sensitivities to international risk factors. However, the fact that international risk remains significant once we explicitly control for liquidity indicators is evidence – though weak – that international risk matters because of the different perceived creditworthiness of the sovereign issuers.

The results of our study have important policy implications. Yields on euro zone government bonds have been increasingly correlated across issuers. This is a sign of enhanced integration that is explained by the common denomination in euro. However, additional policy steps to increase financial market integration by means of increased efficiency both in primary and secondary markets, although desirable, would not deliver a 'seamless' bond market in the euro area.

The risk of default, though small, remains an important factor explaining movements in the yield differentials. This evidence points to incomplete fiscal consolidation and to the need for further convergence of debt-to-GDP ratios. In this process, yield differentials would be important policy indicators, as they would signal market perception of fiscal vulnerability. Furthermore, since higher bond yields imply higher debt service costs, yield differentials reflecting default risk impose market discipline on fiscal policies of the national governments within the euro zone. Although such a role now appears somewhat reduced compared to the pre-EMU period, also because of the limited changes currently observed in budget deficits, it is likely that the risk component of bond yields would continue to work as a deterrent for irresponsible fiscal policies if such policies were ever implemented.

Discussion

Richard Portes
London Business School, and CEPR

This paper is a significant analysis of an important issue: the integration of the euro-area government bond markets. This matters for at least three reasons:

- Governments want the lowest possible yields on their debt, both to minimize the burden of debt service and because there is a welfare loss to residents from debt interest payments to non-residents.
- An integrated government bond market is important for the monetary trans-mission mechanism, it underpins much financial sector activity (hedging, pricing private debt), and it supports the international role of the currency (Portes and Rey, 1998).
- Insofar as yield gaps reflect liquidity differentials, they also reflect market ineffi-ciencies with associated costs.

But there are two meanings or measures of integration in securities markets. The authors stress the elimination of yield differentials across countries. But one might also look for unified and transparent price discovery, as exhibited in benchmarks that are valid for the entire euro area (Dunne *et al.*, 2002). Here the authors use only 10-year yields and take German yields as reference rates. In this case Germany does seem to be providing the benchmark, but that does not seem to be true for shorter maturities (*ibid.*), and it would indeed be useful to extend the analysis here to the 5-year maturity, for example.

The authors explain clearly the alternative hypotheses – default risk versus liquidity as the source of yield differentials (and hence market segmentation) – and their contrasting policy implications. If it is the fundamentals, in particular, government debt levels, then market integration requires further convergence, so the markets provide an incentive to fiscal discipline. But liquidity differentials could be eliminated by improvements in debt management and market microstructure.

There is a major difficulty, however, in viewing differences in debt-to-GDP ratios as a major source of government bond market segmentation in the euro area: the differences are just not very large, for the most part. As of end-1999, say, five of the nine countries studied here in monthly data had debt-to-GDP ratios between 59 and 64%. France and Ireland were significantly lower, Belgium and Italy were signific-antly higher. And indeed, of the nine, only three show a significantly and correctly signed effect of this variable on yield differentials, and only for Italy and Spain is this a substantial component of the observed differential. In particular, Belgium, France and Ireland show no default risk effect. Not surprisingly, there is only very weak evidence for the authors' preferred hypothesis.

Although Table 4 shows clear evidence for the role of international risk factors, that is not the same as country default risk, as the authors themselves carefully explain. If we then look at the liquidity variables, the key determinant is transactions volume, which is correctly signed for eight of ten countries and significant for four of these. This is not surprising. There is an extensive literature going back at least to Amihud and Mendelson (1986) showing that an asset's liquidity is valued in the market, and Amihud and Mendelson (1991) apply this to US Treasury securities. Most recently, Goldreich *et al.* (2003) find a clear (time-varying) liquidity premium in the US Treasury market; here, quoted (not effective) bid-ask spread and transactions volume have the most explanatory power.

So although I find the authors' work very interesting, I cannot accept their conclusion that default risk is primary and liquidity influences secondary in accounting for the remaining market segmentation in the euro-area government bond market. But perhaps it does not matter – if yield differentials are our criterion, the markets seem to be integrating very rapidly! As of 30 June 2003, the *Financial Times* shows '10-year constant' (adjusted for residual maturity) bond spreads relative to Germany ranging from –1 basis point for Finland to only 11 basis points for Italy, with only that country, Portugal and Greece having spreads greater than one (!) basis point. Perhaps we should focus on price discovery and benchmarks instead.

Marcel Thum
Dresden University of Technology, ifo Dresden and CESifo

The EMU has completely eliminated exchange rate risks for the holders of European government bonds. However, yield differentials still persist for various reasons. Codogno, Favero and Missale argue that there are basically three explanations for the remaining yield differentials. First, some countries are more likely to default on their outstanding debt and, therefore, have to pay a risk premium (default risk). Secondly, bonds that can be more easily traded are preferred by investors; a higher liquidity thus translates into lower returns (liquidity risk). Thirdly, international risk factors generate movements in yield differentials between euro zone government bonds.

Using daily and monthly data of government bond yields, Codogno, Favero and Missale arrive at the conclusion that the default risk and general international factors dominate the liquidity effect in explaining yield differentials. This result suggests that yield differentials reflect fundamentals rather than inefficient or incomplete markets.

The authors have used an innovative approach in analysing the sources of yield differentials, so it is not surprising that there still are some open questions where further research is needed. One of the main objectives of the paper is to sort out as to what extent yield differentials are caused by liquidity factors and default risks. In the following, I will discuss these two explanations in turn.

The *default risk* is exclusively measured through debt-to-GDP ratios. It turns out to be significant for yield differentials only in the cases of Italy and Spain. I wonder whether refinements or alternative measures might be needed here. The debt-to-GDP ratio is a rather weak indicator for potential default. The explicit government debt is usually only a small fraction of all outstanding obligations. In many countries under consideration, the implicit debt which mostly comes from comprehensive public pension systems is much larger than the explicit debt. In Germany, for instance, the implicit debt is more than three times the explicit debt.[12]

---

[12] See Raffelhüschen (2001); this is a fairly conservative estimate for the implicit debt in Germany.

The inclusion of the implicit debt might not affect the empirical results if the implicit debt grows in line with the explicit debt. In the period under consideration, however, several countries planned or executed major reforms of their public pension systems. From 1999 until 2002, reform measures were undertaken in Austria, Finland, France, Germany, Italy, the Netherlands and Spain. Most of the reform measures have aimed at reducing the implicit debt of public pension systems. Taking up the example of Germany again, the reform in 2001 reduced the implicit debt from public pensions by more than 10 percentage points of GDP (from 214.9 to 204.3% of GDP; see Raffelhüschen, 2001). Hence, the impact of the pension reform on total government debt is certainly much larger than the impact of policies aiming at the explicit debt.

While default risk is definitely an economically sound argument for yield differentials, *liquidity factors* are more obscure from a theoretical point of view. As a non-expert in this field, I was a bit surprised by the strong focus on liquidity as a possible explanation of yield differentials. I am not aware of a generally accepted theory of liquidity premia, so in reading the paper I would have appreciated more guidance and more detail on theoretical treatments of liquidity as a relevant factor.

Panel discussion

Stijn Claessens doubted whether liquidity and default risk may be reliably identified separately, since they are not independent. Carlo Favero replied, also referring to Richard Portes' discussion, that the paper's identification strategy is based on the idea that the effect on spreads of international perceptions of risk affect depends on fiscal fundamentals. Steve Cecchetti pointed out that risk aversion and perceived uncertainty matter separately as determinants of the risk premium, and that a country's expected fiscal policy can change dramatically (mentioning Brazil as an important example). Carlo Favero replied that the paper simply uses the current value of debt as the indicator of fiscal fundamentals, on the basis of forward solution of the government budget constraint. In reply to Marcel Thum's discussion he agreed that it would be desirable, but does not appear possible, to use a more comprehensive measure for total government liabilities.

Stijn Claessens thought it would be important to exploit information regarding financial market structure across countries and time. Patrick Honohan added that variation in liquidity across different government bonds could also be exploited to disentangle country-specific effects from liquidity factors. Lorenzo Codogno replied that, in order to focus on macro structural issues, the paper chooses to disregard bond-specific phenomena and concentrate empirical efforts on the 10-year benchmark bond. Jonathan Haskel asked for an economic interpretation of the persistence parameter lambda in the regressions, and wondered whether the very different estimates of that parameter across countries may offer useful information.

REFERENCES

Afonso, A. and R. Strauch (2003). 'Fiscal policy events and interest rate swap spreads: some evidence from the EU', mimeo, European Central Bank.

Amihud, Y. and H. Mendelson (1986). Asset pricing and the bid-ask spread, *Journal of Financial Economics*, 17, 223–49.

—— (1991). Liquidity, maturity and the yields on US Treasury securities, *Journal of Finance*, 46, 1411–25.

Arora, V. and M. Cerisola (2001). 'How does US monetary policy influence sovereign spreads in emerging markets?', *IMF Staff Papers*, 48(3), 474–98.

Barnes, K. and W. Cline (1997). 'Spreads and risks in emerging markets lending', Institute of International Finance Working Paper No. 97-1.

Blanco, R. (2001). 'The euro-area government securities market: recent developments and implications for market functioning', Banco de Espana-Servicio de Estudios Working Paper 0120.

Dungey, M., V.L. Martin and A.P. Pagan (2000). 'A multivariate latent factor decomposition of international bond yield spreads', *Journal of Applied Econometrics*, 15, 697–715.

Dunne, P.G., M.J. Moore and R. Portes (2002). 'Defining benchmark status: an application using euro-area bonds', CEPR Discussion Paper No. 3490.

Eichengreen, B. and A. Mody (2000). 'What explains changing spreads on emerging market debt?' in S. Edwards (ed.), *Capital Flows and the Emerging Economies: Theory, Evidence, and Controversies*, NBER Conference Report series, University of Chicago Press, Chicago and London, 107–34.

Favero, C.A., F. Giavazzi and L. Spaventa (1997). 'High yields: the spread on German interest rates', *The Economic Journal*, 107, 956–85.

Favero, C.A., A. Missale and G. Piga (1999). 'EMU and public debt management: one money one debt?', CEPR Policy Paper No. 3, December.

Fleming, M.J. (2001). 'Measuring treasury market liquidity', Federal Reserve Bank of New York Staff reports, No. 133.

Fleming, M.J. and E.M. Remolona (1999). 'Price formation and liquidity in the US treasury market: the response to public information', *Journal of Finance*, 54(5), 1901–15.

Galati, G. and K. Tsatsaronis (2001). 'The impact of the euro on Europe's financial markets', BIS Working Papers No. 100.

Giovannini, A. and G. Piga (1994). 'Understanding the high interest rate on Italian government securities', in Conti Hamaui and Scobie (eds.), *Bond markets, Treasury and Debt Management*, Chapman and Hall, London.

Gómez-Puig, M. (2003). 'Monetary integration and the cost of borrowing', mimeo.

Goldreich, D., B. Hanke and P. Nath (2003). 'The price of future liquidity: time-varying liquidity in the US Treasury market', CEPR Discussion Paper 3900.

Goodhart, C. and J. Lemmen (2001). 'Credit risk and European government bond markets: a panel data econometric analysis', *Eastern Economic Journal*, 25(1).

Gravelle, T. (1999a). 'Liquidity of the Government of Canada securities market: stylized facts and some market microstructure comparisons to the United States treasury market', Bank of Canada Working Paper No. 99-11.

—— (1999b). 'The market microstructure of dealership equity and government securities markets: how they differ' in *Market Liquidity: Research Findings and Selected Policy Implications BIS-CGFS Study* No. 11, May.

—— (1999c). Markets for Government of Canada securities in the 1990s: liquidity and cross-country comparisons', *Bank of Canada Review* (Autumn).

Kamin, S.B. and K. von Kleist (1999). 'The evolution and determinants of emerging market credit spreads in the 1990s', Board of Governors of the Federal Reserve System, International Finance Discussion Paper: 653, November.

Kumar, M.S. and A. Persaud (2001). 'Pure contagion and incestors' shifting risk appetite: analytical issues and empirical evidence', IMF Working Paper.

McCauley, R. and E. Remolona (2000). 'Size and liquidity of government bond markets', *BIS Quarterly Review*, November.

Portes, R. and H. Rey (1998). 'The emergence of the euro as an international currency', *Economic Policy*, 26, 305–43.

Poterba, J.M. and K.S. Reuben (2001). 'Fiscal news, state budget rules, and tax-exempt bond yields', *Journal of Urban Economics*, 50, 537–62.

Raffelhüschen, B. (2001). 'Eine Generationenbilanz der deutschen Wirtschafts- und Sozial-politik', in O. Graf Lambsdorff (ed.), *Grundsätze liberaler Sozialpolitik*, Frankfurt am Main, 241–60.

Scalia, A. and V. Vacca (2001). 'Does market transparency matter?', contribution to the Study Group on Market Liquidity set up by the Committee on the Global Financial system of the G10 central banks.

Fiscal policy

SUMMARY

Economists, policy-makers, and the media often argue that the Maastricht Treaty and the Stability and Growth Pact make it difficult for governments of EMU countries to stabilize their economies with appropriate fiscal policy and to provide adequate public investment. Our empirical analysis offers little support to this view. Discretionary budget deficits have actually become more counter-cyclical in EMU countries after the Maastricht Treaty, as well as in the other EU and non-EU industrialized countries we study. And while public investment has declined recently in EMU countries, a similar tendency is apparent in other countries and started well before the Maastricht Treaty was signed.

— *Jordi Galí and Roberto Perotti*

Fiscal policy and monetary integration in Europe

Jordi Galí and Roberto Perotti

CREI, Universitat Pompeu Fabra and CEPR; European University Institute and CEPR

1. INTRODUCTION

The fiscal apparatus of stage three of economic and monetary union (EMU) is increasingly regarded by many as an unnecessary and harmful straightjacket on national fiscal policies, or even as downright 'stupid'.[1] According to a common argument, the Maastricht Treaty (MT) and the Stability and Growth Pact (SGP) constrain the use of fiscal policy precisely when EMU countries need it the most, having lost their autonomous monetary policy. In particular, critics complain that recessions can only be deepened by efforts to raise taxes and cut spending when cyclical downturns increase deficits towards the SGP's ceiling. Since the SGP fiscal targets do not take cyclical conditions into account, the need to stabilize the budget over the cycle may imply a procyclical fiscal policy and amplify economic fluctuations in EMU countries. A second criticism frequently levelled at the MT and the SGP is that they have

For comments and discussions we thank *Economic Policy* Panel members, our discussants, an anonymous referee, Alberto Alesina, Sandro Momigliano, and seminar participants at CREI–Universitat Pompeu Fabra, ECARES–Université Libre de Bruxelles, the European University Institute, the European Commission, the Bank of Spain and Bocconi University. We thank Gabriele Giudice and Jonas Fischer for providing the European Commission data on fiscal policy. Peter Claeys provided excellent research assistance. Galí acknowledges the financial support of MCyT and the Generalitat de Catalunya.

The Managing Editor in charge of this paper was Giuseppe Bertola.

[1] Interview with Romano Prodi in *Le Monde*, 17 October 2002.

impaired the ability of EMU countries to maintain and increase the public capital stock. This could have long-run consequences on the growth potential of these coun tries that go well beyond their implications for the cyclical properties of fiscal policy.

Our first objective in the present paper is to assess the extent to which the constraints associated with the MT and the SGP have affected national fiscal policies *in practice*: we ask the data whether and how those constraints have made fiscal policy in EMU countries more procyclical. The second objective is to assess empirically whether the alleged negative effects of the MT and SGP on public investment can indeed be seen in the data.

1.1. Methods and results

Regarding the cyclical behaviour of fiscal policy, we test using available data two hypotheses associated with the criticisms mentioned above. The first hypothesis is that, because of the constraints imposed by the MT and the SGP, national fiscal policies can no longer fulfil the stabilizing role they had traditionally played. The second hypothesis is that the loss of an autonomous monetary policy calls for more strongly counter-cyclical fiscal policies in EMU countries. In order to test these hypotheses we estimate empirical fiscal policy rules for eleven EMU countries over the period 1980–2002, and perform a variety of tests for stability of the coefficient capturing the fiscal response to output gap fluctuations in the pre- and post-Maastricht periods. We compare the results with those of similar regressions on data for the three EU countries that did not join EMU, as well as for five OECD countries that do not belong to the EU.

From a methodological point of view, we restrict our analysis to measures that can be reasonably interpreted as indicators of *discretionary* fiscal policy, the component of fiscal deficit whose variation does not result from the automatic influence of the cycle or other non-policy influences. In the short and medium run, this is more likely to be affected by the MT and SGP constraints than the cyclical component of fiscal deficits, which depends on country-specific features that change very slowly over time, like the overall size and composition of government spending and the progressivity of the tax system. We also recognize that our cyclical indicators might be affected by exogenous fiscal shocks, and address this issue with an instrumental variables procedure.

We detect very little evidence that the Maastricht-related constraints have significantly impaired *in practice* the stabilization role of fiscal policy in EMU countries. If anything, we find evidence of the opposite: EMU countries' fiscal policy in the pre-Maastricht period seems to have been significantly procyclical, a feature that largely disappears during the post-Maastricht period. Overall, we detect what appears to be a global trend towards more counter-cyclical fiscal policies. Interestingly, EMU countries seem to lag behind the rest of OECD countries in terms of that trend. It is not yet possible to tell whether this may be a consequence of the MT and SGP constraints or of other factors or, indeed, a rationale for them.

Regarding the effects of the MT and SGP on public investment, we find that the decline in government investment as a share of total spending appears to be a global trend that started well before Maastricht. In fact, in the post-Maastricht period government investment declined *less* than in the 1980s, and *less* in EMU countries than in the other OECD countries.

We should clearly emphasize at the outset what our paper does not and cannot say. Our results do not imply that deficit limits are irrelevant: obviously, if a country is already close to the deficit limit and it is hit by a negative shock, then the limit will be relevant (to the extent, of course, that it is indeed enforced *ex post*). What we document is that in the circumstances so far experienced, there is no evidence of less counter-cyclical behaviour of fiscal policy after the MT – quite the contrary. But the potential for problems from as-yet unrealized crises simply cannot be assessed with our method.

2. DEBTS AND DEFICITS: THE RECORD

Box 1 reviews the key institutional constraints imposed on national fiscal policies by the Maastricht Treaty and the Stability and Growth Pact.[2] To provide some

---

Box 1. Fiscal policy constraints for EMU countries

The 1992 Maastricht Treaty and then the Stability and Growth Pact established targets on the size of debt and deficits, other obligations, and penalties. Article 104 (ex Art. 104c) of the Treaty establishes that 'member sates shall avoid excessive government deficits' (para. 1), and that compliance with budgetary discipline will be judged on the basis of two criteria (para. 2):

'(a) whether the ratio of the planned or actual government deficit to gross domestic product exceeds a reference value, unless:
  – either the ratio has declined substantially and continuously and reached a level that comes close to the reference value;
  – or, alternatively, the excess over the reference value is only exceptional and temporary and the ratio remains close to the reference value
(b) whether the ratio of government debt to gross domestic product exceeds a reference value, unless the ratio is sufficiently diminishing and approaching the reference value at a satisfactory pace.'

---

[2] For other detailed accounts we refer the interested reader to European Commission (2000) and European Central Bank (1999). Artis and Buti (2000), Buiter *et al.* (1993), Buiter and Grafe (2002), Buti and Giudice (2002), and Eichengreen and Wyplosz (1998) also provide good discussions of the institutional aspects of the Maastricht Treaty and of the Stability and Growth Pact, and detailed economic analyses of their rationale and impact.

As is well known, these two reference values were set at 3% and 60%, respectively.

The first criterion was also used, among other criteria like price stability, when a decision was made on which countries would be admitted to stage III of the EMU (the single currency) in May 1998. The Stability and Growth Pact was designed to provide concrete content to several provisions of the Treaty regarding economic policies in the EU. It consists of a Resolution of the European Council and of two ECOFIN Council Regulations (No. 1466/97 and No. 1467/97). The Resolution reaffirms the commitment to fiscal discipline and introduces the notion of 'medium-term budgetary objective of positions close to balance or in surplus', to be respected by member states, in order to 'allow all Member States to deal with normal cyclical fluctuations while keeping the government deficit within the reference value of 3% of GDP'.

Regulation No. 1466/97 clarifies the procedures to be followed for an implementation of the surveillance of the Pact, as envisioned in general terms in Art. 99 (ex Art. 103) of the Treaty. Member states must submit every year an update to the *stability programme* (called convergence programme for non-EMU members), containing a *medium-term objective* for the budgetary position, and a description of the *assumptions* and of the main economic policy *measures* the country intends to take to achieve the targets. The Council, on a recommendation from the Commission, delivers an *opinion* on each programme and its yearly updates and, if deemed necessary, a recommendation. There are three possible types of *recommendations*. First, a recommendation that the programme be adjusted if deemed deficient in some respect. Second, if after approving the programme the Council identifies a 'significant divergence of the budgetary position from the medium-term budgetary objective, or the adjustment path towards it', the Commission can issue a recommendation (*early warning*), in accordance with Art. 103(4). Third, if the divergence persists, the Council can issue a recommendation to take corrective action, and can make the recommendation public.

Regulation 1467/97 offers a more precise definition of the 'exceptional and temporary' excess of the deficit over the 3% of GDP threshold, introduced by Art. 104 (ex Art. 104c) of the Treaty. Deficits are 'exceptional and temporary' if they are the result of 'an unusual event outside the control of the Member State concerned' or of 'a severe economic downturn', more specifically 'if there is an annual fall of real GDP of at least 2%' or 'exceptional' circumstances can be argued on the basis of 'the abruptness of the downturn or on the accumulated loss of output relative to past trends'. This Regulation also clarifies the *Excess Deficit Procedure* set out in Art. 104 (ex Art. 104c) of the Treaty, including the imposition of fines.

background for our assessment of their practical relevance, we start by looking at a few descriptive statistics on the medium-term evolution of the size of debt and deficits of the general government (the union of the central and local governments and of the social security funds). We do so for the current EMU countries, as well as for two other groups of countries. The first, dubbed EU 3 in what follows, comprises the three EU countries that do not belong to the EMU (Denmark, UK and Sweden). The second, dubbed OECD 5, comprises five non-EU OECD countries for which we were able to assemble a consistent set of budget data: Norway, Australia, Japan, Canada and the United States.

While the OECD 5 countries we consider are clearly not affected by EMU fiscal constraints, the position of the EU 3 group is less clear. In principle, the MT and SGP fiscal constraints described in Box 1 apply to all EU member countries, but EU countries that have not adopted the euro are not subject to penalties in case their deficits exceed 3% of GDP (whether such fines would indeed be imposed on EMU member countries is far from clear, however; see Box 2 for a discussion).

Columns (a) and (b) in Table 1 display the average deficit/GDP ratio for the above groups of countries during two different five-year periods (1988–92 and 1997–2001); column (c) displays the difference between the first two columns. The first such period corresponds to the years immediately before the adoption of the MT, whereas the

---

Box 2. Enforcement of fiscal rules for EMU members and other EU countries

Several aspects of the SGP are not fully clear, and this might impair the actual stringency of the provisions of the pact.

The notion of a 'medium-term target' is ambiguously defined. The expression 'sound budgetary positions close to balance or in surplus' was initially identified with a position such that the budget deficit would still be less than 3% of GDP if the automatic stabilizers were allowed to operate during a deep recession, a subjective and controversial 'minimal benchmark'. The Commission computes it on the basis of the worst-case scenario for the output gap, taken to be the largest negative output gap since 1960, or two times the standard deviation of the output gap (see for example European Commission, 1999, p. 4). However, the revised Code of Conduct on the content and format of the stability and convergence programmes, endorsed by the ECOFIN Council in 2001, requires additional margins to cope with unforeseen budgetary risks and to reduce high debts and introduces a distinction between the notions of 'appropriate medium-term target' and the notion of 'close to balance or in surplus' which constitutes the key obligation of the SGP. A stricter bound on deficits might be justified in view of several considerations, like providing for the costs of an ageing population, to create room for discretionary fiscal policies, etc. (see European Commission, 2002, p. 33).

An 'actual or expected significant divergence of the budgetary position from the medium-term budgetary objective' could trigger an early warning, but it is also less than unambiguously defined in the SGP framework. While cyclically adjusted budget balance could be used in making this assessment, the SGP does not refer to cyclical adjustment. Yet the new Code of Conduct states that 'cyclically adjusted balances should continue to be used, in addition to nominal balances, as a tool when assessing the budgetary position', and the 2002 Council Opinions on the programmes of six members mentions the notion of cyclically adjusted balances. However, the role of cyclical adjustment remains unclear. A country may be exempted from the 3% deficit limit for an unspecified period of time if 'exceptional circumstances' define a 'severe' recession even though GDP falls by less than 2%. This notion is also less than clearly defined, making the Excess Deficits Procedure prone to endless bargaining and controversy.

The SGP is also partly ambiguous as regards constraints imposed on EU countries that have not adopted the euro. Regulation 1467/97 establishing the SGP states that para. 1 of Art. 104 (ex Art. 104c) of the Treaty – 'Member States shall avoid excessive government deficits' – does not apply to the UK unless it moves to the third stage. However, the UK is still under the obligation of para. 4 of Art. 116 (ex Art. 109e) – 'In the second stage, Member States shall endeavour to avoid excessive government deficits'. The Council has also interpreted the SGP in the sense that the obligation to pursue a goal of 'close to balance or surplus in the medium term' applies to the UK (see, e.g., the '2002 Council Opinion' on the updated convergence programme).

In contrast to the UK, the resolution and the two regulations establishing the SGP fail to state explicitly that Art. 104(1) does not apply to Denmark. In fact, the 2002 Council Opinion on the updated convergence programme for Denmark states that 'Denmark is also expected to be able to withstand a normal cyclical downturn without breaching the 3% of GDP deficit reference value.'

However, both Denmark and the UK are explicitly exempted from the requirement of paras 9 and 11 of Art. 104 (ex Art. 104c), which establish the right of the Council to request specific actions and to impose non-interest bearing deposits and fines, in cases of a deficit in excess of 3%.

While Denmark and the UK have an *opt-out* from participation in stage 3 of the EMU (the single currency), technically speaking Sweden only has a *derogation*. The practical consequence for the applicability of the SGP, however, appears to be the same as for Denmark; Art. 122(3) of the Treaty establishes that paras 9 and 11 of Art. 104 do not apply to countries with a derogation.

Table 1

	Deficit/GDP ratio (%)			Debt/GDP ratios (%)		
	1988–92 (a)	1997–2001 (b)	(b) − (a) = (c)	1982 (d)	1992 (e)	2001 (f)
AUT	2.8	1.8	−1.0	40.3	57.2	61.7
BEL	7.4	0.7	−6.7	98.9	131.4	108.2
DEU	1.9	2.1	0.2	37.5	41.8	60.3
ESP	3.9	1.5	−2.4	31.1	52.4	69.1
FIN	−2.1	−2.7	−0.6	14.1	40.6	43.6
FRA	2.6	2.0	−0.6	33.5	44.7	64.8
GRC	13.1	1.9	−11.2	29.6	97.6	99.7
IRE	2.9	−2.3	−5.2	79.2	100.1	36.5
ITA	11.4	2.2	−9.2	65.1	116.1	108.7
NLD	4.8	−0.1	−4.9	54.2	77.6	53.2
PRT	4.0	3.1	−0.9	42.6	54.8	55.6
DNK	0.8	2.0	1.2	60.2	66.3	44.7
GBR	1.6	−0.4	−2.0	53.7	49.2	52.5
SWE	−0.4	−2.1	−1.7	60.2	69.0	52.9
NOR	−1.1	−9.4	−8.3	31.9	32.4	26.8
AUS	2.3	−0.4	−2.7	18.4	14.5	10.1
JPN	−1.5	6.2	7.7	60.1	63.5	132.8
CAN	6.4	−1.6	−8.0	68.4	110.4	101.6
USA	4.4	−0.5	−4.9	49.3	74.1	59.5
ALL	3.4	0.2	−3.2	48.9	68.1	65.4
EMU	4.8	0.9	−3.9	47.8	74.0	69.2
EU3	0.7	−0.2	−0.8	58.0	61.5	50.0
OECD5	2.1	−1.1	−3.2	45.6	590.7	66.2

Notes: Deficit is cyclically unadjusted general government deficit. Averages for different groups are unweighted.

Source: OECD *Economic Outlook* database, December 2002 issue.

second sub-period includes the first five years for which the constraints associated with the MT and/or the SGP were in place. (The decision about the set of countries qualifying to join EMU from its birth in 1999 was made in May 1998 on the basis of 1997 fiscal figures, among other factors). The table confirms the well-known substantial decline in the deficit/GDP ratio in all EMU countries except one (Germany). The average decline in the deficit/GDP ratio in EMU countries was close to 4.0 percentage points; Greece had the largest adjustment – more than 11 percentage points, followed closely by Italy with 9.2 percentage points. The only outlier among EMU countries, Germany, experiences a small increase of 0.2 percentage points (albeit starting from one of the lowest deficit ratios among EMU countries, 1.9% in the early sub-period).

To what extent was such a fiscal consolidation restricted to current EMU countries? Interestingly, the performance of our control groups suggests that sizeable consolidations were also taking place over the same period in non-EMU countries. The OECD 5 group experienced an average decline of 3.2 percentage points in the deficit/GDP ratio, a decline that becomes much larger (6.0 percentage points) if one excludes Japan. The EU 3 group shows a smaller reduction in the deficit/GDP ratio, about 0.8 percentage points; this can largely be explained by the much more favourable initial position, an average deficit ratio of 0.7% in the 1988–92 sub-period.

One interpretation of the above evidence is that, while the MT and SGP may have provided political cover and hence facilitated the necessary adjustments in EMU countries, the economic rationale for fiscal consolidation could well be deeper than the requirements for monetary union. The substantial fiscal consolidations experienced by EMU countries in the 1990s, in fact, can be seen as part of a global trend common to most industrialized countries (with Japan as a major exception). The evolution of the debt/GDP ratios suggests a good reason for these worldwide fiscal consolidations. The last three columns in Table 1 show the value of that ratio in three selected years (1982, 1992 and 2001), pointing to the non-sustainability of the fiscal position that most industrialized countries were maintaining in the 1980s. In particular, the average debt/GDP ratio for current EMU members increased from 48% to 74% between 1982 and 1992, and from 52% to 62% among the OECD 5 countries. Only the EU 3 countries, which started their fiscal consolidation process at an earlier stage, managed to contain the rise in the debt/GDP ratio to only 3 percentage points, from 58% to 61%. It was only after the fiscal consolidations of the 1990s that most industrialized countries began to experience a decline or at least a deceleration in their debt/GDP ratios.

3. DECOMPOSING FISCAL POLICY

In order to study the issues set out in the introduction we first need to distinguish between changes in fiscal policy that are due to discretionary measures taken by policy-makers, and those that are due to the 'automatic' response of fiscal variables to business cycle fluctuations. In this paper, we focus primarily on the former; as mentioned in the introduction, the cyclical behaviour of the latter component is determined by the size and composition of government spending and taxation, and the structure of the tax system, all features that are difficult to change significantly in the short to medium run. We do, however, also study changes in the cyclical behaviour of the latter component, and find similar results, although quantitatively weaker, as expected.

We can think of the budget deficit in a given year as the sum of two components:

(1) The 'cyclical' or 'non-discretionary' deficit is the component whose variations are due (at least in the short run) to causes outside the direct control of the fiscal authorities, like business cycle fluctuations in unemployment and in the tax bases. In the case of taxes, these variations can be interpreted as changes in tax revenues due to changes in income, for given tax rates and for given definitions of the tax bases.[3] Among primary expenditures, only unemployment benefits probably have a non-negligible built-in

[3] For simplicity, we abstract here from automatic responses to inflation and interest rates. These are more difficult to estimate. For such an attempt, see Fatás and Mihov (2002b), Perotti (2002), and Canzoneri et al. (2002).

response to output fluctuations. Debt interest payments are also an element of this component, since interest rates are largely outside the control of the fiscal authorities.

(2) The 'structural', 'cyclically adjusted' or 'discretionary' deficit is the value that would be observed if output were at some reference 'potential' level. By removing the cyclical component, it aims at measuring the fiscal stance intentionally chosen by the policy-maker, rather than the result of uncontrolled economic fluctuations. Within this second component we can in turn define two components:

(a) The 'systematic' or 'endogenous' component of the cyclically adjusted deficit corresponds to policy decisions affecting structural spending or revenues in response to changes in the actual or expected cyclical conditions of the economy. For instance, policy-makers wishing to pursue an active counter-cyclical policy could reduce tax rates or increase government consumption whenever the economy is in a recession, and the opposite in an expansion. The possible counter-cyclical behaviour of this component of the structural deficit is thus the result of a deliberate policy decision, rather than of automatic stabilizers.

(b) The 'non-systematic' or 'exogenous' component of the cyclically adjusted deficit captures budgetary changes that do not correspond to systematic responses in cyclical conditions, but are instead the consequence of exogenous political processes or extraordinary non-economic circumstances (e.g., war spending efforts).

These definitions are conceptually straightforward, but the actual implementation of any cyclical adjustment is subject to a large element of subjectivity. As our benchmark, we use cyclically adjusted data constructed by the OECD according to the methodology described in Box 3.

As mentioned, most of our empirical analysis below focuses on a measure of the structural (or cyclically adjusted) primary deficit, which we interpret as an indicator of the stance of discretionary fiscal policy. By varying the structural primary deficit through changes in either taxes or government purchases the fiscal authority can influence aggregate demand and, hence, a country's level of aggregate economic activity. We do not have strong views as to whether the level or the change in the deficit is the appropriate measure of fiscal stance. The choice of the indicator of the fiscal policy stance depends very much on the underlying model of the economy and the notion of policy stance that one has in mind. In a simple IS-LM model, for example, the level of the budget deficit determines the position of the IS curve and its change in the budget surplus determines movements of this curve; 'expansionary' fiscal policy may be either a high deficit (and output) or an increasing deficit (and output). To ease comparability with the literature, we present all our results in terms of deficit levels. Note, however, that the fiscal rules estimated below feature the lagged structural deficit as an independent variable, to imply that if the dependent variable were the change rather than the level of the structural deficit the other coefficients of the regression would be the same as those we report.

Box 3. The structural budget deficit

Let Y^* be the reference value of GDP, and α and β the output elasticity of tax revenues and spending, respectively. Then the structural tax revenues and spending, T_t^* and G_t^*, are computed from the expressions:

$$\frac{T_t^*}{T_t} = \left(\frac{Y_t^*}{Y_t}\right)^{\alpha} \; ; \quad \frac{G_t^*}{G_t} = \left(\frac{Y_t^*}{Y_t}\right)^{\beta}$$

In words, the revenue elasticity α is used to evaluate the value revenues would take if output were at its reference level T_t^* instead of its actual value Y_t, and similarly for government spending. Dividing T_t^* and G_t^* by the reference value of GDP, we obtain the 'structural' budget deficit as a share of reference GDP:

$$d_t^* = g_t^* - t_t^*$$

where d_t^*, t_t^*, and g_t^* are the structural primary deficit, primary revenues, and primary spending, all as shares of reference GDP. Thus, the output of the structural adjustment depends on the reference value of GDP used. Typically, this is some measure of smoothed output, like trend or HP-filtered GDP, or of potential output. In our benchmark results, based on data cyclically adjusted by the OECD, the reference value of GDP is potential output, constructed following a standard production function approach (see Giorno et al., 1995; or OECD 2002). For robustness we also use different cyclically adjusted fiscal data, computed by the European Commission and based on two alternative reference GDPs: HP-filtered GDP and potential output based on the Commission's production function approach (see European Commission, 2002; the European Commission has just started using potential output in its cyclical adjustment, in addition to HP-filtered GDP, with the November 2002 release). A second source of variation in cyclical adjustment procedures is the elasticities used. The OECD elasticities are constructed starting from the tax code and the distribution of taxpayers by income brackets (see Giorno et al., 1995 and van den Noord, 2002). The same elasticities are used by the European Commission. Some studies use elasticities estimated from a regression of tax revenues on GDP or the tax base. If taxes have a contemporaneous effect on output (as is likely in yearly data), the estimates so obtained are inconsistent. This would impair our estimates of the reaction of discretionary fiscal policy to cyclical conditions.

As a summary indicator of the cyclical conditions of an economy at any point in time, we use a conventional, production function-based output gap measure, also constructed by the OECD using the same measure of potential output used in the construction of the cyclically adjusted figures.

4. HAS DISCRETIONARY FISCAL POLICY CHANGED SINCE MAASTRICHT?

Our objective in this section is to ascertain the extent to which European governments have used *discretionary* fiscal policy as a stabilizing tool over the past two decades, and whether constraints on fiscal policy associated with Maastricht and the SGP may have hampered their ability and/or motivation to pursue active counter-cyclical fiscal policies.

4.1. Fiscal rules

Several researchers have estimated a relation of the form:

$$d_t = \phi_0 + \phi_x x_t + u_t$$

where d_t is the cyclically unadjusted total deficit (or some of its components) as a share of GDP and x_t is either the output gap or GDP growth (see Box 4 for a brief discussion of the recent literature on the subject; existing contributions include additional explanatory variables in the regression). This type of regression can provide a useful descriptive statistic of the cyclical relation between budget variables and economic activity, but it cannot identify discretionary policy reactions to cyclical conditions, because an important component of the budget deficit reflects automatic variations in government revenues and expenditures resulting from output and interest rate fluctuations that are outside the control of the fiscal authorities.

Box 4. The cyclical sensitivity of fiscal policy

Several recent papers also estimate the cyclical sensitivity of fiscal policy in OECD countries. There are two main differences with our investigation. First, in all this literature the fiscal variables are cyclically unadjusted, thus making it impossible to separately identify the automatic from the discretionary responses of fiscal policy to cyclical conditions, an issue which is the focus of our analysis. Second, in most papers the indicator of cyclical conditions is not instrumented, thus preventing a structural interpretation of the coefficient of the cyclical condition if fiscal policy has a contemporaneous effect on GDP in yearly data. To facilitate a comparison with our results, we will discuss these contributions as if their dependent variable were the deficit, although in most of them it is actually the surplus. Fatás and Mihov (2002a, b) regress the (cyclically unadjusted) primary deficit (or its first difference) on cyclical

---

indicators like the output gap, inflation and interest rate, and interpret the residual of this estimated equation as the indicator of the discretionary fiscal stance. In our terminology, they estimate the 'non-systematic' component of discretionary fiscal policy (subject to the caveat above that they do not instrument for the contemporaneous output gap on the right-hand side). They show that the average (across countries) standard deviation of this estimated residual has fallen in the 1990s, and interpret this result as evidence that EU countries have been less able to conduct counter-cyclical fiscal policy in the Maastricht years. Arreaza *et al.* (1999), Hercowitz and Strawczynski (1999) and Lane (2002) characterize the cyclical properties of fiscal policy in OECD countries by estimating similar regressions to Fatás and Mihov (2002a, b) both on a panel of OECD countries and on individual countries. These papers also look at how the cyclical behaviour of fiscal policy is affected by institutional and political factors, and they also disaggregate the deficit into its main spending and revenue components. Like Fatás and Mihov they use cyclically unadjusted data; only Lane (2002) instruments the cyclical indicator. Both Arreaza *et al.* (1999) and Lane (2002) find that the deficit/GDP ratio is counter-cyclical; Hercowitz and Strawczynski (1999) show that this is mostly due to recessions; in expansions, the deficit/GDP ratio is essentially acyclical.

A number of papers try to assess the automatic stabilizing properties of fiscal policy. Melitz (1997) and Wyplosz (1999) estimate similar regressions on a panel of European countries (typically including more variables, such as the debt/GDP ratio). They also find and note a counter-cyclical behaviour of the deficit/GDP ratio. Wyplosz (2002) regresses the cyclically unadjusted deficit/GDP ratio on the output gap in four countries: USA, UK, Germany and Italy. His regressions are most closely comparable to ours because he allows for a break in 1992. The differences in results are substantial. For instance, in the pre-1992 sample, he finds that the deficit is counter-cyclical in USA and Italy, and acyclical in Germany and UK; in contrast, we find that the structural deficit is essentially acyclical in USA, UK and Italy, and procyclical in Germany (see Table 2). Like us, Auerbach (2002) finds that the effects of the output gap on the legislated changes in the surplus (analogous to our measure of discretionary fiscal policy) have become slightly more counter-cyclical in the USA after 1992.

Of course, since the automatic response of revenues to the cycle would show up as a counter-cyclical response of the cyclically unadjusted deficit, in general we tend to find a less counter-cyclical behaviour of the deficit than in previous studies above, particularly in the first part of the sample and for the current EMU countries. For the purpose of assessing the possible changes induced by EMU constraints on fiscal policy, it is important to distinguish properly the discretionary and the cyclical component of the deficit.

To address this issue we decompose the general government deficit into its discretionary and cyclical components, and use each component as a dependent variable in turn. When the dependent variable is the discretionary component of the deficit, there is still a second problem. The disturbance term of the fiscal rule, which represents exogenous deficit shocks, is likely to be positively correlated with the output gap if such shocks affect the level of economic activity. This correlation will most likely generate an upward bias (and possibly even a sign switch) in the estimate in the coefficient on the output gap in the fiscal policy rule. To address this problem we use an instrumental variables (IV) procedure, regressing the deficit on a component of the output gap which is uncorrelated with exogenous discretionary fiscal shocks.

A third problem with the above specification of the fiscal policy rule is that it might not properly take into account the timing of fiscal policy decisions implied by the budgetary process of most countries. Since many discretionary fiscal parameters (e.g. tax rates) are largely determined the year before they become effective, any policy rule seeking to respond to output gap variations will have to be based on the *expectation* of the latter, conditional on information available in the previous period. In practice, this calls for replacing x_t with its expectation $E_{t-1}x_t$ in the relationship of interest. Following the lead of several authors (see, e.g., Bohn, 1998; Ballabriga and Martinez-Mongay, 2002; and Wyplosz, 2002), we also incorporate a debt stabilization motive by adding a measure of the size of the debt outstanding (relative to potential GDP) at the time of the budget decision, and which we denote by b_{t-1}. Finally, we account for the likely autocorrelation of budget decisions (possibly resulting from gradual adjustment to a target budget, or just from the serial correlation in the exogenous shocks) by adding the lagged dependent variable as a regressor.

The resulting specification of the fiscal rule is thus:

$$d_t^* = \phi_0 + \phi_x E_{t-1}x_t + \phi_b b_{t-1} + \phi_s d_{t-1}^* + u_t \tag{1}$$

In words (viewing the structural or cyclically adjusted deficit as the dependent variable for now), a negative value of ϕ_x indicates that policy-makers use discretionary fiscal policy in a systematic counter-cyclical way: when cyclical conditions are expected to improve (an increase in $E_{t-1}x_t$), discretionary fiscal policy becomes more restrictive, and the structural deficit falls. A negative value of ϕ_b, as well as a value of ϕ_s less than 1, indicates that the higher the initial debt, or the higher the initial deficit, the lower the structural deficit policy-makers set discretionarily.

We will be mostly interested in studying whether there was a detectable change in the value of ϕ_x, the coefficient of the expected output gap, in the post-Maastricht period in EU countries. More precisely, if the MT and SGP rules reviewed in Box 1 effectively prevent policy-makers from engaging in counter-cyclical fiscal policy, we would expect an increase in this coefficient after Maastricht, i.e. we should be able to detect a fall in the counter-cyclicality (or an increase in the procyclicality) of fiscal policy. To assess this effect, we estimate a version of Equation (1) that allows the output coefficient to differ before and after the possible regime change: formally,

$$d^{*}_{t} = c_{BM} + c_{AM} + \phi_{x,BM}E_{t-1}x_{t} + \phi_{x,AM}E_{t-1}x_{t} + \phi_{b}b_{t-1} + \phi_{s}d^{*}_{t-1} + u_{t} \tag{2}$$

where the subscripts 'AM' and 'BM' stand for 'after Maastricht' and 'before Maastricht', respectively. Thus, $\phi_{x,BM}$ and $\phi_{x,AM}$ are the values of the coefficient of $E_{t-1}x_{t}$ in the pre- and post-Maastricht periods, respectively: the estimation allows for a break in the coefficient of $E_{t-1}x_{t}$ in 1992, and the constant is also allowed to differ before that same year. The budget deficit variable refers to the general government. To estimate Equation (2) we replace $E_{t-1}x_{t}$ with x_{t}, and instrument the latter using x_{t-1} and the lagged value of the output gap of an alternative country or group of countries. Specifically, we use as instruments the EU 15 output gap for the US, and the US output gap for all other countries. The rationale of this choice is that we need to instrument the gap of each country with that of another country (or group of countries) with which it is likely to be correlated for reasons other than the existence of coordinated fiscal policies. We discuss extensively the robustness of this benchmark specification in the web appendix.[4]

4.2. Baseline results

Table 2 displays the results for our baseline specification over the sample period 1980–2002. It reports for each country estimates of the coefficients on the expected output gap in the pre-Maastricht (1980–91) and the post-Maastricht (1992–2002) periods, test statistics for significance of estimated changes of that coefficient, and estimates of the coefficients on lagged debt and deficit. At the bottom, the table shows average values for the EMU, the EU 3 and the OECD 5 groups.

As regards country-group averages, in the pre-Maastricht period discretionary fiscal policy was mildly procyclical in EMU countries. By contrast, it was counter-cyclical in the other groups: strongly in the EU 3, largely as a result of the very negative value estimated for Denmark; mildly in the OECD 5. Most interestingly, in all groups there is a clear trend towards a smaller value of the expected output gap coefficient in the post-Maastricht period. On average, between the two sub-periods this coefficient falls by about 0.5 in EMU and OECD 5 countries, and by 0.3 in EU 3 countries. Only Greece among EMU countries displays a higher output gap coefficient, and the difference is far from significant. In all other EMU countries there is evidence of more counter-cyclical discretionary fiscal policy after Maastricht. Among the EU 3 countries, only Denmark and Australia display a higher point estimate of the output gap coefficient in the post-Maastricht period, but again the difference is entirely insignificant.[5]

---

[4] Notice that Equation (1) can be interpreted also as the reduced form of a structural model of determination of the structural deficit, in which policy-makers have a target value of the debt/GDP ratio and there are costs in changing the structural deficit over time. Such an interpretation generates non-linear constraints among the reduced form coefficients. This is the route taken by Ballabriga and Martinez-Mongay (2002), who estimate such rules for EU countries over the whole period 1980–2000. Our focus, however, is on the difference between the pre- and post-Maastricht periods, and we also look at revenues and spending separately.

[5] We also find that the higher initial debt/GDP ratios, the lower the deficit, given last year's deficit; thus, the debt does exert a constraint on the deficit. In the EMU countries, we typically find that an extra 10 percentage points of debt/GDP ratio is associated with a lower deficit of about 0.8 percentage points the next year. The coefficient on the lagged discretionary deficit is lower than 1; on average, in the EMU countries, only about 40% of an increase in the structural deficit survives the next year, other things equal.

Table 2

	$\phi_{x,BM}$ E(gap)$_{BM}$		$\phi_{x,AM}$ E(gap)$_{AM}$			ϕ_b debty{1}		ϕ_s defy{1}	
	(1)	(2)	(3)	(4)	(5)	(6)	(7)	(8)	(9)
AUT	−0.05	(−0.24)	−0.59	(−1.17)	(0.34)	−0.02	(−0.59)	0.41	(1.80)
BEL	0.38	(1.52)	−0.84	(−1.06)	(0.15)	−0.07	(−2.18)	0.57	(3.17)
DEU	0.41	(3.40)	0.32	(0.84)	(0.83)	−0.02	(−0.38)	0.46	(3.18)
ESP	0.10	(0.92)	−0.06	(−0.37)	(0.44)	−0.05	(−2.05)	0.60	(4.49)
FIN	0.23	(0.64)	−0.35	(−1.81)	(0.18)	−0.03	(−0.55)	0.18	(0.64)
FRA	0.14	(1.55)	0.10	(0.56)	(0.87)	−0.10	(−3.86)	0.34	(1.74)
GRC	0.12	(0.55)	0.35	(0.68)	(0.69)	−0.03	(−0.85)	0.45	(2.49)
IRE	0.26	(1.10)	−0.07	(−0.23)	(0.21)	−0.05	(−1.05)	0.73	(4.78)
ITA	0.35	(1.53)	−0.86	(−1.24)	(0.13)	−0.07	(−2.36)	0.08	(0.36)
NLD	0.29	(0.98)	−0.72	(−1.11)	(0.19)	0.01	(0.17)	0.39	(1.69)
PRT	0.49	(5.24)	0.16	(0.90)	(0.10)	−0.36	(−4.60)	0.06	(0.44)
DNK	−1.40	(−2.11)	−0.24	(−0.47)	(0.25)	−0.00	(−0.06)	0.42	(2.32)
GBR	0.11	(1.81)	−0.90	(−2.92)	(0.01)	−0.05	(−1.01)	0.49	(4.05)
SWE	−0.52	(−1.18)	−1.61	(−2.39)	(0.06)	−0.13	(−2.21)	0.30	(1.16)
NOR	−0.39	(−1.12)	−1.22	(−2.66)	(0.12)	0.07	(0.54)	0.44	(1.81)
AUS	−0.19	(−0.66)	−0.13	(−0.62)	(0.83)	−0.14	(−1.63)	0.87	(6.45)
JPN	0.16	(1.57)	−0.33	(−0.85)	(0.23)	−0.01	(−0.82)	0.81	(13.37)
CAN	−0.15	(−0.75)	−0.39	(−0.76)	(0.67)	−0.02	(−0.65)	0.68	(3.06)
USA	−0.04	(−0.23)	−1.07	(−3.53)	(0.00)	0.00	(0.04)	0.25	(1.16)
ALL	0.02		−0.44			−0.06		0.45	
EMU11	0.25		−0.23			−0.07		0.39	
EU3	−0.60		−0.91			−0.06		0.40	
OECD5	−0.12		−0.63			−0.02		0.61	

Notes: This table displays country-specific estimates of the fiscal rule

$$d_t^* = c_{BM} + c_{AM} + \phi_{x,BM}E_{t-1}x_t + \phi_{x,AM}E_{t-1}x_t + \phi_b b_{t-1} + \phi_s d_{t-1}^* + u_t$$

where d_t^* is the primary deficit of general government, cyclically adjusted, divided by potential output. x_t is the output gap; b_t is the general government debt to potential GDP ratio.
IV estimation, using own lagged output gap and the lagged output of the EU15 countries for the US, and the lagged output of the US for all other countries.
Sample: 1980–2002 for all countries. BM refers to 1980–91 (Before Maastricht); AM refers to 1992–2002 (After Maastricht).
Column (1): estimate of $\phi_{x,BM}$, the coefficient of expected gap in 1980–1991 period. Column (2): t-statistics. Column (3): estimate of $\phi_{x,AM}$, the coefficient of expected gap in 1992–2000 period. Column (4): t-statistics. Column (5): p-value of the hypothesis that the two coefficients in columns (1) and (3) are equal. Column (6): estimate of ϕ_b, the coefficient of the lagged debt / potential GDP ratio. Column (7): t-statistics. Column (8): estimate of ϕ_s, the coefficient of the lagged structural deficit / potential GDP ratio. Column (9): t-statistics. Estimates of the constants in the two periods, c_{BM} and c_{AM}, are omitted for lack of space.
Averages for different groups are unweighted.

Source: OECD *Economic Outlook* database, December 2002 issue (2002 data are preliminary forecast).

Thus, there appears to be no evidence of a less counter-cyclical or more procyclical discretionary fiscal policy in the EMU countries in the post-Maastricht period.

Since there are few degrees of freedom in our specification, the country-specific regressions above offer rather imprecise estimates. We have also estimated a panel version of the fiscal rule that, while restricting the parameters to be the same across

Table 3

	(1)	(2)	(3)	(4)
	EMU (No. obs. = 238)			
$E(gap)_{BM}$	0.17	(3.47)		
$E(gap)_{AM}$	−0.08	(−0.98)	−0.25	(0.01)
$debty\{1\}_{BM}$	−0.05	(−4.70)		
$debty(1)_{AM}$	−0.05	(−3.46)	0.00	(0.95)
$defy\{1\}_{BM}$	0.54	(10.01)		
$defy(1)_{AM}$	0.55	(6.58)	0.00	(0.98)
	EU3 (No. obs. = 66)			
$E(gap)_{BM}$	−0.09	(−0.74)		
$E(gap)_{AM}$	−0.76	(−2.62)	−0.67	(0.04)
$debty\{1\}_{BM}$	−0.10	(−3.30)		
$debty(1)_{AM}$	−0.05	(−1.29)	0.05	(0.34)
$defy\{1\}_{BM}$	0.58	(5.19)		
$defy(1)_{AM}$	0.65	(4.48)	0.08	(0.68)
	OECD5 (No. obs. = 110)			
$E(gap)_{BM}$	−0.14	(−1.29)		
$E(gap)_{AM}$	−0.72	(−3.40)	−0.58	(0.02)
$debty\{1\}_{BM}$	−0.00	(−0.08)		
$debty(1)_{AM}$	−0.00	(−0.08)	0.00	(0.99)
$defy\{1\}_{BM}$	0.76	(7.96)		
$defy(1)_{AM}$	0.60	(5.13)	−0.16	(0.30)

Notes: This table displays panel estimates of the same fiscal rule as in Table 2.
Country-fixed effects are included, and are allowed to have a break in 1992.
Column (1): value of the coefficient in each sub-period. Column (2): *t*-statistics. Column (3): difference 'After Maastricht' − 'Before Maastricht'. Column (4): *p*-value of the test of the null hypothesis that the coefficients 'Before Maastricht' and 'After Maastricht' are the same.
See Table 2 for other details and sources.

countries, can allow all the coefficients of the equation (and the country dummies) to differ before and after the Maastricht treaty. Table 3 displays the panel estimates of Equation (2), with country fixed effects, for the three groups of countries.[6] For each of the three groups of countries, we report estimates of the coefficient on $E_{t-1}x_t$ in the pre- and post-Maastricht periods, the difference between the two sub-periods, and a test for its statistical significance. The other rows of Table 3 are structured similarly.

The pattern that emerges is very similar to that of the country-specific regressions, but now the standard errors are considerably smaller. In all groups of countries, there is evidence of a significant *increase* in the degree of counter-cyclicality of discretionary fiscal policy. In the EMU group, discretionary fiscal policy was procyclical before Maastricht and becomes essentially acyclical after Maastricht; in the EU 3 and

[6] Because of the lagged endogenous variable on the right-hand side, the standard fixed effect estimator of our fiscal policy would be inconsistent. However, we are mostly interested in the *difference* between the estimates of the coefficients between the two periods. If the 'inconsistency' in the estimates were approximately the same in the two sub-periods, the difference would be largely unaffected. Because the small-sample properties of the consistent estimators that have been proposed in the literature are not well understood, and our sample size is small (10 years for each period), we have chosen to present results with a standard IV fixed effect estimator.

OECD 5 groups, it was acyclical before Maastricht and becomes significantly counter-cyclical after Maastricht. In all three cases, the difference in the output gap coefficient between the two periods is highly significant, and is estimated to be close to the average difference from the country-specific regressions, especially for the EMU and the OECD 5 countries.

The estimated coefficient of debt is negative in the EMU and EU 3 groups, but essentially zero in the OECD 5 group. In no case is it significantly different across the two periods. The average EMU country typically reduces the structural deficit by 0.05 percentage points for each additional percentage point of debt in the previous year – a number which is very close to the average of the same coefficient in the country-specific regressions. Similarly, the estimated coefficient on the lagged deficit is very close in all three groups of countries, ranging between 0.55 and 0.75, and again there is no evidence that it has increased after Maastricht. Thus, we find no evidence that, holding constant the expected cyclical conditions of the economy, in the post-Maastricht period the initial fiscal conditions exerted a stronger pressure on discretionary fiscal policy.

The estimates reported in Table 4 are derived from a similar specification for the two main components of the budget deficit, spending and revenues, as dependent variables. When cyclically adjusted primary spending is the dependent variable, the estimated value of the expected output gap coefficient falls for the three groups of countries in the post-Maastricht period, but only in the EMU group is the difference significant at the 10% level. Conversely, when we use cyclically adjusted primary revenues as the dependent variable, we detect some evidence of more counter-cyclical policy for the EU 3 and OECD 5: there is statistical evidence of a larger output gap coefficient for these groups of country (though only significant at the 0.16 level for the latter), but not for the EMU countries. Thus, the evidence suggests a more important role of spending policies in EMU as a counter-cyclical tool in the post-Maastricht or, to be more precise, an end to their procyclical pattern, which characterized the pre-Maastricht period. In the case of the EU 3 and the OECD 5 the evidence points to more proactively counter-cyclical revenue policies in the post-Maastricht period.

5. CHANGES OVER TIME IN NON-DISCRETIONARY FISCAL POLICY

We now provide some evidence on the responsiveness of the non-discretionary (or cyclical) component of fiscal policy to changes in cyclical conditions. That evidence can give us an indication of the role and importance of *automatic stabilizers* as a fiscal tool in euro area countries, as well as in the other countries in our sample. It should be viewed as complementary to the evidence on the stabilizing role of discretionary fiscal policy presented above.

To that end, we estimate a policy rule like in the form

$$d_t^{nd} = c_{BM} + c_{AM} + \phi_{x,BM} x_t + \phi_{x,AM} x_t + \phi_b b_{t-1} + \phi_d d_{t-1}^{nd} + u_t \qquad (3)$$

Table 4

	Spending				Revenues			
	(1a)	(2a)	(3a)	(4a)	(1b)	(2b)	(3b)	(4b)
	EMU (No. obs. = 238)							
$E(gap)_{BM}$	0.20	(4.50)	(0.00)		0.05	(1.36)	(0.17)	
$E(gap)_{AM}$	0.04	(0.49)	−0.17	(0.06)	0.01	(0.19)	−0.04	(0.53)
$debty\{1\}_{BM}$	−0.03	(−3.40)	(0.00)		−0.00	(−0.06)	(0.95)	
$debty(1)_{AM}$	−0.01	(−0.88)	0.02	(0.21)	0.03	(2.38)	0.03	(0.06)
$itemy\{1\}_{BM}$	0.83	(19.58)	(0.00)		0.82	(14.94)	(0.00)	
$itemy(1)_{AM}$	0.80	(8.95)	−0.03	(0.75)	0.67	(9.14)	−0.14	(0.12)
	EU3 (No. obs. = 66)							
$E(gap)_{BM}$	−0.19	(−2.03)	(0.05)		0.01	(0.10)	(0.92)	
$E(gap)_{AM}$	−0.45	(−2.85)	−0.26	(0.16)	0.41	(2.22)	0.41	(0.05)
$debty\{1\}_{BM}$	−0.04	(−1.95)	(0.06)		0.05	(2.40)	(0.02)	
$debty(1)_{AM}$	−0.02	(−0.80)	0.02	(0.61)	0.03	(0.95)	−0.03	(0.48)
$itemy\{1\}_{BM}$	0.18	(0.91)	(0.37)		0.70	(8.17)	(0.00)	
$itemy(1)_{AM}$	0.66	(6.01)	0.48	(0.04)	0.45	(2.12)	−0.26	(0.26)
	OECD5 (No. obs. = 110)							
$E(gap)_{BM}$	−0.11	(−1.19)	(0.24)		0.06	(0.79)	(0.43)	
$E(gap)_{AM}$	−0.26	(−2.06)	−0.15	(0.35)	0.27	(2.20)	0.20	(0.16)
$debty\{1\}_{BM}$	0.03	(1.39)	(0.17)		0.03	(1.45)	(0.15)	
$debty(1)_{AM}$	−0.01	(−0.49)	−0.04	(0.16)	0.01	(1.01)	−0.02	(0.48)
$itemy\{1\}_{BM}$	0.71	(6.40)	(0.00)		0.70	(8.65)	(0.00)	
$itemy(1)_{AM}$	0.76	(7.61)	0.05	(0.74)	0.73	(6.03)	0.03	(0.85)

Notes: This table displays panel estimates of the same fiscal rule as in Table 2, except that the dependent and lagged dependent variables itemy(.) are: spey(.), the primary spending of the general government, cyclically adjusted, divided by potential output in the left panel; and revy(.), primary revenues of the general government, cyclically adjusted, divided by potential output in the right panel.
Column (1): value of the coefficient in each sub-period. Column (2): *t*-statistics. Column (3): difference 'After Maastricht' − 'Before Maastricht'. Column (4): *p*-value of the test of the null hypothesis that the coefficients 'Before Maastricht' and 'After Maastricht' are the same.
See Table 2 for other details and sources.

where d_t^{nd} is the difference between the total primary deficit and the cyclically adjusted primary deficit, expressed as a share of potential GDP. We interpret the resulting variable as a measure of the non-discretionary component of fiscal policy, as defined in Section 4. The only difference with respect to (2), besides the different dependent and lagged dependent variables, is use of the actual rather than expected output gap measure on the right-hand side. This is justified by the very nature of non-discretionary fiscal policy, which represents movements in budget items that arise 'automatically' in response to changes in economic conditions without a deliberate *ex ante* policy decision. For example, variations over time in the volume of unemployment subsidy payments or personal income tax revenues (for any given tax rates) clearly depend on the actual, not the expected behaviour of output.

Table 5 displays the estimates of the coefficients on the expected output gap in the pre-Maastricht (1980–91) and the post-Maastricht (1992–2002) periods, respectively, with *t*-statistics in parentheses. As in the discretionary policy case we attempt to

Table 5

	$\phi_{x,BM}$ E(gap)$_{BM}$		$\phi_{x,AM}$ E(gap)$_{AM}$		ϕ_b debty{1}		ϕ_s defy{1}	
	(1)	(2)	(3)	(4)	(5)	(6)	(7)	(8)	(9)
AUT	−0.29	(−6.53)	−0.39	(−6.62)	(0.08)	0.00	(0.11)	−0.09	(0.74)
BEL	−0.60	(−53.9)	−0.63	(−28.8)	(0.15)	0.00	(0.57)	0.00	(0.21)
DEU	−0.49	(−4.24)	−1.06	(−4.33)	(0.04)	−0.03	(−1.57)	−0.10	(0.67)
ESP	−0.37	(−9.61)	−0.40	(−10.5)	(0.05)	0.01	(2.66)	−0.06	(−0.71)
FIN	−0.62	(−15.9)	−0.70	(−21.5)	(0.01)	−0.00	(−0.48)	0.01	(0.21)
FRA	−0.37	(−35.8)	−0.40	(−33.5)	(0.00)	0.00	(0.27)	0.00	(0.21)
GRC	−0.30	(−8.25)	−0.42	(−8.95)	(0.01)	−0.00	(−0.24)	0.45	(0.05)
IRE	−0.38	(−29.6)	−0.34	(−38.4)	(0.01)	−0.00	(−0.77)	−0.02	(−1.03)
ITA	−0.42	(−6.13)	−0.82	(−4.26)	(0.03)	−0.00	(0.38)	−0.22	(−1.45)
NLD	−0.70	(−8.68)	−0.80	(−12.6)	(0.30)	0.00	(0.32)	−0.02	(0.28)
PRT	−0.33	(−6.03)	−0.53	(−6.34)	(0.01)	0.01	(0.61)	−0.09	(−0.68)
DNK	−0.74	(−13.2)	−0.80	(−30.1)	(0.21)	0.00	(0.07)	0.01	(0.23)
GBR	−0.46	(−5.52)	−0.85	(−4.06)	(0.04)	0.04	(0.95)	−0.09	(−0.55)
SWE	−0.70	(−35.3)	−0.68	(−52.0)	(0.03)	0.00	(0.72)	−0.01	(−0.38)
NOR	0.63	(0.84)	−0.25	(−0.37)	(0.32)	−0.12	(−0.58)	0.78	(2.34)
AUS	−0.23	(−13.5)	−0.26	(−13.2)	(0.11)	0.00	(0.91)	0.01	(0.26)
JPN	−0.21	(−10.5)	−0.23	(−5.03)	(0.69)	−0.00	(−0.30)	−0.05	(−0.68)
CAN	−0.34	(−10.0)	−0.39	(−13.3)	(0.02)	−0.00	(−0.64)	0.03	(0.57)
USA	−0.24	(−61.2)	−0.26	(−68.4)	(0.01)	0.00	(0.62)	−0.01	(−1.35)
ALL	−0.38		−0.54			−0.00		0.01	
EMU11	−0.44		−0.59			−0.00		−0.05	
EU3	−0.63		−0.78			0.01		−0.03	
OECD5	−0.08		−0.28			−0.02		0.15	
(−NOR)	−0.26		−0.28			−0.00		−0.01	

Notes: This table displays country-specific estimates of the fiscal rule

$$d_t^{nd} = c_{BM} + c_{AM} + \phi_{x,BM}x_t + \phi_{x,AM}x_t + \phi_b b_{t-1} + \phi_s d_{t-1}^{nd} + u_t$$

which is the same as that estimated in Table 2 except that the dependent and lagged dependent variables are the non-discretionary component of primary deficit, divided by potential output. See Table 2 for other details and sources, and for an explanation of the structure of this table.

control for the potential endogeneity of the output gap by instrumenting the latter variable with its own lag and the lag of the US output gap (the EU 15 output gap in the US case). The rest of the table has a structure identical to Table 3, with the third column test for equality of the output gap coefficients in the two periods, followed by the estimates of the coefficients on lagged debt and deficit. Again, averages for groups of countries are shown in the bottom panel.

Looking first at the averages, we observe in all groups a clear counter-cyclical behaviour of non-discretionary fiscal policy in the two sample periods considered. The only exception lies in the OECD 5 group in the pre-Maastricht period, which is close to being acyclical. The latter result, however, reflects the influence of Norway which, with a procyclical non-discretionary component in that sub-period, is a clear outlier. In fact, the average estimate of the output gap coefficient for the OECD 5

Table 6

	(1)	(2)	(3)	(4)
	EMU (No. obs. = 238)			
$E(gap)_{BM}$	−0.22	(−6.19)		
$E(gap)_{AM}$	−0.47	(−10.6)	−0.25	(0.00)
$debty\{1\}_{BM}$	−0.01	(−2.89)		
$debty(1)_{AM}$	−0.02	(−4.55)	−0.01	(0.12)
$defy\{1\}_{BM}$	0.34	(4.65)		
$defy(1)_{AM}$	0.17	(2.53)	−0.17	(0.08)
	EU3 (No. obs. = 66)			
$E(gap)_{BM}$	−0.21	(−2.35)		
$E(gap)_{AM}$	−0.83	(−8.33)	−0.62	(0.00)
$debty\{1\}_{BM}$	−0.05	(−3.84)		
$debty(1)_{AM}$	0.03	(1.71)	0.08	(0.00)
$defy\{1\}_{BM}$	0.49	(3.71)		
$defy(1)_{AM}$	−0.21	(−1.52)	−0.70	(0.00)
	OECD5 (No. obs. = 110)			
$E(gap)_{BM}$	0.20	(0.91)		
$E(gap)_{AM}$	−0.17	(−0.91)	−0.37	(0.20)
$debty\{1\}_{BM}$	−0.05	(−1.45)		
$debty(1)_{AM}$	−0.00	(−0.02)	0.05	(0.21)
$defy\{1\}_{BM}$	0.75	(3.57)		
$defy(1)_{AM}$	0.58	(3.31)	−0.17	(0.54)

Notes: This table displays panel estimates of the fiscal rule

$$d_t^{nd} = c_{BM} + c_{AM} + \phi_{x,BM}x_t + \phi_{x,AM}x_t + \phi_b b_{t-1} + \phi_3 d_{t-1}^{nd} + u_t$$

which is the same as in Table 2 except that the dependent and lagged dependent variables are the non-discretionary component of the general government primary deficit, divided by potential output.
See Table 2 for other details and sources, and Table 3 for an explanation of the structure of this table.

group excluding Norway (shown in the last row of the table) suggests a non-negligible role for automatic stabilizers for that group as well, though one that is quantitatively less important than in EMU or EU 3 countries.[7]

Perhaps most interestingly, we notice among all groups an increase in the degree of counter-cyclicality of non-discretionary fiscal policy in the post-Maastricht period, as reflected in a smaller (i.e., more negative) value of the output gap coefficient. Quite strikingly, this finding appears to hold almost uniformly across countries, the only exceptions being Ireland and Sweden.

The basic evidence just described is also reflected in the panel-based estimates, reported in Table 6. In particular, we see an increasingly counter-cyclical non-discretionary fiscal policy in EMU countries and elsewhere.

Overall, we conclude that there is no evidence that the Maastricht Treaty and the SGP may have prevented automatic stabilizers in EMU countries from doing their job. On the contrary, EMU countries appear to have been able to join other industrialized economies in strengthening the counter-cyclical nature of that component of fiscal policy.

---

[7] This observation is consistent with the less progressive fiscal systems and smaller transfer programmes of the non-European countries of our sample.

6. ALTERNATIVE EXPLANATIONS

The most natural interpretation of our statistical evidence is that EMU-related constraints have not impaired the ability of EMU and countries to use discretionary fiscal policy as a counter-cyclical tool. On the contrary, the Maastricht Treaty seems to have brought to an end an era of procyclical discretionary fiscal policies in those countries.

We can think of several possible objections to this interpretation of our results. In this section, we discuss these objections in some detail, and provide what empirical evidence we can to address them. Some further robustness analysis is presented in the web appendix.

6.1. Does the loss of country-specific monetary policy matter?

It is often argued that a country that has given up the monetary instrument in a monetary union might need to run more of a stabilizing fiscal policy than before. This might explain why counter-cyclical discretionary fiscal policy has become more pronounced in EMU countries. Since the common monetary policy in place since 1999 is supposed to focus exclusively on euro area-wide conditions, and disregard national developments, one could think that in those circumstances fiscal policy should be used at the margin as a surrogate for the missing self-oriented monetary policy.

To what extent does this argument apply in practice to the EMU experience so far? In order to assess the merit of the 'surrogate' hypothesis we make use of a simple conventional indicator of deviations from appropriate monetary policy. The latter is approximated by a Taylor rule of the form:

$$r_t = \alpha + 1.5(\pi_t - \pi) + 0.5x_t$$

where r_t is the short-term nominal interest rate and π^* is the medium-term inflation target. This rule, originally proposed by John Taylor as a simple description of US monetary policy under the Greenspan mandate, can be viewed as a good first approximation to the behaviour of central banks that have been successful in stabilizing inflation and the output gap.[8] Such a rule has desirable properties when embedded in a dynamic optimizing model with realistic frictions.[9] We should emphasize, however, that in this section we use this rule exclusively to get a measure of the deviation of monetary policy from an appropriate country-specific configuration, without viewing it necessarily as a good approximation to the actual monetary policy rules followed by all the countries in the sample in all periods.

To assess the 'surrogate' policy hypothesis we introduce the deviation from the Taylor rule interest rate as an additional variable in our empirical fiscal policy rule. We allow its coefficient, like that of all other variables, to differ across the two sub-periods. Thus we do not need to assume a common inflation target for all countries

---

[8] See, e.g., Taylor (1993), Clarida et al. (1998, 2000).

[9] See, e.g., some of the contributions in Taylor (1999).

Table 7

	(1)	(2)	(3)	(4)
	EMU (No. obs. = 238)			
$E(gap)_{BM}$	0.20	(3.88)	(0.00)	
$E(gap)_{AM}$	0.03	(0.24)	−0.17	(0.27)
$debty\{1\}_{BM}$	−0.06	(−5.12)	(0.00)	
$debty(1)_{AM}$	−0.05	(−3.58)	0.01	(0.48)
$defy\{1\}_{BM}$	0.60	(9.87)	(0.00)	
$defy(1)_{AM}$	0.50	(5.57)	−0.10	(0.36)
$tayl\_dev_{BM}$	0.16	(2.21)	(0.00)	
$tayl\_dev_{AM}$	0.12	(1.05)	−0.03	(0.82)
	EU3 (No. obs. = 62)			
$E(gap)_{BM}$	0.12	(0.83)	(0.41)	
$E(gap)_{AM}$	−0.55	(−1.13)	−0.67	(0.19)
$debty\{1\}_{BM}$	−0.14	(−3.44)	(0.00)	
$debty(1)_{AM}$	−0.05	(−1.29)	0.08	(0.16)
$defy\{1\}_{BM}$	0.72	(5.33)	(0.00)	
$defy(1)_{AM}$	0.68	(4.45)	−0.05	(0.82)
$tayl\_dev_{BM}$	0.31	(1.65)	(0.00)	
$tayl\_dev_{AM}$	0.14	(0.55)	−0.17	(0.59)
	OECD5 (No. obs. = 110)			
$E(gap)_{BM}$	−0.12	(−0.64)	(0.53)	
$E(gap)_{AM}$	−1.06	(−2.86)	−0.94	(0.03)
$debty\{1\}_{BM}$	−0.00	(−0.08)	(0.93)	
$debty(1)_{AM}$	0.01	(0.32)	0.01	(0.78)
$defy\{1\}_{BM}$	0.77	(5.62)	(0.00)	
$defy(1)_{AM}$	0.55	(3.68)	−0.22	(0.27)
$tayl\_dev_{BM}$	0.03	(0.22)	(0.00)	
$tayl\_dev_{AM}$	−0.20	(−1.33)	−0.22	(0.25)

Notes: This table displays panel estimates of the same fiscal rule as in Table 2, but including the deviation from the Taylor rule (tayl_dev) as an independent variable. Dependent variable: general government primary deficit, cyclically adjusted, divided by potential output.
See Table 2 for other details and sources, and Table 3 for an explanation of the structure of this table.

and sample periods: possible variations in the latter will be captured in the intercept of our regression, which is allowed to differ across countries, and to have a break in each country in 1992.

The results of that exercise are reported in Table 7. In the EMU countries, the decline in the expected output gap coefficient becomes smaller and insignificant; in EU 3 countries the decline does not change; in OECD 5 countries it becomes bigger. The coefficient on the Taylor rule deviation is typically positive in both periods in EMU and EU 3 groups, but close to zero for the OECD 5. That finding suggests that, at least for EMU and EU 3 countries, fiscal policy and monetary policy may indeed have often acted as substitutes: when monetary policy is tight, discretionary fiscal policy loosens (relative to what it would otherwise be). The coefficients, however, are not large: when the short-term interest rate exceeds the Taylor rule interest rate by 1 percentage point, the discretionary deficit increases by between 0.1 and 0.3 percentage points of GDP, on average.

Table 8

	(1)	(2)	(3)	(4)
	EMU (No. obs. = 110)			
$E(gap)_{92-97}$	0.02	(0.17)	(0.87)	
$E(gap)_{98-02}$	−0.11	(−0.27)	−0.13	(0.76)
$debty\{1\}_{92-97}$	−0.07	(−4.12)	(0.00)	
$debty(1)_{98-02}$	−0.10	(−1.36)	−0.02	(0.77)
$defy\{1\}_{92-97}$	0.36	(3.51)	(0.00)	
$defy(1)_{98-02}$	0.38	(1.63)	0.02	(0.94)
	EU3 (No. obs. = 30)			
$E(gap)_{92-97}$	−0.64	(−1.21)	(0.24)	
$E(gap)_{98-02}$	0.14	(0.16)	0.79	(0.47)
$debty\{1\}_{92-97}$	−0.11	(−1.29)	(0.21)	
$debty(1)_{98-02}$	0.07	(0.70)	0.19	(0.19)
$defy\{1\}_{92-97}$	0.90	(4.16)	(0.00)	
$defy(1)_{98-02}$	−0.36	(−0.59)	−1.26	(0.07)
	OECD5 (No. obs. = 50)			
$E(gap)_{92-97}$	−1.03	(−3.20)	(0.00)	
$E(gap)_{98-02}$	−0.28	(−0.45)	0.76	(0.28)
$debty\{1\}_{92-97}$	−0.00	(−0.06)	(0.95)	
$debty(1)_{98-02}$	−0.05	(−0.83)	−0.04	(0.63)
$defy\{1\}_{92-97}$	0.75	(5.14)	(0.00)	
$defy(1)_{98-02}$	0.73	(1.67)	−0.03	(0.95)

Notes: This table displays panel estimates of the fiscal rule in the form reported in Table 2, for the same specification as in Table 3, but on a different sample: 1992–2002.
See Table 2 for other details and sources, and Table 3 for an explanation of the structure of this table.

6.2. Did actual EMU implementation make a difference?

A second and related argument is that the true test of the impact of the SGP is in the years after monetary unification became effective, or at least after the exchange rates became irrevocably locked in. Obviously we will have to wait some time for an evaluation of this argument. But we can still try to say something with the available time series. Table 8 displays estimates of our fiscal rule over the period 1992–2002, allowing for a structural break in the coefficients of all variables in 1998, when the exchange rates were locked in and decisions on membership were made. Again, we do not find any evidence that in the EMU countries fiscal policy has become more procyclical (or less counter-cyclical) from 1998 onwards. We do find evidence of a larger expected output gap effect after Maastricht in EU 3 and OECD 5 countries, although the difference is not statistically significant.

6.3. Does discretionary fiscal policy respond differently to recessions?

Since the Maastricht-related constraints are only likely to become binding in a recession, one could think that in order to assess their effect one should only look at the

Table 9

Fiscal policy during recession episodes

	Early 1980s			Early 1990s			Early 2000s		
	Δ output gap	Δ primary c.a. deficit	Ratio	Δ output gap	Δ primary c.a. deficit	Ratio	Δ output gap	Δ primary c.a. deficit	Ratio
AUT	-3.45	-0.45	0.13	-3.07	0.19	-0.06	-2.78	-0.28	0.10
BEL	-5.82	-1.7	0.29	-4.88	-1.44	0.30	-3.23	-0.89	0.28
DEU	-8.08	-4.88	0.60	-4.49	-2	0.45	-2.1	1.16	-0.55
ESP	-1.83	1.1	-0.60	-6.74	-1.67	0.25	-1.08	-0.29	0.27
FIN	-2.58	0.66	-0.26	-15.85	1.81	-0.11	-4.1	1.82	-0.44
FRA	-5.78	-0.44	0.08	-3.82	1.84	-0.48	-1.52	0.86	-0.57
GRC	-13.64	-0.51	0.04	-4.51	-2.67	0.59			–
IRE	-7.74	-6.82	0.88	-7.97	-1.94	0.24	-5.04	5.09	-1.01
ITA	-6.72	-1.88	0.28	-4.46	-6.87	1.54	-1.4	-0.08	0.06
NLD	-5.5	-1.94	0.35	-2.76	-4.41	1.60	-4.25	0.42	-0.10
PRT	-12.06	-7.12	0.59	-8.37	-0.95	0.11	-3.85	-0.8	0.21
DNK	-5.01	-0.04	0.01	-2.74	1.1	-0.40	-1.68	-0.15	0.00
GBR	-8.15	-4.85	0.60	-8.41	3.84	-0.46	-1.55	2.58	-1.66
SWE	-3.36	-0.92	0.27	-10.34	8.83	-0.85	-1.83	1.24	-0.68
NOR	-4.39	-2.88	0.66	-0.36	4.46	-12.39	-0.87	-0.2	0.23
AUS	-6.59	0.32	-0.05	-5.76	4.72	-0.82	-1.58	0.93	-0.59
JPN	-3.7	-3.85	1.04	-4.43	4.87	-1.10	-2.93	-0.14	0.05
CAN	-8.45	-0.75	0.09	-7.63	1	-0.13	-2.07	0.89	-0.43
USA	-9.47	0.57	-0.06	-4.16	0.4	-0.10	-3.6	4.3	-1.19
ALL	-6.44	-1.91	0.30	-5.83	0.58	-0.10	-2.53	0.91	-0.36
EMU	-6.65	-2.18	0.33	-6.08	-1.65	0.27	-2.94	0.70	-0.24
EU3	-5.51	-1.94	0.35	-7.16	4.59	-0.64	-1.69	1.22	-0.73
OECD5	-6.52	-1.32	0.20	-4.47	3.09	-0.69	-2.21	1.16	-0.52

Notes: This table displays the cumulative change in the output gap, in the primary cyclically adjusted deficit, and the ratio between the two, in the three recession episodes in the three periods indicated.

Source: OECD *Economic Outlook* database, December 2002 issue.

recent mini-recessions of 2001–2. To address this argument, we analyse the behaviour of fiscal authorities during three recession episodes.

We begin by identifying for each country the years in which its output gap experiences a decline, during the three main global recession waves since 1980: the early 1980s, the early 1990s, as well as the most recent global downturn in the early 2000s. For each country and recession episode we compute the cumulative output gap decline (i.e., the cumulative output losses relative to trend), and the cumulative increase in the primary, cyclically adjusted budget deficit, measured as a share of GDP. These statistics are shown in Table 9, which also reports the ratio between the cumulative deficit change and the cumulative output gap decline. The latter ratio can be interpreted as a simple statistic that captures the sign and intensity of the discretionary fiscal response. Thus, a negative sign for the ratio is evidence of a deliberate counter-cyclical fiscal stance, whereas the size of the ratio captures the strength of that response relative to the size of the output gap decline. Like previous tables, Table 9 also reports averages for each variable and group of countries (EMU and control groups).

Consider first the fiscal behaviour of current EMU countries during the three recession episodes. In the recession of the early 1980s the average cumulative change in the primary adjusted deficit is negative, with a corresponding average ratio to cumulative GDP losses of 0.33. Only in Spain and Finland is the fiscal policy stance counter-cyclical. And fiscal behaviour during that recession in our control groups (EU 3 and OECD 5) does not differ significantly from that of EMU countries. Only Australia and the US show a (very weak) counter-cyclical stance among the non-EMU countries.

During the recessions of the early 1990s the average fiscal stance of EMU countries remained largely unchanged, with a ratio of cumulative deficit change to output losses of 0.27, indicating again a procyclical discretionary policy (most pronounced in Austria, Finland and especially France). Interestingly, however, the picture now becomes quite different for the two groups of non-EMU countries, which both feature counter-cyclical discretionary fiscal responses to the recession, on average as well as uniformly (in sign) across countries.

The most relevant data are those that measure the fiscal stance among EMU countries during the most recent downturn, which happens to be the first one where the constraints developed by the MT and the SGP have been effectively in place. Surprising as this may be for its critics, the SGP has not prevented EMU countries from pursuing counter-cyclical fiscal policies during the recent recession, the average ratio becoming negative (−0.24).[10]

---

[10] Still, this ratio is smaller in absolute value for the two control groups, suggesting a weaker counter-cyclical policy in the average EMU country. And the pattern is not uniform across EMU countries: Germany, France and Ireland account for much of the change in the average.

6.4. Is fiscal policy's stabilizing Influence declining?

The ability of fiscal policy to stabilize the economy might have fallen in the 1990s. To compensate for this, EMU countries might have liked to use counter-cyclical discretionary policy *more intensively* after Maastricht. We do not have much to say on this point. While there is some evidence that the impact of fiscal policy shocks on GDP and its components has dampened in the last 20 years in 5 OECD countries (see Perotti, 2002), it would be extremely hard to assess whether the process has intensified in the 1990s relative to the 1980s.

6.5. Is fiscal policy's cyclical sensitivity declining?

Finally, the cyclical (non-discretionary) component of fiscal policy might have become less responsive to cyclical conditions after Maastricht – for instance because of a decline in the progressivity of income taxes or less generous unemployment benefits and tighter eligibility rules – thus providing less automatic stabilization. Once again, EMU countries might have liked to use discretionary fiscal policy more counter-cyclically than before to compensate for this effect. However, we have seen in Section 6 that exactly the opposite seems to have occurred: the cyclical component of the deficit has, if anything, become more counter-cyclical after Maastricht.

7. PUBLIC INVESTMENT AFTER MAASTRICHT

It is often argued that, for political economy reasons, government investment is the easiest component of government spending to cut in the short run. As a consequence, if the Maastricht-related constraints are binding they should have affected disproportionately government investment, thereby imposing long-term costs besides the (alleged) short-run costs from reduced stabilization.

In this section, we evaluate this claim by comparing the behaviour of government investment over time and across countries. Before doing this, it is important to clarify the nature of the data on government investment we use. First, one may worry that privatizations might impair the comparability of the data over time and across countries (as different countries have privatized in different degrees and at different times). However, it is important to note that the data we use refer to the general government, while the privatization process has concerned mostly state owned enterprises (like banks, airlines, telecoms) that were originally in the public sector, but not in the general government.

Second, we use gross investment proper rather than net capital expenditure by the government. The latter is sometimes used to answer the question we address here, but it includes (as a negative item) net capital transfers received. While in general net capital transfers are small and stable, over this period they include revenues from UMTS spectrum auctions, which were considerable in some countries. For instance,

Table 10

	1978–82 (1)	1988–92 (2)	1998–01 (3)	(3)–(2)
AUT	4.40	3.16	1.67	−1.49
BEL	4.52	1.91	1.65	−0.26
DEU	3.53	2.67	1.82	−0.85
ESP	2.12	4.63	3.21	−1.42
FIN	3.35	3.47	2.77	−0.71
FRA	3.22	3.57	3.05	−0.51
GRC	2.81	4.97	3.78	−1.19
IRE	5.57	2.01	3.38	1.37
ITA	3.19	3.23	2.38	−0.85
NLD	3.72	2.99	3.12	0.13
PRT	3.80	3.53	4.15	0.61
DNK	3.02	1.79	1.75	−0.03
GBR	2.21	1.99	1.17	−0.83
SWE	4.11	3.23	2.61	−0.61
NOR	3.93	3.62	3.20	−0.42
AUS	3.22	2.65	2.39	−0.27
JPN	5.86	5.02	5.31	0.29
CAN	3.02	2.86	2.29	−0.57
USA	3.41	3.62	3.28	−0.35
ALL	3.63	3.21	2.79	−0.42
EMU	3.66	3.29	2.82	−0.47
EU3	3.12	2.34	1.85	−0.49
OECD5	3.89	3.56	3.29	−0.26

Notes: The table displays the average government investment/potential GDP ratio in the three periods indicated. The last column displays the difference between the 1988–92 average and the 1998–2001 average.

Source: OECD *Economic Outlook* database, December 2002 issue.

in 2000 they were 2.5% of potential GDP in Germany, 1.2% in Italy, 0.7% in the Netherlands, and 0.4% in Greece (not all countries recorded the whole amount of auction revenues as net capital transfers received).

Table 10 reports government investment as a share of potential output in three separate five-year periods: 1978–82, 1988–92, and 1997–2001. We take averages over five years to minimize the contribution of cyclical or electoral variation in government spending. Again, the table reports indicators separately for the 19 countries in our sample, and also on average for the 11 EMU countries, the 3 EU, non-EMU countries, and the 5 remaining OECD countries.

The table makes two points. Between the 1988–92 period and the 1997 2001 periods, government investment as a share of potential GDP did fall in the EMU countries by 0.47 percentage points on average, but it also fell by 0.49 percentage points in the EU 3 countries and by 0.26 percentage points in the OECD 5 countries. Thus, there is a clear overall trend fall in government investment as a share of GDP. Second, this trend started well before Maastricht: between 1978–82 and 1988–92, the decline in the government investment/potential output share was also very similar

Table 11

	1978–82 (1)	1988–92 (2)	1997–01 (3)	(3)–(2)
AUT	9.77	6.83	3.62	−3.21
BEL	9.28	4.64	4.10	−0.54
DEU	8.16	6.57	4.33	−2.24
ESP	6.99	11.94	9.08	−2.86
FIN	9.12	7.70	6.39	−1.31
FRA	7.49	7.87	6.70	−1.18
GRC	8.80	14.09	10.67	−3.42
IRE	13.18	5.99	11.19	5.21
ITA	8.27	7.69	6.06	−1.63
NLD	8.07	6.69	7.88	1.19
PRT	10.36	10.01	10.87	0.86
DNK	6.20	3.58	3.39	−0.19
GBR	5.84	5.36	3.36	−2.00
SWE	7.66	6.00	5.30	−0.70
NOR	6.94	6.12	5.39	−0.73
AUS	10.92	9.23	7.78	−1.45
JPN	22.44	18.78	16.60	−2.18
CAN	8.83	7.75	7.28	−0.46
USA	12.45	12.73	12.09	−0.64
ALL	9.51	8.40	7.48	−0.92
EMU	9.04	8.19	7.35	−0.83
EU3	6.56	4.98	4.02	−0.96
OECD5	12.32	10.92	9.83	−1.09

Notes: The table displays the average government investment/cyclically adjusted spending ratio in the three periods indicated. The last column displays the difference between the 1988–92 average and the 1998–2001 average.

Source: OECD *Economic Outlook* database, December 2002 issue.

to the decline in the next decade in the EMU and OECD 5 countries, and actually considerably larger in the EU 3 countries.

The claim we wanted to address, however, is a statement about the impact of the Maastricht-related constraints on government investment *relative* to the rest of government spending. Hence, it should perhaps be assessed comparing the behaviour of government investment relative to total government spending. Table 11 displays the same information as Table 10, but this time government investment is expressed as a share of total primary government spending. The conclusions are the same: here too we find an OECD-wide trend towards a fall in the share of government investment in total spending, which started well before Maastricht.[11]

The Maastricht-related constraints may have a stronger impact on the cyclical behaviour of government investment than on its average value. Lane (2002) indeed

---

[11] The figure for the EMU average is somewhat influenced by Ireland, where the share of government investment in total primary spending increased by almost 6 percentage points between 1988–92 and 1997–2001. However, the qualitative conclusions would hold even if one excluded Ireland.

Table 12

	(1)	(2)	(3)	(4)
	EMU (No. obs. = 239)			
E(gap)$_{BM}$	0.04	(2.58)	(0.01)	
E(gap)$_{AM}$	0.04	(1.80)	0.00	(1.00)
debty{1}$_{BM}$	−0.00	(−1.63)	(0.10)	
debty(1)$_{AM}$	−0.01	(−3.02)	−0.01	(0.08)
giy{1}$_{BM}$	0.82	(19.42)	(0.00)	
giy(1)$_{AM}$	0.54	(6.49)	−0.28	(0.00)
	EU3 (No. obs. = 66)			
E(gap)$_{BM}$	0.02	(1.32)	(0.19)	
E(gap)$_{AM}$	−0.09	(−2.67)	−0.11	(0.00)
debty{1}$_{BM}$	−0.01	(−1.62)	(0.11)	
debty(1)$_{AM}$	−0.00	(−0.64)	0.00	(0.53)
giy{1}$_{BM}$	0.60	(5.52)	(0.00)	
giy(1)$_{AM}$	0.50	(2.92)	−0.10	(0.61)
	OECD5 (No. obs. = 110)			
E(gap)$_{BM}$	0.03	(1.20)	(0.23)	
E(gap)$_{AM}$	−0.04	(−1.66)	−0.07	(0.04)
debty{1}$_{BM}$	−0.00	(−0.52)	(0.60)	
debty(1)$_{AM}$	−0.02	(−5.20)	−0.01	(0.02)
giy{1}$_{BM}$	0.63	(8.61)	(0.00)	
giy(1)$_{AM}$	0.35	(2.92)	−0.28	(0.05)

Notes: This table displays panel estimates of a fiscal rule in the form reported in Table 2, except that the dependent and lagged dependent variables are the general government investment to potential output ratio ('giy'). Sample: 1980–2002 for all countries.
See Table 2 for other details and sources, and Table 3 for an explanation of the structure of this table.

finds that government investment is the most cyclical component of government spending. Table 12 reports estimates of our baseline fiscal policy rule, with the cyclically adjusted deficit replaced by government investment as a share of potential output. We do find some evidence of a mildly procyclical behaviour of government investment in EMU countries: in the pre-Maastricht period, on average the government investment/ potential output ratio increased by about 0.04 percentage points for every extra percentage point in expected gap. However, there is no evidence that the cyclical behaviour of government investment has changed in the post-Maastricht period in any group of countries. And when we compare the cyclical behaviour of government investment in the 1992–97 and 1998–2002 periods, we find that in the EMU countries the coefficient of the expected gap declined in the second period by 0.17 (with the difference significant at the 14% level).

8. CONCLUSIONS

As the debate on the pros and cons of the SGP heats up, a popular view is that the constraints on fiscal policy have significantly impaired the ability of EU governments to conduct an effective counter-cyclical stabilization policy and to provide an adequate level of government services and of public infrastructure.

We do not find much support for this view. We document that discretionary fiscal policy in EMU countries has become more counter-cyclical over time, following what appears to be a trend that affects other industrialized countries as well. There is still some way to go before EMU countries' discretionary fiscal policy becomes as counter-cyclical as that of other industrialized countries. Whether the SGP will become an impediment to this remains to be seen.

The decline in public investment (as a share of GDP) observed over the past decade among EMU countries is also hard to view as a consequence of the MT and SGP constraints. Empirical evidence indicates that industrialized nations not subject to those constraints have experienced an even greater decline recently, and that the decline in public investment was even greater before Maastricht.

To conclude, we want to stress our desire not to read in the data more than they can tell us, and to keep in mind the necessary limitations associated with an empirical analysis of the sort provided in our paper. In particular, there is a caveat the reader must not ignore: real recessions have been quite rare among EMU countries during the post-Maastricht period, hence it may be that the available data cover a period when the constraints associated with the SGP were not really binding. If and when an active counter-cyclical fiscal policy is really needed in the future, the impact of the SGP could well be different from that we detect in the experience to date. Our findings can offer useful empirical caveats to an appealing but simplistic view, rather than a precise answer to a question that will likely remain open for some time to come.

APPENDIX

Available at http://www.economic-policy.org

Discussion

Philip R. Lane
Institute for International Integration Studies (IIIS), Trinity College Dublin and CEPR

This paper documents two shifts in fiscal policy between 1980–91 ('before Maastricht' or BM) and 1992–2001 ('after Maastricht' or AM). First, discretionary fiscal policy has become more counter-cyclical over time. Second, public investment has declined in importance relative to overall government spending. The former result challenges the concern that the Maastricht Treaty and the Stability and Growth Pact constrains European governments from using fiscal policy as a stabilization device; the latter trend in fact has been weaker in EMU countries than elsewhere in the OECD, such that it is hard to attribute to the binding nature of these fiscal agreements. The authors do a good job in developing their empirical work, addressing many potential objections but remaining suitably cautious in interpreting the results, in view of the inevitably short time interval.

The authors go further and explore a range of hypotheses as to why discretionary fiscal policy has become more counter-cyclical in recent years. Perhaps most importantly, they show that the automatic non-discretionary component of fiscal policy has also become more counter-cyclical in recent years, such that the shift in the behaviour of discretionary fiscal policy is not substituting for less-active automatic stabilizers.

However, one candidate explanation that they do not address is the Talvi and Vegh (2000) prediction that fiscal procyclicality is positively correlated with the degree of output volatility. Their argument is based on the political infeasibility of running large surpluses during boom times. For a high-volatility country, the appropriate surplus required during an expansion phase may be quite large as a ratio to GDP. However, a large surplus may unleash intense political pressure to increase public spending. In contrast, the required surplus in a low-volatility country may be quite small and may not attract the same degree of political opposition. The net result is that fiscal procyclicality is much more likely for countries or periods in which the amplitude of the business cycle is large.

In addition to the Talvi–Vegh political economy story, there is also a straightforward technical reason why volatility affects the cyclical performance of fiscal policy. Making a correct decomposition between the trend and cyclical components of output growth is centrally important in determining the appropriate stance for fiscal policy: for instance, a permanent increase in production may call for an increase in government investment to augment the public capital stock, whereas a temporary boom requires expenditure restraint. The more volatile is output growth, the greater is the likelihood of making a serious error in identifying the path for potential output and hence inadvertently adopting a procyclical fiscal stance.

In fact, the period studied by Galí and Perotti offers some evidence of a relation between volatility and fiscal cyclicality. Table 13 shows that volatility fell almost everywhere between 1982–91 and 1992–2001, thereby relaxing procyclical pressures on fiscal policy. Moreover, Figure 1 shows that, across countries and the two sub-periods, the positive correlation is reasonably strong between output volatility and the country-specific cyclicality coefficients estimated by Galí and Perotti (the point estimate is 0.41).[12]

It is also quite possible that the Maastricht Treaty and the Stability and Growth Pact have positively contributed to the improved cyclical behaviour of fiscal policy among EMU member countries, rather than being a negative or neutral force. This is based on the notion that fiscal consolidation is a precondition for an effective cyclical stabilization policy. For instance, if a fiscal position is deemed to be unsustainable, a government may be forced to run a procyclically tight fiscal policy even during a recession in order to satisfy financial markets. In contrast, if fiscal control is well established, a counter-cyclical fiscal policy will not call forth an increase in financial risk premia. The EMU member countries achieved a substantial improvement in the

[12] See also the results in Lane (2002).

Table 13. Standard deviation of the output gap, 1980–91 and 1992–2001

	1980–1991	1992–2001	Change
Australia	2.16	0.82	−1.34
Austria	2.00	0.83	−1.17
Belgium	2.83	0.98	−1.86
Canada	3.46	1.55	−1.91
Germany	2.27	0.63	−1.64
Denmark	2.23	0.75	−1.48
Spain	3.01	1.77	−1.24
Finland	4.47	3.24	−1.23
France	2.04	1.36	−0.68
United Kingdom	3.88	0.79	−3.10
Greece	2.10	1.61	−0.49
Ireland	2.38	3.42	1.04
Italy	1.59	0.71	−0.88
Japan	2.05	1.51	−0.53
Netherlands	2.27	1.11	−1.16
Norway	2.28	1.11	−1.18
Portugal	4.47	1.56	−2.92
Sweden	3.23	1.45	−1.78
United States	2.46	1.01	−1.45
Mean	2.69	1.38	−1.32

Note: Data from OECD *Economic Outlook* Database.

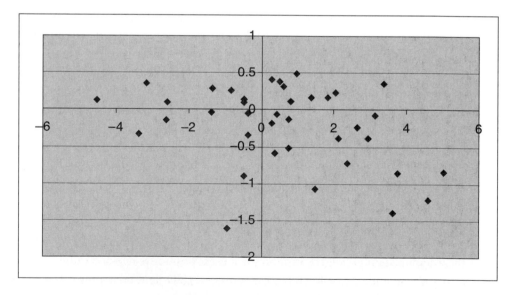

Figure 1. Scatter plot of cyclicality coefficients against output gap volatility

Note: Correlation is 0.41.

Source: Data from OECD *Economic Outlook* Database.

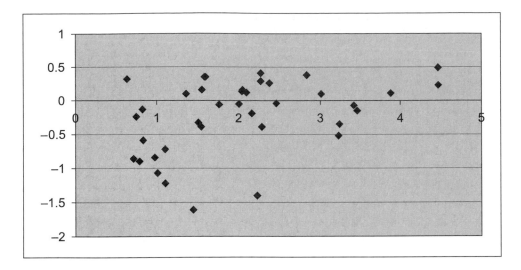

Figure 2. Scatter plot of cyclicality coefficients against average primary surplus

Note: Correlation is 0.36.

Source: Data from OECD *Economic Outlook* Database.

average primary surplus between BM and AM: a mean increase of 2.2 percentage points of GDP (the OECD average increase was 1.56 percentage points). Moreover, Figure 2 shows a significant negative correlation between the average primary surplus and the estimated cyclicality coefficient. In this way, to the extent that the Maastricht Treaty and the Stability and Growth Pact have facilitated fiscal adjustment (for example, by reducing the domestic political costs of debt reduction strategies), they may have indirectly also improved the cyclical performance of fiscal policy.

As the authors highlight, the trend in deficit reduction has also been evident in other major industrial countries. As such, it is clear that the EMU fiscal framework is not the only institutional mechanism that can deliver fiscal stabilization. However, just as the causes of the original debt accumulation differed across countries (e.g. between the US and Continental Europe), so it is natural that there was heterogeneity in how countries engaged in the fiscal adjustment process. Further research on establishing the appropriate counterfactual for the EMU countries (what would have happened without the Maastricht Treaty) would be very interesting.

Another significant result in this paper is that fiscal policy remains significantly less counter-cyclical in the EMU countries than in some other major industrial nations. Again, this may be consistent with the Maastricht Treaty and the Stability and Growth Pact (or the high debts that still persist in some EMU countries) constraining counter-cyclical policy to some degree. However, it may also reflect the lack of coordination among national fiscal policies in Europe: the effectiveness of a fiscal stimulus in any individual country is limited by the highly open nature of the individual European countries, such that the payoff to a more aggressive stabilization policy is limited. In this way, to the extent that output gaps among EMU countries have a common component, the lack of an effective fiscal coordination mechanism (or a larger federal budget) may limit the capacity for counter-cyclical fiscal policy.

Regarding public investment, the authors note that, in contrast to the aggregate picture, public investment has not become more counter-cyclical AM relative to BM. It follows that the shift in aggregate fiscal cyclicality is attributable to some other component(s) of public spending. Lane (2002) found that the public sector wage bill played a key role in the cyclical behaviour of fiscal policy. It is interesting to speculate as to why public sector pay and/or employment may have turned more counter-cyclical in recent years. One possibility is that governments and taxpayers may have become more resistant to aggressive public-sector wage claims during boom times, in response to the large run-up in such spending during the 1970s and 1980s. Another is that the preferences of public sector unions have shifted in favour of greater stability over the cycle, moderating claims during expansions in order to protect incomes during downturns. A third is that the private-sector wage bill may have become more counter-cyclical, spilling over into a similar pattern in the government sector. Research on these questions would make for a potentially fruitful future project in this area.

Although the empirical work in this paper is quite extensive, I would have liked to see two more exercises. First, it would be interesting to allow the data to identify endogenously country-specific break points over the 1982–2001 period: in this way, it would be revealed whether the change in fiscal behaviour dates to the introduction of the Maastricht Treaty or to some other event. For instance, the change in fiscal behaviour in Ireland dates back to the much-studied adjustment undertaken in 1987 rather than being related to EMU.[13] Second, in line with my previous comments, it would also be informative to include interaction terms in the regression analysis: for instance, does the cyclicality coefficient vary with the level of output volatility or the level of the average fiscal surplus?

Finally, I concur with the authors' caveat that the evidence in this paper may not be relevant in predicting what would happen in the event of a large or sustained negative shock. Although the SGP does have an escape clause for large declines in output, it may be too cumbersome and retrospective in its procedures to permit an early and aggressive response to a major slump. The recent Japanese experience deserves close study in designing a new fiscal framework for Europe.

Wolfram F. Richter
University of Dortmund, CESifo and IZA

This paper is good news for the supporters of the Maastricht Treaty and the Stability and Growth Pact, or SGP. There have been widespread concerns that the SGP, instead of promoting stability and growth, would effectively achieve just the opposite.

---

[13] Favero and Monacelli (2003) identify 1987 as dating a shift in the US macroeconomic policy regime.

Instead of constraining overly active fiscal management, the SGP would keep participating countries from taking the measures needed to fight recessions and economic
breakdowns. And instead of directing public policy towards growth, the SGP would
curtail governments' scope of financing public investment. This is so as investment
expenditures are often said to be among the first to be axed when budget deficits
force governments to cut spending.

It may well be too early to make ultimate statements about the justification of such
concerns. After all, SGP-based policy is still in its infancy and the excessive deficit
procedure has not passed any hard test. However, Galí's and Perotti's paper shows
that from today's perspective any such concerns are unwarranted. The authors find
some evidence of mildly procyclical behaviour of government investment in EMU
countries, but there is no evidence that the cyclical behaviour has changed in the
period after Maastricht.

All this is good news, and it is reassuring to see that the results are robust and well
substantiated. I have only two comments to make, one on the authors' motivation for
their analysis, the other on the way the authors model budgetary policy. I start with
the latter.

The authors use the (expected) output gap and the outstanding debt to explain the
cyclically adjusted primary budget surplus. Of course these variables capture two
objectives of budget policy, that of output stabilization and that of debt stabilization.
Other plausible objectives, however, have not been studied as extensively by
theories of budget policies, yet cannot be ignored when interpreting the empirical
evidence. One is the political objective to cut down the government sector: it is hard
to believe that deficits would have been reduced as much over the years as they have
been reduced effectively without broad public consent to reduce government activity.
Another is the objective to finance government investment, which I will address
below.

As to motivation, the authors refer to critiques of SGP. It is true that many are
critical of that policy framework; however, this may be motivated by concerns different to those suggested by Galí and Perotti. I agree that there had been concerns in
the 1990s that too far-reaching co-ordination of national fiscal policies could prove
to be a harmful straitjacket when fighting asymmetric shocks. However, I believe
that this kind of critique has decreased and not increased over the years. The reasons
are both theoretical and empirical. The empirical ones are the subject of the present
paper. There is little, if any, empirical evidence corroborating the straightjacket
hypothesis.

The theoretical evidence points in the same direction. A careful reading of the
SGP indicates that it is medium-term oriented. The Resolution of the European
Council of 17 June 1997 where it says that the member states 'commit themselves to
respect the medium-term budgetary objective positions close to balance or in surplus
set out in their stability or convergence programmes'. All that the SGP tries to do is
to restrain overly active fiscal management. The underlying idea is that governments

should choose their medium-term targets and let automatic stabilizers play symmetrically over the business cycle (Buti, 2001). The only understandable concern would have to rely on the fear that adherence to a medium-term objective unduly hampers demand management in the short run. Whether this concern is effectively substantiated is, however, a very debatable subject.

The other concern motivating Galí and Perotti's work is even less justified by a reading of the SGP. It is the concern that compliance with the SGP could negatively affect public investment. To be frank, I have difficulties seeing this problem. The SGP makes a strict difference between expenditures for investment and expenditures for consumption. According to the SGP a necessary requirement for an excessive deficit is a government deficit that exceeds government investment expenditure. This is the so-called 'golden rule' of budget discipline. According to the golden rule public deficits raise a problem only if they exceed government investment. The rule is well anchored in the Basic Law for the Federal Republic of Germany (Article 115) and it has played a prominent role in the discussion surrounding the SGP. I cannot imagine that the excessive deficit procedure is brought against a member state that can justify deficits by investments. Since governments are aware of this provision I cannot see why the SGP should harm the propensity to invest. At most, the SGP could be said to hamper a policy of public investment that produces budget deficits in the future. If this outcome were to be feared I would rather put the quality of investment up to discussion before I would put any blame on the SGP.

To be fair, there is some discussion about the SGP which deserves to be taken seriously. But this discussion has a different focus. The focus is not that the SGP is too strict. The focus is instead that the SGP is incomplete. It is claimed to be incomplete insofar as it does not acknowledge the role of fiscal externalities. That might be a severe impediment to successfully coping with severe symmetric shocks. There are economists who see the world on the verge of an economic breakdown. If this assessment is correct, some co-ordinated fiscal policy by the world's leading economies may be the required remedy. The SGP, however, provides no basis for policy co-ordination and the Broad Economic Policy Guidelines are not legally binding (Directorate General, 2002). Hence Europe might have a constitutional problem. The available instruments for policy co-ordination might be insufficient to cope with exceptional challenges. However, the literature conveys no clear picture on this matter. It is a debatable subject whether Europe needs more closed forms of fiscal policy co-ordination.

Panel discussion

In reply to Philip Lane, Jordi Galí stated that the authors tried to address the Talvi–Vegh hypothesis by allowing for non-linear terms in the econometric specification, but found them to be insignificant.

David Miles thought that the results of the paper show that the SGP is malleable or ignored, so the results cannot necessarily be called good news. David Begg and Mike Artis pointed out that the results including the effects of automatic stabilizers are crucial if the total effect of fiscal policy is of interest, and felt that the distinction between the discretionary and automatic components is somewhat arbitrary. Ignazio Angeloni added that more attention needs to be paid to the automatic stabilizers of fiscal policy: if fiscal policy is more sustainable in the medium term, automatic stabilizers work better so that there is more scope for the discretionary part of fiscal policy.

David Begg pointed out that one benefit of counter-cyclical fiscal policy is to contain inflationary fears. In general, the endogeneity of output and inflation to the monetary policy regime change could be analysed in more depth. Mike Artis pointed out the similarity of the endogeneity problems in the paper with the literature investigating whether the ERM or EMS decreases inflation. The worldwide downward trend indicates that institutions, such as the SGP, may well be endogenous to deeper factors.

Ignazio Angeloni was not surprised by the better fit of Taylor rules in recent years, when exchange rate volatility is no longer present. Carlo Favero expressed concern with using the Taylor rule for the first part of the sample, when omitting variables such as exchange-rate volatility is not appropriate.

Karen Helene Midelfart Knarvik was intrigued by the common trend towards a counter-cyclical fiscal policy and the observed differences between EMU countries and the control groups. Concerning Norway she argued that tax reforms had facilitated counter-cyclical fiscal policy and she wondered whether this could also be the case for other countries.

Steve Cecchetti pointed out that measures of the net-present value of government liabilities would be a better measure of fiscal stance than current deficits, which can be manipulated by governments.

REFERENCES

Arreaza, A., B.E. Sørensen and O. Yosha (1999). 'Consumption smoothing through fiscal policy in OECD and EU countries', in J.M. Poterba and J. von Hagen (eds.), *Fiscal Institutions and Fiscal Performance*, University of Chicago Press, Chicago, 59–80.

Artis, M. and M. Buti (2000). 'Close to balance or in surplus: a policy maker's guide to the implementation of the Stability and Growth Pact', *Journal of Common Market Studies*, 38(4), 563–602.

Auerbach, A.J. (2002). 'Is there a role for discretionary fiscal policy?', in *Rethinking Stabilization Policies*, Federal Reserve Bank of Kansas City, 109–50.

Ballabriga, F. and C. Martinez-Mongay (2002). 'Has EMU shifted policy?', Economic Papers, European Commission, Directorate General for Economic and Financial Affairs, No. 166, available at http://europa.eu.int/comm/economy-finance.

Beetsma, R., X. Debrun and F. Klaassen (2001). 'Is fiscal policy coordination in EMU desirable?', *Swedish Economic Policy Review*, 8, 57–98.

Bohn, H. (1998). 'The behaviour of US public debt and deficits', *Quarterly Journal of Economics*, August, 949–63.

Bouthevillain, C., P. Cour-Thimann, G. vand den Dool, P. Hernández de Cos, G. Langenus, M. Mohr, S. Momigliano and M. Tujula (2001). 'Cyclical adjusted budget balances: an alternative approach', European Central Bank Working Paper No. 77, September.

Buiter, W., G. Corsetti and N. Roubini (1993). 'Excessive deficits: sense and nonsense of the Treaty of Maastricht', *Economic Policy*.

Buiter, W.H. and C. Grafe (2002). 'Patching up the Pact: some suggestions for enhancing fiscal sustainability and macroeconomic stability in an enlarged European Union', CEPR Discussion Paper No. 3496.

Buti, M. (2001). 'Comment on Beetsma, Debrun and Klaassen: is fiscal policy coordination in EMU desirable?', *Swedish Economic Policy Review*, 8, 99–105.

Buti, M. and G. Giudice (2002). 'Maastricht's fiscal rules at ten: an assessment', *Journal of Common Market Studies*, 40(5), 823–48.

Canzoneri, M.B., R.E. Cumby and B.T. Diba (2002). 'Should the European Central Bank and the Federal reserve be concerned about fiscal policy?', paper presented at the Federal Reserve Bank of Kansas City's symposium on 'Rethinking Stabilization Policy', Jackson Hole, August 2002.

Clarida, R., J. Galí and M. Gertler (1998). 'Monetary rules in practice: some international perspectives', *European Economic Review*, 42, 1033–67.

— (2000). 'Monetary policy rules and macroeconomic stability: evidence and some theory', *Quarterly Journal of Economics*, February, 147–80.

Directorate General for Economic and Financial Affairs (2002). 'Co-ordination of economic policies in the EU: a presentation of key features of the main procedures', *Euro Papers* No. 45.

Eichengreen, B. and C. Wyplosz (1998). 'The Stability Pact: more than a minor nuisance?', *Economic Policy*, April, 67–113.

European Central Bank (1999). *Monthly Bulletin*, May, 45–61.

European Commission (1999). 'European Economy: Supplement A. Budgetary Surveillance in the EMU', March.

— (2000). 'European Economy:. Public Finances in EMU', Reports and Studies No. 3.

— (2002). 'European Economy: Public Finances in EMU', Reports and Studies No. 3.

Fatás, A. (1998). 'Does EMU need a fiscal federation?', *Economic Policy*, April.

Fatás, A. and I. Mihov (2002a). 'Fiscal policy and EMU', mimeo, INSEAD.

— (2002b). 'On constraining fiscal policy in EMU', mimeo, INSEAD.

Favero, C. and T. Monacelli (2003). 'Monetary-fiscal mix and inflation performance: evidence from the US', mimeo, IGIER-Bocconi.

Giorno, C., P. Richardson, D. Roseveare and P. van den Noord (1995). 'Potential output, output gaps, and structural budget balances', *OECD Economic Studies*, 24, 167–209.

Hercowitz, Z. and M. Strawczynski (1999). 'Cyclical bias in government spending: evidence from the OECD', mimeo, Tel Aviv University.

Lane, P. (2002). 'The cyclical behaviour of fiscal policy: evidence from the OECD', *Journal of Public Economics*, forthcoming.

Melitz, J. (1997). 'Some cross-country evidence about debt, deficits, and the behaviour of monetary and fiscal authorities', CEPR Discussion Paper No. 1653, CEPR, London.

OECD (2002). 'Economic Outlook, Sources and Methods', http://www.oecd.org/eco/out/source.htm

Perotti, R. (2002). 'Estimating the effects of fiscal policy in OECD countries', mimeo, European University Institute.

Talvi, E. and C. Vegh (2000). 'Tax base variability and procyclical fiscal policy,' NBER Working Paper No. 7499.

Taylor, J. (1993). 'Discretion vs. policy rules in practice', *Carnegie-Rochester Series on Public Policy*, XXXIX, 195–214.

— (ed.) (1999). *Monetary Policy Rules*, University of Chicago Press, Chicago.

van den Noord, P. (2002). 'Automatic stabilizers in the 1990s and beyond', in M. Buti, J. von Hagen and C. Martinez-Mongay (eds.), *The Behaviour of Fiscal Authorities*, 130–48, Palgrave, New York.

Wyplosz, C. (1999). 'Economic policy coordination in EMU: strategies and institutions', *ZEI Policy Paper*, B11.

— (2002). 'Fiscal discipline in EMU: rules or institutions?', mimeo, Graduate Institute for International Studies, Geneva.

Life on the outside

SUMMARY

The European economic and monetary union (EMU) is now over 4 years old. In this paper we assess whether monetary union has begun to have significant economic effects by comparing countries in EMU with the EU countries outside. We focus principally on trade creation between EMU member countries, using a methodology that controls for the fact that the decision to join the monetary union was not random but was more likely to be taken by countries whose prospects of trading with other EMU members were already high. We find that the trade effects of monetary union are significant. We estimate that had the UK been inside EMU the sum of its imports and exports could have been substantially greater. For comparative purposes, we also make preliminary estimates of the effect of monetary union on three other dimensions of economic performance: foreign direct investment, the development of financial markets and overall macroeconomic performance, though we recognize that our ability to control for other factors is more limited in respect of these other indicators. The evidence suggests that inward investment in the countries outside would have been greater had they joined EMU, but that the impact of this on GDP would be no more than 0.3% of GDP per annum for the UK and less than that for the other 'outs'. Financial market activity shows no clear sign of having been affected by EMU, and London's position as Europe's financial centre remains, as yet, largely unchallenged. On standard measures of aggregate performance inflation, unemployment and output – no clear pattern of EMU effects has yet emerged.

– David Barr, Francis Breedon and David Miles

Life on the outside: economic conditions and prospects outside euroland

David Barr, Francis Breedon and David Miles

The Business School, Imperial College London

1. INTRODUCTION

What can we learn about the potential benefits and costs of the European monetary union by comparing the performance of the 'ins' and 'outs' over the past few years? Those who are strongly in favour of 'outs' staying out or of 'outs' jumping in implicitly take the view that the answer to this question is 'a lot'. Those sceptical about whether the UK, Sweden and Denmark should adopt the euro point out that unemployment in those countries has stayed lower than in the euro area, that inflation has remained low and that there are no signs from financial markets that the credibility of monetary policy in controlling inflation has been harmed. The euro enthusiasts – particularly in the UK – have focused on the (largely) unwelcome strength of the 'out' currencies against the euro for much of the period since 1999 and have highlighted the relative weakness of foreign direct investment inflows into the 'outs'.[1] Sorting out what we

The Managing Editor in charge of this paper was Paul Seabright.

[1] See, for example, Layard et al. (2002).

can, and particularly what we cannot, learn about the implications of adopting the euro from recent economic events within Europe is important. It is what we try to do in this paper. We take the view that overall real macro performance – output and unemployment – is as yet unlikely to have been affected by the introduction of the euro in ways which make it clear how the outs and ins have done relative to each other by dint of their decisions on the currency. But in three areas – trade, foreign direct investment (FDI) flows and financial market activity – effects are potentially important and likely to show up more quickly than with the usual economic aggregates where trends and cycles having little to do with EMU probably still dominate recent outcomes. In the event it is only the trade effect that shows up clearly in the data so far: our estimates of the effect on FDI and financial markets serve mainly to indicate that, to the extent that any effects can be discerned at all, they are of a much lower order of magnitude than the trade effects. We focus mainly on the relative performance of the euro countries with the EU 'outs' – Denmark, the UK and Sweden. But we also sometimes consider the performance of the EFTA countries.

It is important to work out at the outset what made some countries adopt the euro. Unless we have some idea about that it is hard to know how much of the recent economic performance of the 'ins' is a result of adopting the euro and how much is just a reflection of the forces, whatever they might be, that made countries wish to adopt the currency in the first place. So the starting place for our analysis is a consideration of what made countries 'ins' or 'outs' in the first (or in the case of Greece, second) place. In Section 2 we start the paper by looking at what distinguished ins and outs before monetary union got going. We then look at three areas where the potential impact of either adopting the euro or retaining the national currency may be large: trade, FDI and the scale and location of financial market activity. In Section 3 we see what we might learn about the impact of the single currency on bilateral trade flows. In Section 4 we concentrate on FDI flows. In Section 5 we briefly survey the evidence on financial market location and activity, while Section 6 widens the analysis to look at overall economic performance in the ins and the outs.

In Section 7 we draw conclusions, paying as much attention to what recent trends do *not* tell us as to the more positive messages from the data.

2. WHY IN? WHY OUT?

Before we can undertake an analysis of the relative performance of EMU ins and outs, we need to have some explanation of why the outs chose to be outs and the ins chose to be ins. Without such an explanation, it is difficult to argue that any observed differences between the ins and outs is due to monetary union as opposed to another factor that explains both the observed difference and the propensity to join EMU.

2.1. An analytical framework

Our starting point for such an explanation is the work of Alesina and Barro (2000) (which is itself an extension of the work of Mundell, 1961). They identify the main economic determinants of the propensity to join a currency union as:

(1) Trade – the more two countries trade already, the greater will be the benefit of forming a currency union (though this result depends on 'reasonable' assumptions about the elasticities of substitution). Alesina and Barro also argue that other variables that may influence trade (such as distance between countries) could have an independent effect on the desire to join a currency union – we ignore those effects in this section.

(2) Co-movements of output – the greater the co-movement of output between countries, the smaller will be the cost of giving up monetary independence through a currency union.

(3) Co-movements of prices – as with output co-movement, greater price co-movement reduces the cost of giving up an independent monetary policy.

(4) History of high and volatile inflation – a country may wish to join an existing currency union, or form a union with a larger partner, in order to gain the discipline and credibility of the anchor currency's monetary policy.

For our purposes, the first three of these determinants are the most relevant as EMU, arguably, has no one 'anchor' currency to which other countries are linked. (Although Germany was the largest single economy in the union, the fact that a new currency and central bank were created suggests that EMU cannot be simply seen as a DM currency zone). Table 1 outlines estimates of these three determinants for

Table 1. Indicators of the propensity to form a currency union (average for the period 1978–91)

	Trade (bi-lateral trade as a share of GDP) (%)	Output co-movement (lower figure = more co-movement) (%)	Price co-movement (lower figure = more co-movement) (%)
All	0.40	2.5	1.8
EMU	0.49*	2.1***	1.7
UK with EMU	0.31	3.1***	1.5
Sweden with EMU	0.34	2.5*	1.7
Denmark with EMU	0.29	3.0***	1.4

Notes: Bilateral trade is the sum of exports and imports divided by 2. Both trade and GDP measured in US dollars and deflated by US GDP deflator.
Output co-movement is the average absolute deviation between output gaps (relative to their time series mean) using OECD output gap measures.
Price co-movement is the standard deviation of the difference between annual inflation rates.
Z-test of the difference in means for the two samples (row labelled EMU shows test of all EMU pairings versus all pairing involving at least one EMU-out. Individual country rows show test of all EMU pairings versus all pairings involving the named country). * significantly different at the 10% level *** significantly different at the 1% level.

Source: All data from OECD database.

countries within the EU and EFTA (excluding Luxembourg and Liechtenstein for data reasons).[2]

Looking at Table 1 in detail, in the row labelled 'All' we present the average value of each of the three determinants (trade, output co-movement and price co-movement) for all possible bilateral pairings in our sample. The row labelled 'EMU' then shows the same calculation but now only for bilateral pairings involving two EMU countries. Focusing on the non-EMU members of the EU we also show the average value of each determinant for all pairings involving each of these countries with every EMU member. So 'UK with EMU' shows the average value of our determinants for all pairings involving the UK and an EMU country – similarly for Sweden and Denmark. For example, for trade we calculate bilateral trade as a share of GDP for every possible pairing in our sample (272 combinations) over the period 1978 to 1991 (up to the signing of the Maastricht Treaty). The row labelled 'All' shows the average of all these combinations, the row labelled 'EMU' shows the average bilateral trade only for combinations involving two (future) EMU members. The 'UK with EMU' row shows UK average trade share with each EMU country, similarly for Sweden and Denmark.

Additionally we test to see if the EMU-ins are significantly different from the outs using a Z-test. For each indicator this involves finding the average value of the indicator for bilateral pairings involving two EMU-ins and comparing that with the average value of the indicator for all bilateral pairings involving at least one EMU out. The individual country tests (for UK, Sweden and Denmark) simply compare the EMU-in sample with the average indicator value for every pairing involving each of those countries. The Z-test is then a test of whether the mean of the EMU-in sample is significantly different from the mean of the out, or individual country, sample.

We find that both in terms of trade and output co-movement the countries that formed EMU were better placed to do so than the rest of our sample (on average). In particular, there is a highly significant relationship between output co-movement and subsequent EMU membership. This perhaps indicates that the issue of economic convergence had a significant impact on the decision to join EMU. Price co-movement (arguably the least important of the three factors, not least because of its interaction with the credibility effect), on the other hand, appears to have no significant link with EMU membership.

A potential problem with our results is that while they appear to help explain *who* will be in the currency union they do not tell us why the union was formed *when* it was. Given our use of time series averages to construct our indicators, the timing of EMU is difficult to gauge. However, Table 2 indicates that when we compare the period 1978–88 with the period 1988–98, all of our indicators are more conducive to a currency union in the later period, indicating perhaps that costs of monetary

---

[2] The countries are Austria, Belgium, Switzerland, Germany, Denmark, Spain, Finland, France, UK, Greece, Ireland, Iceland, Italy, the Netherlands, Norway, Portugal and Sweden.

Table 2. Indicators of the propensity to form a currency union (period averages, all countries)

	Trade (average bi-lateral trade as a share of GDP) (%)	Output co-movement (lower figure = more co-movement) (%)	Price co-movement (lower figure = more co-movement) (%)
1978–88	0.39	2.2	1.6
1988–98	0.41	1.7	1.1

Note: Variable definitions as in Table 1.

union have fallen and the benefits risen over time. This goes some way to explaining why monetary union did not occur earlier.

Overall, it seems that we can find economic variables that help explain why some countries chose to join EMU and some did not. In particular, output co-movement proves to be an important predictor of the subsequent decision to join. Not only does such a result undermine the argument that the decision was purely political and unrelated to economic considerations, these predictors are invaluable in determining whether EMU has had significant economic effects. In essence, they help us unravel the economic impact of EMU from the economic determinants of EMU. We discuss this in more detail below.

3. DID BEING OUT OF EMU INFLUENCE TRADE?

One of the key benefits of joining a currency union is its potential effect on trade. A large and growing literature has identified the existence of different currencies as a surprisingly large barrier to trade. If that is so, trade by the EMU outs might be expected to suffer relative to the ins.

Rose (2000) was the first to estimate the effect of currency unions on trade and his work found a remarkably large impact (over 200% increase in trade for members of a union). His approach, based on a standard gravity model (where bilateral trade flows are positively related to GDP of the two countries and negatively related to their distance from one another), attempts to control for the main factors that influence trade, and then includes a dummy variable for currency union. The coefficient on this dummy is then interpreted as the currency union effect on trade. Following Rose's work a number of authors have attempted to overturn his result with varying degrees of success. But most studies have actually confirmed a large currency union effect. However, two important criticisms of Rose's study have arisen. The first concerns sample selection: Rose's sample of currency unions was small (less than 1% of the total sample) and dominated by developing countries. Thom and Walsh (2001) studied Ireland's break from sterling and found no significant trade effects, suggesting perhaps that Rose's estimates do not apply to developed country unions. The second criticism centres on the endogeneity issue discussed below. If it were the case that countries expecting a large increase in trade tend to form currency unions, then the estimated relationship between trade and currency unions cannot be interpreted as a currency union effect.

Ever since Rose's results first appeared, the most significant criticism of this approach has been the issue of endogeneity. If this is a problem, the estimated impact of currency unions may to a significant extent be due to the impact of a third variable that predicts entry into a currency union and more trade. To assess the impact of EMU on trade we need to address this endogeneity issue. While this problem is familiar to most economists, in the context of a panel estimate (which combines cross section and times series) it becomes slightly more involved.

The underlying problem can be expressed most simply using two equations:

$$\text{TRADE} = \alpha + \beta(\text{EMU}) + \gamma X + \theta Z + \varepsilon \tag{1}$$

$$\text{EMU} = \psi + \delta Z + \chi W + \xi \tag{2}$$

Here trade is a function of EMU membership, variable X and variable Z (Equation 1). EMU entry is a function of variable W, and is also a function of variable Z (Equation 2). When we estimate the impact of EMU on trade we must attempt to control for all possible variables that can influence trade other than EMU. In particular, were we to leave out variable Z from our model, then the estimate of β (the trade impact of EMU) would be biased since it would include both the impact of EMU and, indirectly, the impact of variable Z. The problem we face is that unless we control for all the variables that influence trade, we cannot be sure that our estimated EMU effect is correct since we may have excluded a variable like Z. The first solution, that of Rose (2000), is to include an extensive range of variables that might influence trade. This approach was criticized by Persson (2001) who pointed out that even if the list of variables was exhaustive, if some of those variables influenced trade in a non-linear way, but were included as having a linear relationship, then the estimate of the currency union effect could still be biased. An alternative approach is to include fixed effects in our model that control for *any* differences in characteristics of EMU and non-EMU countries. This involves allowing for a dummy variable for every country and means that the EMU effect is only significant if there is a *change* in trade post-EMU rather than just higher trade on average for EMU-ins. As a result, even if we cannot explicitly identify all the differences in characteristics between countries, the fixed effect will pick them up.

However, even allowing for fixed effects there is still a potential endogeneity problem. This arises if the variable we inadvertently exclude predicts both the decision to join EMU and higher trade post-EMU. For example, if a country observes a change in its circumstances that will increase trade with EMU countries in the future, it may choose to join EMU as a way of maximizing the benefit of that change. As a result, we will observe the decision to join EMU being followed by higher trade, so even the fixed effect estimate will ascribe the increase in trade to EMU. To get around this problem, we need an instrumental variable – something that predicts EMU entry, but cannot have been influenced by the potential trade increase post-EMU (such as variable W in Equation 2). If we can find such a variable (or variables), then we can use it to assess the probability that a country will join EMU, and see if that probability predicts higher trade post-EMU. If it does then we can ascribe the increase in trade to EMU membership since, if the instrument is valid, it could not have been influenced by the post-EMU increase in trade. It is this instrumental variables approach that we take in this paper.

3.1. The trade impact of EMU

In this and the following section we aim to estimate the effect of EMU on trade. Our approach is to start by estimating the standard gravity model of Rose (2000) for the period 1978Q1 to 2002Q1 for a panel of European countries (quarterly data is used to maximize our post-EMU sample and extend it to the introduction of euro notes and coins). Our sample of countries is once again all of the EU and EFTA except Luxembourg and Liechtenstein, thus giving us 11 EMU ins and 6 outs. Given that we are looking at every bilateral combination of our 17 countries, we have 136 different time series each covering the period 1978Q1 to 2002Q1 giving us a total panel sample of 13,192 observations.

Since the range of variables that might influence trade is myriad, the range of possible specifications of the gravity model is virtually limitless. Therefore we narrow the field by focusing on Rose's original simple specification (though we exclude former colonizer effects for obvious reasons). The column headed OLS in Table 3 outlines the results.[3]

Generally speaking, the model has similar coefficients to Rose's original model with all the variables entering significantly and with the expected sign. We also find a positive and significant effect for membership of the monetary union of about 29%[4] (and of the EU). An alternative specification including fixed effects (which requires us to drop variables such as distance that have no time series variation) gave an EMU effect of 27%.

Our estimates of the currency union effect are significantly smaller than that found by Rose (29% rather than 240%), though offset somewhat by the fact that the exchange rate volatility effect is larger in the Rose specification (12% trade impact for every 1% change in standard deviation rather than the 2% trade impact found by Rose). Our high estimate for the impact of exchange rate volatility is a little surprising given that De Grauwe and Skudelny (2000) find a much smaller (but still significant) impact of exchange rate volatility using a similar sample to ours. Certainly, in our robustness checks using alternative specifications, this volatility effect was smaller (though still significant) in most of the other specifications we looked at

---

[3] We experimented with a range of different specifications that gave similar results. For example, a fixed effect version of the model above gave a significant currency union coefficient of 0.24.

[4] 29% is exp(0.254).

Table 3. Gravity trade model (log of bilateral trade as a function of)

	OLS	IV
Currency union	0.25 (0.033)	0.21 (0.04)
Exchange rate volatility	−0.12 (0.009)	−0.15 (0.009)
Log(output)	1.23 (0.010)	1.23 (0.008)
Log(output per capita)	0.23 (0.031)	0.23 (0.028)
Log(distance)	−1.24 (0.016)	−1.24 (0.016)
Contiguity	0.19 (0.019)	0.18 (0.024)
Language	0.25 (0.016)	0.26 (0.020)
EU membership	0.46 (0.016)	0.45 (0.017)

Notes: Bilateral trade: sum of exports and imports divided by 2. Both trade and GDP measured in US dollars and deflated by US GDP deflator (as above). Exchange rate volatility: standard deviation of monthly log changes in bilateral exchange rate for the year prior to observation date. Output: sum of GDP in both countries measured in US dollars deflated by GDP deflator. Per capita GDP: sum of GDP divided by sum of populations. Distance: great circle distance between capital cities. Contiguity: 1 for countries that share a common border. Language: 1 for countries with languages from the same group (i.e. similar languages such as Norwegian and Swedish as well as common languages) mixed language family pairs get fractional values (e.g. for France and Belgium the dummy takes the value 0.5). EU dummy takes value 1 for country pairs that are both in EU at the time. EMU dummy similarly. All economic data from the OECD. Robust standard errors in brackets, constant and time dummies not reported.

(for example, as low as 0.01 in the fixed effect version). These checks also confirm that, unsurprisingly, the volatility effect interacts quite strongly with the EMU effect (excluding volatility from the Rose specification increases the EMU effect to about 40%). A number of these checks are presented in the appendix.

3.2. Instrumental variables estimation

While our version of the gravity equation avoids one of the criticisms of this type of currency union model – namely an excessive reliance on currency unions involving developing countries – it does not, as it stands, avoid the second: we have not yet allowed for the possibility that the propensity to join the currency union is related to factors that increase trade.

As discussed above, instrumental variables can help to overcome this problem and so we use the price and output co-movement variables discussed in Section 2 as instruments.[5] As we have seen, output co-movement in particular has a very strong relationship with subsequent EMU entry, so it and price co-movement seem good candidates as instruments. Certainly, by focusing on co-movement for the period 1978 to 1991 (before the Maastricht Treaty was signed) we can be fairly confident

---

[5] Tenreyro and Barro (2003) propose another highly ingenious instrument – namely the joint probability that two client countries adopt the same anchor currency – on the assumption that bilateral trade between the two clients is not influenced by the anchor economy, only by the common currency. Unfortunately, this instrument is not appropriate for our study as EMU has no defined anchor currency, or any alternative anchors.

that these co-movement variables are independent of the prospective trade impact of EMU. So, even though there is evidence that increased trade can increase co-movement (see, e.g., Frankel and Rose, 1997), greater co-movement is unlikely to be caused by *future* increases in trade.

However, both our co-movement variables have the limitation that they have no time series variation (recall that they are defined as the average co-movement over the period 1978 to 1991). As a result, although they can be used to predict which countries will enter EMU, they cannot be used to predict when EMU will occur. Fortunately, since the entry timing decision is highly correlated across countries (i.e. other than Greece the timing of entry is identical across countries), the information lost through not explaining the time series variation in entry decision is minor. In fact, when we use these two co-movement variables as instruments for EMU membership and exchange rate volatility (both defined as above) we find very similar results to the OLS regression (see column marked IV in Table 3) – though the standard errors attached to these estimates are larger.

Once again, we tested the robustness of these estimates through both alternative specifications of instruments (for instance introducing some limited time variation by splitting our averaging period into two sub-samples) and through alternative specifications of the underlying model (e.g. a fixed effects version of the model). None of these changes had a significant impact on the estimated coefficients (see the web appendix for details).

Some may find it surprising that our estimates using instrumental variables are so similar to the OLS version, since many would expect the OLS estimate to be significantly biased upward (arguing that countries with potential for significant growth in trade are more likely to form currency unions). However, as Barro and Tenreyro (2000) point out, the biases could go either way, and their later study (Tenreyro and Barro, 2003), actually finds stronger currency union effects on trade once the currency union dummy has been instrumented. The fact that we do not get the same result probably relates to our more homogeneous sample (no developing countries or high inflation countries) so that the endogeneity effect is only minor in the case of EMU. It is also worth noting that although our two sets of estimates are similar, Durbin-Wu-Hausman tests of endogeneity indicate that instrumentation is appropriate.

The fact that our instrumental variables estimate suggests that it is membership of EMU that is responsible for almost all the increase in trade within EMU (rather than vice versa), need not mean that all of the trade impact is due to the mere act of entering EMU. It is possible that countries that expected to enter EMU altered their policies in ways that encouraged more trade (thus the trade impact is still caused by EMU, but only indirectly). While it is difficult to unravel the direct from the indirect impact of EMU, it is interesting to note that if we estimate our trade model with time dummies just for the EMU-in countries, it appears that EMU is already affecting trade well before EMU actually occurs (as far back as 1994 for the fixed effect version of the model and 1998 for the Rose specification – see appendix). This suggests that

Table 4. Implied trade effect of entering EMU (average increase in trade with EMU member states as a result of joining EMU)

	Pure currency union effect (%)	Exchange rate volatility effect (%)	Total impact (%)
Denmark	29	4	33
Sweden	29	20	49
United Kingdom	29	43	72

Note: Based on Rose's OLS specification.

the trade impact of EMU is more than just the impact of the single currency – the policy preparations seem to have influenced trade as well.

Although our approach is independent of and very different to that of Micco, Stein and Ordoñez in this volume (i.e. our approach focuses more on the endogeneity issue), it is instructive to compare our results with theirs since the question we address here – namely the trade impact of EMU – is the same. Using a comparable, but shorter, data set, they also find a significant impact of EMU on trade. However, the estimated coefficient in their preferred fixed effect specification is significantly smaller than ours (ranging from 9% to 20% for the most comparable sample), while using a Rose-type specification their results are very similar to ours (an EMU effect ranging from 21% to 37%). Experimentation using a shorter data sample (see appendix) reveals that when we reduce our sample to the period 1993 to 2002, the fixed effects version of our model gives a lower estimate of the EMU effect (9%) while the Rose specification gives very similar estimates (30%). Therefore, it seems that their shorter sample (1992–2003) explains the difference between the results of Micco, Stein and Ordoñez and those presented here. Given that the analysis discussed above suggests that the EMU effect on trade began as early as 1994 it is likely that some of the EMU effect is subsumed into country fixed effects in a shorter sample. However, it is also possible that the lack of a dynamic specification introduces more biases into a longer time series such as the one we use.

3.3. The trade effect of being out

Armed with these results, we can now estimate the trade impact of being *out* of EMU. Table 4 shows estimates of the possible increase in trade the non-EMU EU countries could have had with EMU countries had they been in the union. The exchange rate volatility effect is estimated by calculating the predicted increase in trade that would have occurred if exchange rate volatility had been zero since 2001 (Greece's entry date).

Even though our estimated currency union effect is significantly smaller than that estimated by Rose, the results are still dramatic. For the UK in particular (which has experienced the highest exchange rate volatility of the three) the estimated trade impact is very large.

At first sight these results suggest an enormous trade cost of not being a member of EMU but two caveats need to be kept in mind.

First, this model only estimates the trade impact with EMU countries. If much of that impact is simply trade that has been diverted from non-EMU countries whose comparative advantage is almost identical to EMU countries then the economic impact might be relatively small. However, we have some evidence against trade diversion. If we assume that EMU has no impact on trade between EMU outs, then trade diversion would imply that the creation of EMU would see a decline in trade between EMU-ins and EMU-outs relative to trade between EMU-outs. Estimating our model with an additional dummy variable for trade between EMU-ins and EMU-outs we find no significant impact.

The second caveat is that there is no simple link between trade and overall GDP. This is more difficult to answer and a survey of the literature on this question would merit a paper in itself. However, in a careful review of the evidence HM Treasury (2003) suggests that 'it seems reasonable to assume that each 1 percentage point increase in the trade to GDP ratio increases real GDP per head by at least 1/3 per cent in the long-run'. Using the figures from Table 4 (including exchange rate volatility effects) and converting the rise in trade with the euro-area to a share of GDP gives a long-run GDP gain of about 7% for the UK and Sweden, and 6% for Denmark.[6] Although this is only a one-off effect on the long-run *level* of GDP, it is not insignificant.

4. FOREIGN DIRECT INVESTMENT[7]

The impact of monetary union on levels of FDI has become one of the key issues in the economic debate between those who see major advantages in the 'outs' adopting the euro and those who see more costs than benefits. In the UK – which has received a disproportionate share of FDI coming from outside Europe – the advocates of entry have highlighted the recent fall in the scale of inflows.

'With Britain outside the Euro zone it will be increasingly difficult to attract (foreign firms) . . . because they can avoid exchange rate risk on the bulk of their European sales by investing instead in one of the 12 euro countries. This will strongly affect US and Japanese investors who currently invest in the UK as the gateway to Europe, and therefore want Britain to join the euro . . . Britain's share of foreign direct investment coming into Europe has fallen by half . . . We should not be complacent. Britain is not the outstanding place to invest that anti-euro propagandists portray' (Layard *et al.*, 2002).

---

[6] Note that although our results suggest that the UK will get the largest trade boost from EMU, UK trade with the euro area is a much smaller share of GDP than Sweden, which in turn has a smaller share than Denmark, so the overall GDP impact is similar for all three.

[7] The authors would like to thank Rachel Griffith and Alexander Klemm of the Institute for Fiscal Studies for helpful conversations on the issues raised in this section and for allowing us to use some data that they had assembled.

In this section we first consider the possible links between the scale of FDI and adoption of the single currency. We then consider the potential benefits of FDI. Then we take a careful look at the latest data and draw some conclusions. Here we focus on the ins and the outs among the EU 15. Given the significance of this to the economic debate on entry for the outs – particularly in the UK – it is important to draw out what we can, and more significantly what we cannot, infer from recent trends.

To assess the impact of being an 'in' or an 'out' on FDI we need to know what motivates such flows. There is a huge literature on the determinants of overseas investment by multinationals. (For good recent reviews see Markusen, 2002 and Lipsey, 2000, 2002). Most FDI flows are from rich, developed countries to other rich developed countries with levels of skills among the workforce which are comparable. Markusen stresses the role of imperfect competition and the desire of firms with information advantages to protect their assets (which include benefits of a good reputation) by setting up production rather than licensing. Such incentives are greater when costs of exporting from the home country are greater. Lipsey stresses the significance of efficiency advantages for some multinationals. He argues that a main motivation of FDI is that it transfers assets and production from less efficient (domestic) owners to more efficient (multinational) ones. 'Inward investment can be viewed in the recipient countries as freeing capital that had been frozen in industries that the owners would prefer to leave'. Neither of these strands in the literature places a great emphasis upon exchange rate variability or the costs of exporting from a host country to other (third) countries. Indeed as De Menil (1999) points out, the impact of bilateral exchange rate variability on FDI inflows is theoretically ambiguous.

4.1. Currency risk and FDI

The impact that adoption of the euro has on the scale and direction of FDI into different European countries depends crucially on the answers to two questions.[8] First, what is the impact of uncertainty about exchange rates between European countries on the location of investment crossing national boundaries? Second, can exchange rate uncertainty be hedged over the time scales that are relevant for long-term investment decisions?

The second issue is relatively clear: for investment projects where cash flows will be generated for many years into the future the ability to hedge any currency risks (for example, those that might occur if costs are incurred in one currency and revenues from sales incurred in another) is severely limited. Foreign exchange forward contracts can be used to hedge risk one or two years ahead – beyond that markets are thin. Whether that reflects some intrinsic problems in long-horizon hedging or an absence of demand for long-term hedging is crucial and really takes us to the

---

[8] A third factor is what the impact of joining a currency union is on competitiveness, particularly relative labour costs. This will depend upon the conversion rate at entry.

Table 5. Stock market – exchange rate correlations

	Change in Real Effective Exchange Rate Index			
	UK	Germany	France	Italy
US stock returns	0.001	−0.013	−0.049	0.064
Japan stock returns	0.032	−0.075	−0.075	0.049
French stock returns	−0.035	−0.087	−0.076	−0.017
German stock returns	−0.020	−0.124	−0.125	0.031
Italian stock returns	0.019	−0.190	−0.095	−0.022
UK stock returns	−0.038	−0.060	−0.059	−0.073

more fundamental issue. But for whatever reason it seems highly likely that for those who now *do* want to hedge currency exposures over periods stretching five, ten or more years into the future the scope to do so is very limited. Furthermore the scale of the risks to be hedged is itself rarely known. Only a company that knew its scale of production, and of costs and revenues and where those revenues were going to come from, would know *how much* to hedge.

It does not follow from this that the existence of currency risks necessarily reduces FDI nor that its reduction (by a country adopting the euro) increases FDI. In the first place it is not clear how harmful currency volatility is. Risk averse investors in a publicly quoted multinational will care about the correlation between the stock price of the company and their consumption, which in turn will reflect the covariance with other elements of wealth. Even if significant investment by a US or German company into Sweden or the UK makes profits exposed to pound-euro or krona-euro exchange rate volatility it is not clear that this is a risk shareholders should worry about. It may be an entirely diversifiable risk.

One simple way to assess how damaging to shareholders in country X is exposure to unpredictable swings in the real exchange rate of country Y, is to calculate the correlation of the stock returns on a diversified portfolio of country X companies with swings in the country Y real exchange rate. Table 5 shows the correlation between monthly (local currency) returns on national stock indices and the percentage change in the real exchange rate of various *other* countries. The first element in the matrix is the correlation between the dollar monthly returns on the S&P 500 index and the change in the UK pound real effective exchange rate index. That correlation is negligible (0.001 over the period January 1980 to December 2001). This suggests that investors in US multinationals – who we implicitly assume are primarily US investors holding a major part of their risky wealth in US stocks – should not be much concerned about any exposure they get to UK real exchange rate risk stemming from a decision by a US multinational to locate investment in the UK as a base for possible re-export (hence generating some exposure to pound exchange rate risk).

It is clear that the great majority of the elements in the matrix are trivially small – the only non-trivial elements are the exposures of French and Italian investors to

German exchange rate risk. UK exchange rate risk should not be very important to investors who are largely exposed to the US stock market, or to the Japanese market or to continental European markets.

How exposed profits from FDI into a country are to fluctuations in the value of that country's currency will itself depend crucially on the motives for FDI. If the great majority of FDI inflows are for production to satisfy the domestic market of the recipient country then the removal of currency risk will more likely reduce inflows than increase them. After currency risk has gone, overseas companies can locate production for sale into the original recipient of FDI in other, potentially lower cost, areas of the currency union. This might be offset by greater inflows of investment for production for export; but for a country without a cost advantage over others such extra inflows might be limited.

If, however, the larger part of FDI inflows into a country are for production of goods to be exported to other regions then the removal of exchange rate risks with those other regions brings an increase in incentives to inward investment (assuming of course that exchange rate risk itself is costly). But the correlations shown above should make us sceptical about how great those risk costs are. And once again it is relevant that attempts to find a significant exchange rate effect on FDI have not yielded robust results.

This obvious theoretical ambiguity in the direction of the impact of changes in exchange rate risk on the scale of FDI is not easily removed by looking at data on FDI. Breakdowns of FDI by broad sector – manufacturing, services, primary sector – offer few clues as to whether production is primarily for the domestic market or for export. Barrell and Pain (1997) find evidence that a 1% rise in the net stock of inward FDI in the UK, Germany, France and Sweden increases exports by about 0.15% implying that inward FDI does significantly boost exports. But neither theoretical nor empirical evidence on the impact of exchange rate uncertainty on overall investment levels is conclusive. Some recent papers (e.g. Davis and Byrne, 2002) find some negative correlations. But De Menil (1999), in a careful analysis, finds that there is actually a positive impact of bilateral exchange rate volatility on bilateral FDI flows.

4.2. Should we really pay lots of attention to FDI anyway?

Suppose, however, it were the case that FDI inflows were to be significantly and negatively affected by a decision to remain outside the European monetary union. Should that be an important factor behind the decision to adopt the common currency? To some the answer is self evident – surely inward investment is an unambiguously good thing. In fact this is not so obvious. First, FDI inflows are not equivalent to extra investment. FDI inflows represent an increase in foreign ownership and control of assets in a domestic country. That could reflect the change in ownership of an existing asset and not be associated with any new (tangible) investment. (In practice a significant proportion of FDI flows finance mergers and acquisitions.[9]) Empirical evidence suggests that there is little relation between the scale of inward FDI into a country and the level of capital formation. Lipsey (2000) finds that, if anything, there is a small (and insignificant) negative relation between capital formation ratios and inward FDI ratios. He concludes that the net flow of FDI does not appear to have any significant effect on aggregate capital formation ratios.

The large empirical literature on the impact of FDI has, in fact, not concentrated so much on whether inflows boost the size of the domestic capital stock but rather on whether productivity in foreign-owned firms is higher and whether there are positive externalities from large inflows of FDI. Externalities may come in a variety of ways – greater competition, better training of workers, domestic firms learning from more advanced production methods used by foreign multinationals.

The evidence suggests that labour productivity in foreign-owned firms is indeed higher than for domestic firms. A series of studies shows that foreign-owned firms in the UK have higher productivity than UK-owned firms (see Griffith and Simpson, 2001; Oulton, 2000; Davies and Lyons, 1991). Doms and Jensen (1998) find a similar result for the US: foreign establishments in the US have higher productivity than all US plants lumped together. But both Doms and Jensen, for the US, and Criscuolo and Martin (2002), for the UK, find evidence that the real difference is not so much between foreign-owned and domestic firms but rather between multinationals and domestic producers. The UK evidence is in fact some-what subtler. Criscuolo and Martin find that *non-US* multinationals operating in the UK have no higher productivity than UK multinationals operating in the UK. But US multinationals seem to have some intrinsic advantage wherever they set up in the world.

Whether it is nonetheless simply a multinational effect or an FDI effect, the scale of the productivity differences do seem to be large. Griffith and Simpson (2001) find that foreign-owned firms have productivity around 24% higher than the average UK firm; Criscolou and Martin estimate the difference to be 22%.

But the fact that foreign-owned firms seem to have higher productivity than the average domestic firm does not in itself show that FDI is highly beneficial or that losing some part of FDI inflows because of foreign exchange risk is a significant cost. First there is a sample selection issue. It may be that foreign multinationals chose to acquire a stake in domestic companies which (already) have above average product-ivity. In this case the fact that inward FDI looks to be of unusually high productivity is illusory. This point only has force for that part of FDI which is the acquisition of existing assets and not net new investment. But since mergers and acquisitions typically make up over half of FDI this is still a large part of inflows. Below we present evidence that takes this sample selection issue into account.

---

[9] Devereux and Griffith (2002) note that the OECD has estimated that mergers and acquisitions account for more than 60% of all FDI. See OECD (2000).

Second, the evidence in Doms and Jensen and in Criscuolo and Martin suggests that the productivity advantage of foreign-owned firms is essentially a multinational effect rather than an FDI effect. So *if* domestic multinational firms undertake more domestic investment when foreign multinationals undertake less, overall productivity may not be affected. But given the estimated size of the difference in productivities between the average of domestic firms and the average of foreign affiliates it would require that all of any reduction in FDI was compensated for by investment by domestic multinationals. This is highly implausible. So even if there are no additional benefits from FDI beyond that such investment had higher productivity than investment by average domestic firms there would still probably be some losses from losing FDI. Such losses would be greater if there were in addition positive externalities from FDI.

The literature on positive externalities from multinational companies is a large one. Early work (e.g. Caves, 1974; Globerman, 1979; Blomstrom, 1989; Barrell and Pain, 1997; and Borensztein *et al.*, 1998) suggested that externalities were large and positive.[10] More recent studies (Harrison and Aitken, 1999; and Griffith *et al.*, 2001) suggest much smaller externalities. Indeed Harrison and Aitken find that negative effects on domestic firms roughly match direct benefits from FDI leaving the overall impact neutral. But their research is based on analysis of FDI into Venezuela and might have limited relevance to FDI into Europe. Baldwin *et al.* (1999) find that higher penetration levels of inward FDI led to more rapid growth in labour productivity; this is consistent with some positive technology spillovers.

Particularly relevant is a recent careful study by Haskel *et al.* (2002). They find some evidence of positive impacts upon domestic firms of foreign presence in an industry. Based on the productivity performance of a very large sample of UK manufacturing firms they conclude that a 10% increase in foreign presence within an industry has a positive effect on the total factor productivity of other, domestic firms of about 0.5%. This is a modest, but statistically well-determined, effect. Having analysed what has happened to FDI flows for the 'ins' and 'outs' we will use the Haskel results to estimate the potential scale of costs to the 'outs' of lower FDI.

4.3. Recent evidence on the scale of FDI

Within Europe the economic significance of FDI is generally high but *very* variable across countries. Table 6 gives an indication. The *stock* of inward FDI as a proportion of GDP varies widely from over 100% in Belgium and Luxembourg to only around 10% for Italy. The UK has the largest stock of inward FDI (close to 20% of the EU total) though employment by foreign affiliates is relatively low as

---

[10] Barrell and Pain estimate that a 1% rise in the stock of foreign-owned capital raises technical progress in German manufacturing by 0.26% and in UK manufacturing by 0.27%. But they find no evidence of a positive impact on stocks of FDI in the UK service sector, and this is where most FDI has gone.

Table 6. FDI Inward stocks in EU 2001

	$ billions	Percentage
United Kingdom	496.7	19
Belgium and Luxembourg	482.1	18
Germany	480.8	18
France	310.4	12
Netherlands	284.2	11
Spain	158.4	6
Italy	107.9	4
Sweden	81.2	3
Ireland	74.8	3
Denmark	64.3	2
Austria	34.4	1
Portugal	32.6	1
Finland	26.2	1
Greece	14.1	1
EU Total	2648.7	100

Source: UNCTAD, World Investment Report Book 2002 FDI inward stock, p. 310.

Table 7. Shares of total stocks of inward FDI in EU in UK, Sweden and Denmark

	1980	1985	1990	1995	1996	1997	1998	1999	2000	2001
UK	0.291	0.239	0.278	0.179	0.191	0.206	0.211	0.218	0.183	0.188
Sweden	0.013	0.016	0.017	0.028	0.029	0.034	0.032	0.041	0.035	0.031
Denmark	0.019	0.014	0.013	0.021	0.019	0.018	0.019	0.023	0.027	0.024
Total	0.323	0.269	0.308	0.228	0.238	0.258	0.262	0.282	0.245	0.243

Source: UNCTAD.

a proportion of total employment, suggesting that in the UK FDI is unusually heavily concentrated in highly capital-intensive sectors with high labour productivity. The (unweighted) country average of FDI as a percentage of GDP in Europe in 1999 was about 28%; the averages of value added by foreign affiliates as a fraction of GDP and of foreign affiliates' employment in the whole economy were 16% and 9% respectively.

Around one-quarter of all FDI stocks in the European Union are currently outside the euro zone, that is, in the UK, Sweden and in Denmark. Of that fraction the overwhelming part is in the UK. The evolution of the stock of FDI in the three 'out' countries is shown in Table 7. Their share has been volatile. It has fallen from around 26% in 1998 to 24% in 2001. But in 1995 it was lower than it was in 2001. But provisional figures suggest that the 'out' share fell further in 2002.

Table 8 shows the shares of *inflows* of FDI into all European countries that have come to the three 'outs'. Once again there is substantial volatility from year to year. But here the downturn post-1999 is clearer. In 2000 and 2001 around 22% of inflows went to the 'outs' – the share had averaged around 35% in the period from 1985 to 1995.

Table 8. Shares of total flows of FDI in the EU in UK, Sweden and Denmark

	1970	1975	1980	1985	1990	1995	2000	2001
UK	0.290	0.336	0.475	0.345	0.338	0.174	0.144	0.167
Sweden	0.020	0.027	0.002	0.008	0.013	0.036	0.040	0.022
Denmark	0.021	0.008	0.012	0.027	0.022	0.126	0.029	0.039
Total	0.332	0.371	0.489	0.380	0.372	0.337	0.213	0.228

Source: UNCTAD.

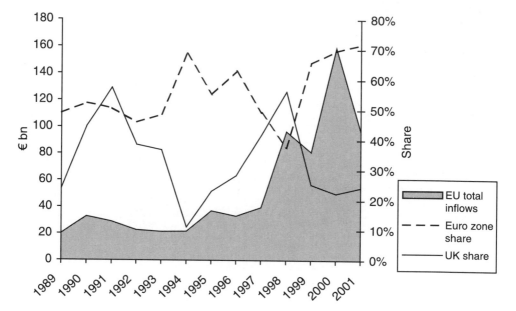

Figure 1. FDI inflows from non-EU countries (€ billions)

Source: Eurostat.

That part of the flows of inward investment to any EU country that comes from *outside* the EU is described in Figure 1 and in Table 9. The share of inward investment from outside the EU going into the countries that formed the monetary union in 1999 increased markedly from that date. Between 1999 and 2001 the share of investment from outside going into the euro zone averaged about 70% of all inflows to the EU; in the previous 10 years the average was 54%. The share of inward investment from outside the EU into the UK fell sharply in 1999 to around 25% and has stayed at around that level. But UK investment as a share of all FDI inflows into the EU had been even lower in 1994 and exhibits huge variability. Inflows into the other EU countries that have not yet adopted the euro are also down: in Sweden FDI inflows had averaged 7% of all inflows into the EU from 1989 to 1998 and have fallen to 5% since then. In Denmark the average fell from 3% to 2%. The share of inward investment into the EU going to the three 'outs' averaged

Table 9. Shares of inflows of FDI from outside EU into EU

	Euro area	Non-euro area	UK	Sweden	Denmark
1989	0.48	0.52	0.23	0.24	0.04
1990	0.52	0.48	0.45	0.02	0.02
1991	0.52	0.48	0.59	−0.12	0.02
1992	0.52	0.48	0.44	0.03	0.01
1993	0.52	0.48	0.40	0.05	0.03
1994	0.74	0.26	0.12	0.09	0.05
1995	0.54	0.46	0.23	0.22	0.02
1996	0.65	0.35	0.29	0.04	0.01
1997	0.49	0.51	0.42	0.07	0.02
1998	0.38	0.62	0.56	0.01	0.05
1999	0.66	0.34	0.25	0.06	0.03
2000	0.71	0.30	0.22	0.06	0.02
2001	0.72	0.28	0.24	0.03	0.01
Average					
1989–1998	0.54	0.46	0.37	0.07	0.03
1999–2001	0.69	0.31	0.24	0.05	0.02

Table 10. Shares of intra-EU 15 inflows of FDI: selected countries

	1995	1996	1997	1998	1999	2000	2001
Denmark		na	na	0.008	0.020	0.040	na
Germany		0.065	0.096	0.144	0.109	0.297	0.103
France		na	0.215	0.165	0.099	0.059	0.180
Ireland		na	na	0.034	0.017	0.009	0.056
Italy		na	na	na	0.011	0.015	0.046
Netherlands		0.071	0.116	0.097	0.066	0.051	0.094
Austria	0.018	0.062	0.020	0.032	0.006	0.011	0.019
Portugal		0.022	0.022	0.009	0.003	0.010	0.023
Finland		0.020	0.020	0.076	0.011	0.013	0.013
Sweden		na	na	na	0.134	0.022	0.040
UK	0.093	0.118	0.134	0.124	0.160	0.123	0.104

Note: The German figure for 2000 is likely to have been significantly influenced by the takeover of Mannesmann by Vodafone which counts as inward FDI.

Source: Eurostat.

31% in 1999–2001 – lower than at any time over the past 15 years with the exception of 1994.

There has been less of a decline in the share of intra-EU FDI inflows coming to the 'outs'. Table 10 shows that the UK received an average of around 13% of all intra-EU FDI inflows between 1999 and 2001, though it has been on a downward trend over that period. The average over the period 1995–8 was just under 12%.

Provisional figures from UNCTAD suggest that in the first half of 2002 the UK share of total FDI inflows to all EU countries fell to only just over 5% – down from around 17% in 2002. The share to France was 19% and to Germany 18% – both shares up on their 2001 levels. Eurostat figures show that in the first three quarters of 2002, UK FDI inflows were running at about one-half the level of inflows into Germany and only about 40% of inflows into France. Provisional OECD figures for the whole of 2002 confirm this picture. They suggest there has been a big fall in inflows into both the UK and Denmark. UK and Danish inflows in 2002 are estimated to have been only around half the level of 2001 – and flows in 2001 were themselves only half the scale of flows in the previous year. In France and Germany there was no fall in FDI inflows in 2002. But data from Ernst and Young for the whole of 2002 suggest that the number of projects coming into the UK may only have fallen by 5%. The number of UK inward investment projects remained the largest in the EU at 19% of the total.

4.4. Assessment

It appears that there has been a fall in both the absolute and the relative amount of FDI coming into the UK in recent years, but FDI has historically been highly volatile so it is hard to say how significant is this recent development. The picture in Sweden and in Denmark is even less clear-cut. How should we interpret this? Is the decline in inflows into the UK (relative to the rest of Europe) an EMU effect or just a reflection of the strength of sterling for much of the period since 1999 and perhaps the weakness of US investment, which has historically gone disproportionately to the UK? If the latter factors are the real ones they may prove temporary. Even if they do not they are not single currency factors *per se* – though of course to the extent that overvaluation of sterling could be removed by adoption of the euro there is a link.

Barrell and Pain (1997) report estimates of the elasticity of *stocks* of FDI to relative labour costs (between host and investing country). They estimate the elasticity of outward FDI stocks from the UK to be around 0.5 in the short run and 1 in the long term (Table 2, p. 1774). They report estimates of the elasticity of the stock of outward investment from Germany to relative labour costs of around 0.2 in the short run and around 0.33 in the long run. In the UK the average real effective exchange rate between 1999 and end 2001 was approximately 12% above the average over the period 1980–2002 and about 20% above the average for the period 1992–8. Suppose we take the degree of deterioration in relative labour costs in the UK between the mid 1990s and the period since 1999 as 15%. If we use the lower of the Barrell and Pain estimates of short-run relative cost elasticity for the stock of FDI (i.e. the 0.2 figure reported for Germany) we would estimate that the stock of UK FDI should have fallen by about 3%. If we use the higher cost elasticity figure of 0.5 the fall would have been about 7.5%. Between 1998 and 2001 the share of total inward FDI stocks in Europe that are in the UK fell from 21.1% to 18.8% (Table 7). This is a fall in the UK share of about 11% – i.e. $100 \times (18.8/21.1 - 1)$. So a substantial proportion of the fall in the relative amount of FDI in the UK – perhaps around one half using the average elasticity estimates of Barrell and Pain – could plausibly be a

Table 11. US FDI flows into Europe

	Europe $ billions	UK $ billions	UK share
1994	34 380	9 615	0.28
1995	52 275	13 830	0.26
1996	40 148	16 421	0.41
1997	48 318	22 961	0.48
1998	86 129	29 094	0.34
1999	99 224	47 839	0.48
2000	92 427	35 763	0.39
2001	56 133	13 231	0.24
2002 H1	49 878	5 676	0.11

Note: 2002 H1 figure is expressed at an annual rate.

Source: US Bureau of Economic Analysis.

result of a, perhaps temporary, rise in UK relative costs rather than as a reaction to failure to adopt the euro.

What about the weakness of FDI flows out of the US in recent years? Might this, rather than EMU, account for the rest of the weakness of inflows into the UK? US inflows into Europe fell by about 40% in 2001 and in the first half of 2002 were down by a further 12% from 2001. So on the face of it weakness in UK overall inflows is perhaps not surprising.

But Table 11 reveals that this explanation does not really add up. Since 1999 there has been a fall in the *share of US FDI inflows coming into Europe going to the UK*. In 1999 the share was 55%. But in 2001 that share fell to 28% and in the first three quarters of 2002 was still only around 30%. This is against an average for the period since 1991 of around 40%.

So the notion that the very recent fall in the share of FDI coming into the UK is largely due to the weakness of US FDI does not hold up since the share of weak US inflows coming into the UK has itself fallen.

Overall we find that while the competitiveness story for the weakness of UK FDI is likely to account for a significant part of the recent flows it still leaves a lot to be explained. The idea that UK weakness is just the mirror image of low US inflows does not stand up. We conclude that there has been a marked relative weakness of FDI inflows into the 'outs' since 1999. Though it is far from clear how much of that weakness is due to not adopting the euro we believe that some significant part may be. But even if that is so does it really constitute a big argument for adopting the euro? *The real issue is what is the loss to the economy from receiving less FDI.* We now present some estimates of an *upper bound* on that loss based on UK data.

4.5. The costs of lower FDI

The evidence we described above suggests that the inflow of FDI into the UK over the first three years after the euro came into existence has been only about one-half what might have been predicted given overall inward FDI into all EU countries and based on the UK share over the previous 20 years. One extreme assumption is that all of this 'lost' inward FDI was due to not adopting the euro. We now take that as an upper bound on the size of any reduction in inflows and try to estimate its effect on the economy.

First we stress again that there is little evidence that any lost inward FDI would reduce the size of overall domestic capital formation – Lipsey (2000) shows that there is *no* link between the scale of capital formation and flows of FDI. So any significant impact on domestic production, wages and productivity of changes in FDI inflows will come about as a result of productivity spillover effects, or because foreign assets have higher productivity or both. The second effect (the potential higher productivity of assets owned and controlled by foreign multinationals) may be overestimated by simply applying the average excess of productivity and wages in foreign firms over domestic firms, since foreign firms may choose to acquire domestic assets that were already of higher average productivity. So the 25% or more average productivity advantage of foreign firms is not a good estimate of the true enhancement to productivity. This is a sample selection/bias issue analogous to that which arises in the trade issue we considered above.

Fortunately there is some very good evidence for the UK that allows us to adjust for the potential impact of this bias. Conyon *et al.* (2002) analyse panels of firms in the UK taken over by domestic and foreign acquirers. They also used matched data for over 600 firms that were not taken over and use difference-in-difference techniques to estimate the productivity effects from assets simply coming under the control of a foreign multinational. They find that the differential effects on wages and on productivity are substantial. Having controlled for a wide range of factors, they estimate that the pure productivity enhancing effect of assets being managed by a foreign acquirer is to increase productivity by 13%. Around half of the higher productivity is reflected in higher wages paid by firms that come to be owned by foreign multinationals.

We take a 10% figure as a central estimate of the direct productivity effect of foreign presence.[11] We add to this the estimate by Haskel *et al.* of the positive spillover effect of foreign presence on domestic firms. Their estimate is of an elasticity of TFP to foreign presence of approximately 0.05 (a 10% rise in foreign presence raises productivity of domestic firms by 0.5%). We take an upper estimate of the induced fall in FDI flows into the UK as a result of not adopting the euro to be that flows are reduced by 50%.

An extreme assumption is that outside the monetary union the flows into the UK will remain at the same relative level as seen since 1999. Combining these estimates

---

[11] We scale down the 13% figure of Conyon *et al.* to allow for the fact that not all the gains accrue to the host economy – they estimate that wages only rose by around half the 13% figure. We consider 10% an upper bound on the effect on domestic residents.

and assumptions we now estimate an upper bound for the impact upon wages and productivity of not adopting the euro. The share of value added from foreign affiliates in the UK in 1999 was just over 4%. Had the UK share of inward investment always been at its 1999–2002 value the stock of foreign capital might have been half that size and foreign affiliates contributed only 2% to GDP. If foreign-owned firms have a 10% productivity advantage the direct effect of lower foreign presence on productivity is then $10\% \times 2\% = 0.2\%$ (i.e. firms that produce 2% of GDP would not be owned by foreign multinationals and would as a result have a level of productivity 10% lower). To this we add the lost benefits of positive spillovers based on an assumed elasticity of 0.05. This generates a further loss of $2\% \times 0.05\% = 0.1\%$.

The overall loss is 0.3% of the level of productivity. This is a long-run, steady-state loss and is based on the assumption of permanently losing half of FDI flows as a result of not adopting the euro. The scale of losses would be far lower than this in the initial periods after not adopting the single currency and would only gradually build up to that level. At current values the long-run level of losses, only experienced after many years outside the single currency area, would be about $5 billion a year in the UK.

That is not a trivial figure. But neither is it large and we consider it very much an upper bound on the long-run cost. It is in any case much smaller than the potential trade effects we discussed in Section 3 above. On the basis of this simple calculation, to base a decision on adopting the euro largely on the possible impact of FDI would be to give it far too much weight.

5. FINANCIAL MARKETS: ACTIVITY AND LOCATION

The introduction of the single currency raised the possibility that the centre of financial activity in Europe would shift from London to Frankfurt. Currency unions, and time zones, typically have a single dominant centre, usually located in the same city as the dominant currency's central bank. With the ECB located in Frankfurt, and London being outside the union, the latter's status as Europe's financial centre was vulnerable. A crucial issue for London is whether it can remain the principal location for euro-denominated financial activity despite not being part of the euro area, particularly if the euro's importance as an international currency grows. The equivalent issue for the ins is whether they will continue to see the bulk of activity in their own currency conducted by one of the outs.

London has many advantages as a financial sector to set against those of Frankfurt including a critical mass of activity; high-volume clearing systems; a high concentration of financial firms, support services, physical assets, labour, and legal and accounting expertise. It also has the advantage of having English as its common language. The probability that the UK will eventually adopt the euro must diminish one of Frankfurt's advantages, leaving it with just the proximity of the central bank in its favour. Even this is diluted to some extent by the presence of the Bank of

England, which would probably have a higher profile in the ESCB were the UK to join. It is significant that most of London's business is denominated in foreign currency (mainly in euros and dollars), while that of Frankfurt and Paris is denominated in local currency.

5.1. Evidence

There is little evidence to suggest that use of the euro has increased relative to that of its legacy currencies since 1999. For example, while the euro is the second most used currency in foreign exchange transactions, its use is only slightly greater than that of the DM in 1999.[12] This pattern is also apparent in international banking, over-the-counter interest rate derivatives, insurance and official reserves. The euro has increased its profile in two areas, however: there has been a significant increase in euro-denominated credit derivatives (although demand for these appears to have come from Europe rather than the US or Japan), and in corporate bonds where the euro's share increased from 29% in 1998 to 36% in 2001. Not surprisingly, activity in euro-denominated government bonds has declined with the introduction of restrictions on European government borrowing. Significantly, however, London's share of euro-denominated Eurobond issuance has increased since 1999, from 50% to 60%.

In terms of size, London is clearly the dominant player in Europe (see Table 12), and there is little sign so far of its share of international business declining, as Table 13 shows. The only area of financial activity in which Frankfurt has grown significantly is in exchange-traded derivatives. Although London appears to have suffered no ill effects from being outside the euro area, there are signs, however, that the smaller

Table 12. Shares of international financial business, 2002 (in %)

	UK	France	Germany
Cross-border bank lending	19	6	10
Foreign equities turnover	56	3	3
Foreign exchange dealing	31	3	5
Derivatives turnover			
– exchange-traded	6	6	13
– OTC	36	9	13
International bonds			
– primary market	60	. . .	. . .
– secondary market	70	. . .	. . .
Holdings of international equities ($bn, end 1999)	London only: 2.5	Paris only: 0.5	Frankfurt only: 0.3

Source: International Financial Services (2003) and Bank of England (2002).

[12] In April 2001 the euro figured in 43% of foreign exchange transactions by value, compared with 85% for the dollar, and 26% for the yen.

Table 13. Recent changes in London's share of international financial business (in %)

...	1998	1999	2000	2001	2002
Cross-border bank lending	20	19	19	19	19
Foreign equities turnover	65	56	48	56	56
Foreign exchange dealing	32	...	...	31	...
Derivatives turnover					
– exchange-traded	11	8	8	7	6
– OTC	36	...	...	36	...
International bonds					
– primary market	...	60	60	60	60
– secondary market	...	70	70	70	70

Source: International Financial Services (2003).

centres in Europe are losing euro-denominated business to Frankfurt, Paris and, significantly, London.

Overall, while four years would probably be sufficient time to see some evidence of a migration from London had EMU significantly altered market participant's location decisions, we can find none.

6. MACROECONOMIC PERFORMANCE

While some of the economic consequences of monetary union, such as changes in FDI, may become apparent quite quickly, others, such as improvements in growth, unemployment and inflation, may take many years to emerge. Although questions about macro performance are not unreasonable even at this stage of the union, as recent experience in Germany has shown, we do not yet have enough data to warrant a detailed econometric investigation. In this section, therefore, we report the results of a very simple, broad-brush search for indications that macroeconomic activity has responded to the single currency.

6.1. Has the performance of the outs differed from that of the single-currency area as a whole?

When the euro was introduced most of Europe had been on much the same macro trajectory since the trough of the early-1990s recession in 1994. The recovery after that was prolonged, remarkably smooth and characterized by declining inflation accompanied by increasing output. Significant changes to the structure of macroeconomic policy also took place in this period as newly independent central banks took aim at inflation targets, and abandoned, or at least downgraded, the use of intermediate targets such as monetary growth. The broad approach to fiscal policy also changed as governments attached increasing weight to balancing their books.

The trends of the previous six years were interrupted in mid-2000 by a negative demand shock worldwide, accompanied by monetary tightening, and fiscal loosening, in most European countries. European economic performance reacted to these changes in a fairly uniform fashion. Growth increased in the first year of the euro, declined dramatically in 2000 through 2001, and began a slow recovery in 2002. Unemployment and inflation too have displayed fairly uniform behaviour across Europe: unemployment has generally declined continuously since 1998, while inflation increased in 1999 towards a peak around 2000, before declining to what appears to be a fairly stable level for 2002, at or above the levels of 1998.

On the basis of data from 1998 to 2001, only a small number of exceptions to the general trends stand out. In particular, the major exception to the common-growth story has been Norway, where growth and unemployment have deteriorated since 1998. The other major trend outlier is Swedish unemployment, where the fall of 3.4% since 1998 considerably exceeds the 2.2% of the euro area. In terms of shocks, the UK appears to have responded best to the slowdown in 2000 (with the arguable exception of Norway), with its growth rate falling by just 0.9% while the euro average fell by 1.4%. In terms of inflation the UK is also slightly out of step with the euro zone in having a rate that was lower in 2002 than in 1998. However, even these differences are minor and cannot easily be attributed to being in or out of EMU, except to the extent that the UK was able to run a tight monetary policy before 2000 and an expansionary one thereafter – something it could not have done as an in.

6.2. Have the outs performed better than individual members of the single currency?

While there appears to be no clear evidence that the outs have performed better or worse than the ins as a group, it is possible that some significant differences might be present on a bilateral basis, since economic performance since 2000 has not been uniform across all the members of the single currency. In Table 14 we present the results of bilateral comparisons of performance in terms of growth, unemployment and inflation. For each country we calculate the average values of each variable for the periods 1995–8 and 1999–2001. We then compare these average levels across countries in each period. Finally, we present a comparison of the change in the average levels across the two periods for each country. In each case we award a score of 1 to the 'winning' country, and enter the sum of all these scores along the rows of the table. So, for example, the first panel of Table 14 shows that Denmark had a higher average level of growth than five of the ins in 1995–8.

In terms of growth the ins clearly score better than the outs taking the two periods together. From a total of 83 bilateral comparisons, the outs come out better in only 27. In terms of the improvement in growth, however, the scores are about even; the outs scoring 20 out of 39. The picture is reversed for unemployment. The outs perform better in 45 of 55 comparisons in 1995–8, and 38 of 50 in 1999–2002. The

Table 14. A scorecard of macroeconomic performance

	Denmark	Norway	Sweden	Switzerland	UK
Growth					
1995–1998	5	9	3	1	5
1999–2001	2	1	7	1	3
Change	3	0	9	7	3
Inflation					
1995–1998	5	5	10	11	4
1999–2001	5	5	10	11	11
Change	6	5	7	0	10
Unemployment					
1995–1998	9	10	7	11	8
1999–2001	7	9	6	10	6
Change	5	4	7	7	5

outs also do better in terms of inflation performance, scoring 35, 42 and 28 out of 55 for the three comparisons.

Overall, taking only the comparisons that involve the EMU period, the outs score 35 out of 80 for growth, 64 out of 100 for unemployment, and 70 out of 110 for inflation. Thus in 169 cases out of 290, i.e. 58%, of the bilateral comparisons the performance of the outs has either been better than that of the ins since 1999, or has improved more in comparison with the pre-euro period, or both. Thus there does not appear to be any strong evidence that the ins have performed better than the outs so far.

7. CONCLUSIONS

Currency unions often last many decades – good ones last many centuries. Can we learn anything from the first four years of the European currency union? In terms of the overall macroeconomic performance of the EU 'ins' relative to the performance of the EU 'outs' there is no killer fact. The outs have, on balance, done slightly better on some things than most of the ins – the ins have generally done slightly better than the outs on a range of other performance measures. But the similarities in overall performance are more striking than the differences. Inflation in most European countries has been low and unemployment has fallen since 1999, net, in most countries.

Not surprisingly, in broad macroeconomic terms it is not yet obvious what difference the monetary union has made. But in one area where we might expect monetary union to have had a significant and relatively rapid effect – trade between currency union members – there are signs that the Euro has made a difference. We find significant evidence for a trade enhancing effect on bilateral trade within Europe from the formation of the single currency; outs might do a lot more trade with ins if they adopted the euro. On FDI the evidence is less clear – there has been a fall in FDI to the non-member countries, but these flows have historically been volatile for many reasons. In addition, such a fall, even if statistically significant, is certainly much less economically significant than the potential trade effects just discussed. In contrast, we find no evidence that EMU has yet influenced financial market location, and that London's position as the principal financial centre in Europe appears to have been unaffected by its being outside of the euro zone.

The potential welfare gains from the outs adopting the euro as a result of enhanced trade and greater FDI are significant. Against those gains should be set the costs of losing some degree of independence over monetary policy. The scale of those costs depends on the likelihood of there emerging substantial divergence from cyclical positions in the rest of the euro area. Little can be learned about that from the experience of the relatively short period since the launch of the euro.

Discussion

David Begg
The Business School, Imperial College London and CEPR

I greatly enjoyed this paper, which provides an early assessment of what we have learned about the consequences of remaining outside the euro. In some respects, of course, it is too soon to say; but in other respects the evidence is already convincing. Broadly, I share the authors' judgments as to which questions have been resolved since the start of the euro and which questions will be answered only after we have much more evidence than is yet available.

On the issue of the trade effects of the euro, we have already learned a lot. Before the advent of the euro, pioneering studies of the effects of currency unions had to rely largely on small and tiny countries about whose relevance to Europe one could never be sure. Now we have evidence from European countries themselves. From this we have learned two things. First, the qualitative conclusion that currency unions promote trade has survived the European transplant. Second, in quantitative terms, the effect is probably between 20 and 50%. The lower end of the range is suggested by the companion paper by Micco, Stein and Ordoñez in this volume. The upper end is the ceiling suggested in the recent assessment by the UK Treasury. Barr, Breedon and Miles come down in the middle of this range.

To the extent that such estimates rely on comparing what happened before and after the launch of the euro, this may still prove to be an underestimate of the eventual effect, for two reasons: first, the 'pre-euro' data display some effects that occurred only because of the anticipation that the euro was on the way; second, the 'post-euro' data are unlikely yet to include all the long-run effects. Hence, the difference between before and after understates the true effect. Barr, Breedon and Miles adopt a central estimate of 29% for the trade-creating effect of the euro, but this may turn out to be an underestimate. Even so, it is much more plausible than the estimates of 200% or more that were derived from earlier data based on currency unions comprising small countries and dependencies of colonial powers.

I note in passing that the UK Treasury's assessment of the '5 tests' for UK membership, published in June 2003, acknowledged that extra UK trade from the euro could be anything up to an annual £1700 in per capita income, or nearly £7000 a year for a family. It is hard to think of any government policy actually being implemented today acknowledged to have benefits this large.

A related issue is whether the formation of a monetary union causes trade diversion that reduces the absolute level of trade between ins and outs. To date, the evidence – whether for Europe or for small countries and dependencies – suggests that no such trade diversion can be detected. For the European outs, this has two implications. First, the formation of the euro zone is unlikely to interrupt the ever-increasing degree of integration that is occurring within Europe. Hence, European outs are likely to adopt the euro sooner or later. Second, by failing to join at the outset, the outs are forgoing trade creation that they could have had.

The welfare cost of forgone trade is much smaller than the level of trade forgone. It must be identified as little triangles of consumer surplus not exploited, as failure to enjoy economies or scale and scope, as profit shifting, as failure to unlock benefits of diversity and competition, or as gains to the greater pursuit of comparative advantage. Any estimate is still subject to a large confidence interval.

The second part of the paper discusses the fall in inward investment to the outs since the start of the euro zone. Broadly speaking, this argument is in three parts: first, investment is down but is volatile, so the confidence interval on any implied reduction is large; second, even if a fall has taken place, our models of FDI are less well developed than our models of trade, so it is more difficult to be sure that the fall should be ascribed to the advent of the euro; and, third, even if it was caused by the euro, the welfare effects may be small.

The UK share of EU inward investment averaged 39% in the decade prior to the launch of the euro, and has averaged 23% in the subsequent three years. Yet it will take several more years of data before we can be sure that there has been any euro effect. The authors argue that some of the reduction in UK FDI should be attributed to the sterling appreciation during 1996–2002. While I agree that this probably inhibited inward investment, I am less sure that it is appropriate to view it as unconnected with the launch of the euro. In particular, if the UK had been the first wave of euro entrants, sterling would have been locked into the euro at a more competitive exchange rate than that which subsequently transpired.

I share the authors' judgment – a point not always recognized – that, although productivity is higher in firms that are foreign owned, it is difficult to infer from this to what extent higher productivity is caused by foreign ownership and to what extent foreign owners simply acquire firms with above average productivity. Although this is an important caveat, I still suspect that technology transfer and investment in knowledge-intensive industries are of increasing importance, especially for the intra-industry trade that so dominates trade within Europe. Hence, in relation to FDI I conclude that, while the case cannot yet be proven beyond doubt, there is little good news for the outs.

The final part of the paper deals with the comparative macroeconomics of ins and outs. This is a bit like viewing an early lap of an Olympic 10 000m race and trying to make inferences about the likely eventual winner. For many purposes, it is simply too short a span from which to draw any reliable judgment. Yes, Germany has been in recession and has adopted the euro, but do Real Madrid victories in the Champions League demonstrate that the euro is good for football too? The people who argue on Mondays, Wednesdays and Fridays that Germany could have reflated but for the strait of the euro are the same people who on Tuesdays and Thursdays point out that most German problems are microeconomic and supply side.

Thus, while I happily endorse the view that there is scope for improving the structural and institutional design of macroeconomic policy in the euro zone, I think that simple scorecards are not informative.

Jonathan Haskel
Queen Mary, University of London

The paper sets out to answer two key questions. First, how are those countries on the outside of the euro doing? Second, and rather harder, how would those countries currently on the outside do if they became insiders?

As the paper rightly points out, getting sensible answers to the first question is hard owing to the short time period. However, the indications are that, if anything, countries outside are doing rather well, the key example being the UK whose output growth, for example, looks very impressive. The authors point out this was likely a consequence of a monetary policy that would not have been feasible with the euro: tight before 2000 and then expansionary thereafter.

Answering the counterfactual of what would have happened to macro policy if the outsiders had been insiders is comparatively easy since there are more or less specified macro rules. It is rather harder to say what would have happened to trade and FDI. Since the pro-euro lobby regards euro membership as being beneficial for both these flows this is a key question that the authors address.

Starting with trade the essential claim is that membership of a currency union benefits trade, as in the upward sloping line in Figure 2. Thus if we knew the slope of the line we would be able to work out how much extra trade would arise were a new member to join the euro. The problem of identifying this relation from actual data is set out in Figure 3. Actual data presents us with a group of countries who are 'in' and a group who are 'out'. But joining is not a random activity. If countries who are 'in' would also have a higher trade relationship anyway (they, for example have good political relations which both raises trade and the chances of being in) then they lie on a higher locus. Hence estimation from observed data will likely overstate the gains from joining, unless this can be corrected for. In a regression framework the problem is that we need to run a regression of

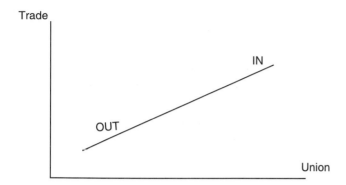

Figure 2. Relation between trade and membership of a currency union

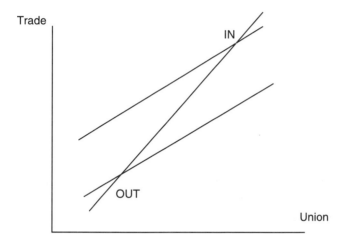

Figure 3. Identifying the relation between trade and membership of a currency union from actual data

$$Y_i = \beta_1 \text{EURO}_i + \beta_2 X_i + v_i \tag{3}$$

where Y is some variable (inflation, FDI, trade etc.), EURO is a dummy for membership and X every other control that might conceivably have any effect on Y and is correlated with EURO. If we omit an element of X the coefficient a_1 is of course a biased predictor of what would happen if a randomly selected country joined the euro.

There are of course two solutions to the problems in (3); to control for X or to find a good instrument for EURO. Both are tried in this paper. The first is to estimate a gravity equation with (log) bilateral trade (Y) as a function of euro membership plus exchange rate volatility, output, output per head, distance, contiguity, language and EU membership. This gives a coefficient on EURO of 0.25, suggesting that trade increases by 25% with EURO membership. A fixed effects estimate gives a coefficient of 0.24. The second method, IV, gives a coefficient of 0.21, where the instrument is output and price co-movement. In sum, all of these measures suggest an increase in trade of about 20–25%.

A number of issues arise from this discussion. First, as the authors point out, these are large effects. While it is true that they are less than some of the original Rose effects (Rose, 2000, for example) this may well be because the trade/union relation is concave and much of the variation in the Rose estimates arose from small countries with little trade initially. Note, however, that the overall effect of euro membership would be 72% taking into account the implied reduction in exchange rate flexibility.

Second, I was somewhat surprised that the fixed effects estimates are so close to the non-fixed effects estimates. This is not the case in the Micco, Stein and Ordoñez paper in this volume, where the use of fixed effects involves large falls in β_1, from 20% to 6%. Indeed their fixed effects estimates are around 6–9%, rather than the 20–25% here. This fall in the estimates seems plausible to me. For β_1 to be downward biased, factors omitted from X which are captured by the fixed effects would have to be those that make trade more likely but joining the euro less likely. It is hard to think of such factors; rather the relation is likely positive making β_1 upward biased. Thus 20% as an upper bound seems sensible to me.

The authors discuss the relation between their findings and those of Micco *et al.* in some detail and document a very interesting finding, namely that restricting their data set from 1978–2002 to 1993–2002 the panel coefficient falls to the much lower 9% effect found in Micco *et al.*, suggesting that it is the short period that accounts for the differences. Given how critical this coefficient has become in the UK public debate on joining EMU (HM Treasury, 2003) this is important and the paper also suggests that quite a lot of the trade effect comes from the anticipation of joining EMU. One problem here is to try to also unravel the effects of the Single Market Programme that was supposed to have been completed in 1992 but might also have had some lagged effects.

Third, and similarly, I was also surprised that the IV and OLS estimates were close together. Recall that IV estimates identify the marginal effect for the particular part of the sample that makes up the instrument. In this case it is the countries with the greater output co-movement whose marginal effect on trade is being identified by the IV result. So can we draw any inference for countries with smaller output co-movement, who from Table 1 are countries currently outside the euro? If the trade/union relation is concave the marginal effect might be greater for the current outs, which would put 21% at an underestimate. On the other hand, if the amount of trade depends on the instrument as well as the included X factors then the estimate is likely biased upwards, since the part of the variation in joining the euro or not that it tries to capture is correlated with trade net of the X factors. This latter possibility seems more likely to me. All in all, the 20% figure looks to be an upper bound on bilateral trade.

Does the evidence on FDI provide more support? The authors start by trying to untangle whether FDI has fallen in the UK while it has been out. This is a hard calculation to make since there is a relatively short time period and there has been a trend shift towards FDI in Eastern Europe since the fall of the USSR. Thus the authors are rightly cautious in concluding there is some indication that the UK is losing out. So is this a good reason to join the euro? There are a number of issues here.

First, as the authors point out, the extent to which currency risk is a current disincentive for FDI to come to the UK depends on the amount of goods that are exported to the EU from UK-located affiliate plants. Direct evidence on this issue for US multinationals is set out in Slaughter (2003) who documents that in 1999 75% of Ireland-based affiliate sales were exported, whereas 75 of UK-based affiliate sales were into the host market. Since the US is by far the largest source of FDI to the UK, other affiliates would have to have hugely opposite figures for the main destination of affiliate sales to be outside the UK. This might explain why the loss, if any, to the UK, of FDI from being outside the euro, is hard to detect.

Second, on the general issue of the desirability of FDI it is important to distinguish between whether foreign firms are desirable simply because they raise productivity via a batting average effect, or whether they might be the source of productivity spillovers. On the batting average effect, if foreign firms are simply more productive, the implied possible decrease in productivity from the loss of FDI follows, depending on the replacement effects there might be from UK firms. If there are spillovers then there may be detrimental effects on productivity directly if FDI is lost.

Regarding the batting average effect, it used to be thought that the observation that foreign firms are more productive was clinching evidence that the loss of foreign firms would reduce host country productivity. With the papers by Criscuolo and Martin (2003) for the UK and Doms and Jensen (1998) for the US, this view has been discredited. A simple comparison of foreign firms operating in country X with domestic firms operating in country X compares foreign firms, who are by definition multinational enterprises (MNEs), with all domestic firms. Since all domestic firms include domestic MNEs and non-MNEs the comparison is not like-with-like. The appropriate comparison is foreign MNEs and domestic MNEs. When one does this, as Criscuolo and Martin (2003) and Doms and Jensen (1998) are able to do, one finds that MNEs generally have about the same total factor productivity (TFP; although US MNEs seem to have higher TFP than everyone), so that the apparent domestic disadvantage arises due to the mixing of domestic non-MNEs and domestic MNEs in the crude calculation. Indeed, Criscuolo and Martin (2003) are able to go further. They document that the source of the MNE advantage, which is in part due to managing plants better, but mostly due to owning better plants in the first place. In sum, the loss of productivity due to the possible loss of FDI and the consequent batting average effect seems likely to be very small.

What about the loss of productivity due to spillovers? Estimates of spillovers from foreign firms are notoriously hard to pin down. Using plant-level data Haddad and Harrison (1993) and Aitken and Harrison (1999) find negative spillovers from increased industry-level FDI for Moroccan manufacturing and Venezuelan manufacturing, which they speculate might be due to unmeasured poor absorption capacity of plants in developing countries. Haskel *et al.* (2002) and Keller and Yeaple (2003) find positive spillovers using plant and firm level data for the UK and US respectively. The former paper finds that the spillover effects seem rather modest; the 10 percentage-point increase in foreign presence in the UK in 1973–92 accounted for about 5% of the observed rise in UK manufacturing TFP. Let us suppose that the UK lost half of its foreign presence, i.e. a decade's worth of FDI, as a consequence of being outside the euro. It would then have had 2.5% less of its rise in TFP; this seems like a small number.

A counter-argument to this is the rather higher numbers estimated in Keller and Yeaple (2003) who find that positive spillovers account for around 15% of US TFP growth in 1986–97. Their only significant spillover findings, however, are in the US high-tech sector for which they document a strong positive relation between US firm TFP growth and foreign presence. Given that the US is likely the productivity leader in this sector it does seem more likely that this coefficient is exaggerated due to reverse causation, i.e. that foreign firms enter the US high-tech sector to learn from the US rather than the other way around.

In sum, I was not convinced that the losses from being on the outside in terms of lost trade and FDI were serious. Thus I agree with the authors' conclusion that on these numbers at least, the case for the UK 'out' becoming an 'in' is not compelling.

Panel discussion

Carlo Favero suggested an explanation for why the coefficient of the trade effect of EMU does not fall much if instruments are used: it is well known in the literature that IV estimation does not affect coefficient estimates if the stochastic trend is dominant. Indeed, compared with the paper of Micco, Stein and Ordoñez the sample contains more time-series observations. He wondered why the authors did not estimate a dynamic model with a lagged dependent variable. Alejandro Micco pointed out that including fixed effects in the regressions does not affect the coefficient estimates because the authors use a longer time period so that endogeneity matters relatively less. Ernesto Stein found it puzzling that the endogeneity bias of OLS estimates might be considered to go in either direction: it is hard to imagine that a country that trades more is less likely to join the currency union. David Miles replied that he agreed that IV estimation should lower the estimate of the currency union effect. Michael Ehrmann suggested that a way of making better use of the data would be to distinguish between those countries that had been more homogeneous pre-EMU and those that had been more heterogeneous.

Jean-Marie Viaene mentioned that the FDI share of euro area countries might be inflated because of a substantial volume of merger and acquisitions (M&A), as for example in Belgium. Thus, the FDI share of the UK and other countries outside the euro area might seem artificially small. He suggested distinguishing between M&A

and truly new capital. Hans-Werner Sinn added that the most important components of FDI are typically M&A and retained earnings and not new capital. David Miles replied that the back-of-the-envelope calculations addressed this comment by assuming that the capital stock remains unchanged whereas the ownership changes. Thomas Moutos argued that even if productivity increased with FDI, this would not imply that welfare increases if competition decreases at the same time. Steve Cecchetti asked whether the decrease of FDI in the UK could be explained by legal and regulatory changes in the continental European countries that have decreased the competitive advantage of the UK over time. David Begg considered this as unlikely because such changes had been well underway for quite some time.

George de Ménil thought that FDI in central Europe is not important quantitatively. Alejandro Micco added that the risk of investors with respect to FDI had increased for EU countries outside EMU so that expected profits for such investments had fallen. Karen Helene Midelfart Knarvik asked for a more detailed analysis of FDI as a consequence of EMU. She expected the UK to be affected more for FDI locating in the UK to serve as an export platform as compared with FDI meant to serve the UK market. David Miles replied that such a disaggregated analysis was not feasible because of data limitations. More importantly, it is quite plausible that EMU affects FDI that serves to supply the UK market.

Finally, Ernesto Stein wondered why the authors dismissed a high inflation history as an important criterion for an optimum currency area after EMU. High inflation history still matters as a motivation for countries like Italy to remain in EMU.

APPENDIX: EXPLORING THE TRADE IMPACT OF EMU

This appendix presents a number of robustness checks and alternative specifications of our estimates of the trade impact of EMU.

Country exclusion tests

Table A1 shows the impact on the EMU coefficient of dropping individual countries (and all the EFTA countries) from both the Rose and fixed effects specifications of the OLS trade

Table A1. Estimated EMU coefficient after removing countries

Country	AU	BE	CH	DE	DK	ES	FI	FR	GB
Rose	0.31	0.21	0.26	0.20	0.12	0.19	0.24	0.29	0.25
Fixed E.	0.29	0.25	0.27	0.28	0.27	0.23	0.28	0.28	0.23

Country	GR	IR	IS	IT	NL	NO	PR	SW	EFTA
Rose	0.23	0.24	0.29	0.25	0.26	0.27	0.28	0.28	0.30
Fixed E.	0.28	0.19	0.26	0.28	0.31	0.27	0.26	0.25	0.26

Table A2. Estimated EMU coefficient after removing variables

Variable dropped	Ex. rate vol.	Output	Output per capita	Distance	EU	Common language	Contiguity
Rose	0.38	0.33	0.24	0.00	0.42	0.27	0.26
Rose excl. ex-rate vol.		0.43	0.37	0.18	0.59	0.40	0.40
Fixed effect	0.26	0.26	0.26		0.32		
Fixed effect excl. vol.		0.27	0.27		0.32		

Table A3. Estimated EMU effect in different sample periods

	1983:1–2002:1	1988:1–2002:1	1993:1–2002:1	1978:1–2001:4	1978:1–2001:1	1978:1–2000:1
Rose	0.28	0.33	0.30	0.27	0.29	0.28
Fixed effect	0.21	0.14	0.06	0.24	0.27	0.28

model. Note that the fixed effect specification drops the variables distance, language and contiguity since they have no time series variation.

In all cases the EMU coefficient remains significant at the 1% level. The largest change comes from dropping Denmark from the Rose specification; this is due to the strong interaction between the EMU effect and the exchange rate volatility effect. It seems that Denmark, as a low volatility non-EMU country, is important in discerning the volatility effect from the EMU effect. Certainly, the fall in the EMU coefficient is mirrored by a rise in the volatility coefficient.

Variable exclusion tests

Table A2 shows the impact on the EMU coefficient of dropping individual variables from the Rose and fixed effect version of the trade model. Given the strong interaction between the volatility effect and the EMU effect in the Rose specification, we also show the impact of dropping further variables after the exchange rate volatility effect has been dropped.

The EMU effect remains significant at the 1% level in all cases except when the distance variable is dropped from the Rose specification. Once again, the interaction of the exchange rate volatility and EMU effects is responsible for this (the volatility effect increases significantly when the distance variable is dropped).

Changes in estimation period

Table A3 shows the impact on the EMU coefficient of changing the sample period used in estimation (the full sample runs from 1978:1 to 2002:1). We show the impact of dropping observations from the beginning of the sample as well as from the end.

The EMU effect remains remarkably stable across sample periods for the Rose specification, but declines significantly in the fixed effect specification when earlier observations are dropped.

Table A4. Impact of alternative instrument specification

	Rose specification		Fixed effect specification	
	EMU coefficient	Volatility coefficient	EMU coefficient	Volatility coefficient
Post EMU	0.21	−15.0	0.26	−0.7
Split sample	0.21	−14.7	0.26	−0.7

As discussed above, this explains the differences between our results and those of Micco, Stein and Ordoñez in this volume, who use a shorter data sample. All coefficients remain significant at the 1% level.

Specification of instrumental variables

As discussed above, while our instruments are appropriate in the sense that they are correlated with the variable they are instrumenting (EMU entry) but independent from factors that might influence trade post-EMU, they do have the limitation that, in the form used above, they have no time-series variation. Table A4 presents alternative specifications of our two instruments (price co-movement and output co-movement) that introduce some time-series variation. Not only may such specifications help identify whether time variation has an impact on the EMU estimates for the Rose specification, time-series variation is a prerequisite for using our instruments in the fixed effect version of our trade model.

We present two alternative specifications of our instruments: First, instead of simply letting the instruments take a single value of the whole time-series sample, we set the instruments equal to zero up until EMU entry (1998:4), and then equal to their 1978–91 averages post entry (1999:1 onwards). The second specification sets the instruments equal to the 1978:1 to 1987:4 average over that period and then to their 1988:1 to 1997:4 average for the period 1988:1 to 2002:1 (i.e. we split the pre-EMU sample in half).

As Table A4 shows, the alternative specifications make little difference to the estimated coefficient. All coefficients are significant at the 1% level except exchange rate volatility in both versions of the fixed effect model in which it is significant at the 5% level.

EMU effect over time

As noted in the text, not all of the impact of EMU need be due to the introduction of a single currency, some may be due to policy changes made by countries that knew they were going to enter, or other anticipation effects. To give some idea of this pre-entry effect we look at the evolution of the EMU effect through time by introducing a whole set of dummy variables that take the value one over a given year for EMU countries. For example EMU93 will equal one for all four quarters of 1993 if the country pair involves two countries that will enter EMU. Figure A1 shows the evolution of the coefficients on these dummies for our two models. In the case of the Rose specification we show the actual coefficients on these dummies, while in the fixed effect version we show the deviation of the dummies from the average coefficient pre-1992.

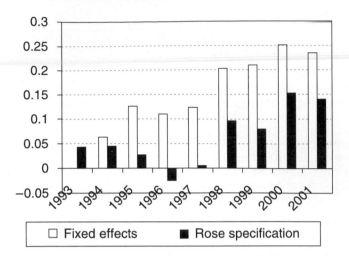

Figure A1. Evolution of the EMU coefficient through time

In both cases it seems that the EMU effect increases most strongly in 1998, the year before EMU entry. However, for the fixed effect model we begin to see significant EMU effects as early as 1994 indicating perhaps that the preparations for EMU had an effect on trade.

WEB APPENDIX

Available at http://www.economic-policy.org

REFERENCES

Aitken, B.J. and A.E. Harrison (1999). 'Do domestic firms benefit from foreign direct investment? Evidence from Venezuela', *American Economic Review*, June, 605–18.

Alesina, A. and R. Barro (2000). 'Currency unions', NBER Working Paper 7927.

Baldwin, R., H. Braconia and R. Forslid (1999). 'Multinationals, endogenous growth and technological spillovers: theory and evidence', CEPR Discussion Paper No. 2155.

Barrell, R. and N. Pain (1997). 'Foreign direct investment, technological change and economic growth within Europe', *The Economic Journal*, 107.

Bank of England (2002). 'Practical issues arising from the euro', Bank of England, London.

Barro, R. and S. Tenreyro (2000). 'Closed and open economy models of business cycles with marked-up and sticky prices', NBER Working Paper No. 8043.

Blomstrom, M. (1989). *Foreign Investment and Spillovers: A Study of Technology Transfer to Mexico*, Routledge, London.

Blomstrom, M., S. Globerman and A. Kokko (2000). 'The determinants of host country spillovers from foreign direct investment', CEPR Discussion paper No. 2350.

Borensztein, E., J. Gregario and J. Lee (1998). 'How does foreign direct investment affect economic growth?', *Journal of International Economics*, 45.

Caves, R. (1974). 'Multinational firms, competition and productivity in host country markets', *Economica*, 41.

Conyon, M., S. Girma, S. Thompson and P. Wright (2002). 'The productivity and wage effects of foreign acquisition in the United Kingdom', *Journal of Industrial Economics*, L (1), 85–102.

Criscuolo, C. and R. Martin (2002). 'Multinationals, foreign ownership and productivity in UK businesses', Working Paper of the Centre for Research into Business Activity, Office for National Statistics, London.

Criscuolo, C. and R. Martin (2003). 'Productivity and American leadership: evidence from the UK', Centre for Research into Business Activity, Working Paper, at www.ceriba.org.uk.

Davies, S. and B. Lyons (1991). 'Characterising relative performance: the productivity advantage of foreign owned firms in the UK', *Oxford Economic Papers*, 43.

Davis, P. and J. Byrne (2002). 'Investment and uncertainty in the G7', National Institute for Economic and Social Research mimeo, London.

De Grauwe, P. and F. Skudelny (2000). 'The impact of EMU on trade flows', *Weltwirtschaftliches Archiv*, 136 (3).

De-Menil, G. (1999). 'Real capital market integration', *Economic Policy*, 28.

Devereux, M. and R. Griffith (2002). 'The impact of corporate taxation on the location of capital: a review', *Swedish Economic Policy Review*, 9.

Doms, M. and J. Jensen (1998). 'Comparing wages, skills and productivity between domestically and foreign-owned manufacturing establishments in the US', in R. Lipsey, R. Baldwin and J. Richardson (eds.), *Geography and Ownership as Bases for Economic Accounting*, University of Chicago Press, Chicago.

Frankel, J. and A. Rose (1997). 'Is EMU more justifiable ex post the ex ante?', *European Economic Review*, 41 (3–5).

Globerman, S. (1979). 'Foreign direct investment and spillover efficiency benefits in Canadian manufacturing industries', *Canadian Journal of Economics*, 12.

Griffith, R. and H. Simpson (2001). 'Characteristics of foreign owned firms in British manufacturing', Institute for Fiscal Studies Working Paper, March.

Griffith, R., H. Simpson and F. Windmeijer (2001). 'Understanding productivity differences between domestic and foreign firms', Institute for Fiscal Studies, London, mimeo.

Haddad, M. and A.E. Harrison (1993). 'Are there positive spillovers from direct foreign investment?', *Journal of Development Economics*, 42, 51–74.

Haskel, J., S. Pereira and M. Slaughter (2002). 'Does inward foreign direct investment boost the productivity of domestic firms?', NBER Working Paper No. 8724.

Harrison, A. and B. Aitken (1999). 'Do domestic firms benefit from direct foreign investment: evidence from Venezuela', *American Economic Review*, 89.

HM Treasury (2003). *EMU and Trade*, HM Treasury, London.

International Financial Services (2003). *International Financial Markets in the UK*, International Financial Services, London.

Keller, W. and S. Yeaple (2003). 'Multinational enterprises, international trade and productivity growth: firm-level evidence from the United States', NBER Working Paper No. 9504, February.

Layard, R., W. Buiter, C. Huhne, W. Hutton, P. Kenen and A. Turner (2002). 'Why Britain should join the euro', *Britain in Europe*, October, London.

Lipsey, R. (2000). 'Interpreting developed countries foreign direct investment', NBER Working Paper 7810.

— (2002). 'Home and host country effects of FDI', NBER Working Paper 9293.

Markusen, J. (2002). *Multinational Firms and the Theory of International Trade*, MIT Press, Cambridge, MA.

Mundell, R. (1961). 'A theory of optimum currency areas', *American Economic Review*, September.

OECD (2000). *Recent Trends in Foreign Direct Investment*, OECD, Paris.

Oulton, N. (2000). 'Why do foreign owned firms in the UK have higher labour productivity?', Bank of England, March.

Persson, T. (2001). 'Currency unions and trade: how large is the treatment effect?', *Economic Policy*, 33.

Rose, A. (2000). 'One market one money: estimating the effect of common currencies on trade', *Economic Policy*, 30.

Rose, A. and E. van Wincoop (2001). 'National money as a barrier to international trade: the real case for currency union', *American Economic Review, Papers and Proceedings*, 91 (2).

Slaughter, M. (2003). 'Host-country determinants of US foreign direct investment into Europe', in H. Herrmann and R.E. Lipsey (eds.), *Foreign Direct Investment in the Real and Financial Sector of Industrial Economies*, Springer Verlag, forthcoming.

Tenreyro, S. and R. Barro (2003). 'Economic effects of currency unions', NBER Working Paper No. 9435.

Thom, R. and B. Walsh (2001). 'The effect of a common currency on trade: Ireland before and after the sterling link', *European Economic Review*, 46 (6).